A Short History of
the Arab Peoples

By the same author

A SOLDIER WITH THE ARABS

THE STORY OF THE ARAB LEGION

BRITAIN AND THE ARABS

WAR IN THE DESERT

THE GREAT ARAB CONQUESTS

THE EMPIRE OF THE ARABS

THE COURSE OF EMPIRE

THE LOST CENTURIES

THE MIDDLE EAST CRISIS

A SHORT HISTORY OF
THE ARAB PEOPLES

Lieutenant-General
SIR JOHN GLUBB
K.C.B., C.M.G., D.S.O., O.B.E., M.C.

Let my son often read and reflect on history.
That is the only true philosophy.
NAPOLEON BONAPARTE

Stein and Day / *Publishers* /'New York

First STEIN AND DAY PAPERBACK edition 1970

Copyright © 1969 by J.B.G. Ltd.
Library of Congress Catalog Card No. 69-16907

Manufactured in the United States of America

Stein and Day/*Publishers*/Scarborough House
Briarcliff Ma..ur, New York 10510

SBN 8128-1351-0

THIRD STEIN AND DAY PAPERBACK PRINTING 1985

Contents

	Author's Note	11
	Introduction	13
I	Before Islam	21
II	Apostle of God	30
III	The First Conquests	42
IV	First Signs of Schism	55
V	The Great Umaiyids	70
VI	The Abbasid Revolution	84
VII	The Age of Wealth and Culture	98
VIII	Disintegration	113
IX	The Seljuq Supremacy	124
X	The Mediterranean	138
XI	The Crusades	154
XII	The Fall of the Kingdom	169
XIII	A Berber Empire	181
XIV	The Mongol Catastrophe	194
XV	The Mamlooks	211
XVI	The Ottoman Period	230
XVII	The Age of Reforms	245
XVIII	North Africa down to our own Times	260
XIX	The Twentieth Century	272
XX	The Value of History	288
	A Short Bibliography	301
	Index	307

List of Maps

		PAGE
1	The Arab countries to illustrate racial origins	14
2	Arabia in A.D. 600 before Islam	22
3	Events in the life of the Prophet	31
4	Operations in Syria and Iraq, 633–638	44
5	The Arab conquest of Egypt	58
6	The Arab conquest of Persia, 636–652	61
7	Civil war between Ali and Muawiya	67
8	Events in the West, 670–717	71
9	Events in the East, 680–712	76
10	Events in the West, 717–775	86
11	Events in the East, 730–775	89
12	Events in the East, 775–833	100
13	The breakaway of the West, 755–833	102
14	Events in the East, 833–975	114
15	The Byzantine military revival, 870–999	121
16	Minor dynasties in the East, 900–1055	125
17	Syria and Iraq under Alp Arslan and Malik Shah, 1063–1092	130
18	North Africa, 800–1095	139
19	Andalus, 755–1097	147
20	The Crusader States, 1097–1150	155
21	Events in the East, 1100–1150	162
22	Routes followed by the Second Crusade	165
23	The Crusader States, 1150–1187	170
24	Campaigns of Saladin and Richard, 1187–1192	177
25	Western Islam, 1100–1269	184
26	Eastern Islam, 1156–1220	186
27	Campaigns of Jenghis Khan	195
28	Events in Syria, 1228–1260	200
29	The Crusade of St. Louis	293

30 The Campaigns of Hulagu   206
31 The end of the Crusader States   212
32 The Il Khan Empire, 1260–1334   214
33 The Mamlook Empire in the reign of Malik al Nasir
      Muhammad, 1310–1341   218
34 The Ottoman Empire   223
35 Campaigns of Tamerlane, 1399–1404   225
36 Vicissitudes of Iraq, 1508–1831   232
37 Syria and Egypt, 1517–1840   239
38 The disintegration of the Ottoman Empire, 1830–1914   247
39 Operations in Arabia, 1901–1924   254
40 North Africa, 1400–1965   261
41 The Arab Revolt, 1916–1918   274
42 Operations in Syria and Iraq in the Second World War   282
43 Situation in Palestine, April 1949   284

List of Genealogical Trees

		PAGE
1	Quraish, the Prophet's family	27
2	The Umaiyid Khalifs of Damascus	74
3	The Great Abbasid Khalifs	92
4	The Puppet Abbasid Khalifs	117
5	The Seljuqs	128
6	Quraish to show the khalifs and imams	141
7	The Fatimid Khalifs of Egypt	143
8	The Royal House of Jerusalem	159
9	The Ayoubids, the family of Saladin	182
10	The Great Muwahhids	189
11	The Mongol Khakans or Supreme Khans	196
12	The Hohenstaufen Emperors	198
13	The Il Khans of Persia	215
14	The Great Othmanli or Ottoman Sultans	221

Author's Note

ARABIC names are often both difficult and confusing to Western readers. The Arabic language is written in an alphabet different from our own and containing a number of extra letters. How to write these letters using the English alphabet is always doubtful. In recent years, learned Arabists have adopted a more-or-less agreed system of transliteration into English, but French, Germans, Italians and others all use different methods.

For Arabists the English method is excellent, but it does not help persons ignorant of Arabic to pronounce correctly. Take a very simple name, Mahmud. The English system spells the second syllable -mud, with the result that those who do not know Arabic pronounce it like the English word "mud". I have ventured to spell it -mood, the correct pronunciation being like the English word "mood".

Where the emphatic syllable is doubtful, I have placed an accent on it the first time the word is mentioned. I have not repeated the accent again. Take as an example "Murábit". (As English people often do not pronounce their r's, this might be written in English, murarbit.)

The construction of Arabic personal names may also be worth a note. The Arabic word for son is *ibn*. Arabs who are not particularly distinguished are often known only by their own names and that of their fathers, such as Ahmad ibn Ibrahim. Distinguished families or royal dynasties need a family name and this often takes the form of *ibn* with the name of a famous ancestor. Thus the ruler of central Arabia is Ibn Saud, though Saud lived two centuries or more ago. Such names are similar to our own Johnson, Harrison or Peterson.

In the plural, however, we say "the Johnsons" but the Arabs say "the sons of John". Thus we shall find Ibn Abbas, the family name of one man, but the collective name for the family is Beni Abbas, the sons of Abbas. (Beni is pronounced benny, not beany.) An alternative way of referring in Arabic to the family of Abbas is to add an

-i, Abbasi.[1] When transliterating a name of this kind, there is a European convention of adding a -d. Thus Abbasi is written Abbasid.

In the years of Arab decadence, an ever-increasing number of honorific titles was given to rulers. At the time of the Crusades, a ruler assumed two titles when he came to the throne, one a throne title, the second a religious. Thus a ruler might be called "the Victorious King, Sun of the Religion, Mahmood".

The only other group of names worthy of mention is that of the slaves of God type. The Prophet himself commended names of this kind. The word *abid* means a slave. The name we write Abdulla is really Abid Allah, Slave of God. In many cases, the word Allah is replaced by some divine attribute. Thus Abid al Rahman, Slave of the Merciful, usually written in English, Abdul Rahman. It will be noted that Abdul Rahman is one name, not a personal name and a family name, like Tom Jones.

As a result, a Muslim cannot be addressed as Abdul, which is half a phrase, "Slave of the". The family name will be added to this phrase, thus—Abdul Rahman ibn Saud, "Slave of the Merciful, the son of Saud".

There are, of course, also family names originating from professions such as Najjar, carpenter, Qassab, butcher, Nahhas, copperworker. Or from place names—Al Bukhari, the man from Bukhara.

The reader may find all this rather complicated to remember but when puzzled by names in the narrative he can refer back to this note.

---

[1] The suffix -er is used in a somewhat similar manner in English to indicate a man's place of origin—a Londoner or a New Yorker.

Introduction

WHEN I began to write this book, two problems immediately presented themselves. The first of these was its title. Should it be called a history of the Arabs, and, if so, who *are* the Arabs?

The name was originally used to designate the nomadic tribes of Arabia and indeed is still used in that sense, as a secondary meaning. The collective name in Arabic for a group of tents is an "Arab".

In the seventh century, however, these nomads established a great empire extending from the Atlantic to the borders of China, north of Tibet. For three or four centuries, the Muslim inhabitants of this empire were known as Arabs. With the disintegration of the Arab Empire in the tenth century, the word reverted to its meaning of "nomads", the peoples of the empire resuming their previous designations of Egyptians, Syrians, Persians or whatever it might be. In the same manner, in the heyday of the Roman Empire an Egyptian, a Syrian or a Spaniard might be a Roman, but with the disintegration of the Roman Empire the name was abandoned by the provincials.

This situation continued until the First World War, except for a partial attempt to impose the name of Ottomans on the subjects of that empire. After the First World War, Syrians and Iraqis began once again to call themselves Arabs, at least in an international sense. Only since the Second World War have Egypt and North Africa been included in the list of "Arab countries".

Since the 1930s a number of studies of the inhabitants of Syria, Jordan, Lebanon and Iraq have been made. By recording such physical characteristics as head shape, height, sitting height, skin, hair, eyes, features and so on, the extraordinary diversity of races[1] in these countries has been revealed.

---

[1] I use the word "race" as it is defined in the Oxford Dictionary as "a group of persons connected by common descent" or "regarded as of common stock". In other words, as an ethnic and not a cultural group.

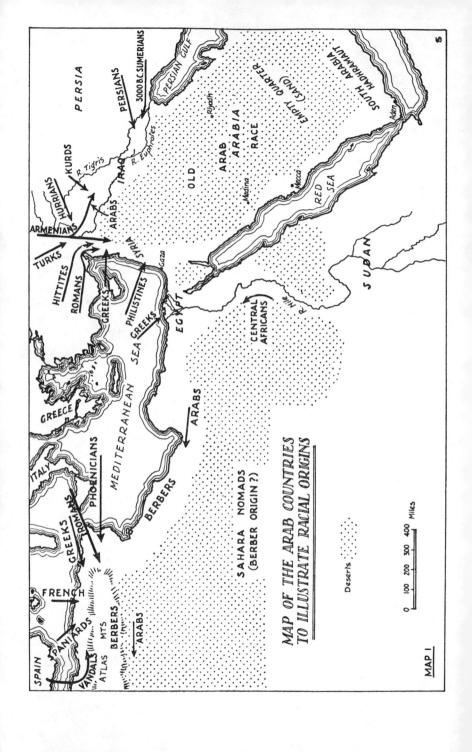

MAP OF THE ARAB COUNTRIES
TO ILLUSTRATE RACIAL ORIGINS

Deserts [dotted]

0   100 200 300 400   Miles

MAP I

For the earliest times, archaeology has come to our aid. We know now that many of the peoples of Syria and Iraq four or five thousand years ago were not racially related to the Arabs. The Sumerians, 3000 B.C., came from the east and settled in Iraq and northern Syria. The Hurrians came from the direction of north Persia, the Hittites from Asia Minor. These races seem to have been Aryans. In historical times, the same processes have continued. For a thousand years, for example, Syria and Palestine were closely connected with, and colonized by Greeks and Romans.

The early Arab historians were aware of these racial diversities. They referred quite correctly to the tribes of Arabia as Arabs and to the subjects of their empire as Arabicized. Some modern writers have preferred to call the people of the Arabian peninsula, Arabians, and the Syrians, Iraqis, Egyptians and North Africans, Arabs. An alternative is to call the inhabitants of the peninsula Arabs, and the remainder Arabic-speaking peoples.

Such devices would be extremely cumbrous in the title of this book. I accordingly decided to use the expression "Arab peoples", the plural being intended to indicate that many different ethnic groups are involved, though all share the Arabic language and culture. I venture to suggest to the reader that the vicissitudes of these people in history will be more easily understood if he remembers that they consist of many diverse races, sharing the same language.

But to explain that the Arabic-speaking peoples all differ from one another is merely academic unless some attempt be made to analyse the characteristics of each. Such an analysis must necessarily be broad, yet, in fact, the differences are in many respects extremely striking.

THE CENTRAL ARABIANS   The majority of these people are now subjects of Saudi Arabia but, in the north, they extend into the desert between Syria and the Euphrates. These northern tribes, many of them still partially or wholly nomadic, are homogeneous with the peoples of Saudi Arabia.

These Arabians, the original Arabs, are an old and almost unmixed race. This means that their characteristics are extremely uniform. Physically, and probably mentally and spiritually also, they resemble one another, with few deviations.

The deserts of Arabia have never attracted foreign invaders. The Holy Cities of Mecca and Medina, on the contrary, have long been inhabited by mixed populations from all Muslim countries and, since

1945, there has been a large influx of other Arabic-speaking races into the oilfields and, more recently, into the capital, Riyadh. There are now, therefore, several centres of mixed population but Saudi Arabia as a whole is still principally inhabited by the ancient Arab race.

These Arabs bear certain resemblances to the peoples of north-west Europe. They are of a practical, realist turn of mind, ready to strike a bargain or to compromise, hardy, enterprising and courageous. They differ from north-west Europeans in their self-reliance and readiness to take the initiative, perhaps the result of thousands of years of existence in a poor country of great open spaces. This individualism often leads to jealous rivalries, to an extreme sensitivity on what they consider to be personal honour and to a certain lack of communal loyalty and public spirit. This old Arab race were the conquerors of the empire of the seventh century and they are still excellent military material, though their ignorance of technology makes them, at the moment, incapable of meeting modern armies.

Perhaps the simplest proof of the paucity of Arabian blood in the other Arabic-speaking peoples is provided by the sparse population of the desert peninsula. The number of inhabitants in the whole vast peninsula of Arabia today is less than half that of the tiny Nile Delta.

When the Arabians broke out of their deserts and conquered their immense empire, they did so with armies of fifteen or twenty thousand men. It has been estimated that, when all the conquests were over, the Arabians represented only one per cent of the population of their empire. The remainder were a medley of many different races. Even today, Arabian blood may well constitute only one or two per cent of that of the people of some of the Arab countries.

THE SYRIANS   (including the Lebanese and the Arabs of Palestine). Syria forms a complete contrast to Saudi Arabia. Whereas no foreign invaders were tempted by Arabia, the history of Syria is little more than a list of foreign invasions. The climate of Syria was tempting to races from colder, northern countries. Moreover the long narrow strip of country from Aleppo to Gaza, confined by the Mediterranean on one side and the desert on the other, constituted an isthmus joining Asia and eastern Europe to Africa. From the dawn of history, an endless succession of invading armies and migrating nations travelled up and down this Syrian causeway.

In 539 B.C., Syria was conquered by the Persians, in 333 B.C. by Alexander the Great. Thereafter, until the Arab conquest in A.D. 636,

Syria remained Greek or Roman for a thousand years, a period during which extensive immigration took place from Greece, Italy and other Mediterranean countries. The Syrians are racially unrelated to the Arabs of Arabia. Many of their characteristics resemble those of the Greeks, particularly their extreme intellectual subtlety. As professors, philosophers and lawyers, they supplied a considerable number of the intellectual leaders of Rome.

Like many intellectuals, they are unpractical in ordinary life and are incapable of compromise. Intellectually a proposition is correct or erroneous. More practical minds accept the statement that half a loaf is better than no bread, but not so the intellectual. Syrians who migrate achieve honours and distinctions in every country but at home their subtlety often lacks realism. They are socially charming, extremely courteous and the heirs of thousands of years of culture. The Syrians are thus not only racially unrelated to the Arabians but, in many ways, their opposites. The Arabians are distinguished by practicality and common sense, the Syrians by subtlety and intellectual theories.

THE IRAQIS   seem to be composed of many racial strains. The peoples of southern Iraq are probably largely of Persian or other eastern origin. Those of northern Iraq are a mixture of Kurds, Turks, early Indo-European races and Arabs. The Iraqis are less intellectual and less polished and courteous than the Syrians but are of a stronger and coarser strain. On the other hand, they differ profoundly from the Arabians.

THE EGYPTIANS   are probably the descendants of the people of the Pharaohs. It is to be noted, moreover, that the Sahara forms an almost 'impassable obstacle between tropical Africa and Mediterranean North Africa. The Nile valley is almost the only connection between central Africa and the Mediterranean. As a result, there is no doubt that from prehistoric times, there has been a continual infiltration of central African blood down the Nile into Egypt.

Closely packed in the damp heat of the Nile Delta, the conditions of the lives of Egyptians for thousands of years have been the exact opposite to conditions in Arabia, where the great open spaces have produced individuality and initiative. The density of population and the enervating climate of the Nile Delta have been destructive of initiative and self-reliance.

Egyptians are, in general, submissive to authority. They can fight stubbornly in a static and defensive position but rarely display enough enterprise for moving warfare. Thus once again we find the characteristics of the Egyptians, like those of the Syrians, to be the exact opposite of those of the Arabians.

THE SOUTH ARABIANS   may be yet another different race, but I have not seen any scientific analysis of their origin. Very old local tradition divided the Arabs into a northern and a Yemenite race. The sand desert, known as the Empty Quarter, separates Central Arabia from Aden and Hadhramaut.

THE NORTH AFRICANS   are quite distinct from the peoples east of Suez. The majority belong to the racial group known as Berbers, who, since prehistoric times, have been located in the area. They are entirely different from Arabs and the two races do not integrate easily. There are also pockets of Arabs here and there, the remains of tribal immigrations many centuries ago.

While the peoples of the Atlas are mainly Berbers, the inhabitants of the coastal plains are of mixed Mediterranean race. Phoenicians, Greeks, Vandals, Italians, Byzantines, Spaniards and French have all contributed to the coastal population, where they have mingled with Berbers and Arabs.

These brief notes will have sufficed to show that the word Arab, as used today, has no racial significance. The "Arabs" are a linguistic group composed of many races, which often show characteristics not only different but diametrically opposed to one another.

The nearest parallel to the "Arab" group of peoples is probably to be found in South America, where many different races share the Spanish and Portuguese languages. In both cases the common religion and language are due to military conquest several centuries ago and have little or no ethnic significance. If the reader keeps these facts in mind, the historical vicissitudes described in this book will be much more easily understood.

*   *   *

The second problem which faced me was where to end my story. This book is intended to be a historical work and I was tempted to end it in 1900 or with the First World War. It seemed to me, however, that it might be annoying for the reader if I stopped fifty or sixty years ago, without connecting the narrative with the situation today.

On the other hand, the last fifty years have been so packed with problems, many of them still burning political issues, that to treat them fully would occupy the whole book, leaving no space for the previous thirteen centuries of history. I have accordingly carried my story up to the 1950s, but have limited myself to a brief summary of events in the last fifty years. To those who wish to study the political problems of today, a vast selection of works is available, a few of which have been included in the bibliography.

I

Before Islam

AT the beginning of the seventh century A.D., the civilized world (omitting India and China) had, for six centuries, been divided between two ancient and cultured empires, the Roman on the west and the Persian on the east. America, Africa south of the Sahara and Australasia were, of course, undiscovered. The frontier between these two great power blocs extended, with occasional gains or losses, from Dura Europus on the Euphrates through Nisibis to Armenia. The Arabian peninsula thus lay south of the imperial boundary and in contact with both empires.

Rome and Persia passed six centuries in constant military, political and commercial rivalry. Although both empires poured out their blood and treasure in these endless struggles, the frontier between them remained virtually unchanged for six hundred years.

In 395, however, the Roman Empire was divided into eastern and western halves under Arcadius and Honorius, the sons of the Emperor Theodosius. In 475, the Western Roman Empire collapsed and most of Italy, Gaul, Spain and Britain were abandoned to the barbarians. The eastern half of the empire, however, survived with its capital at Byzantium or Constantinople. The eastern Roman provinces of Greece, Asia Minor, Syria and Egypt had always been wealthier and more civilized than Gaul, Spain and Britain, and the Eastern or Byzantine Empire was able to survive the loss of the West. In regard to military defence against Persia, however, the Byzantines were soon in difficulties. When the whole Roman Empire was at the height of its glory, it had barely been able to hold its ground against the Persians. Now the eastern half was left to defend itself alone.

The great Byzantine Emperor Justinian, who reigned from 527 to 565, set his heart on the reconquest of the West. Under his famous commander Belisarius, North Africa and part of Italy were reconquered by Constantinople but the effort required to achieve these

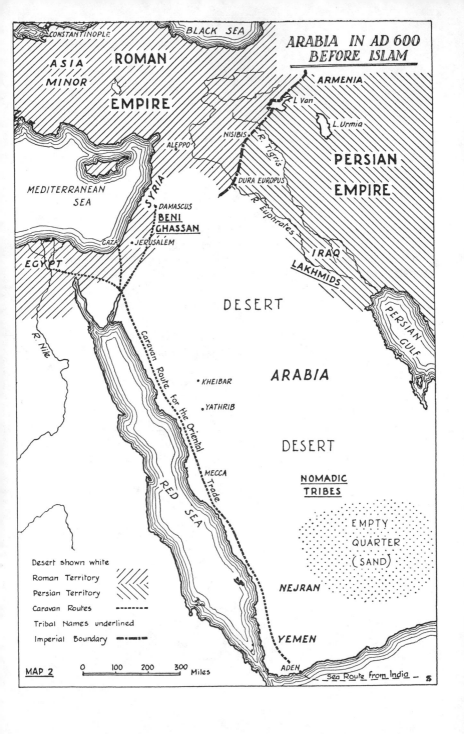

ARABIA IN AD 600
BEFORE ISLAM

CONSTANTINOPLE   BLACK SEA

ASIA
MINOR   ROMAN

EMPIRE   ARMENIA

L.Van

L.Urmia

MEDITERRANEAN
SEA   NISIBIS

ALEPPO   PERSIAN

DURA EUROPUS   EMPIRE

SYRIA   DAMASCUS

BENI
GHASSAN   IRAQ

GAZA   JERUSALEM   LAKHMIDS

EGYPT

DESERT   PERSIAN
GULF

R. Nile

ARABIA

KHEIBAR

YATHRIB   DESERT

MECCA   NOMADIC
TRIBES

RED SEA   EMPTY

QUARTER

(SAND)

NEJRAN

Desert shown white
Roman Territory
Persian Territory
Caravan Routes   - - - - -
Tribal Names underlined
Imperial Boundary   -·-·-·

YEMEN

MAP 2   0   100   200   300 Miles   ADEN   Sea Route from India

Caravan Route for the Oriental Trade

victories necessitated a weakening on the Persian frontier. With his armies engaged in the West, Justinian was obliged to buy peace in the East by the payment of indemnities and the surrender of cities and territory to the King of Persia.

The Byzantine Empire fell into confusion after the death of Justinian. In 602, profiting by a mutiny in the Byzantine army, the King of Persia, Chosroes Parwiz, invaded Byzantine territory almost unopposed. In 613 he captured Damascus, in 614 Jerusalem, and in 616, his armies occupied both Egypt and Asia Minor. The Eastern Roman Empire seemed to be about to disappear as the Western had done in 475.

In this moment of crisis, the Byzantine Empire was saved by the genius of the Emperor Heraclius who, in five years of brilliant fighting, defeated the Persians and drove them from Roman territory. In 628, Chosroes Parwiz was assassinated and the Persian Empire collapsed in anarchy. After twenty-six years of war, during which both empires had been reduced to bankruptcy and exhaustion, peace was concluded on the basis of the frontiers of 602.

*   *   *

The greater part of the peninsula of Arabia consisted of deserts, inhabited by nomadic tribes, breeders of camels, sheep and goats. North of the actual peninsula, the same desert extended as far as Aleppo, thereby separating the settled and cultivated lands of Syria and Iraq. The camel provided the only means of transport in the desert, which was completely impassable to the cavalry and infantry of the Byzantine and Persian armies. As a result, military operations between the two empires were limited to a front extending from the Euphrates to the Caucasus.

This boundary was heavily studded with fortresses but neither empire had constructed any defences to protect its territories from the Arabs of the desert, who were not considered to constitute any military threat to the imperial armies. To provide against raids by the desert tribes, however, both empires maintained subject dynasties of Arab princes.

In eastern Syria and Damascus, the princely family of Beni Ghassan held sway, the head of the family enjoying the title of a Roman patrician. On the lower Euphrates, the Arab Lakhmids were subject princes of the Great King. The two Arab dynasties occupied themselves in endless desert warfare and raiding against each other. This system of Arab satellite princedoms guarding the desert flanks of both empires broke down, by a curious coincidence, a few years before the Muslim invasions.

The official religion of the Byzantine Empire was Orthodox Christianity. The Greeks, who formed a large part of the subjects of that empire, have always been the possessors of highly subtle intellects. For several centuries, their cleverness had found scope in hairsplitting discussions of religious dogma. These subtle disputations were often conducted with a singular absence of Christian charity and led to furious hatreds and persecutions.

In the sixth century, the inhabitants of Syria and Palestine were of the Christian Monophysite sect, which had been pronounced heretical by the Orthodox or established church of the empire. In 581, as a result of these religious differences, the prince of Beni Ghassan was arrested and conveyed to Constantinople. Thereafter the Arab tribes of eastern Syria remained in anarchy and semi-rebellion.

In 605, Naaman ibn al Mundhir, the Lakhmid prince, quarrelled with the Great King, who abolished the privileged position hitherto enjoyed by the family as defenders of the desert frontier, with the result that the Arab tribes along the Euphrates revolted against Persia.

In 628, therefore, when both empires lay exhausted after twenty-six years of war against one another, their Arab satellites along the desert frontiers were everywhere disaffected or in open revolt.

*   *   *

The importance of Arabia to the rest of the world had always been due to its geographical position, lying as a barrier between two seas. The climate of the countries round the Indian Ocean and eastwards to China differed fundamentally from that of the Mediterranean basin. As a result, the products of East Africa, India, Indonesia and China were considered rare and exotic in the West and commanded high prices. To reach the Mediterranean, these oriental goods could be conveyed by sea up the Red Sea or the Persian Gulf.

Navigation in the Red Sea was dangerous, however, owing to coral reefs and to pirates, with the result that a large proportion of the eastern trade was landed in the Yemen and conveyed by camel caravan up the eastern shores of the Red Sea to Egypt and Syria. From very early times, this lucrative trade had produced a wealthy and civilized Arab community in the Yemen, variously known as Minaeans or Sabaeans. The Queen of Sheba, who paid a famous visit to Solomon, was probably queen of what we call the Yemen. South

Arabia also earned a large revenue from its own production of spices, which sold at high prices in the West. Half way between the Yemen and the Byzantine frontier lay a small desert settlement called Mecca, which was a staging post for this caravan trade.

*   *   *

The greater part of the peninsula of Arabia, as already explained, was inhabited by nomadic Arab tribes, who lived by breeding camels and sheep. The principal interest of their lives was provided by wars between one another. Living in semi-isolation from the rest of the world, the tribes had produced a culture of their own, particularly in so far as concerned their wars.

The nomads lived in a state of perpetual war but their hostilities were conducted according to a strict code of honour. No tribe really aspired to exterminate or enslave another. Indeed, compared with the ruthless methods used by the "civilized" nations of the twentieth century, Arab tribal wars were scarcely more than a game.

The object of the Arab warrior was not so much to win the war as to gain glory. This attitude produced a certain "sporting" spirit between the combatants. No glory could be won by treachery or stealth, even if they resulted in a victory. Before a battle, time was allowed for champions to fight one another between the armies—a process quite irrelevant to military tactics but one which allowed the maximum number of persons to win glory before a large audience. Sometimes the date and place of a battle were fixed by agreement long before the event, to ensure that neither side stole an unfair advantage.

A life spent as a herdsman, watching grazing animals in the vast emptiness of the desert, is doubtless one of wearisome monotony. Tribal wars and the exploits of rival heroes lent excitement and glamour to this dull routine. Moreover the Arab nomads were passionate poets and every incident of these chivalrous encounters were immortalized in verse and recited every night around the camp fires which flickered here and there in the empty vastness of the desert peninsula.

The nomadic tribes of Arabia at the beginning of the seventh century were worshippers of idols or rather perhaps of spirits. They made pilgrimages to sacred stones and trees, which they kissed and on which they hung offerings. These sacred objects were probably thought of as the residences of the spirits peculiar to a well or spring.

This worship of the native spirits may have been influenced by the

Chaldaeans of the lower Tigris and Euphrates valley, who were famous as astronomers. Thus before Islam, we find Arabs with the name of Abid Shems, servant of the sun. The temple of Mecca, a small cubical stone building called the Kaaba, was said to contain three hundred and sixty-five idols.

On the frontiers of Syria and Iraq, however, Christianity had largely replaced idolatry. The Syrian tribes were all Christian. On the borders of Persia, the Nestorians, a Christian sect denounced as heretical by the Orthodox Byzantine Church, had made many converts along the Euphrates. In the Yemen and Nejran, there were also Christian communities.

Judaism had penetrated Arabia before Christianity and there were large colonies of people professing the Jewish faith at Kheibar, Medina (then called Yathrib) and in the Yemen. Thus while the tribes of the peninsula were still idolaters, the more civilized Arab communities along the fringes of the desert had already been penetrated by Judaism and Christianity.

*   *   *

We have already mentioned the desert town of Mecca in two connections. Firstly as a staging post for commercial caravans from the Yemen to Egypt and Syria, and secondly as the site of an important idol temple. This little town of Mecca was dominated by an Arab clan called Quraish, who were both merchants and also guardians of the idol fane.

Quraish were not mere caravaners or camel drivers but were also men of business. They met the ships from India and Africa in the harbours of south Arabia, bought the merchandise, transported it to Syria and sold it at a large profit. With the proceeds they bought the products of Egypt and Syria, and sold them in Mecca and in the other oases of Arabia.

The Meccans even turned their religious duties into financial profit. Once a year, the tribes of the peninsula made a pilgrimage to the temple of Mecca. Their worship of the idols was combined with an annual fair at which the traders of Quraish were able to dispose at a profit of the piece-goods which they had brought down from Damascus.

The merchants of Mecca were, therefore, men of the world, engrossed in their money-making ventures. The more wealthy of them had visited the Byzantine court or had paid their respects in Persia to the Great King. As most of their business was with Syria

1. GENEALOGICAL TREE OF QURAISH, THE PROPHET'S FAMILY

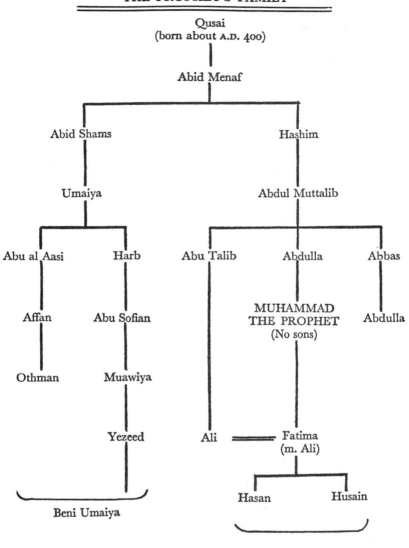

NOTES

(1) Abu Sofian of Beni Umaiya was Muhammad's chief opponent.

(2) The Prophet had no surviving sons. Two families of Beni Hashim were in the future to join in the struggle for power, the descendants of Ali and those of Abbas.

(3) The persons listed had many other sons but only those mentioned in the text are shown.

and Egypt, however, their sympathies lay with the Byzantines rather than with the Persians in the long "World Wars" of the time.

*   *   *

Quraish owed their powerful position in Mecca to their ancestor Qusai, who had seized possession of the place from its previous owners. A great-grandson of Qusai, known as Abdul Muttalib, born in 497, likewise achieved a position of considerable influence. He had five sons of whom one, Abdulla, died an early death in 570. A few months later, on 20th August, 570, his wife gave birth to a son who was named Muhammad.

It was the custom of Quraish to give their children to be suckled by women of the neighbouring tribes, the free air of the desert being thought healthier than that of the dusty little town. Muhammad was thus given to a woman of the Beni Saad tribe outside Mecca.

When he was six years old the child returned to his mother in Mecca, but within a year she died, leaving him an orphan. He was looked after by a slave girl until his grandfather, Abdul Muttalib, took him in. Two years later, however, Abdul Muttalib died and the boy found refuge with his uncle Abu Talib. At the age of twelve, the young Muhammad accompanied his uncle on a business trip to Damascus.

The future prophet, perhaps as a result of these vicissitudes, grew up quiet and pensive. His kind uncle Abu Talib was poor and Muhammad had inherited nothing. Sometimes he worked as a shepherd, at others he made a small profit in business transactions, as did all the Meccans. At the age of twenty-five, his uncle secured him a job to conduct a trading caravan to Syria. As he already enjoyed a reputation for honesty, he was made responsible for the disposal of the merchandise and the purchase of Syrian piece-goods for resale in Mecca.

The caravan belonged to a rich widow of Quraish who managed her own commercial affairs. Muhammad performed the duties entrusted to him to her complete satisfaction, with the result that, soon afterwards, she sent him a proposal of marriage. Khadija[1] was much older than Muhammad but, in other respects, the match was a good one. Muhammad consented and the marriage was an unqualified success. She bore him two sons and four daughters, though both the sons died in infancy.

His marriage to the rich widow absolved Muhammad from the

---

[1] Pronounced Khadeeja.

necessity of earning his living. Freed from financial anxieties, he was able increasingly to indulge his taste for solitude and meditation. Generally reserved and silent, he nevertheless relaxed in congenial company and was often playful and humorous. A quiet, kindly, affectionate man, he was the devoted husband of his rather middle-aged wife, Khadija, whom he consulted on all his problems.

NOTABLE DATES

Division of the Roman Empire into two halves	395
Collapse of the Western Roman Empire	475
Attempt of the Emperor Justinian to reconquer the West	527–565
Birth of Muhammad	20th August, 570
Marriage of Muhammad to the widow Khadija	595
Occupation of Syria, Egypt and Asia Minor by the Persians	616
Assassination of Chosroes Parwiz } Conclusion of Roman–Persian peace }	628

PERSONALITIES

Byzantine Emperor Justinian
Byzantine Emperor Heraclius
Chosroes Parwiz, King of Persia
Muhammad, the future prophet
His uncle Abu Talib
His wife Khadija

II

Apostle of God

AS he grew older, Muhammad spent more and more of his time in meditation. Escaping from the dusty lanes and the jostling crowds of Mecca, he would take refuge in lonely caves in the craggy mountain peaks which overlooked the town. Rocky gorges, bare precipices and the absence of all vegetation gave the landscape a stern and savage character beneath the blistering sun. Here he would ponder on the joys of heaven, the endless tortures of hell-fire and the vast power of a single Almighty God.

Returning home, he would pour his fears and hopes into the sympathetic ear of Khadija, who combined for him the love of a wife with the solicitous care of the mother whom he had lost as an infant. One night in 610, when he was forty years old, he was sleeping in a cave in the mountains when he was visited by the Archangel Gabriel, who commanded him to read:

> "Read in the name of the Lord who created,
> Who created man of blood coagulated.
> Read! The Lord is the most beneficent,
> Who taught by the pen,
> Taught what they knew not to men."

Muhammad, fearing that he was possessed by some evil spirit, ran from his cave to throw himself over a precipice, when suddenly he saw the Archangel Gabriel "in the form of a man, with his feet astride the horizon". Shattered by these experiences, he hastened home to confide his visions to Khadija, who declared her belief that he was to be the prophet of the Arabs. His cousin Ali, the son of his uncle Abu Talib, and Zeid, a boy whom he had adopted, formed, with Khadija, his first three converts. A Meccan merchant called Abu Bekr, a quiet, pleasant man, became his fourth disciple.

Three years after his vision of Gabriel, Muhammad received the order to preach. His doubts seemed to be ended and he stood up in the public square to address his fellow citizens. His teaching was

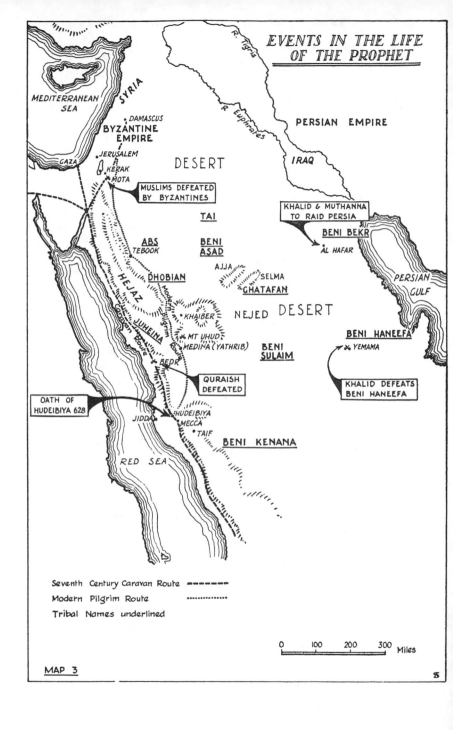

EVENTS IN THE LIFE
OF THE PROPHET

MEDITERRANEAN
SEA

SYRIA

• DAMASCUS

BYZANTINE
EMPIRE

• JERUSALEM

GAZA

KERAK

MOTA

MUSLIMS DEFEATED
BY BYZANTINES

DESERT

TAI

ABS

TEBOOK

BENI
ASAD

DHOBIAN

AJJA

SELMA

GHATAFAN

HEJAZ

JUHEINA

KHAIBER

NEJED DESERT

MT UHUD

MEDINA (YATHRIB)

BENI
SULAIM

BEDR

QURAISH
DEFEATED

OATH OF
HUDEIBIYA 628

JIDDA

HUDEIBIYA

MECCA

• TAIF

BENI KENANA

RED SEA

R. Tigris

PERSIAN EMPIRE

IRAQ

R. Euphrates

KHALID & MUTHANNA
TO RAID PERSIA

BENI BEKR

AL HAFAR

PERSIAN
GULF

BENI HANEEFA

YEMAMA

KHALID DEFEATS
BENI HANEEFA

Seventh Century Caravan Route   --------

Modern Pilgrim Route   ············

Tribal Names underlined

0   100   200   300 Miles

MAP 3

simple. God, he alleged, was One and idols must be swept away. He
himself was a messenger, or apostle, sent by God. One day the dead
would rise again, the righteous to eternal happiness, the idolaters to
hell-fire.

He claimed to have learned these facts by divine revelation. Sometimes, he said, the Archangel Gabriel spoke to him, man to man.
Sometimes he heard an interior voice. As soon as such a revelation
was over, he would recite to his disciples a passage in sonorous
rhyming prose, which they learned by heart. These revelations,
collated after his death, went to form the Qoran.

The new Apostle[1] claimed that the faith which he was preaching
was not new, but was, on the contrary, the religion of Abraham,
which, he alleged, had subsequently been distorted by the Israelites.
Eventually Jesus had been sent to bring religion back from Jewish
heresies to the true path. Muhammad stated that Jesus was the Spirit
of God, but that, after a time, his followers also had adulterated his
teaching.

Now, Muhammad claimed, he too had been sent to restore the
religion of Abraham. The revelations which he received and recited
to his followers were not, he alleged, composed by him. They were
the actual words of God, which he only repeated verbatim. He called
this new way of life Islam—surrender to God. Those who adopted it
were to be known as Muslims or surrendered persons.

In spite of Muhammad's earnestness, his preaching met with little
response. After four years of his ministry, his disciples only numbered
about seventy. The Meccans particularly resented two factors in his
doctrine. Firstly they were proud of their idol temple. Moreover
men from all over Arabia came to it as pilgrims and bought many
commodities which the Meccans imported. If Muhammad insisted
on the destruction of the idols, both the prestige and the commerce of
Mecca would suffer. Secondly the Prophet alleged that their fathers
and ancestors were all suffering in hell, for they in their lifetime had
worshipped such idols.

Family feeling was too strong to allow his enemies to inflict physical
injury on Muhammad. His relatives would have been bound to
protect him, even if they did not believe in his preaching. Several of
his converts, however, were slaves or servants and without tribal
protection. Some of these were subjected to actual persecution.
Muhammad himself suffered many humiliations and annoyances.

[1] Muhammad was known to his followers both as the Apostle of God and also as the
Prophet. I have used both designations.

In 615, five years after his first vision of Gabriel, fifteen of his converts, harassed by ridicule and violence, sailed for the Christian
Kingdom of Abyssinia.

In 619, the Prophet suffered two personal misfortunes in the
death of the faithful Khadija and of Abu Talib, the uncle who had
brought him up. In March 620, however, Muhammad met seven
men from Yathrib (later to be known as Medina) who had come to
Mecca on a pilgrimage. As the result of a private talk, the seven
declared themselves converted.

A year later, the seven again came on the pilgrimage, and brought
five more with them. The twelve met the Prophet secretly at night in
a little valley east of Mecca and pledged their loyalty to him, returning to Yathrib full of enthusiasm. Muhammad's hopes were now
fixed on Yathrib and he almost ceased preaching in Mecca, as a
result of which persecution was relaxed.

In March 622, seventy-three men came from Yathrib and swore
allegiance secretly to the Prophet. A few days later, he instructed his
Meccan disciples to slip away unostentatiously, one by one, and to
reassemble in Yathrib, two hundred and fifty miles further north.
Muhammad showed considerable courage by himself remaining in
Mecca until all had left. Only his cousin, Ali, the son of Abu Talib,
and his faithful friend Abu Bekr remained with him.

The Meccan leaders had now noticed the disappearance of the
Apostle's followers and held a council, at which it was decided to kill
Muhammad. The latter, however, heard of their resolve, slipped out
of his house and took refuge in that of Abu Bekr. "God has given me
permission to emigrate," he told his friend. As darkness fell, the two
men clambered out of a back window of Abu Bekr's house and
scrambled up the rocky mountainside behind the town, where they
hid themselves in a cave.

As soon as the escape was known, the Meccans offered a large
reward for the apprehension of the two fugitives. The hue and cry
lasted for three days. On the fourth evening, Abdulla, the son of Abu
Bekr, who had stayed in Mecca to watch events, brought three riding
camels to the cave and reported that the way was clear. Asma, Abu
Bekr's daughter, had prepared a bag of food which she tied to her
father's saddle. Silently the three camels padded down the mountain
track and across the desert to the north.

If some passing herdsman had recognized the three riders and
given the alarm, the history of the world would have been very
different. As it was, on 28th June, 622, just after noon, the weary

travellers topped a pass in the rocky Hejaz mountains and saw at their feet the cool green fields and the gardens of plumed date palms of the oasis of Yathrib, thenceforward renamed Medinat al Nebi, or the Prophet's city.

*   *   *

The date of Muhammad's escape from Mecca to Medina has ever since marked the commencement of the Muslim calendar. It also marks a complete turning point in his career. Twelve years had passed since his first vision of the archangel. Throughout this period, the Apostle had shown an extraordinary degree of patience and humility under insult, discouragement and ill treatment. His revelations, couched in glowing and poetic terms similar to those used by Isaiah, Jeremiah or Ezekiel, had seemed to reveal the burning and passionate conviction of his heart.

But once established in Medina his attitude changed. Gabriel, he announced, had told him that God now ordered the Muslims to fight the unbelievers. The most powerful factor in promoting the great Arab conquests, which were soon to follow, was the promise of the immediate admission to paradise of all Muslims who fell in battle against non-Muslims. Moreover the detailed descriptions of that paradise with its cool, flowing streams, delicious fruits and above all its houris, beautiful virgins perpetually young, were precisely such as to tempt the poor bedouins, whose lives were an endless struggle against physical hardships.

The fact that Mecca earned its living from the caravan trade between the Yemen and the Mediterranean world has already been explained. Medina (for we will now drop its name of Yathrib) lay two hundred and fifty miles north of Mecca and was thus well placed to cut the caravan route on which the livelihood of Mecca depended.[2] For the unbelievers whom the Apostle ordered the Muslims to fight were not at this stage the Byzantine Christians but the idolaters of Mecca, who had for twelve years scorned and rejected his message.

In March 624, a caravan of a thousand camels belonging to the Meccans was due to pass Medina, returning from Damascus. The Muslims in Medina resolved to intercept it. Their intention, however, became known and the leader of the caravan, one Abu Sofian, was informed of it while still in Syria. He immediately despatched a swift camel rider to Mecca, urging Quraish to send an armed force to meet him and to escort the caravan past Medina.

[2] Map 3, page 31.

Muhammad set out from Medina with three hundred and four-teen men to intercept the caravan at the wells of Bedr, where it was expected to water. Abu Sofian, however, an old caravaner, seeing that no escort had come to meet him, changed his course so as to avoid Bedr and slipped by in a long forced march before the Prophet and his disciples reached the wells.

Meanwhile, however, unknown to the Muslims or the caravan, an escort of a thousand men had left Mecca to meet the caravan. In the evening, the three hundred Muslims camped by the wells of Bedr. Next morning the Meccans arrived, three times as numerous as the Muslims. Quraish, however, were not all anxious to fight. They had come to protect their caravan, which, they had now heard, had already passed safely. The Meccan emigrants who were with Muhammad included men from every clan in the city and tribal feeling was strongly opposed to shedding the blood of kinsmen.

The Muslims, on the other hand, had been obliged to escape from Mecca, leaving all their property behind. They were penniless exiles, longing to avenge their wrongs. Moreover God, the Prophet said, had ordered them to fight and those who were killed, freed from the anxieties and privations of this hard world, would be welcomed by bevies of lovely virgins into the glowing gardens of paradise.

After a few single combats between champions, Quraish advanced and for some time a wild and furious mêlée ensued. The Prophet had remained behind the battle line, calling loudly upon God for victory. The fierce enthusiasm of the Muslims was not to be withstood and the Meccans at last broke in flight. Out of about one thousand men of Quraish, forty-nine were killed, and a similar number were taken prisoners. The Muslims then returned in triumph to Medina.

More than half the inhabitants of the oasis of Medina were Jews. The Prophet, claiming to preach the religion of Abraham, had at first hoped for their support. The Jews, however, were well versed in the Old Testament and some of them laughed at Muhammad's claims. Returning flushed with victory from Bedr, the Muslims surrounded Beni Qainuqa, one of the Jewish tribes, and compelled them to migrate to Syria. Their property, houses, and gardens were con-fiscated and provided homes and a livelihood for the exiled Meccans.

Among the Arabs, poetry was a passion. Topical poems, passing from mouth to mouth, served as propaganda among a people largely illiterate and the sarcasms of the local poets were greatly feared by Arab rulers. The Prophet, who was sincerely and passionately serious about his mission, was deeply outraged by the biting ironies of certain poets of Medina, and caused three of them to be murdered by his disciples.

At the same time, he engaged a number of men to defend him in verse, of whom the best known was Hassán[3] ibn Thábit. "How can you manage," enquired Muhammad, "to satirize Quraish without injuring me, seeing that I am myself of that tribe?" "I shall know how to pick you out from their midst," replied the facetious Hassan, "as a man picks a hair out of the stew."

It will be noticed that the Prophet, so patient, humble and devoted under persecution in Mecca, commenced to use power politics after his arrival in Medina. Not only does he resort to war against the Meccans, but in Medina he drives the Jews into exile and arranges for his own opponents to be assassinated. Muhammad himself, however, claimed that he preached the same religion as Abraham, Moses and Jesus.

Their respective attitudes to the legitimacy of physical force has, ever since then, been one of the most marked contrasts between Muslims and Christians. Individual wars may be right or wrong, but war in general cannot be condemned by Muslims, because it was used by the Prophet himself. The fact that Muslims believe that war can sometimes be a religious duty has resulted in the fact that Muslim soldiers are often extremely religious and enjoy a far higher status than they do in Christian countries.

Muslims in general do not believe that men can be made righteous by moral example or by intellectual persuasion alone, but consider that force is also necessary. To Christians, war has always presented a problem. Violence appears, at first sight, to be contrary to the Gospels, yet Christian governments have never been able to avoid wars. Murder is merely an extension of the same principle. The Prophet, it is true, only used war and murder against the enemies of Islam, who were obstructing the propagation of the faith. Nevertheless, once violence is admitted, it is all too easily abused.

Soon after his arrival in Medina, Muhammad married Aisha, the daughter of Abu Bekr. She is said to have been nine years old, while he was fifty-three. Before he died, the Apostle married eleven wives. His followers were permitted only four wives but he claimed for himself a divine revelation, permitting him to exceed the statutory number. Yet it is remarkable that he had been for twenty-five years the faithful husband of Khadija, a woman considerably older than himself. Most of his marrying was done in his late fifties, partly, per-

[3] Accent on the second syllable.

haps, in the hope of having a son as a successor—a hope which was never realized.

He himself, however, made no secret of his fondness for women. He once said, "I love most in the world women and perfume, but the apple of my eye is prayer." Although he had eleven wives and allowed his followers four, he was very strict concerning extra-marital indulgence. It was said that he would not so much as touch a woman's hand except in the case of his wives. He was never interested in money, even when he could have acquired considerable wealth. He died penniless in a rude hut which we would consider unfit for a stable.

The Arabs before Islam were addicted to drinking. While living in Medina, apparently as the result of a case of drunkenness, the Prophet forbade his followers to use alcohol. Muslim jurists, however, classify drunkenness as detestable but not as mortal sin.

*   *   *

The strategy followed by the Muslims in Medina was to intercept all caravans going from Mecca to Syria, thereby ruining the Meccans. The open deserts crossed by the Meccan caravans were inhabited by nomadic tribes, whose co-operation was obviously necessary for this blockade. The Prophet had won over the tribe of Juheina, which camped between Medina and the Red Sea, but the tribes of Ghatafan and Beni Sulaim further east were allies of Quraish.[4] Thus a subsidiary war developed between the Muslims and their confederate tribes on the one hand, and the tribes allied to Mecca on the other.

These alarms were causing considerable damage to the caravan trade and, in 625, Quraish marched on Medina, determined to put an end to Muhammad and his sect, once and for all. The Meccan force was commanded by Abu Sofian, who had led the caravan to safety at the time of Bedr. It consisted of three thousand men, including two hundred cavalry. The followers of Muhammad could muster only seven hundred men and no horses, less than a quarter of the strength of Quraish.

The Muslims nevertheless sallied out of the town and a battle was fought at the foot of Mount Uhud, some two miles north of Medina. The Muslims were completely defeated, Muhammad himself was wounded and his uncle Hamza was killed. The remnants of the Muslims, carrying the wounded Prophet, fled for refuge to the rocky

[4] Map 3, page 31.

crags of Mount Uhud. Quraish could probably have ended the war by occupying Medina, but the old Arabs did not practise total war. Final victory was not to them a familiar concept. Abu Sofian, standing in the plain below, called up to the fugitives clinging to the rocks of Uhud, "Today is in exchange for Bedr. We will meet again next year." Quraish then remounted their camels and rode away.

The fact that the Apostle had claimed that divine aid had been responsible for the victory of Bedr made it all the more difficult to explain away the defeat at Uhud. A special divine revelation came to him, however, now incorporated in Chapter III of the Qoran. God, it said, had allowed the Muslims to be defeated in order to try their faith. Meanwhile morale was soon restored by a series of plundering raids against the tribes favourable to Quraish.

Two years after Uhud, the Meccans once again marched on Medina, this time with ten thousand men. Four thousand of these were Quraish, the remainder being from their allied tribes, Ghatafan, Beni Sulaim and Beni Kenana. The Muslims, unable to face so large a force in the open, shut themselves into the town. The fickle tribesmen, who enjoyed their galloping desert battles, had no taste for the drudgery of a siege. After blockading Medina for three weeks, the Meccans and their allies withdrew.

One of the Jewish tribes of Medina, Beni Quraidha, had placed itself in communication with the enemy during the siege. No sooner had the Meccans retired than the Prophet gave orders for the siege and capture of the Beni Quraidha settlement. All the men, to the number of seven hundred, were put to death in cold blood.

*   *   *

Before Islam, the idolatrous Arabs recognized four sacred months in the year, during which raiding and fighting were forbidden. In March 628, which was one of these months of truce, Muhammad declared his intention of making a pilgrimage to the temple of Mecca. According to generally accepted practice, Quraish had no right to resist him. In fact, however, the Meccans were by no means convinced that the Muslims would observe the code and they consequently mobilized their forces and took up a position to defend the city.

The Muslims halted at Hudeibiya, a short day's march from Mecca. They had not come armed to fight a battle and their position was precarious. Standing beneath one of those thorny trees which are to be found here and there among the sand and rocks of these arid mountains, Muhammad called on all those present to swear to fight to the death. Long years afterwards, when the Arabs had built up a great empire, the deepest respect was always shown firstly, to the men who had fought at Bedr and secondly, to those who had taken the oath at Hudeibiya.

Emissaries passed between the two sides and a truce was eventually concluded. The Muslims were to return to Medina but were to be allowed to make the pilgrimage after the expiry of one year. These events took place in 628, the year, it will be remembered, in which the exhausted empires of Byzantium and Persia at last made peace after twenty-six years of war.

In 629, two thousand Muslims claimed their right to make the Meccan pilgrimage. Quraish had evacuated the city and camped on the surrounding mountains. The Prophet went straight to the Kaaba, touched the Black Stone[5] and performed the seven circuits of the building prescribed by the heathen ritual. It was soon clear that Muhammad's idea of making a pilgrimage was a political master-stroke. Much of the opposition to him in Mecca had sprung from the belief that he wished to discredit the temple, on which the prestige of the city depended. Now he announced that the Kaaba was the House of God and had been built by Abraham, whose religion he was himself preaching. The Meccans had sinned by placing idols in the Kaaba and these must be removed. But when this had been done, the Kaaba would remain the House of God and pilgrimage to it would be a Muslim obligation.

In 629, a Muslim raid was sent against the Kerak[6] district, within the Byzantine border. At Mota, a village five miles south of Kerak, the Muslims encountered a Byzantine force and were completely defeated. The expedition was to have momentous results.

In January 630, the Apostle of God once more called the Muslims to arms and, with ten thousand followers, set out for Mecca. Abu Sofian, the victor of Uhud and the leader of the opposition, realizing that the game was up, met the advancing Prophet on the way and accepted Islam. Next day, the Muslims entered Mecca unopposed.

Standing before the Kaaba, Muhammad ordered the idols to be cast down, broken and thrown away. A general amnesty was then proclaimed and the men and women of Mecca were made to swear loyalty. Although many of those who had formerly persecuted him

[5] The Black Stone, apparently a meteorite, was considered sacred and was built into the wall of the Kaaba or sanctuary. It is still kissed by Muslim pilgrims.
[6] Now in Jordan. Map 3, page 31.

were still living in the city, the Apostle won all hearts by his clemency on this day of triumph.

In September 630, Muhammad led a force northwards to Tebook. The local Arab chiefs hastened to pay their respects and agreed to pay tribute, though some of them were Byzantine subjects. The Prophet then returned to Medina, where he continued to live, even after the capture of Mecca.

In March 632, Muhammad himself led a vast crowd of Muslims on the pilgrimage to Mecca. He preached the sermon to the assembled faithful, looking up to heaven at the conclusion and crying, "O Lord, I have delivered my message and fulfilled my mission." One day in June of the same year, he complained of fever and headache. For a week his condition steadily deteriorated, and he delegated Abu Bekr to lead the public prayers.

On the tenth day, the Prophet's symptoms were greatly aggravated, he was racked with pain and at times delirious. The following morning, however, he rallied and wished to stand up, but his strength was insufficient and he fell back on his bed, probably a mere mattress on the floor.

Then he rallied again, called for water and wet his face. "O Lord," he cried, "I beseech thee to assist me in the agonies of death." Aisha, the daughter of Abu Bekr, gently supported his head. He prayed in a faint whisper, "Lord, grant me pardon. Eternity in paradise. Pardon . . ." Suddenly Aisha noticed that his head had grown heavy in her lap. The Prophet of Arabia had gone to meet his Lord.

NOTABLE DATES

Birth of Muhammad	20th August, 570
Marriage of Muhammad to Khadija	595
Vision of the Archangel Gabriel	610
Commencement of preaching	613
Flight of the Prophet to Medina	28th June, 622
Battle of Bedr	624
Battle of Uhud	625
Truce of Hudeibiya	628
Conclusion of peace between Byzantium and Persia	628
Muslim pilgrimage to Mecca	March 629
Muslim occupation of Mecca	January 630
Death of Muhammad	June 632

PERSONALITIES

Muhammad, the Apostle of God
Abu Talib, his uncle
Ali ibn abi Talib, his cousin
Abu Bekr, Muhammad's companion
Abu Sofian, leader of the opposition in Mecca
Khadija, the Prophet's first wife
Aisha, his favourite wife after the death of Khadija

III

The First Conquests

DURING the last two years of his life, the Prophet had received the submission of most of the tribes of Arabia. This did not, of course, mean that the peninsula constituted a political unity, governed and administered from Medina. Submission involved two actions only: a nominal adherence to the Muslim religion and the payment of an annual tax.

The Prophet died without leaving any instructions regarding his successor. No sooner was it known that he was dead than the people of Medina gathered together and decided to elect their own chief. Muhammad had been a Meccan and his principal lieutenants had all been from Quraish. The Medinis had found themselves in a subordinate position in their own town. They had tolerated the situation while the Prophet was still with them, but now they were determined to shake off the yoke of Quraish.

Abu Bekr, now old, frail and stooping, faced the clamouring crowd without fear. "The Arabs will not accept a leader except from Quraish," he said firmly. Then, pointing to two men beside him, Umar ibn al Khattáb and Abu Ubaida, he invited the crowd to choose one or the other. "No, indeed," cried the impulsive Umar. "The Prophet, when he was ill, named you to lead the prayers. We swear allegiance to you." Seizing Abu Bekr's hand, he pronounced the oath of loyalty to him. A few Meccans present and some tribesmen followed his example. Abu Bekr, a man of simple and loyal character, was generally trusted. Gradually the Medinis came up one by one and swore. The crisis was passed but civil war between the Muslims had only been narrowly averted.

The modest Abu Bekr adopted the title of khalif,[1] the successor of the Prophet. Ominously, however, Ali ibn abi Talib, the Prophet's cousin, son-in-law and close intimate had not been present and did

---

[1] This word is often spelt "caliph" after the Greek transliteration. "Khalif" is nearer the Arabic.

not take the oath until six months later. Rival claimants to the khalifate were to give rise to endless Muslim civil wars, which might perhaps have been avoided if Muhammad had laid down rules for the
succession. The Arabs, however, are individualists and jealousy of
one another is one of their chief faults. It is, therefore, by no means a
foregone conclusion that such rivalries would have been avoided,
even if the Prophet had established a procedure for the selection of
the khalifs.

No sooner did the tribes of the peninsula hear of the death of the
Apostle of God than most of them renounced Islam and refused any
longer to pay the tax, a movement known in Arab history as the
Apostasy. Abs and Dhobian, two tribes north of Medina, offered to
remain Muslims if the tax were abolished. At this crucial moment,
the gentle Abu Bekr showed an unexpected determination, which
revived the enthusiasm of the Muslims of Medina.

Muhammad had been so successful that rival prophets had
appeared in the field. The most dangerous of these appeared to be
a certain Tulaiha at the head of the tribe of Beni Asad. A Muslim
column, four thousand strong, was sent against him under the command of a distinguished fighter, Khalid ibn al Waleed. Beni Asad
were defeated and the column marched on to defeat Musailima,
another false prophet at the head of Beni Haneefa.[2] Musailima is
alleged to have written to Muhammad during his lifetime, offering
to share with him. "From Musailima the Apostle of God to Muhammad the Apostle," he is said to have written. "Let us divide the earth
between us, half to you and half to me." The reply, however, was
discouraging. "From Muhammad the Apostle of God to Musailima
the Liar. The earth is the Lord's. He causes such of his servants to
inherit it as he pleases."

Beni Haneefa offered a desperate resistance, but were eventually
defeated at Yemama, though the Muslims are alleged to have
suffered twelve hundred dead, out of a force of some five thousand
men. Among the dead was Zeid, the brother of Umar ibn al Khattáb
who was to be the next khalif. When Umar's son, Abdulla, returned
to Medina in safety, his father reproved him for having survived his
uncle's death. "Father," the young man is said to have replied, "he
asked God for martyrdom and his prayer was granted. I did the
same but my petition was refused."

The defeats of Beni Asad and Beni Haneefa reduced nearly all the
peninsula to obedience. Fighting dragged on in Oman, Hadhramaut

[2] Map 3, page 31.

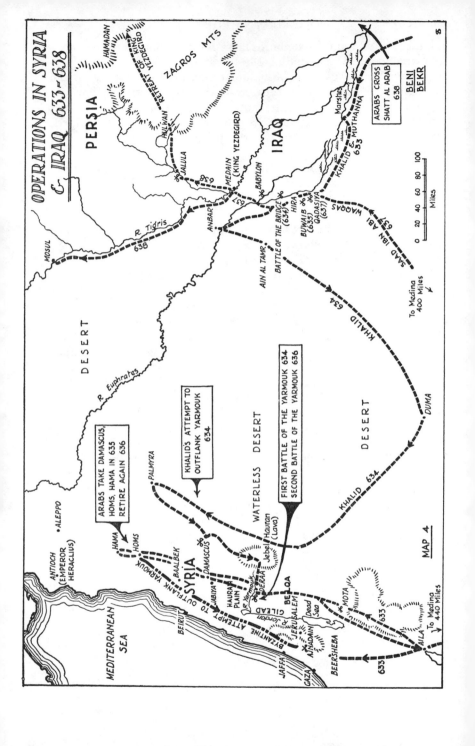

OPERATIONS IN SYRIA & IRAQ 633-638

PERSIA

HAMADAN

ZAGROS MTS

RETREAT OF KING YEZDEGIRD

HULWAN

JALULA 638

MEDAIN (KING YEZDEGIRD)

BABYLON

IRAQ

Marshes

ARABS CROSS SHATT AL ARAB 638

BENI BEKR

KHALID & MUTHANNA 633

637

MOSUL

R. Tigris

638

ANBAR

637

HIRA

BUWAIB (635)

QADASIYA (637)

BATTLE OF THE BRIDGE (634)

SAAD IBN ABI WAQQAS

AIN AL TAMR

Miles

0 20 40 60 80 100

To Medina 400 Miles

KHALID 634

DESERT

R. Euphrates

PALMYRA

KHALID'S ATTEMPT TO OUTFLANK YARMOUK 634

ARABS TAKE DAMASCUS, HOMS, HAMA IN 635 RETIRE AGAIN 636

WATERLESS DESERT

DESERT

FIRST BATTLE OF THE YARMOUK 634 SECOND BATTLE OF THE YARMOUK 636

DUMA

KHALID 634

ANTIOCH

ALEPPO

HAMA

HOMS

BAALBEK

SYRIA

BYZANTINE ATTEMPT TO OUTFLANK YARMOUK

DAMASCUS

HABIYA

HAURAN PLAIN

Jebel Hauran (Lava)

DERAA

R. Yarmouk

GILEAD

R. Jordan

JERUSALEM

Dead Sea

BEISAN

MEDITERRANEAN SEA

BEIRUT

JAFFA

GAZA

BEERSHEBA

AJNADAIN

MOTA

633

AILA

To Medina 440 Miles

633

MAP 4

and the Yemen until the spring of 633. A year after the Prophet's
death, the Apostasy had been suppressed.

*   *   *

In the summer of 633, Arabia was at peace. Unending tribal warfare, raids, battles and feats of arms had been the background of the
lives of the Arabs for thousands of years. But the Prophet had forbidden wars between Muslims. How long would it be possible to
keep the Arab tribes at peace with one another? It is difficult to say
whether or not Abu Bekr appreciated this problem and devised the
idea of launching the tribes on a career of conquest. On the Persian
front at least, hostilities seemed to begin naturally, without orders
from Medina.

The desert west of the head of the Persian Gulf was occupied in
633 by the large bedouin tribe of Beni Bekr ibn Wail, the ancestors of
the modern tribe of Aneza. These people had formerly been the
loyal followers of the Arab Lakhmid princes, satellites of the Persian
King of Kings. We have already seen, however, that in 605 the King
of Kings had abolished the Lakhmid dynasty, since which time Beni
Bekr had been in revolt against Persia. One of the chiefs of Beni Bekr,
Muthanna ibn Haritha, invited Khalid to join him in a few lucrative
raids into Persia. Muthanna professed Islam, rode to Medina and
obtained the khalif's consent.

In March 633, Khalid and Muthanna concentrated at Al Hafar,[3] a
group of wells, where they were also joined by a force from the tribe
of Tai. The key to Arab operations for the next four years was the
fact that, riding on camels, they could move freely in the desert,
which was impassable to the regular armies of Persia or Byzantium.
Arab strategy, therefore, was to skirt along the border of the desert,
raiding towns and villages and defeating local forces sent to repulse
them. If, however, the troops sent against them appeared to be too
strong, the Arabs could always vanish into the desert, where they
could not be overtaken.

Acting on this principle, Khalid and Muthanna moved northwards up the Euphrates, twice defeating the local tribes, stiffened by
Persian troops. In the spring of 633, they reached the town of Hira,
which had formerly been the capital of the Arab Lakhmid dynasty.
The people of Hira were Arab Christians and readily came to terms.
Khalid occupied the city as his headquarters. In September 633, he
captured Anbar, likewise on the edge of the desert and populated by

[3] Map 3, page 31.

Arabs. In December 633, he took the oasis of Ain al Tamr, the modern Shitata. Thus in nine months, from March to December 633, Khalid had overrun all the desert up to the River Euphrates and had captured two important towns.

It may well be asked what the Persian king was doing, allowing these ragged tribesmen to capture two cities only some fifty miles from his capital at Medain.[4] After the twenty-six year war between Persia and Byzantium had ended in 628 with the murder of Chosroes Parwiz, anarchy had ensued and all the male heirs to the throne had been massacred.

In the ensuing four years, 628 to 632, nine claimants ascended the throne, only to be deposed. Several of these were princesses, as no male princes could be found. In the summer of 632, however, immediately after the death of Muhammad, a boy of fifteen called Yezdegird was discovered. He was said to be of royal descent and to have been concealed during the massacres. He was, however, still too young to wield authority. It was during this period of anarchy in Persia that Khalid ibn al Waleed arrived on the Euphrates.

*   *   *

As we have seen, the Khalif Abu Bekr had not sent Khalid to invade Persia. The suggestion had been made by Muthanna, the Beni Bekr chief, who had obtained the khalif's consent to some raiding.

In fact, however, Quraish, who were still in complete control of policy, were much more interested in Syria. They had nearly all been to Gaza and Damascus in their caravan days and Syria was much nearer and more familiar than Persia. But perhaps the most important factor in Abu Bekr's opinion was that the Prophet himself had sent the force which had been defeated by the Byzantines at Mota. To follow the example of the Apostle of God could not be wrong.

Accordingly, early in 633, the Khalif Abu Bekr organized three columns to invade Byzantine territory. One of these defeated a Byzantine force in southern Palestine and overran the plains of Beersheba. The other two columns moved northwards together, keeping along the edge of the desert and across the Belqa.

The northern end of the Belqa plain, however, is closed by a

---

[4] Seleucia on the Tigris had been founded by Seleucus Nicator, the successor of Alexander the Great. The Persians built Ctesiphon, on the other side of the river, the two cities being joined by bridges. The Arabs called the two together Medain, the plural of Medina, "the cities".

mountainous area of extinct volcanoes, so thickly strewn with lava as to be impassable to mounted men, and in places even to men on foot. This area, formerly called Jebel Hauran, is now known as the Jebel Druze. To the east of this tangle of dead volcanoes lay waterless desert. To the west lay the mountains of Gilead and the thousand-foot-deep rift of the Jordan valley. From the volcanic mountain bloc to the Jordan valley ran a narrow stream called the River Yarmouk, most of the course of which was in a deep, almost impassable, ravine.

A narrow gap existed immediately west of the lava, where the Yarmouk still ran on the surface before falling into its gorge. This narrow passageway was commanded by the town of Deraa. Damascus was only accessible from the south through this narrow defile. When the Arabs arrived from the south, they found the Deraa gap strongly held by the Byzantines, and a deadlock ensued. The Arabs could not force the fortified lines of the Byzantine army, and the latter was unwilling to venture into the open plains to do battle.

In these circumstances, Abu Bekr recalled Khalid ibn al Waleed from the Euphrates, leaving only the bedouins under Muthanna to confront the Persians. Khalid crossed the desert to Duma, the modern Jauf, and then moved northwards on the right flank of the army facing the Yarmouk. Thence, being now used to desert travel, he crossed the waterless desert east of the lava (nearly dying of thirst) to Palmyra, whence he attempted, by an attack on Damascus from the east, to compel the Byzantine army to withdraw from the Yarmouk. His attack was repulsed and the Yarmouk position held firm.

The Emperor Heraclius was at Homs and, early in 634, sent a force southwards through Palestine to outflank the Arabs. In July 634, however, this Byzantine column was completely defeated at Ajnadain. Perhaps Arab morale was raised by this victory and that of the Byzantines depressed. Fighting on the Yarmouk became more active and, in September 634, the Arabs captured the position. The doorway to Syria had been forced open.

*   *   *

Meanwhile, on 23rd August, 634, the old Khalif Abu Bekr had died in Medina. Before doing so, he had nominated as his successor Umar ibn al Khattab, who had supported him on the day of the attempted revolt of the people of Medina, immediately after the death of the Prophet. Umar, a close associate of Muhammad, was as simple and as dedicated as Abu Bekr himself. In other ways, however, the two men differed. Abu Bekr had been quiet, humble and patient, though he had shown great determination in moments of crisis. Umar, on the contrary, was inclined to violence of temper.

Abu Bekr had used the title of khalif or successor to the Prophet. Umar consulted his intimates as to what title he should use. "You are the Prince of the Faithful," said one, and the title was thereafter to be used by all his successors.

*   *   *

As has already been told, the Arabs overran the Yarmouk position in September 634. In February 635, they advanced northwards up the Hauran plain and, in March, they laid siege to Damascus. Invincible in battle on an open plain, the Arabs had no knowledge of siege warfare, nor did they possess any equipment. Khalid ibn al Waleed, however, apparently made friends with a Christian bishop inside the city. The bishop was presumably a Monophysite, a sect persecuted by the Orthodox Byzantine church. Thus a Monophysite bishop might well be disaffected.

One day, probably early in September 635, the bishop informed Khalid that the walls that night would be lightly guarded. He also supplied two ladders. A party of Muslims mounted the walls in the dark and opened the city gates from the inside. When the Arabs flooded into the city at dawn, the Byzantine governor surrendered on terms. All non-Muslims were to pay a poll-tax of one dinar[5] per year and a measure of wheat for the maintenance of the army. The cathedral was divided in half by a partition wall, the Muslims in future praying in one half, the Christians in the other. There was no killing or looting. These terms were of extraordinary generosity. Cities taken by storm were, in Europe, liable to be sacked, even as recently as in the Napoleonic wars.

From Damascus the Arabs pressed on northwards, taking Baalbek, Homs, and Hama. The Emperor Heraclius withdrew to Antioch. Refusing to abandon hope, he summoned fresh armies to resume the struggle. Four or five months after the fall of Damascus, he had gathered an army stronger than before. When the Byzantines marched southwards from Antioch, the Arabs abandoned Homs, Hama and Damascus and withdrew southwards through the Deraa gap on to the Belqa plains.

The Arab retirement, after so many victories, followed their usual strategy. If they had fought a pitched battle in close country amid

[5] Approximately equivalent to one pound sterling or two U.S. dollars and fifty cents.

towns and villages, they would have been exterminated in the event of defeat. They preferred to withdraw from the cultivated area to a place where they had the desert at their backs, a safe refuge should they suffer a reverse. No sooner had the Arabs gone than the Byzantines reoccupied the Deraa gap. The door to Syria was slammed shut once more.

Heraclius had only been able to raise so large an army by making heavy demands on the Armenians for support. The army was in part Byzantine and in part Armenian and the two portions quarrelled with one another. The Arabs were mobile and enterprising, infiltrating round behind the Byzantine position, raiding convoys and seizing prisoners, while the morale of the Byzantines was lowered by a policy of passive defence.

On 20th August, 636, a hot dust-storm blew from the desert into the faces of the Byzantines. On such occasions, it is impossible for a man to stand facing the sandstorm with his eyes open. Advancing from the south-east, the Arabs had the wind at their backs, could fight with their eyes open and succeeded in overrunning the position. Detachments had already been sent round the flanks to cut off the enemy retreat. Before nightfall, the Byzantine army had been exterminated, Theodorus, the brother of the Emperor Heraclius, being killed.

When the emperor heard in Antioch of the extermination of the army which he had made such great efforts to raise, he decided that the decision was final and rode sadly away across the Taurus Mountains. The thousand-year-old Graeco-Roman dominion in Syria was ended. The Arabs quickly fanned out over the northern plains until they reached the foot of the Taurus. Jerusalem did not surrender until the winter of 637–638. The Patriarch Sophronius insisted that he would only surrender the keys to the Khalif Umar in person. The ragged old khalif duly made the journey and guaranteed the safety and the religious freedom of the Christians.

*   *   *

In December 633, when Khalid ibn al Waleed was called from Iraq to assist in the Syrian campaign, he left Muthanna in charge of operations against Persia. The accession of the young Yezdegird had put an end to the disturbances in Persia and, in 634, the national leaders decided to mark the recovery of their imperial unity by driving out the marauding Arab tribesmen.

The Persian column, which was accompanied by an elephant,

engaged Muthanna's tribesmen near the ruins of Babylon.[6] It was still among the Arabs a point of honour for the commander to lead the attack in person and Muthanna himself engaged the elephant and brought it down. The Arabs then pressed forward and the Persian column was obliged to retreat.

Muthanna, however, had spent many years in guerilla raids against the Persians and was aware that, though they had still not recovered from their civil wars, they would soon be able to send overwhelming forces against him. He took advantage of the lull to ride to Medina, where he arrived the day before the death of the Khalif Abu Bekr. With his dying breath, the old khalif ordered his successor Umar to send reinforcements to the Persian front.

Muthanna himself made a speech in the mosque in Medina, calling for volunteers and expatiating on the vast quantities of plunder to be obtained by those who went to fight for God in Iraq. The two ideas of loot and the service of God blended harmoniously in early Islam. The Prophet himself had said that God would enrich the Believers in this world and in the next.

In spite, however, of these exhortations, recruits came forward slowly. The military reputation of the Persians seems to have been more formidable than that of the Byzantines. The first recruit to offer himself was a certain Abu Ubaid of Medina. The new Khalif Umar, indignant at the slowness of recruiting, nominated the obscure Abu Ubaid to be commander-in-chief, as being the man most eager to die for God.

This extraordinary incident illustrates the mentality of the first Muslims. Unaware of, or at least indifferent to, the need for military experience or training, they relied solely on God for victory. A thousand years later, Oliver Cromwell was to exclaim, "It matters not who is our commander-in-chief if God be so," and the Khalif Umar might well have used the same words.

On the present occasion, the result was not entirely satisfactory. Abu Ubaid led the Arabs across the Euphrates and fought the Persians in enclosed country broken up by gardens and irrigation channels. The Persians, preceded by their elephants, opened the attack. Abu Ubaid ran forward against the leading elephant and was immediately trampled to death. The Arabs gave way and the fatal error committed by their inexperienced commander was immediately obvious. Always before they had fought with the desert at their backs. Now they found themselves hemmed

[6] Map 4, page 44.

in with the Euphrates behind them, spanned by only one bridge.

By almost superhuman efforts, Muthanna extricated a remnant of the Muslims, but four thousand had already been killed or drowned in the Euphrates, and two thousand more deserted. This action was named by the Arabs the Battle of the Bridge.

Nevertheless, a year later, in November 635, Muthanna had sufficiently raised the morale of the Muslims to enable him to defeat a Persian force sent against him at Buwaib. (In Syria, Damascus had been captured in September 635 and, in November, the Arabs had taken Homs.) Muthanna died soon after his victory at Buwaib, of wounds received at the Battle of the Bridge.

The second Battle of the Yarmouk, in August 636, completed the conquest of Syria. The Khalif Umar immediately ordered the switch of a part of the army of Syria to the Persian front. At the same time, he sent a new commander-in-chief to the Euphrates. Saad ibn abi Waqqás was a man of Quraish and a cousin of the Prophet. An early convert, he had fought at Bedr and was now a veteran campaigner. Short and thickset, with a large head and shaggy hair, his selection, unlike that of Abu Ubaid, seemed eminently suitable.

Late in 636, Saad ibn abi Waqqas arrived in the desert south of the Euphrates. Unlike the enthusiastic Khalif Umar, he was aware of the need for training. Three months he kept his new forces in the desert, eighty miles from the Euphrates, where the Persians, mounted on horses, were unable to interfere with them. For the first time, we read of a rudimentary military organization, all the men being divided into sections of ten, each under its own section commander.

The Persians had now ceased to underestimate the Arabs, and had collected a great army under their commander-in-chief, Rustem. The Muslim historians estimate their strength at anything from sixty to a hundred and twenty thousand men. A more probable estimate might be twenty to thirty thousand, but they brought with them a formidable "armoured division" of thirty-three elephants.

Rustem's plan of campaign, however, differed from that of the young King Yezdegird. The veteran commander realized that the Arabs only fought with confidence in the desert. When they crossed the Euphrates into the alluvial plain, covered with villages and intersected by canals, they were easily defeated by the Persians. Rustem, therefore, proposed to remain on the east bank of the Euphrates. If the Arabs crossed over to him, he would defeat them. If they remained in the desert, they did no harm. The young king, however, had no patience with such Fabian strategy, and ordered his commander to cross the Euphrates immediately and drive away these desert rats who had ventured to encroach on the dominions of the King of Kings. Rustem was unwillingly forced to obey.

The decisive battle was fought at Qadasiya, probably between the modern towns of Nejf and Abu Sukhair. The exact date cannot be traced, but February 637 is the most likely month. The Persians crossed, perhaps below Hira, and drew up on the desert plain. While they were doing so, Chapter VIII of the Qoran was read out before each Arab tribal contingent. "O Prophet, urge on the believers to battle. If there be of you twenty steadfast, they shall conquer two hundred . . ." The Muslims stood in silence while these stirring passages were read, preparing themselves for the alternative joys of victory or of martyrdom and instant admission to the endless bliss of paradise.

Saad ibn abi Waqqas had discovered a small tower or building immediately behind the centre of the Arab line. Pleading illness, he took up his position on the roof, from which he commanded a view of the whole battlefield. The Arabs, however, who believed it to be the duty of a commander to lead the charge, accused him of cowardice. "We fought patiently," sang the Arab poet:

> "We fought patiently until God gave us victory,
> "While Saad was safe inside walls at Qadasiya."

It is tempting to believe that Saad was a serious soldier, who knew that a commander was of more value directing the battle than performing romantic exploits with sword and lance.

The Persians began the action, preceded by the dreaded elephants, swaying their great trunks to and fro, the howdahs on their backs crowded with archers and waving flags. Some of the Arabs were thrown into confusion, until Asim, a chief of Beni Temeem, with a few picked kinsmen, formed an "elephant-hunting team". Their tactics were to slip under the bellies of the huge animals and cut the girths, bringing the howdahs crashing to the ground. When darkness fell and the fighting ceased, the Arabs had only just succeeded in avoiding defeat.

On the second day of the battle, the Arabs did better. No elephants appeared, presumably owing to the damage to their crews and equipment the day before. It will be remembered that, after the completion of the conquest of Syria, the Khalif Umar had ordered part of the army of Syria to reinforce the Persian front. On the afternoon of the second day of battle at Qadasiya, the advance guard of the army of Syria began to arrive on the field, led by the gallant Qaqaa, the chief of Beni Temeem.

The early part of the third day was spent clearing the dead from the field to allow the troops to move. Just as fighting was recommencing, the Arabs were encouraged by the arrival of the main body of the reinforcements from Syria, but their anxieties were increased by the reappearance of the Persian elephants.

This time Qaqaa was ordered by Saad to deal with the elephants. While his followers plied the "crews" on the elephants' backs with missiles, Qaqaa and one companion crept up on foot, armed with lances. Watching their opportunity, they suddenly pierced an elephant's eyes with a quick lunge of their lances. When two elephants, thus blinded, rushed round the field in panic, trumpeting loudly, the remainder stampeded and galloped off, trampling alike on friend and foe. At the end of the third day's fighting, the Arabs had slightly gained the advantage but the Persians were still fighting strongly.

After dark had fallen, however, some of the Arabs decided to harass the enemy at night. This unpremeditated attack, which had not been ordered by Saad, led to a general battle in the darkness. To the bedouins, living in frail tents or beneath the sharp desert stars, the night is as familiar as the day. When the day dawned after this "Night of Fury", the fighting was still going on. The struggle had become a battle of attrition, in which victory would go to the side which was able to summon the last ounce of energy and determination.

When daylight came, it was the Arabs who were able to mount the attack, led in person by the fiery Qaqaa, supported by the incredible hardihood of the bedouins. They broke through the Persian centre, and killed Rustem. Two formations were able to withdraw across the Euphrates. Thirty Persian "regiments" disdained to flee and were killed to a man. The remainder scattered in flight, some being cut down as they fled, others being drowned in the river. The Great King's army was exterminated. According to the Arab historian Tabari, the Muslims lost eight thousand five hundred killed, out of thirty thousand men, heavy casualties even for a modern battle.

The Arabs were too exhausted to pursue. After two months' rest on the battlefield, they moved northwards and, in the late summer of 637, blockaded the Persian capital of Medain. Early in 638, the Great King sent proposals of peace. When these were rejected by Saad, Yezdegird abandoned his imperial capital of Ctesiphon,[7] and

---

[7] See page 46, footnote.

withdrew to the mountains, establishing his headquarters at Hulwan. In December 638, the Persians were again defeated at Jalula and Yezdegird retired beyond the Zagros. At the end of 638, the victorious Arabs had occupied Mosul in the north and, in the south, had crossed the combined Tigris and Euphrates—now called the Shatt al Arab.

NOTABLE DATES

Death of Muhammad	June 632
The War of the Apostasy	June 632—June 633
Campaign of Khalid ibn al Waleed on the Euphrates	March to December 633
Battle of Babylon in Iraq	Spring 634
Battle of Ajnadain in Palestine	July 634
Death of the Khalif Abu Bekr	23rd August, 634
First Battle of the Yarmouk	September 634
Battle of the Bridge in Iraq	October 634
Siege of Damascus	March to September 635
Battle of Buwaib in Iraq	November 635
Second Battle of the Yarmouk	20th August 636
Conquest of Syria completed	20th August 636
Battle of Qadasiya	February 637
Occupation of Medain (Ctesiphon)	March or April 638
Battle of Jalula	December 638

PERSONALITIES

Abu Bekr, Muhammad's first khalif or successor
Umar ibn al Khattab, the second khalif
Khalid ibn al Waleed, Muslim commander
Muthanna ibn Haritha, chief of Beni Bekr
Saad ibn abi Waqqas, the victor of Qadasiya
Heraclius, Byzantine Emperor
Yezdegird, King of Persia
Rustem, Persian commander-in-chief

IV

First Signs of Schism

HAVING conquered the extensive and wealthy provinces of Syria, Palestine and Iraq, the Khalif Umar decided to consolidate before undertaking any further advances.

As already explained in the introduction, the populations of Syria and Palestine were of mixed origin. The sea coast of the Mediterranean was inhabited by people only partly Semitic, mixed with Philistines (originally from Greece), Hittites (from Asia Minor), Romans and Greeks. In the eastern half of Syria, "Arab" blood probably predominated but the cities, including Damascus, were largely Greek. The total population of Syria and Palestine in 638 may well have been five million, nearly all of them Christians.

The conquering Arabs who had arrived in the previous five years probably did not exceed a hundred thousand, including their women and children. They constituted thus about one-fiftieth of the inhabitants. If they were allowed to mix with the natives, Umar feared that the Arabs would lose their fighting spirit, for the Syrians had shown few martial qualities. Moreover the puritan khalif viewed with horror the music and dancing, the rich clothing and the wine drinking of the pleasure-loving Syrians. He accordingly decided to segregate the Muslim Arabs, establishing them in a military cantonment at Jabiya,[1] a few miles south-west of Damascus.

In Iraq, he ordered the army to withdraw from the luxurious Persian capital at Medain and to establish military bases in the desert west of the Euphrates, at Kufa[2] and Basra.

The end of active operations, however, and the segregation of the Muslims in military bases, gave rise to difficulties. In the six years since the Prophet's death, the Muslim warriors had never been paid. Their services had ostensibly been given to God, but, in fact, their continuous victories had provided ample plunder. Muhammad himself had laid down the procedure for its distribution. After a battle, the loot was collected in one place. One-fifth was separated, loaded

---

[1] Map 4, page 44.   [2] Map 6, page 61.

on caravans and sent to the treasury in Medina. The remaining four-fifths was equally divided between the soldiers. The end of hostilities however, meant the end of plunder.

If, therefore, peace were to be maintained, the troops would have to be paid. This, firstly, involved the preparation of nominal rolls, though scarcely anyone among the Arab soldiers could read or write. Secondly, no money was available. The statutory fifth of the loot, sent to the treasury in Medina, had hitherto been immediately distributed by the khalif to the poor of the town. The khalif himself had no money, went barefoot, had only one shirt and ate the same simple diet as his fellow-citizens.

Financial difficulties were partly overcome by the fact that wherever the Muslims had occupied a conquered country, they had imposed a poll-tax on the non-Muslim inhabitants. This money could be collected and used to pay the troops. As, however, the Arabs had as yet no civil service, Byzantine or Persian officials were employed to collect the taxes.

The actual payment of the men, however, had to be carried out by the Arabs themselves. The army still fought in tribal contingents and the money for the tribal unit was paid to the chief, who distributed it to the men with the assistance of elders. It is perhaps some tribute to the genuine religious enthusiasm which moved these simple and unlearned men that we do not at this period hear of any charges of peculation involving the pay of the troops.

Judicial problems also arose. For the Muslims, the Qoran and the example of the Prophet contained the answers to all the problems of life and no code of laws was needed. But the former subjects of Byzantium and Persia had their own well-established legal procedure, administered by trained judges and lawyers. The Arabs were always tolerant and easy-going. Christians, Jews and Zoroastrians were each allowed to govern themselves by their own laws, while Muslims alone were obliged to obey the Qoran. This forbearance, contrasting so strongly with the compulsory uniformity enforced in Europe in later centuries, has survived until our own times.

*   *   *

While, however, the cautious Khalif Umar was hoping for a period of peace, the Arabs had tasted the sweets of victory and were anxious for more. Amr ibn al Aasi had been one of the original three column commanders who had invaded Syria and Palestine in 633. His special area had been Palestine and he had besieged Jerusalem and occupied the harbours on the coast.

According to an old tradition, when Umar came to accept the surrender of Jerusalem, Amr ibn al Aasi asked the khalif's permission to invade Egypt. The khalif seems to have hesitated and the matter remained open. In the autumn of 639, however, Amr ibn al Aasi, who had been at Caesarea, marched southwards down the coast of Palestine with only three thousand six hundred men.

He had reached Rafah, on the border between Palestine and Sinai, when he received a letter sent post-haste by the khalif from Medina. Before opening the despatch, Amr, crossing the Palestine-Egypt border, marched on to Al Arish,[3] where he read the khalif's letter. "If, when you receive this letter, you are still in Palestine," Umar had written, "you should abandon the operation. If, however, you have already crossed into Egypt, you may proceed." Amr ibn al Aasi enquired innocently from those standing near, whether he was in Palestine or Egypt. When they replied that they were in Egypt, he ordered the continuation of the march. This incident occurred on 12th December, 639.

Unskilful as usual in siege warfare, the invaders were delayed for a month at Farama and another month at Bilbeis. Then they pressed on to the fortress of Babylon,[4] at the southern tip of the delta. Here a considerable Byzantine force had been concentrated. The Governor of Egypt, the Patriarch Cyrus, was also in the fortress.

Amr's ragged bedouins were incapable of besieging Babylon, so they passed the time raiding the Faiyum, probably to obtain supplies. On 6th June, 640, however, twelve thousand reinforcements from Medina arrived at Heliopolis, some six miles north-east of Babylon, from which it was separated by a sandy plain. In the middle of July 640, the Byzantine commander marched out of Babylon to attack Heliopolis, but was completely defeated and obliged to take refuge again behind the walls of the fortress, which the Arabs were unable to assault. Fortunately for them, however, Cyrus the governor was ready to negotiate.

Prior to the arrival of the Arabs, Cyrus, a patriarch of the Orthodox Church, had made himself hated in Egypt by his persecution of the Monophysite sect. Aware of his own unpopularity, he may have felt himself in no position to resist the invaders. Accordingly, after a

[3] Pronounced Al Areesh.
[4] It is not exactly known how this castle acquired this name. Ancient Babylon, of course, was in Iraq.

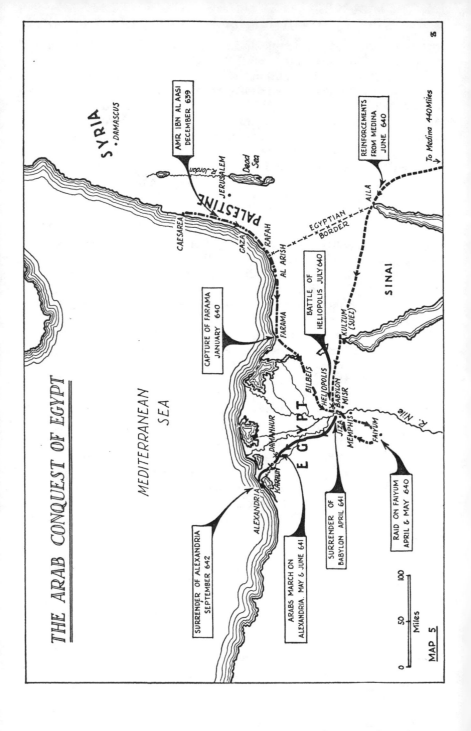

THE ARAB CONQUEST OF EGYPT

MAP 5

SYRIA
• DAMASCUS

AMR IBN AL AASI
DECEMBER 639

REINFORCEMENTS
FROM MEDINA
JUNE 640

To Medina 440 Miles

PALESTINE

CAESAREA

JERUSALEM

Dead Sea

R. Jordan

GAZA
RAFAH

AL ARISH

EGYPTIAN
BORDER

AILA

SINAI

CAPTURE OF FARAMA
JANUARY 640

FARAMA

BATTLE OF
HELIOPOLIS JULY 640

KULZUM
(SUEZ)

MEDITERRANEAN
SEA

BILBEIS

HELIOPOLIS
BABYLON
MISR

EGYPT

KARIUN

DAMANHUR

ALEXANDRIA

JIZA
MEMPHIS
FAIYUM

R. Nile

SURRENDER OF ALEXANDRIA
SEPTEMBER 642

ARABS MARCH ON
ALEXANDRIA, MAY & JUNE 641

SURRENDER OF
BABYLON APRIL 641

RAID ON FAIYUM
APRIL & MAY 640

0   50   100
         Miles

MAP 5

5

few brief negotiations, he signed an agreement for surrender, stipulating that the Christians would pay tribute to the conquerors, but be free to practise their own religion. A clause was added making the agreement subject to ratification by the Emperor Heraclius.

In Constantinople, however, the emperor categorically refused to ratify the surrender. Hostilities were resumed but, in March 641, the garrison was discouraged by news of the old emperor's death. The Arabs secretly prepared scaling ladders and, at dead of night, a party of Muslims reached the top of the battlements, led by Zubair ibn al Awwám, a companion of the Prophet. When day dawned the walls had been scaled by only a small party, which could have been thrown down by a determined counter-attack. But the siege had lasted seven months, the morale of the garrison was low and the commander agreed to surrender. On 9th April, 641, the Byzantines withdrew in boats down the Nile.

It was doubtless with joy and exhilaration that the Arabs crossed the Nile a few days later to Jiza and set out once more through clean, dry desert in search of fresh fields to conquer. The Byzantines in Alexandria had been reinforced and Theodore, the commander-in-chief, offered strong resistance at Damanhur and again at Kariun before withdrawing, in July 641, within the defences of Alexandria.

The city, which had over a million inhabitants, was one of the greatest in the world and, in addition to strong walls, was largely surrounded by lakes and canals. Amr ibn al Aasi, therefore, left a small force to observe Alexandria and himself withdrew to Babylon in August 641.

The Byzantines could probably have held Alexandria for years, but Constantinople was in confusion after the death of Heraclius and Cyrus was determined to resume negotiations. On 8th November, 641, he signed a new agreement surrendering the whole of Egypt. The inhabitants would be allowed the free practice of their religion and the Muslims were not to demolish any more churches. The Byzantine army was allowed a year's grace to evacuate the country. In September 642, the withdrawal was completed.

Egypt had been conquered by the initiative of Amr ibn al Aasi, for the khalif had attempted to prevent the invasion. No sooner was the conquest complete than a messenger arrived from the Khalif Umar, with a letter accusing the victorious commander of having grown rich. "I have enough experience of dishonest officials," wrote Umar ibn al Khattab, "and have sent Muhammad ibn Maslama to bring me half your possessions." "It is an evil age in which we can be treated in this way," Amr is said to have remarked crossly. "Hush," answered the khalif's inquisitor, "had it not been for this age which you hate, you would today be bending in the courtyard of your house at the feet of a goat, whose abundance of milk would please you, or whose scarcity would cause you dismay."

This vivid little dialogue, one thousand three hundred years old, serves to remind us of the humble origins of these men who now ruled nations as if they were emperors. It also gives us an insight into the extraordinary enthusiasm of the first years of Islam, when a single messenger from a barefoot old man in a far desert oasis could deprive a victorious commander of the rewards of a hard-fought campaign. Amr ibn al Aasi was not one of the most pious of the Muslims but the simple religious enthusiasm of his men made it impossible for him to resist the khalif's orders.

*   *   *

Umar ibn al Khattab had forbidden Saad ibn abi Waqqas to cross the Zagros Mountains into Persia. If the Great King had been willing to limit his dominions to Persia, history might have been different. But Yezdegird was still young and was determined to drive the Arabs back into their deserts. As the years 639, 640 and 641 passed by, a great army was built up, armed and trained in Persia.

When Saad ibn abi Waqqas reported this, the Khalif Umar realized that peace could not be won until the throne of the King of Kings had ceased to exist. Reinforcements were gathered from all over Arabia and an army of thirty thousand men was sent over the Zagros. In 642, a great battle was fought at Nehawand in which, after desperate fighting all day long, the Persians were ultimately completely defeated.

The messenger bearing the good news took with him also to the khalif two large chests filled with precious stones from the treasures of the Great King. As there was no treasury or strong-room in Medina, the chests were deposited for the night in a room in Umar's house. But the old man was worried at the presence of such wealth. The hoarding of treasure, he felt, showed a lack of faith in God's power to provide. In the morning, he summoned the messenger and told him to take the chests away, sell the contents and distribute the proceeds among the soldiers.

Yezdegird was never again able to raise a great army. The Arabs accordingly fanned out into a number of columns, which set out to pacify the interior of Persia. Whereas, however, Syria and Egypt

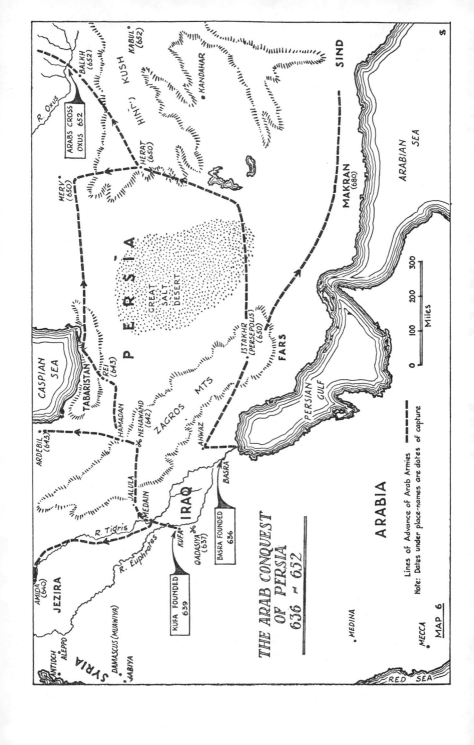

THE ARAB CONQUEST
OF PERSIA
636 ~ 652

Lines of Advance of Arab Armies ▬ ▬ ▬

Note: Dates under place-names are dates of capture

MAP 6

had offered no resistance once the Byzantine army had been defeated, the Persians continued to offer strong local opposition, assisted by the many mountain ranges and deserts in their country. Ten years of fighting followed the great Arab victory of Nehawand. In 652, however, Yezdegird was murdered and the Arabs completed the pacification of the country, as far east as the Oxus and the borders of India.

*   *   *

We have seen how Saad Ibn abi Waqqas had established a military base at Kufa at Umar's orders. Saad had marked out the cantonment on a piece of open desert and had built a mosque and a house for himself in the middle. Shacks, huts and then houses were erected around it and soon Kufa was a town. Complaining that visitors, petitioners and even the merely curious were constantly in and out of his house, so that it was impossible for him to discuss public business with his staff, Saad enclosed a small forecourt in front of the building.

A few weeks later the khalif's inquisitor, Muhammad ibn Maslama, arrived in Kufa with a letter. "I hear that you built yourself a mansion," wrote Umar ibn al Khattab, "and have erected a door between you and the people . . . Come out of it and do not erect a door to keep people out and to banish them from their rights, so that they have to wait until you receive them."

Muhammad ibn Maslama does not appear to have found any neglect of duty on the part of Saad, except that he had erected a door to prevent everybody walking into his house. Nevertheless the victor of Qadasiya was summarily dismissed from his post. Of Umar's dedication to his duties, his modesty and his asceticism, there can be no doubt. His relationship to the army commanders, however, is worthy of study. He seemed to be the implacable enemy of any leader who won great victories. Khalid ibn al Waleed had been dismissed and disgraced. Amr ibn al Aasi, who on his own initiative had conquered Egypt, was bullied and insulted. Saad ibn abi Waqqas, who had defeated the Persians, was summarily dismissed.

Was Umar jealous of his most famous commanders? Did he fear that a victorious soldier might rebel? Or did he believe that victories were won by God and that it was therefore more important that the commander be pleasing to God than experienced in war? Umar's selection of a successor for Saad seemed to support the last theory. Ammár ibn Yásir had been a slave in Mecca when the Prophet had begun to preach. He had been converted and, as a result, had suffered a good deal of persecution. Abu Bekr had rescued him by buying him from his master and setting him free. Since then, he had lived in poverty, asceticism and piety. Already old, his reputation for sanctity entitled him, in Umar's opinion at least, to be governor and commander-in-chief in Iraq.

On 3rd November, 644, Umar was leading the prayers soon after sunrise in the mosque of Medina when a Persian slave called Abu Lulu suddenly rushed upon him from behind and stabbed him in the body in six places. The old khalif was carried to his house adjoining the mosque, perfectly conscious though obviously dying. He summoned Ali ibn abi Talib, the Prophet's cousin and son-in-law, Othmán ibn Affan, one of the earliest converts, Zubair ibn al Awwam, who had scaled the walls of Babylon in Egypt, Saad ibn abi Waqqas, the conqueror of Iraq and Abdul Rahman ibn Auf. These five he appointed to be a selection committee to choose his successor and then quietly passed away.

Umar ibn al Khattab was, perhaps, the greatest of all the khalifs. In his ten years of rule, the Arabs had conquered an empire. Although he had humbled the Byzantine and Persian Emperors, he remained always pious, simple and compassionate. Prisoners-of-war brought to Medina expected to see palaces and imperial pageantry such as they had witnessed in Constantinople or in Ctesiphon. Instead, in the glaring, dusty square of a little mudbrick town, they would find a circle of Arabs sitting on the ground. One of them, a tall lean man, barefoot and wearing a coarse woollen cloak, would prove to be the world's most powerful emperor.

The readiness with which he listened to complaints against his army commanders and governors—dismissing an army commander on a complaint from a soldier—undermined discipline and resulted in disastrous disorders once his own powerful personality was removed from the scene. In spite, or perhaps because of his humility and his profound piety, his word was law from one end of the empire to the other.

*   *   *

No sooner was Umar buried than the selection committee assembled to choose his successor. All of them were, of course, members of Quraish, the Prophet's tribe. It was soon evident, however, that Ali ibn abi Talib and Othman ibn Affan were the only two serious candidates. Before Islam, the two clans of Beni Umaiya and Beni Hashim had been rivals for supremacy over Quraish. The Prophet had been of Beni Hashim and it was no accident that the principal opponent of Muhammad had been Abu Sofian of Beni Umaiya.[5] Now there were two candidates to the khalifate, Othman of Beni Umaiya and Ali of Beni Hashim. Twelve years after the death of the Apostle of God, family rivalries were reappearing.

It was twenty-two years since Muhammad had arrived in Medina, escaping from persecution in Mecca. In those twenty-two years, a new world empire had risen on the ruins of Persia and of Rome. But the seeds of the destruction of that empire were already being sown. Quraish had built it and Quraish were to destroy it.

*   *   *

On the fourth morning that the selection committee had been in session, relations were growing tense in Medina between the factions of Othman and of Ali. Finally all agreed to abide by the decision of Abdul Rahman ibn Auf, a member of the committee who had himself refused to stand for election. After a short hesitation, he chose Othman. Once again the problem of the selection of a new khalif had nearly led to civil war.

Othman was already seventy years old. He was handsome, genial, and lenient but, after the stern and puritan Umar, he was to show himself unfortunately weak. Meanwhile the conquests continued. Othman dismissed Amr ibn al Aasi and appointed his own foster-brother to be governor of Egypt. Muawiya, the governor of Syria, was also of the Umaiyid family, but was a man of outstanding ability. Under him, the Arabs embarked on the sea and conquered Cyprus.

The assassination of Umar ibn al Khattab—and by a Persian at that—had been followed by new popular risings in Persia, and fighting continued for the first five years of Othman's khalifate, 644 to 649. Meanwhile Othman had nominated his own half-brother, Waleed ibn Uqba, to be governor of Kufa and commander-in-chief of operations in northern Persia. Waleed's father, Uqba, had been taken prisoner fighting at Bedr for Quraish, and had been condemned to death by the Prophet himself. To his anguished cry, "Who will take care of my little children?" Muhammad had replied coldly, "Hellfire." The new governor of Kufa was one of those children whom the Prophet had thus consigned to perdition.

Unfortunately Waleed was also a drunkard and had to be removed but he was replaced by Saad ibn al Aasi, another Umaiyid. The governor of Basra, who controlled operations in southern Persia, was also dismissed and replaced by an Umaiyid, Abdulla ibn Aamir. It must be admitted that the Umaiyid nominees were often extremely capable. By 652, eight years after the election of Othman, the revolts in Persia had been completely suppressed and Abdulla ibn Aamir had captured Balkh, Herat and Kabul, and had crossed the Oxus. In spite of this, however, it was being widely said with some bitterness that no one who was not an Umaiyid could any longer hope for high office although, in the Prophet's time, Beni Umaiya had led the opposition to Islam.

It will be remembered that Umar ibn al Khattab had been faced with the dilemma of whether to allow the Arabs to mix with the conquered races or to segregate them in military camps and keep them as a separate sovereign race, whose duty was to rule and to fight.

In 652, twenty years after the death of the Apostle of God, the Arabs still exhibited in war the same reckless courage and patient endurance as before. But with the reduction in active operations, many thousands of them now passed idle lives in their cantonments. Several factors appeared which tended to introduce internal schisms, as the white-hot religious enthusiasm generated by the Prophet began to cool.

Firstly, the allegiance of the Arabs from time immemorial had been to their tribes. Religious enthusiasm had, for a time, caused these rivalries to disappear but now once again they revived.

Secondly, Umar ibn all Khattab had encouraged soldiers to bring to him their complaints against their commanders and had thereby sown the seeds of insubordination.

Thirdly, Quraish had become a kind of ruling clique over all Arabs, due to the prestige they had acquired from the Apostle, but now the Arabs began to resent the arrogance of this new aristocracy.

Fourthly, as we have seen, Quraish were divided against themselves. The old jealousy between Beni Umaiya and Beni Hashim had reappeared and had produced two rival candidates for the khalifate, Othman and Ali.

Fifthly, Othman seemed to be under the influence of his relatives, and all important commands had been given by him to Beni Umaiya.

The idleness of the soldiery in the cantonments and the weakness and nepotism of Othman brought all these troubles to a head. In 655, open disaffection broke out in the Kufa cantonment and Saeed, the Umaiyid governor, fled to Medina. The same disaffection prevailed in Egypt. Soon secret messengers were passing back and forth between Kufa and Fustat, the great military cantonment in Egypt.

Early in 656, mutinous armies set out simultaneously from Fustat, Kufa and Basra, and marched on Medina. It was noticeable that Syria, the governor of which, Muawiya, was also an Umaiyid, was quiet. Muawiya had abandoned Umar's system of segregating the Arabs in cantonments. He had made Damascus his capital and allowed his men to mix freely with the populace.

The aged khalif, now eighty-two years old, was besieged in his home in Medina. On 17th June, 656, a screaming mob of soldiers broke into the khalif's house. Othman, who was sitting on the floor reading the Qoran, behaved in his last moments with fearless calm and dignity. But the mutineers burst into his room and hacked him to death, his blood soaking the manuscript of the Qoran which he had been reading.

*   *   *

Everything in the Arab world was changed by the murder of Othman. For twenty-five years, the Muslims had lived in a dream. God had chosen them to conquer and rule the world, after which they would pass into the unimaginable joys of paradise. The dream had suddenly evaporated and they found themselves once again surrounded by war, violence and bloodshed.

Four leaders of the Muslims had been in Medina at the time of the murder of the Khalif Othman—Ali ibn abi Talib, who had opposed his election, Zubair ibn al Awwam, Talha ibn Ubaidullah and Saad ibn abi Waqqas, the victor of Qadasiya. All these, except Talha, had been on the selection committee which had appointed Othman. They had done little or nothing to save his life, perhaps because they themselves cherished ambitions to succeed him.

Five days after the murder of Othman, the Prophet's cousin and son-in-law, Ali ibn abi Talib, was acclaimed as khalif and the mutineers returned to their garrisons. Ali faced an immediate decision. Should he, or should he not, avenge the death of Othman? Muawiya, the Umaiyid governor of Syria, refused to acknowledge Ali as khalif until the murderers were punished. But Ali took no action, pleading the need for the restoration of discipline before the offenders could be brought to book. Muawiya replied by charging Ali with complicity in the murder.

The two most senior elders of the Muslims, Zubair and Talha, slipped out of Mecca and, crossing the desert, raised the standard of revolt in Basra. Ali set out with an army in pursuit. Halting outside

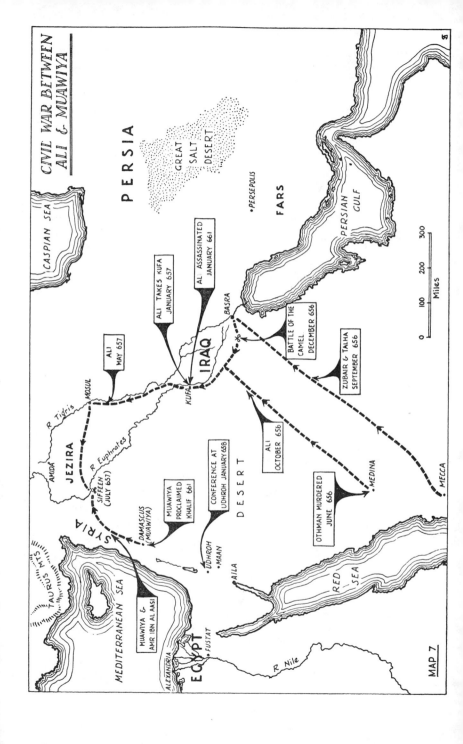

MAP 7

CIVIL WAR BETWEEN ALI & MUAWIYA

PERSIA

CASPIAN SEA

GREAT SALT DESERT

• PERSEPOLIS

FARS

PERSIAN GULF

ALI ASSASSINATED JANUARY 661

ALI TAKES KUFA JANUARY 657

ALI MAY 657

0   100   200   300
Miles

BASRA

R Tigris

MOSUL

IRAQ

KUFA

BATTLE OF THE CAMEL DECEMBER 656

ZUBAIR & TALHA SEPTEMBER 656

AMIDA

JEZIRA

R Euphrates

Siffeen (JULY 657)

DAMASCUS (MUAWIYA)

SYRIA

MUAWIYA PROCLAIMED KHALIF 661

CONFERENCE AT UDHROH JANUARY 658

DESERT

ALI OCTOBER 656

OTHMAN MURDERED JUNE 656

• MEDINA

• MECCA

• UDHROH

MAAN •

AILA •

TAURUS MTS

MEDITERRANEAN SEA

MUAWIYA & AMR IBN AL AASI

EGYPT

ALEXANDRIA

FUSTAT

RED SEA

R Nile

Basra, he sent emissaries to invite Zubair and Talha to negotiate. Peace might have been restored but the mutineers who had killed Othman feared that a settlement would lead to their trial, and seem to have deliberately precipitated a fight.

The Battle of the Camel, so-called because Aisha, the Prophet's widow, riding a camel, was with the rebels, was fought in December 656. Ali was victorious and both Talha and Zubair were killed. In January 657, seven months after the murder of Othman, Ali occupied Kufa and established his capital there.

From Kufa, Ali again summoned Muawiya to acknowledge his authority, but the governor of Syria replied that he would do so as soon as the murderers of Othman had been punished. Seeing further negotiation to be useless, Ali marched to the upper Euphrates with an army of fifty thousand. At Siffeen, he found the army of Damascus awaiting him.

Both sides hesitated long before committing such large armies of Muslims to fratricidal butchery. For several weeks, emissaries went back and forth in vain. At last, in July 657, a general battle commenced. For two days the slaughter continued with extreme ferocity. On the morning of the third day, the army of Syria began slowly to give ground. Amr ibn al Aasi, the conqueror of Egypt, now fighting for Muawiya, had a sudden inspiration. A force of cavalry moved forward with Qorans tied to their lances, calling out, "Let the word of God decide." The army of Ali immediately took up the cry and both armies ceased to fight.

A conference was agreed upon, at which arbitrators from both sides should meet to decide the conflict. The assembly took place at Udhroh, in Jordan, thirteen miles north-west of Maan, in January 658, but failed to agree. Ali seems to have lacked the power to lead, for at this stage a mutinous movement began in his own army. The malcontents, who became known as Kharijites, or Outsiders, were extreme puritan equalitarians, like the Levellers who opposed Oliver Cromwell. Sickened by the rivalries of their leaders, they demanded a theocracy, ruled only by God.

On 20th January, 661, a fanatical Kharijite, Muhammad ibn Muljam, assassinated Ali ibn abi Talib at the door of the mosque in Kufa. The first convert made by the Prophet after his wife Khadija, Ali appears to have been of a mild and kindly disposition, insufficiently ruthless to dominate so turbulent a community.

The death of Ali left the field clear for his Umaiyid rival, Muawiya. By a remarkable irony, the new Prince of the Faithful was the son of Abu Sofian, who in the Prophet's life-time had been his bitterest opponent.

NOTABLE DATES

Invasion of Egypt by Amr ibn al Aasi	12th December, 639
Battle of Heliopolis	July 640
Death of Heraclius	11th February, 641
Surrender of Egypt	8th November, 641
Battle of Nehawand } Conquest of Persia	642
Assassination of Umar ibn al Khattab	3rd November, 644
Death of Yezdegird, King of Persia	652
Murder of the Khalif Othman	17th June, 656
Battle of the Camel outside Basra	December 656
Battle of Siffeen	July 657
Assassination of Ali ibn abi Talib	20th January, 661
Muawiya sole khalif	July 661

PERSONALITIES

The Khalif Umar ibn al Khattab
Amr ibn al Aasi, conqueror of Egypt
The Khalif Othman ibn Affan
The Khalif Ali ibn abi Talib, cousin and son-in-law of the Prophet
Muawiya ibn abi Sofian, governor of Syria, then khalif

V

The Great Umaiyids

MUAWIYA, like his father Abu Sofian, had been a bitter opponent of Muhammad until the latter took Mecca, whereupon he became a Muslim. The Prophet, anxious to reconcile his enemies, made him his secretary, a fact which also indicates that he was above the average in education.

The sanctity of the khalifate had been undermined by the murder of Othman and the civil war between Ali and Muawiya. When, after the assassination of the former, the Arabs gave their loyalty to Muawiya, it was not so much for religious as for personal reasons. For although all through their history they have shown a tendency to anarchy, they willingly accord their allegiance to a man whom they consider to be worthy to rule.

Muawiya assumed the rôle of the democratic Arab chief of tradition. He circulated freely in the streets without an escort, and engaged in conversation in public with his enemies as much as with his friends. When addressed with bitterness or with insolence, he would give a quiet and conciliatory reply, often tinged with dry humour. Yet in spite of his equalitarian attitude, or perhaps because of it, he was the only Arab khalif against whom there was never a rebellion.

One of the most remarkable of Muawiya's lieutenants was Zayyad "the-son-of-his-father". He was the son of Sumaiya, a vagrant slave girl of Mecca, whose favours had been so promiscuously bestowed that Zayyad's father could not be identified. Zayyad had been made governor of southern Persia by Ali, his headquarters being in Persepolis, once the capital of Cyrus and Darius. After the murder of Ali, Zayyad transferred his allegiance to Muawiya, who made him governor of both Kufa and Basra. He was thus the viceroy of Muawiya for Iraq and Persia, the whole eastern half of the empire.

With the end of the civil war, the Arabs resumed their advance in the East. Zayyad the-son-of-his-father crossed the Oxus and took

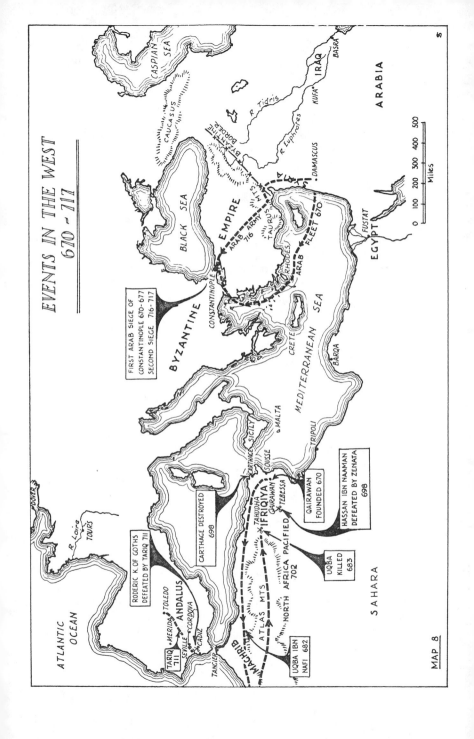

EVENTS IN THE WEST
670 - 717

ATLANTIC OCEAN

R. Loire
TOURS

ANDALUS
TOLEDO
MERIDA
SEVILLE
CORDOVA
CADIZ

RODERIC K. OF GOTHS DEFEATED BY TARIQ 711

TARIQ 711

TANGIER

MAGHRIB

ATLAS MTS

UQBA IBN NAFI 682

NORTH AFRICA PACIFIED 702

TAHUDHA

IFRIQIYA
TEBESSA
QAIRAWAN
SOUSSE
CARTHAGE
SICILY
MALTA

CARTHAGE DESTROYED 698

QAIRAWAN FOUNDED 670

HASSAN IBN NAAMAN DEFEATED BY ZENATA 698

UQBA KILLED 683

SAHARA

TRIPOLI

BARQA

MEDITERRANEAN SEA

CRETE

RHODES

ARAB FLEET 670

FUSTAT

EGYPT

ARAB ARMY 716

TAURUS MTS

DAMASCUS

BYZANTINE BORDER

R. Euphrates

R. Tigris

KUFA

BASRA

IRAQ

ARABIA

BYZANTINE EMPIRE

CONSTANTINOPLE

BLACK SEA

CAUCASUS

CASPIAN SEA

FIRST ARAB SIEGE OF CONSTANTINOPLE 670- 677 SECOND SIEGE 716- 717

0 100 200 300 400 500
Miles

MAP 8

Bukhara.[1] Soon afterwards, Samarqand also was taken by Saeed, the son of the murdered Khalif Othman. Further south, the Arabs invaded Sind, in modern Pakistan.

*   *   *

At sea, there was even greater activity than on land. In 670, an Arab fleet sailed through the Dardanelles and laid siege to Constantinople itself. In 672, another fleet captured Rhodes and later on twice raided Sicily. In 677, however, the Arabs abandoned their fruitless attacks on the walls of Constantinople.

*   *   *

Muawiya reappointed Amr ibn al Aasi as governor of Egypt, of which he had been the original conqueror. In Roman times, the name of Africa had been applied only to the area which we now call Tunisia and to eastern Algeria. Morocco had been referred to as Mauretania. The Arabs transformed the word Africa into Ifriqiya, but Mauretania they called the Maghrib, the land of the sunset. Cyrenaica was known to them as Barqa.

The area from the Atlantic to Carthage consisted of three strips of country, running west to east. The coastal plain, averaging perhaps a hundred miles wide, was Mediterranean. From the earliest historical times, it had been settled by many races, Phoenicians, Greeks, Romans, and even Vandals from northern Europe. These plains were closely cultivated and dotted with wealthy cities, which shared in the commerce of the Mediterranean.

South of the coastal plain lay the great Atlas range, a tangle of mountains a hundred miles wide and one thousand two hundred and fifty miles long, and inhabited by a hardy race known as the Berbers. South of the Atlas and shut off by the mountains from the rainfall of the Mediterranean, lay the Sahara, sparsely peopled by nomadic tribes.

No sooner had Amr ibn al Aasi first conquered Egypt than, in 642, he had sent troops to occupy Barqa. In 643 and again in 647, the Arabs plundered Tripoli but returned with the loot to Barqa. In 665, they defeated the Byzantines near Sousse, but again withdrew.

When Amr was once more made governor of Egypt by Muawiya, he sent his nephew, Uqba ibn Nafi, to conquer North Africa. Uqba reached modern Tunisia, fifteen hundred miles from his base in

- [1] Map 9, page 76.

Egypt. Here, realizing that the country could not be controlled without a local capital, in 670 he established a military base at Qairawan, as the early Muslims had done at Kufa and Basra.

The struggle in North Africa was three-cornered. The Byzantines, with their provincial capital in Carthage, held a number of coastal fortresses extending as far west as Tangier. The interior of the country was held by the Berbers. Now the Arabs had arrived on the scene.

Uqba was a man of remarkable courage, enterprise and simple loyalty but he was no politician. In 682, he carried out an extraordinary military foray. From the newly established base at Qairawan, he marched twelve hundred miles to the west until he reached the River Sus in modern Morocco. Here tradition depicts him as riding his horse into the Atlantic Ocean and declaiming, sword in hand, "God is most great! If my course were not stopped by this sea, I would still ride on to the unknown kingdoms of the west, preaching the unity of God, and putting to the sword the rebellious nations who worship any other god but him."

Riding carelessly back to the east, elated by this splendid march, he was ambushed at Tahudha by the Berbers in 683. He and his men fought on until all were killed. As soon as his death was known, all the Berbers rose in revolt, Qairawan was lost and the Arab frontier was back again in Barqa. Uqba had failed to exploit the political possibilities of the situation by playing off the Berbers against the Byzantines. Instead, with early Muslim enthusiasm, he had attacked both simultaneously.

*   *   *

Before Muawiya became sole khalif, the Arab conquests had been halted by the six years of civil war between Ali and himself. As he grew old, his chief preoccupation was to avoid the resumption of civil war between Beni Umaiya and Beni Hashim after his death. Eventually he decided to nominate as his heir his son Yezeed, to whom he succeeded in persuading most of the notables to swear allegiance.

Muawiya died in April 680 and Yezeed was acclaimed in Damascus as khalif. But it was soon apparent that all was not well. The Arabs have never entirely accepted hereditary right to succession. They invariably scrutinize the person of the candidate, accept him if he appears worthy to rule and reject him if he seems likely to prove inadequate.

2. THE UMAIYID KHALIFS OF DAMASCUS

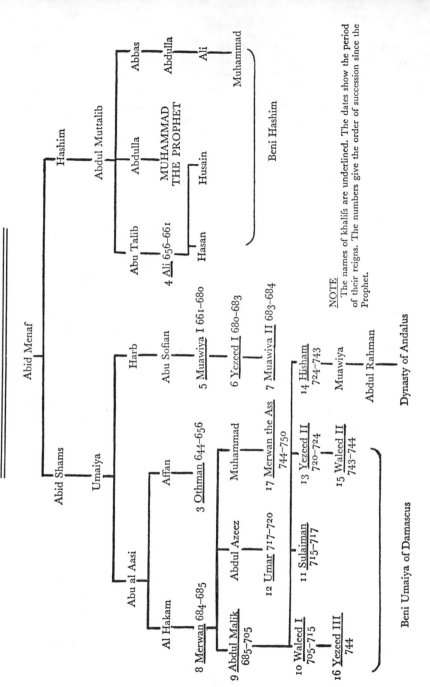

NOTE

The names of khalifs are underlined. The dates show the period of their reigns. The numbers give the order of succession since the Prophet.

Yezeed was perhaps inclined to be frivolous and was not conspicuously religious. Moreover his position was logically weak. If his right to the khalifate were based on heredity, the previous khalifs had all left sons, who had as good a right as he. If, on the other hand, the post should go to the most suitable candidate, then many were obviously better qualified than Yezeed.

Medina had always resented the transfer of the capital to Damascus. Moreover all Yezeed's rivals were already collected in the Prophet's city. His most formidable competitor was Husain, who was not only the son of Ali, a former khalif, but also the grandson of the Prophet himself through his daughter, Fatima.[2] Moreover Husain was pious, serious and virtuous, in contrast to the frivolous Yezeed.

At this critical moment, letters reached Husain from Kufa, inviting him to come and assume the leadership in Iraq. After much hesitation, he decided to go and left Mecca to cross the Arabian deserts to Kufa, without an army and accompanied only by his family.

The news that Husain was going to Kufa caused alarm in Damascus, where the civil wars between Ali and Muawiya were still vividly remembered. Zayyad the-son-of-his-father was dead, but he had left behind him a son called Ubaidullah, who was as ruthless as he. While Husain was riding slowly across the desert, Ubaidullah was appointed governor of Kufa by Yezeed. In a few days, the new governor had arrested and executed Husain's principal supporters and completely established his own authority.

When Husain's little convoy approached Kufa, it was met and surrounded by a large force of cavalry, and was forced to halt in the desert without water at a place called Kerbela. Entreaties for a little water for the women and children fell on deaf ears. Husain claimed that he had done nothing wrong and was willing to go and confront Yezeed in Damascus. Ubaidullah, however, insisted on unconditional surrender.

At length, on 10th October, 680, the cavalry closed in. Husain drew up his seventy-two relatives and retainers for battle. The cavalry were about four thousand strong. For several hours, Husain's little party were subjected to constant sniping by archers till all his men, and several of his children, had been killed. At length Husain, bleeding from several wounds, stood at bay alone, except for the women crouching in the tents behind him. At the command of an

[2] Genealogical tree 1, page 27.

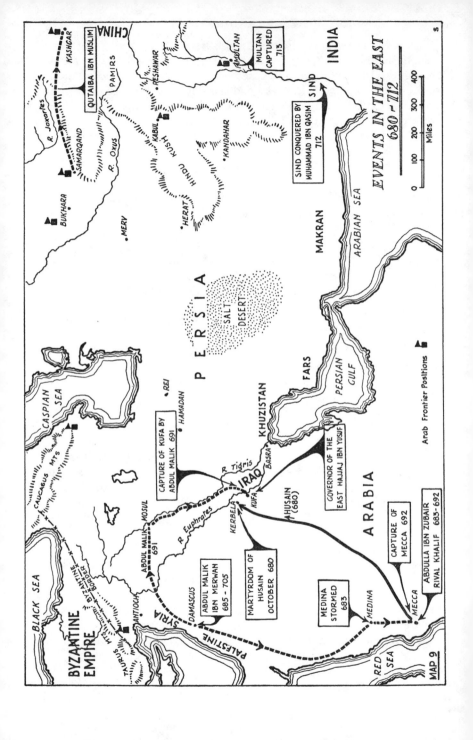

EVENTS IN THE EAST
680 ~ 712

Miles
0   100   200   300   400

MAP 9

BYZANTINE EMPIRE

BLACK SEA

CASPIAN SEA

CAUCASUS MTs

BYZANTINE BORDER

TAURUS Mts

ANTIOCH

SYRIA

DAMASCUS

ABDUL MALIK IBN MERWAN 685-705

PALESTINE

RED SEA

Medina

MEDINA STORMED 683

MECCA

CAPTURE OF MECCA 692

ABDULLA IBN ZUBAIR RIVAL KHALIF 685-692

ARABIA

MARTYRDOM OF HUSAIN OCTOBER 680

ABDUL MALIK 691

MOSUL

R. Euphrates

IRAQ

R. Tigris

KERBELA

KUFA

CAPTURE OF KUFA BY ABDUL MALIK 691

HAMADAN

• REI

PERSIA

SALT DESERT

BASRA

HUSAIN (680)

GOVERNOR OF THE EAST HAJJAJ IBN YUSUF

KHUZISTAN

FARS

PERSIAN GULF

MAKRAN

ARABIAN SEA

MERV

• HERAT

KANDAHAR

HINDU KUSH

KABUL

PESHAWAR

PAMIRS

R. Oxus

BUKHARA

SAMARQAND

QUTAIBA IBN MUSLIM

R. Joxartes

KASHGAR

CHINA

MULTAN

MULTAN CAPTURED 715

SIND

SIND CONQUERED BY MUHAMMAD IBN QASIM 712

INDIA

Arab Frontier Positions

5

officer called Shemmer, the troops closed in, and Husain fell beneath their swords. His head and those of his seventy-two retainers were cut off and sent to Ubaidullah.

It is easy to imagine the fear and anxiety felt in Damascus at the prospect of another civil war between Beni Umaiya and Beni Hashim. The temptation to dispose of the principal Beni Hashim candidate was a strong one. Yet the brutality of the action, and the fact that Husain was a grandson of the Prophet himself, provoked an intense reaction against the Umaiyids all over the Muslim world. The martyrdom of Husain elicited passionate devotion from his adherents, and has divided the Muslim world into two parts from that day to this. Those who support the claims of Ali and his sons are called Shiites,[3] while the remainder of the Muslims are termed Sunnis.

The elimination of Husain did not bring peace to Yezeed. In the autumn of 682, two years after the tragedy of Kerbela, Medina openly revolted. On 26th August, 683, an army from Damascus, commanded by Muslim ibn Uqba, the son of Uqba ibn Nafi, the first conqueror of Africa, took the city by storm.

Meanwhile Mecca also had revolted and was besieged but, in November 683, Yezeed died in Damascus. Chaos followed immediately. Muawiya II, the son of Yezeed, though still a child, was acclaimed in Syria. Ubaidullah, after a momentary bid for power himself, joined the Umaiyids in Damascus. In Mecca, Abdulla ibn Zubair, son of that Zubair who had rebelled against Ali, proclaimed himself khalif. Then the child Muawiya II died and, in 684, Merwan was raised to the khalifate in Damascus.[4] In 685, however, Merwan died and his son Abdul Malik ibn Merwan was proclaimed in Syria as his successor.

The situation which confronted Abdul Malik in 685 seemed to be almost desperate. Only Syria, Palestine and Egypt recognized his accession. In Mecca the rival khalif, Abdulla ibn Zubair, was firmly in control. Persia was in anarchy and, in Iraq, the Shiites and the Kharijites were in rebellion.

Not until 691 was Abdul Malik strong enough to take the field. He commenced by invading Iraq. Defeating and killing the brother of Abdulla ibn Zubair, he took Kufa in December 691. The loss of Iraq rendered hopeless the position of Abdulla ibn Zubair in Mecca. Early in 692, an army left Damascus to capture the Holy City.

[3] Collective—the Shia or the party.
[4] Genealogical tree 2, page 74.

The siege of Mecca lasted for eight months. The Umaiyid commander, Hajjáj ibn Yusuf, had placed mangonels[5] on the mountains which, on all sides, overhung the little desert town and a continuous bombardment of rocks was maintained. On 3rd October, 692, when further resistance was impossible, Abdulla ibn Zubair, sword in hand, sallied out alone against the Damascus army. A missile struck him in the face and blood poured down his beard and clothes. He paused for a moment, to recite in stentorian tones—he was famous for the power of his voice—these lines from a classical Arab poet:

"No craven wounds our backs shall stain with shame,
    But down our breasts our glorious blood shall flow."

Then, moving forward again alone, he fell riddled with arrows.

Such were the ancient Arabs. War and poetry were their joy. Even in their endless and bloodsoaked feuds, they maintained a noble spirit of courage, dignity and drama.

*   *   *

The fratricidal civil war had lasted for twelve years. At last, on 3rd October, 692, Abdul Malik was sole khalif of the Muslims, though Iraq was still disturbed by the rival activities of the Shiites and the puritan Kharijites. Hajjaj ibn Yusuf had won fame by his defeat of Abdulla ibn Zubair. In January 695, Abdul Malik wrote to Medina to inform Hajjaj that he was transferred to the governorship of Kufa.

Hajjaj set out immediately, rode six hundred miles across the desert with an escort of only twelve camelmen, and arrived in Kufa before anyone knew that he had left Medina. Next day, his face muffled in his headdress, he mounted the pulpit in the mosque. Suddenly uncovering his face, he announced grimly, "I see in front of me heads ripe to be cut off, the blood spurting from beneath the beards." He was as good as his word. All opposition was ruthlessly suppressed and both the Shiites and Kharijites vanished like melting snow.

After fourteen years, the Arab war-banners again moved forward. Bukhara, Samarqand and Kabul, which had been lost during the civil wars, were reoccupied. Hajjaj, like his equally capable predecessor, Zayyad the-son-of-his-father, was made governor of Kufa, Basra and all the eastern half of the empire.

*   *   *

[5] The mangonel was a long wooden beam which, when bent back, threw rocks as missiles.

We have already seen the exploits of Uqba ibn Nafi in North Africa, his foundation of the base at Qairawan[6] and the withdrawal of the Arabs to Barqa after his death. In 695, after the termination of the civil wars between Abdul Malik and Abdulla ibn Zubair, the advance was resumed once again.

Hassán ibn Naamán re-established the base at Qairawan, took Carthage in 698 and levelled it with the ground. At this moment, however, the Zenáta, a nomadic tribe of Berbers from the Sahara, overran Ifriqiya, completely defeating Hassan ibn Naaman at Tebessa. The remnant of the Arab forces escaped with difficulty to Barqa.

In 702, however, Abdul Malik ibn Merwan was at the height of his power. Hassan ibn Naaman, powerfully reinforced, defeated the Zenata and re-established Qairawan. After sixty years of alternate victory and defeat, the Berbers submitted and were converted to Islam. North Africa was pacified as far as the Atlantic coast.

*   *   *

While the Arab career of conquest was thus resumed during the reign of Abdul Malik, the administrative consolidation over which he presided was no less striking. Although sixty years had elapsed since the Arab conquest of Syria, the public accounts were still kept in Greek. Under Abdul Malik, the accounts and all official correspondence were transacted in Arabic. The government in Damascus was organized in diwans or "ministries"—a secretariat, a finance diwan, an army diwan and so forth. Copies of all letters issued were retained and filed. A highly organized postal service radiated from Damascus to every part of the empire, provincial postmasters being also responsible for secret political intelligence. Carrier pigeons did duty for the modern telegraph system.

Taxation was still on the simple basis instituted by Muhammad. The Poor Tax, collected from all Muslims, was distributed to the indigent members of the community. Land Tax was paid by all who cultivated and poll-tax was collected from non-Muslims. Tribute was paid by certain conquered districts and one-fifth of war plunder belonged to the treasury.

Abdul Malik ruled according to the ancient Arab tradition, which may be described as equalitarian autocracy, or perhaps patriarchy— the system which, to this day, seems most congenial to the Arab temperament. It is largely based on the accessibility of the ruler, or

[6] Map 8, page 71.

of his delegated representative, to the complaints of the public, with which he deals benevolently in person. It is, in many ways, the antithesis of modern Western bureaucracy, under which senior officials are inaccessible to the ordinary man. In addition, the Arab benevolent autocrat is expected frequently to consult with the leaders of the nation.

Abdul Malik died on 8th October, 705. It was he who consolidated the imperial greatness of the Arabs. An exceptionally capable man, he was careful to appear religious, was well educated, a man of letters and a poet, but with the strength of character to command obedience. He was succeeded by his son Waleed.

*   *   *

In 531, a hundred and seventy years earlier, the Goths had conquered Spain, where they had become an idle aristocracy, abandoning the use of arms and living in luxury and pleasure.

In 705, Musa ibn Nusair succeeded Hassan ibn Naaman as governor of North Africa. In 710, tradition relates that a certain Count Julian, at enmity with Roderic, King of the Goths, suggested to Musa an Arab invasion of Spain. When the proposal was referred to the Khalif Waleed, the latter considered the project too risky, but authorized a reconnaissance in force. In April 711, Musa sent a force of twelve thousand men across the Straits of Gibraltar, under a Berber freedman of his own, called Tariq ibn Zayyad. Tariq established his base on the rock of Gibraltar, ever since known by his name, Jebel Tariq, Tariq's mountain.

The decisive battle was fought a few miles east-south-east of Cadiz.[7] The Goths were completely defeated and King Roderic killed. Tariq, with remarkable daring, marched straight on and occupied the Gothic capital, Toledo. The following summer, Musa ibn Nusair himself crossed to Spain, took Seville and Merida and joined Tariq.

The Arab conquerors in Spain behaved with their usual leniency. The churches were divided between Muslims and Christians. Crown lands, or those of landowners who had fled the country, were confiscated and Christians and Jews were obliged to pay a poll-tax. The conquest was indeed not an unmitigated disaster for the people. The Arabs were, on the whole, more tolerant than the Goths. Serfs and slaves, by professing Islam, could obtain their freedom. The

[7] Map 8, page 71.

Jews particularly, who had been persecuted by the Goths, were under the Arabs free to practise their religion.

The pacification of Spain was quickly completed, except for a remnant of Christians in the mountains of Galicia. The Arabs were rarely very successful in mountains and the omission completely to subdue Galicia was to cost them dear, for the Christian reconquest was to commence from there.

In the summer of 714, Musa received peremptory orders to report immediately to Damascus, where he found himself accused and then disgraced. An old and broken man, he ended his days in poverty in a small oasis near Medina. His success, like that of Warren Hastings, had produced jealousy at home.

*   *   *

While Musa and Tariq had been conquering Spain, known to the Arabs as Andalus, Hajjaj ibn Yusuf was still viceroy of the eastern half of the empire. Qutaiba ibn Muslim, a commander appointed by him, crossed the River Jaxartes[8] and the Pamirs to Kashgar in Sinkiang. From there a delegation was sent to the Emperor of China to demand his submission, a suggestion apparently received with philosophic good humour by the Son of Heaven. Perhaps more important was the fact that the Arabs learned from the Chinese the secret of the manufacture of paper, which they introduced into their own dominions and subsequently passed on to Europe.

While Qutaiba ibn Muslim was advancing into Central Asia, Muhammad ibn Qasim, a cousin of Hajjaj, was in what is now called Pakistan. In 712, while Musa was conquering Andalus, he defeated and killed the Brahman King of Sind and, in 713, he took Multan.

*   *   *

Sulaiman, the brother of Waleed, succeeded him as khalif in February 715. The most notable event in his brief reign was the second Arab siege of Constantinople, which lasted from 716 until 717. The siege was conducted by Maslama ibn Abdul Malik, a brilliant soldier and brother of the khalif. The massive walls of Constantinople were attacked in vain again and again, the city being probably impregnable to an eighth century army. The Byzantines also enjoyed the advantage of their possession of the Greek fire, an inflammable liquid apparently containing naphtha,

[8] Map 9, page 76.

which could be discharged from nozzles fitted in the bows of Byzantine ships. By this means, they were able to destroy the Arab fleet without which a blockade could not be maintained, for the city on three sides was surrounded by water. The flaming liquid could also be poured from the battlements on troops attempting to mount the walls.

Unfortunately for the Arabs, the winter 716–717 was exceptionally cold and thick snow covered the Arab lines for three months. The loss of their fleet made it impossible for them to obtain supplies or clothing and many died of starvation and exposure.

In the spring of 717, the dauntless Emperor Leo the Isaurian persuaded the Bulgars to attack the Arabs in the rear. While desperate fighting was still in progress, the Khalif Sulaiman died in Damascus. His successor, Umar ibn Abdul Azeez, sent orders for the abandonment of the siege and the return of the army to Syria.

NOTABLE DATES

Foundation of Qairawan	670
First Siege of Constantinople	670–677
Death of Muawiya	April 680
Martyrdom of Husain	10th October, 680
Revolt in Medina	682
Death of Yezeed I	November 683
Accession of Abdul Malik ibn Merwan	685
Siege of Mecca	February to October 692
Death of Abdulla ibn Zubair	3rd October, 692
Operations of Hassan ibn Naaman in Ifriqiya	695–702
Death of Abdul Malik	8th October, 705
Arab Conquest of Spain	711–712
Capture of Kashgar	713
Capture of Multan	713
Second Siege of Constantinople	716–717

PERSONALITIES

The Umaiyid Khalifs

Muawiya ibn abi Sofian	661–680
Yezeed I, son of Muawiya	680–683
Muawiya II, son of Yezeed	683–684

Merwan ibn al Hakam	684–685
Abdul Malik ibn Merwan	685–705
Waleed ibn Abdul Malik	705–715
Sulaiman ibn Abdul Malik	715–717

Other Personalities

Abdulla ibn Zubair, claimant to the khalifate in Mecca
Husain ibn Ali, grandson of the Prophet, the Martyr of Kerbela
Zayyad the-son-of-his-father, viceroy of the East
Ubaidullah, his son
Hajjaj ibn Yusuf, viceroy of the East
Musa ibn Nusair, the conqueror of Spain

VI

The Abbasid Revolution
717–775

ALTHOUGH the Khalif Sulaiman ibn Abdul Malik left sixteen brothers and several sons when he died, he nominated his cousin, Umar ibn Abdul Azeez[1] as his successor. This was a good example of the ancient Arab system of succession, which required the heir to be the most suitable candidate available from the ruling family, but not necessarily the son of the previous ruler. Through his mother, Umar ibn Abdul Azeez was the great-grandson of the Prophet's second successor, Umar ibn al Khattab, who, it will be remembered, went barefoot and possessed only one shirt, while the immense treasures of Byzantium and Persia were spread at his feet.

Seventy-three years had passed since the assassination of the first Umar. The khalifs had ceased to be barefoot tribesmen living in mud shacks in desert oases, and had become great emperors, escorted by guards with drawn swords through the gay and worldly streets of Damascus. Amid these magnificent surroundings, Umar ibn Abdul Azeez aspired to imitate the austerities of his great-grandfather. He too possessed only one shirt, was said to live almost entirely on lentil soup and to pass his nights in prayer.

But Umar was no mere fanatic. Ever since the days of Muawiya I, the Arab world had been torn by the violent feud between Beni Hashim and Beni Umaiya. Umar did all in his power to heal the rift. In the same way, when the Kharijite puritans raised yet another revolt in northern Iraq, he did not send an army but invited a rebel delegation to Damascus to explain their grievances.

Financially, however, Umar failed to solve the problem which was to contribute to the overthrow of the Umaiyid dynasty. The Prophet, it will be remembered, had forbidden the persecution of Jews and Christians but had ordered them to pay a poll-tax, in return for

[1] Genealogical tree 2, page 74.

which their lives and property would be protected. This tax formed a substantial part of the revenue. But if such persons were converted to Islam, they ceased to be liable to poll-tax.

Seventy-five years had passed since the conquest of Syria, Persia and Egypt and every year increasing numbers of the conquered races had professed Islam. If all converts had been excused the poll-tax, the treasury would have been bankrupt. In practice, therefore, converts were, more often than not, obliged to continue payment. Exemption had, in fact, become largely an Arab privilege, which Muslims of other races did not enjoy.

Umar ibn Abdul Azeez, guided by the actions of the Prophet himself, ruled that no Muslim should pay poll-tax. Not only was the treasury immediately in difficulties, but the exemption caused great numbers of persons of other religions to be converted, most of them doubtless not from conviction, but to avoid taxation.

To the pious khalif the issue was simple—should he or should he not obey the Prophet's orders? Twelve centuries later, we can see the problem in a different light. When Muhammad was alive, there was no empire and indeed no government and no paid army. What revenue came in to Medina was immediately distributed to the poor. But in Damascus, eighty-six years after the Prophet's death, an immense empire had to be administered and regular armies had to be maintained from the shores of the Atlantic to the borders of India and China. The financial system sufficient for the little theocratic community of Medina was hopelessly inadequate for the great Arab empire. Complete fiscal reorganization was long overdue.

Umar ibn Abdul Azeez died on 10th February, 720, after a reign of only two years and nine months. He was succeeded by Yezeed II ibn Abdul Malik,[2] brother of the two previous khalifs, Waleed and Sulaiman. Yezeed II was a weak and frivolous character, who reigned for only four years, dying on 28th January, 724. He was succeeded by yet another son of Abdul Malik, Hisham.

The new khalif was capable, steady, hard-working and conspicuous for his common sense. He avoided the frivolity of his two brothers, Sulaiman and Yezeed II, and the somewhat narrow views of the pious Umar ibn Abdul Azeez. In his reign of nineteen years, the Umaiyids recovered much of their shaken prestige and the empire seemed to be at the height of its glory and strength.

The decision of Umar ibn Abdul Azeez that non-Arab Muslims were exempt from poll-tax had been reversed under Yezeed II, in

[2] Genealogical tree 2, page 74.

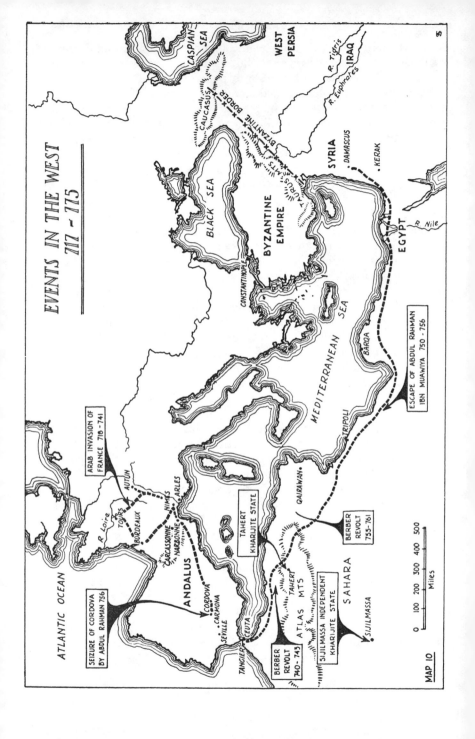

EVENTS IN THE WEST
717 – 775

WEST PERSIA

CASPIAN SEA

R. Tigris
IRAQ
R. Euphrates

BYZANTINE BORDER

CAUCASUS

BLACK SEA

CONSTANTINOPLE

TAURUS MTS

BYZANTINE EMPIRE

AURUS MTS

SYRIA
• DAMASCUS
• KERAK

EGYPT
R. Nile

MEDITERRANEAN SEA

ESCAPE OF ABDUL RAHMAN
IBN MUAWIYA 750 – 756

BARQA

TRIPOLI

ATLANTIC OCEAN

ARAB INVASION OF
FRANCE 718 – 741

R. Loire
TOURS
AUTUN
BORDEAUX
NIMES
CARCASSONNE
ARLES
NARBONNE

SEIZURE OF CORDOVA
BY ABDUL RAHMAN 756

ANDALUS
SEVILLE
CORDOVA
CARMONA
TANGIER
CEUTA

TAHERT
KHARIJITE STATE

ATLAS MTS
TAHERT
QAIRAWAN •

BERBER
REVOLT
755 – 761

BERBER
REVOLT
740 – 743

SIJILMASSA INDEPENDENT
KHARIJITE STATE

SAHARA
SIJILMASSA •

MAP 10

0 100 200 300 400 500
Miles

order to re-establish the solvency of the government. A rebellion in
Khurasan, the north-eastern province of Persia, was the result. The
situation was rendered extremely dangerous by the fact that the
Turkish tribes of Central Asia had recently established a powerful
confederation in the Illi valley.[3] The Khurasan rebels appealed to
the Turks and the Khakan, or paramount khan, invaded Khurasan.
Only after ten years of hard fighting, from 738 to 748, in the often
snow-covered foothills of the Pamirs and on the plains of Trans-
Oxiana, was the authority of the government eventually re-
established.

*   *   *

The Berbers of North Africa had, as we have seen, been conquered before 710 and the great majority had professed Islam. This,
however, did not make them resigned to Arab rule. On the contrary,
it produced the same grievance as in Khurasan. Berber Muslims
were still required to pay poll-tax.

Frequent reference has already been made to the Kharijites of
Iraq, those puritan Levellers who sought a theocratic republic and
who recognized no earthly princes. "No ruler but God" was their
motto. Moreover, although the original Kharijites had been Arabs,
their fundamentalism recognized no racial differences. A negro
slave, they said, could be khalif, if he possessed the necessary moral
qualities.

After the death of Abdul Malik in 705, the Kharijite heresy infiltrated into Ifriqiya, where it spread like wildfire. Ironically enough,
the Berbers, so recently converted to Islam by the Arabs, now
claimed to be truer Muslims than the "worldly" dynasty of Damascus. In 740, all the Berbers from Tangier to Qairawan rose in
rebellion. The Arab forces were not only defeated but exterminated,
for they still possessed enough of their ancient glory to prefer death
to surrender.

In 741, a fresh army of twenty-seven thousand men sent by
Hisham from Damascus was likewise destroyed, a hundred miles
south of Tangier. The indefatigable Hisham sent another army in
742, but no sooner did it reach the base at Qairawan than it found
itself besieged by large numbers of Berbers. Supplies soon ran low
and no further relief could be expected from Damascus.

The Arab commander, Handhala ibn Safwan, a man of noble
character and high courage, decided that so desperate a situation
required a desperate remedy. At dawn, the garrison sallied forth,

[3] Map 11, page 89.

every man drawing his sword and throwing away the scabbard. The Arabs fought with savage fury until, after many hours of bitter struggle, discipline won the day. The Berber tribesmen broke and fled and, in 743, Arab domination was re-established.

*   *   *

We left Andalus in 714, when Musa ibn Nusair was recalled by the Khalif Waleed. No other governor seems to have been sent and the Muslims—Arabs and Berbers together—were left to their own devices. In 718, they broke through the eastern end of the Pyrenees into France, and occupied Carcassonne and Narbonne. In 725, they took Nîmes and their columns, moving up the Rhone valley, reached Autun. Early in 732 they took Bordeaux but, in October 732, they were defeated at Tours by the Franks under Charles Martel. Six years later, in 738, the Arabs were still holding Arles. In 741, however, civil war broke out between the Arabs and the Berbers in Spain and, perhaps for this reason, the invasion of France seems to have been abandoned.

*   *   *

The Khalif Hisham died in 743 at the age of fifty-four. He had been a diligent and scrupulous ruler. He himself constantly examined the public accounts and supervised the administration. He was extremely painstaking in his legal decisions. In appearance, he was thickset and suffered from a squint. He was particularly interested in farming and passionately fond of horses—an open-air, practical country squire.

Masudi, one of the earliest of the famous Arab historians, writes that Beni Umaiya produced three really great rulers, Muawiya I, Abdul Malik ibn Merwan and Hisham ibn Abdul Malik.

*   *   *

After the death of Hisham, the Umaiyids declined rapidly. The new khalif was Waleed II, a son of the frivolous but harmless Yezeed II. Waleed II was a libertine, a drunkard, a blasphemer and a cynic. He was killed after a reign of only fifteen months. On 17th April, 744, his head, transfixed on the point of a lance, was paraded through the streets of Damascus.

The revolt had been led by Waleed's cousin, Yezeed III, the son of Waleed I. Immediately acclaimed as khalif, Yezeed seemed to be conscientious, pious and serious but he died in October 744, after a reign of only six months.

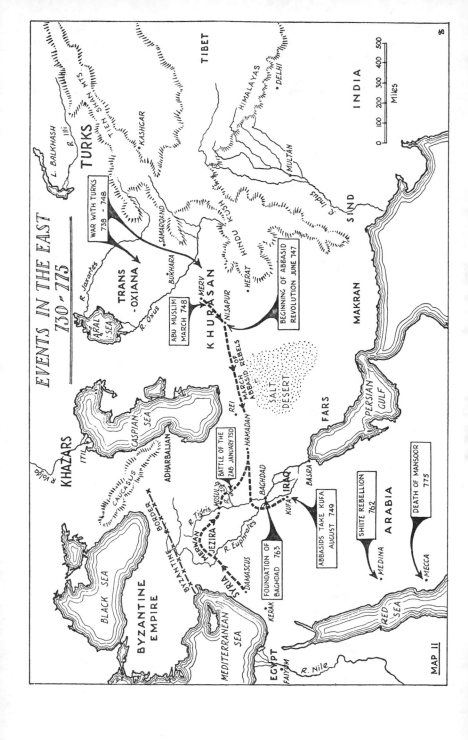

EVENTS IN THE EAST
730 – 775

L. BALKHASH

R. ILI

TURKS

TIEN SHAN MTS

KASHGAR

TIBET

HIMALAYAS

DELHI

INDIA

500
400
300
200
100
0
Miles

WAR WITH TURKS
738 – 748

R. Jaxartes

SAMARQAND

TRANS-
OXIANA

BUKHARA

R. Oxus

ARAL
SEA

MERV

ABU MUSLIM
MARCH 748

KHURASAN

NISAPUR

HINDU KUSH

HERAT

MULTAN

R. Indus

SIND

BEGINNING OF ABBASID
REVOLUTION JUNE 747

MAKRAN

MARCH OF ABBASID REBELS

REI

SALT
DESERT

FARS

PERSIAN GULF

KHAZARS

ITIL

R. Volga

CASPIAN SEA

CAUCASUS

ADHARBAIJAN

HAMADAN

BATTLE OF THE
ZAB JANUARY 750

R. Zab

MOSUL

R. Tigris

MERWAN

JEZIRA

BAGHDAD

BASRA

IRAQ

KUFA

ABBASIDS TAKE KUFA
AUGUST 749

SHIITE REBELLION
762

ARABIA

MEDINA

DEATH OF MANSOOR
775

MECCA

BYZANTINE EMPIRE

BLACK SEA

BYZANTINE BORDER

SYRIA

DAMASCUS

R. Euphrates

FOUNDATION OF
BAGHDAD 763

KERAK

MEDITERRANEAN SEA

EGYPT

FAIYUM

R. Nile

RED SEA

MAP II

89

For twelve years, from 732 to 744, Merwan ibn Muhammad ibn Merwan[4] had been the military commander-in-chief and governor of the Jezira and Adharbaijan. His front included most of the Byzantine border in the west and that of the Caucasus, occupied by the warlike Khazars, on the north. In 737, in a brilliant campaign, he had utterly defeated the Khazars and occupied their capital, Itil, at the mouth of the Volga.

Merwan was a dedicated soldier, indifferent to women, luxury and ease, always in the field with his troops. His endurance had earned for him the nickname of Merwan the Ass, for to the Arabs the ass was proverbial, not for its foolishness, but for its patient endurance.

The collapse of the Umaiyid dynasty stirred Merwan to action. He marched on the capital and was acclaimed as khalif in Damascus on 23rd November, 744.

*   *   *

The Arabs have always been individualists, violent in their mutual jealousies, carrying their love of independence to the extent of anarchy. The Umaiyid Empire, bestriding the world like a colossus from the Atlantic to the borders of China, was torn internally by innumerable feuds. The principal causes of these dissensions may here be explained.

The discontent of non-Arab Muslims has already been mentioned. Although the Prophet had stated that all Muslims were equal, the Arabs in fact constituted a sovereign race.

Ever since the civil war between Ali and Muawiya and the subsequent martyrdom of Husain, the Muslim world had been divided into two, the partizans of the descendants of Ali, known as Shiites, being bitterly hostile to the followers of the Umaiyids, who were called Sunnis. Spasmodic Shiite rebellions continued to break out in Iraq. The religious picture was further complicated by the puritan Kharijites, who were now firmly established in Ifriqiya.

A third problem, and one which seems to us entirely unnecessary, was the division of the Arabs themselves into two groups, known as Adnan and Qahtan or Qais and Yemen. Their tradition, perhaps truthfully, alleged that the Arabs had originally consisted of two races, one originating from the northern half of the peninsula and known as Adnan or Qais,[5] the other, called Qahtan, from the

[4] Genealogical tree 2, page 74.
[5] Pronounced like the English word "case".

Yemen. Many of the Yemenites, however, had migrated to northern Arabia before Islam. In the great conquests, all had intermingled. Nevertheless, in Iraq and Syria, even in Andalus and Turkestan, the feud between Qais and Yemen was maintained.

A fourth and even more pressing schism now arose. We have seen that Quraish, the Prophet's tribe, were divided between Beni Umaiya and Beni Hashim, whose claim for leadership had hitherto been represented by the descendants of Ali. But Hashim had another grandson, Abbas, the uncle of the Prophet and of Ali.[6] The descendants of Abbas had quarrelled with the Umaiyids, and lived in obscurity south of Kerak, in modern Jordan.

The head of the Abbasid clan was a certain Muhammad ibn Ali ibn Abdulla ibn Abbas. This man seems to have possessed a genius for political organization worthy of the Communists of today. He inaugurated a political underground which carried on vigorous propaganda against the alleged worldliness of the Umaiyids. This secret campaign was conducted in the name of "the family", a vague term which the Shiites interpreted as meaning the descendants of Ali. In Persia, and especially in turbulent Khurasan, the movement exploited the grievances of the non-Arab Muslims, who still paid poll-tax.

Merwan the Ass, the new khalif, was an enthusiastic partizan of the Qais faction among the Arabs, with the result that the conspirators secured the adherence of many Arabs of the Yemen party. At the same time the Kharijites, though not allied to the new movement (for they opposed all princes), seeing the government in difficulties, staged a rebellion in Iraq. Merwan the Ass, a vigorous soldier, marched back and forth defeating one enemy after another, but he was no politician. He did not separate his enemies by conciliating one group and crushing another.

At this moment of crisis, the conspirators discovered a born leader in the person of one Abu Muslim, who seems to have been a Persian resident in Kufa. Small, of dark complexion, with a persuasive manner and a constant courage which never faltered, Abu Muslim, in June 747, raised the standard of revolt in Khurasan. Establishing his headquarters in Merv, he administered an oath of allegiance in the name of Beni Hashim. As this appellation covered the descendants of Ali, the Shiites took the oath with alacrity.

The rebels pressed on triumphantly in Persia until, in August 749, they occupied Kufa. At this stage, the Abbasid family secretly

[6] Genealogical tree 2, page 74.

3. THE GREAT ABBASID KHALIFS

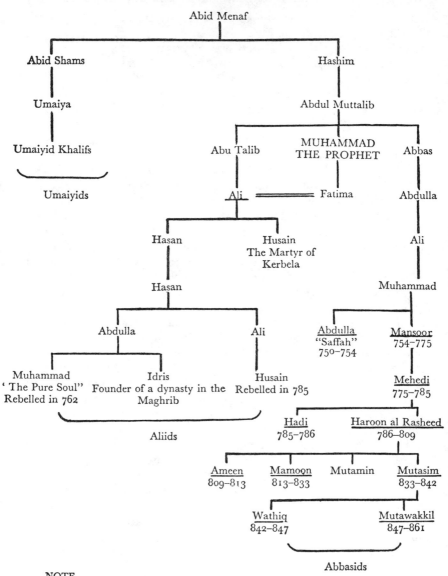

NOTE
Khalifs are underlined.

abandoned their home in Jordan and, crossing the desert by camel, appeared in Kufa, where the rebel army hailed Abdulla ibn Muhammad ibn Ali ibn Abdulla ibn Abbas as the rightful Prince of the Faithful. The Shiites, suddenly disillusioned, attempted to acclaim a descendant of Ali, but were quickly suppressed.

On 25th January, 750, the decisive battle was fought on the River Zab, eighty miles south of Mosul. The loyalty of the Umaiyid army had already been undermined by propaganda. Many units refused to fight and Merwan was completely defeated.

The disaster was irretrievable. Merwan fled to Syria with the Abbasids in hot pursuit. Unable to pause long enough to organize any resistance, he continued his flight to Egypt, where, on the night of 5th August, 750, he was surprised and killed by Abbasid cavalry in the little village of Busir in the Faiyum. All the members of the Umaiyid family who could be found in Syria were indiscriminately massacred.

*   *   *

The Battle of the Zab was one of the decisive battles of the world because it resulted in the orientalization of Islam. The Umaiyid Empire had been a Mediterranean power. Damascus had been for a thousand years part of the Graeco-Roman world, as had Palestine, Egypt, North Africa and Spain. Persia, the Punjab and Turkistan had been colonies of this Mediterranean empire. But the Abbasids had achieved power principally with the support of Persians. They made their capital at Kufa in Iraq, which for more than a thousand years had been part of Persia.

The Khalif Abdulla, the first Abbasid Prince of the Faithful, did not reign long to enjoy his triumph. He died of smallpox on 9th June, 754, though he had already earned the nickname of Saffah, the Shedder of Blood. He was succeeded by his brother Abu Jafar, who was acclaimed khalif in Kufa with the title of Mansoor, the Victorious.

While the Blood-Shedder was still alive, Mansoor had urged him to dispose of Abu Muslim, by whose efforts the Abbasids had been raised to power. "If you do not lunch off him today, he will dine off you tomorrow," he remarked cynically. But the Blood-Shedder had hesitated to murder the man to whom he owed his throne, for fear of a mutiny of the Khurasan army. Mansoor, however, was more determined. Abu Muslim had become a national hero and as such was dangerous. The khalif accordingly invited him to court and caused him to be assassinated when he was his guest. The hero's body was rolled up in a carpet and quietly dropped into the Tigris.

*   *   *

The most famous action connected with the name of Mansoor was the founding of Baghdad. Ever since the days of Ali and Husain, the people of Kufa had acquired a reputation for treachery, and the new khalif was anxious to found a city in which he could settle his own partizans. After careful personal reconnaissances, he chose the site of modern Baghdad. Here the Euphrates was joined to the Tigris by a navigable canal. Moreover the site was on a main road to Persia, leading through the mountains to Hamadan.

Baghdad was thus centrally placed between Arabia, Egypt and Syria on the one hand, and Persia, Trans-Oxiana and the Punjab on the other. But it was extremely remote from Spain and North Africa. The boundary between East and West in the eighth century (and indeed to some extent even today) does not lie along the eastern shores of the Mediterranean but along the ancient border between Rome and Persia, the present frontier between Syria and Iraq. The movement of the capital from Damascus to Baghdad thus resulted to a large extent in the orientalization, not only of the Arab Empire, but of the world of Islam itself.

Mansoor's new city was made completely round within a double circle of walls. At the centre of the circle was the khalif's palace. The walled city was occupied only by the palace, the khalif's body-guard and some blocks of government offices. The suburbs outside the walls were settled by the supporters of the dynasty, chiefly natives of Balkh, Merv, Bukhara, Khiva and north-east Persia, where Abu Muslim had first raised the banner of revolt.

This splendid isolation of the Prince of the Faithful in his palace, surrounded by double walls and by carefully chosen retainers, forms a remarkable contrast to the simplicity of the early Muslim society of Medina, when the Prophet and his first successors, barefoot and in peasant's dress, mingled without ceremony with the crowds in the bazaar.

Mansoor was passionately interested in building, and super-intended in person the distribution of bricks and mortar and the payment of the wages of the workmen. By this means he acquired a reputation for parsimony and was nicknamed Old Farthings.[7]

*   *   *

[7] Abu al Dawanik.

The Abbasids had obtained power by what today we should call subversive propaganda. Under the rule of the Prophet's own family, it had been claimed, the iniquities of the wicked Umaiyids would cease and the reign of peace, mercy, justice and happiness would spread over all the earth. These dreams had been quickly dispelled by the Blood-Shedder and his successor. If the Abbasids were no worse than the Umaiyids, they were certainly no better.

In the Roman revolution which, in the century before Christ, transformed the old Roman Republic into an empire, another change had occurred less obvious than the constitutional innovations. The Roman Republic had been ruled by Italians, the empire was an interracial, Mediterranean commonwealth.

The Arab revolution of 750, in the same manner, transformed the purely Arab empire of the Umaiyids into a Muslim state. The Abbasids were, of course, Arabs, the official language was Arabic, as the language of the Roman Empire had been Latin, but advancement was henceforward open to all races alike.

*   *   *

Disillusionment followed rapidly on the assumption of power by "the Prophet's family", and resulted in a crop of rebellions. Even in Khurasan, home of the Abbasid rising, revolt broke out. In 762, a desperate Shiite rebellion took place in Medina, led by Muhammad ibn Abdulla ibn Hasan. This Hasan was the brother of Husain and a grandson of the Prophet. Muhammad ibn Abdulla, nicknamed the Pure Soul, a man of genuine religious faith, was defeated and killed. His brother Idris,[8] a great-great-great-grandson of the Prophet, later escaped to the Maghrib, where he founded a dynasty.

In 755, a rebellion broke out in Ifriqiya, and Qairawan was taken and sacked.[9] Not until 761 were the rebels repressed and Qairawan reoccupied. Ten years later, the Berbers, now all Kharijites, were again in arms, but were defeated by the governor Yezeed ibn Hatim and suppressed with great severity.

The government, however, made no attempt to control the Berbers of the Atlas mountains, who had set up a number of small, independent Kharijite states. Most prominent of these were Tahert, under a dynasty known as the Beni Rustem, and Sijilmassa, south of the Atlas, the "landfall" of the trans-Saharan caravan trade from

[8] Pronounced Idrees. See Genealogical tree 3, page 92.
[9] Map 10, page 86.

Ghana and Nigeria. The Kharijites were extremely equalitarian, observed a high standard of morality, even of asceticism, and passed their time in theological discussions.

*   *   *

The most sensational of all the revolts in the reign of Mansoor was, however, that of Andalus or Spain. In the almost complete extermination of the Umaiyids in Syria, a grandson of the Khalif Hisham had escaped. His name was Abdul Rahman ibn Muawiya.[10] Disguised, and accompanied by one devoted servant, he wandered across Palestine, Egypt, Barqa and into the Atlas mountains. After five years as penniless vagabonds, they reached Ceuta, on the Straits of Gibraltar. Andalus had been conquered in the time of Umaiyid glory and many Syrians had settled there. These welcomed the fugitive prince who, in May 756, occupied Cordova, the capital.[11]

Civil war, however, continued until 763, when Ala ibn Mughith, sent by Mansoor to reconquer Andalus for the Abbasids, arrived on the scene. Abdul Rahman the Umaiyid was besieged in Carmona and his situation seemed to be completely hopeless. But the young prince was a man of desperate courage. Collecting seven hundred picked men, he sallied suddenly from the town gate, took the besiegers by surprise, killed Ala ibn Mughith and won a complete victory. The head of Ala ibn Mughith, pickled in camphor and salt and wrapped in Mansoor's diploma appointing him governor, was sent, a gruesome gift, to the khalif by a well paid messenger.

Thus only thirteen years after the seizure of power by the Abbasids, the western end of the empire began to break away.

*   *   *

Mansoor died in October 775 in his camp near Mecca, while on a pilgrimage. He was sixty-four years old and had reigned for twenty-one years. Tall, thin and sallow, he was of a serious disposition and well read. He frowned on frivolity and would not allow any kind of music. A capable and extremely hard-working administrator, he killed a great many people early in his khalifate, including Abu Muslim to whom he owed his throne. In the later part of his reign, however, when he began to feel secure, he displayed more moderation. Where no political motive was suspected, he was careful and painstaking in the enforcement of justice.

[10] Genealogical tree 2, page 74.   [11] Map 10, page 86.

NOTABLE DATES

Arab invasion of France	718–732
Berber revolt in Ifriqiya	740
Defeat of Berbers by Handhala	742–743
Accession of Merwan the Ass	23rd November, 744
Rebellion of Abu Muslim	747
Battle of the Zab	25th January, 750
Landing of Abdul Rahman ibn Muawiya in Andalus	755
Abdul Rahman ruler of Andalus	763
Foundation of Baghdad	763
Death of Mansoor	775

PERSONALITIES

Umaiyid Khalifs

Umar ibn Abdul Azeez	717–720
Yezeed II ibn Abdul Malik	720–724
Hisham ibn Abdul Malik	724–743
Waleed II ibn Yezeed II	743–744
Yezeed III ibn Waleed I	744
Merwan II the Ass	744–750

Abbasid Khalifs

Abdulla al Saffah (the Blood-Shedder)	750–754
Mansoor	754–775

Other Personalities

Abdul Rahman ibn Muawiya, ruler of Andalus
Abu Muslim, leader of the Abbasid revolution

VII

The Age of Wealth and Culture
775—833

SAFFAH and Mansoor had grown up as conspirators and, after their seizure of power, had lived in constant fear of rebellions. Mehedi, the son and successor of Mansoor, had been brought up as a prince. Young, handsome and generous, he was thirty-three years old when he succeeded his father in October 775. "Old Farthings" had accumulated great sums of money in the treasury, but Mehedi, ashamed perhaps of his father's reputation for parsimony, spent lavishly.

Mansoor had disapproved of wine, music and frivolity but here also the new khalif offered a contrast to his father. In a poem celebrating his friendship with one of his boon companions he wrote:

> My good fortune I pray that my God may prolong
> Through Abu Hafs, the friend of my leisure.
> For the joy of my life is in wine and in song,
> Perfumed slave girls and music and pleasure.

The Abbasid propaganda which had caused the fall of the Umaiyids had made great play with their addiction to wine and women in Damascus. Now, however, that they were themselves in power, the dream of a return to true religion under the Prophet's own family seemed to have evaporated, while luxury continued to increase. The Umaiyids had retained much of ancient Arab tradition and, when in need of relaxation, camped in the desert to hunt gazelle. When, in September 777, Mehedi went on pilgrimage to Mecca, he was accompanied by long trains of camels carrying containers packed with snow to cool his drinks.

History shows many examples of an aristocracy limiting the power of its king, a process which occurred again and again in England. Louis XIV, to overcome this check on his despotism, brought the nobles to court and made them his servants, with the result that, in the French Revolution, king and nobles were guillotined together. The resulting "classless society" soon fell under the dictatorship of Napoleon, in the manner of most complete democracies.

The change from the Umaiyid to the Abbasid régime produced similar results. The turbulent Arab chiefs had kept the power of the Umaiyid khalifs in check but the Abbasids had turned away from the Arabs, and enlisted mercenary troops from Persia. The loss of influence of the great Arab families left the power of the khalifs unchecked.

The Prophet had sanctioned the use of prisoners-of-war as slaves and, in the century and a half since his death, large numbers of foreign slaves had poured into Syria and Iraq. But the Apostle had also said that the emancipation of a slave was a meritorious action, with the result that many of these slaves had been freed and had mingled with the population. According to the ideas of the time, however, the freedman was still under an obligation of loyalty to the owner who had liberated him. Many examples can be found of freedmen giving their lives in defence of their patrons.

The Abbasids, having weakened the Arab aristocracy, were nevertheless obliged to find an increasing number of provincial governors and civil officials and this they did, more and more, by appointing their own freedmen. The significance of the change was twofold. Firstly the former chiefs of the Arabs had considered themselves almost the equals of the khalifs and had not hesitated to oppose them. Moreover, the chiefs themselves were important citizens with a substantial interest in the prosperity of the state. The freedmen, on the contrary, were not the servants of the nation but the personal dependents of the khalif. Secondly, being former slaves, they were not even Arabs.

Under Mehedi, therefore, both heads of departments in Baghdad and governors of provinces tended increasingly to be freed slaves of the Abbasid family. Mehedi introduced an innovation in the form of a wazeer, or chief minister, who was the head of the government. "Old Farthings" had supervised every item of the administration himself. The presence of a chief minister, however, was to encourage future khalifs to leave the task of government to him.

We can recognize these tendencies because we can look back, knowing what happened later. But to his contemporaries, the reign of Mehedi seemed to be glorious—the empire at the height of its

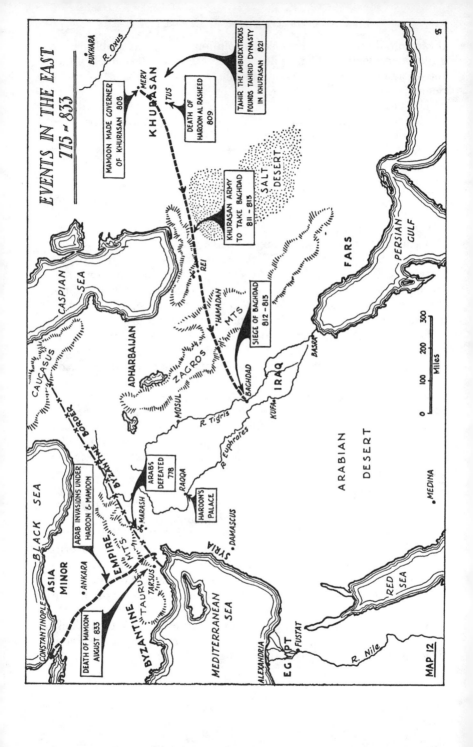

EVENTS IN THE EAST
175 – 833

MAMOON MADE GOVERNOR OF KHURASAN 808

DEATH OF HAROON AL RASHEED 809

TAHIR THE AMBIDEXTROUS FOUNDS TAHIRID DYNASTY IN KHURASAN 821

KHURASAN ARMY TO TAKE BAGHDAD 811 – 815

SIEGE OF BAGHDAD 812 – 815

ARABS DEFEATED 778

HAROON'S PALACE

ARAB INVASIONS UNDER HAROON & MAMOON

DEATH OF MAMOON AUGUST 833

BUKHARA
R. Oxus
MERV
TUS
KHURASAN
SALT DESERT
REI
CASPIAN SEA
ADHARBAIJAN
ZAGROS MTS
MOSUL
HAMADAN
BAGHDAD
IRAQ
KUFA
BASRA
FARS
PERSIAN GULF
R. Tigris
R. Euphrates
CAUCASUS
BLACK SEA
ASIA MINOR
ANKARA
CONSTANTINOPLE
BYZANTINE EMPIRE
BYZANTINE BORDER
TAURUS MTS
TARSUS
MARASH
RAQQA
SYRIA
DAMASCUS
MEDITERRANEAN SEA
ARABIAN DESERT
MEDINA
RED SEA
EGYPT
FUSTAT
ALEXANDRIA
R. Nile

0   100   200   300
Miles

MAP 12

wealth and power and the khalif, unlike his immediate predecessors, debonair, generous and popular.

*   *   *

The great Umaiyids had made a point of maintaining a dominant military position against the Byzantines, whose government was the only well-organized empire in the world which was in the same class as the Arabs'. The Taurus Mountains, which formed the boundary between the two empires, were pierced by a small number of difficult passes. Thus whichever side held the passes was secure from invasion and could raid the open country belonging to the other.

After the death of Hisham ibn Abdul Malik in 743, the decline of the Umaiyids, followed by the civil wars which brought the Abbasids to power, had caused a relaxation of vigilance. The Emperor Constantine V, the son of Leo the Isaurian, seized the Taurus passes, pushing the Arabs down into the plains on the east. In 778, the Arabs were defeated at Marash, twenty-five miles east of the Taurus.

Mehedi determined to recover the dominating position previously held by the Umaiyids. The Emperor Constantine V had been succeeded in 775 by Leo IV, who died in 780, leaving his widow, the Empress Irene, as regent. In February 782, Haroon, the second son of the khalif, invaded Byzantine territory with ninety-five thousand men. Sweeping almost unopposed across Asia Minor, he camped on the shores of the Bosphorus, immediately opposite Constantinople. Irene was compelled to accept a humiliating peace, by which she promised to pay the khalif an annual tribute of seventy thousand gold dinars. Arab military predominance was completely reasserted.

On 4th August, 785, Mehedi was killed in a riding accident while hunting gazelle in the Persian mountains. He was forty-three years old and had reigned ten years.

*   *   *

Musa, surnamed Al Hadi, the eldest son of Mehedi, succeeded his father. Tall, handsome and socially pleasant, he appears to have been a somewhat weak character. His reign lasted only fourteen months, for he died on 15th September, 786.

Only two incidents of his short reign deserve record. In 785, a further Shiite rebellion took place in Mecca, in the name of one Husain, a great-great-grandson of Ali ibn abi Talib and a cousin of Muhammad, the Pure Soul, who had rebelled in 762.[1] It was on

[1] Page 95. Genealogical tree 3, page 92.

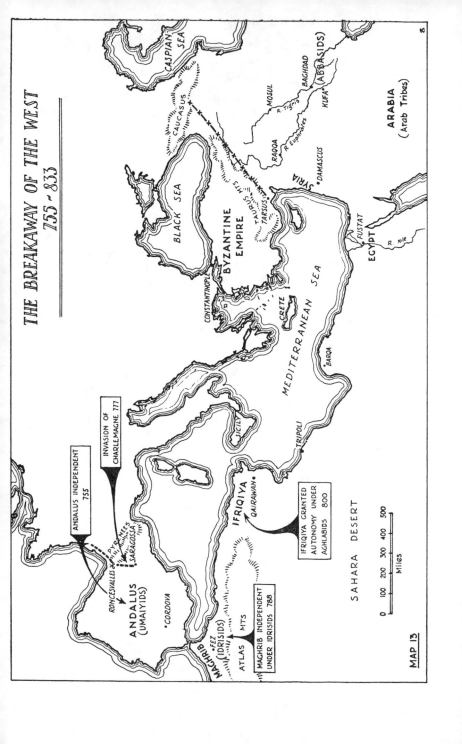

THE BREAKAWAY OF THE WEST
755 – 833

ANDALUS INDEPENDENT 755

INVASION OF CHARLEMAGNE 777

RONCESVALLES • PYRENEES
SARAGOSSA

ANDALUS
(UMAIYIDS)

• CORDOVA

MAGHRIB
• FEZ
(IDRISIDS)
ATLAS MTS

MAGHRIB INDEPENDENT
UNDER IDRISIDS 788

SAHARA DESERT

IFRIQIYA
• QAIRAWAN

IFRIQIYA GRANTED
AUTONOMY UNDER
AGHLABIDS 800

TRIPOLI

SICILY

• BARQA

CRETE

MEDITERRANEAN SEA

CONSTANTINOPLE

BLACK SEA

BYZANTINE
EMPIRE

TAURUS MTS
TARSUS

ANTI-LEBANON MTS

CAUCASUS

CASPIAN
SEA

SYRIA
DAMASCUS

RAQQA

MOSUL

R. Tigris

R. Euphrates

BAGHDAD

KUFA • (ABBASIDS)

ARABIA
(Arab Tribes)

FUSTAT

EGYPT

R. Nile

0   100 200 300 400 500
Miles

MAP 13

this occasion that Idris, a brother of Muhammad, the Pure Soul, escaped from Mecca. Like Abdul Rahman the Umaiyid, who had made himself the ruler of Andalus, Idris crossed North Africa in disguise, accompanied only by one devoted freedman. He reached Volubilis in the Maghrib, where the remains of ruined temples and colonnades still attest the departed glories of Rome. A man of remarkable personality, surrounded, as a descendant of the Prophet, by a halo of sanctity, he received a warm welcome from the local Berbers. Soon he made himself ruler of the area, where he built himself a capital at Fez.

The three rival clans of the Prophet's family had now established themselves each on an independent throne. The Umaiyids had founded a dynasty in Spain and the descendants of Ali and Fatima had done the same in Morocco, though both still left the title of khalif to the Abbasids in Baghdad.

No sooner was Al Hadi dead than Haroon al Rasheed, the second son of Mehedi, was proclaimed khalif in Baghdad. A brilliant and energetic young man of twenty-two, he was to become one of the most famous rulers in history and is probably the only Arab khalif whose name is today familiar to great numbers of persons in the West.

A Persian, called Yahya the Barmecid, had been the tutor of Haroon when he was a boy, and a strong bond of friendship had grown up between master and pupil. No sooner was Haroon on the throne than he appointed Yahya the Barmecid as his wazeer, abandoning to him the detailed administration of the whole empire.

The accession of the new khalif was marked by the distribution of a liberal cash donative to the troops, an ominous sign reminiscent of the later Roman Emperors. The Arab Empire had changed fundamentally since the early days of enthusiasm under the Umaiyids. The army now included fewer and fewer Arabs, and was increasingly recruited from foreign mercenaries, particularly Khurasanis from eastern Persia and from Turks. In exactly the same manner, the later Roman armies had consisted of barbarians, who fought for hire.

The system of government had likewise changed. We read of persons admitted to the presence of the khalif falling down to kiss his feet, and we remember the early khalifs like Umar ibn al Khattab, rubbing shoulders unescorted with the crowds in the narrow and dusty alleyways of Medina.

Haroon, however, was no *roi fainéant*. If he left the details of administration to Yahya the Barmecid—the office work we might say—he himself was always on the move, visiting the outlying portions of the empire. In 796, he performed the pilgrimage to Mecca, walking two hundred and fifty miles of the journey on foot to gain greater merit. Then he visited the Byzantine frontier, Mosul, Kufa, Persia and finally Raqqa on the Euphrates, where he had built himself a palace.[2] There can be little doubt that his immense prestige was largely due to the fact that so many of his subjects knew him personally.

Haroon, however, showed little interest in North Africa. In 800, an officer called Ibrahim ibn al Aghlab agreed with the khalif to keep Ifriqiya quiet without asking for military assistance, if he were given a free hand. Haroon was perhaps glad to be quit of responsibility for a turbulent province. Ibrahim, a man of outstanding character, founded the Aghlabid dynasty, which was to rule Ifriqiya for a hundred years in virtual independence, though paying lip-service to the distant khalif. Ifriqiya was thus the first imperial province to receive "dominion status".

Meanwhile at home the Arab tribes, the original conquerors of the empire, were becoming increasingly estranged from the imperial government. Recent anthropological research has shown the nomadic tribes of the desert to be ethnologically a different race from the inhabitants of Syria and Iraq. Hardy, warlike, practical and outspoken, these original Arabs had been the first soldiers of Islam, but their sturdy individualism and insistence on personal freedom fitted uneasily into a complicated, civilized and intellectual society.

Under Haroon, the empire achieved its high noon of glory and wealth, comparable perhaps to Victorian England. The aggressiveness of the Umaiyids had disappeared. No one wanted any more to conquer the world for God. On the contrary, Andalus and the Maghrib had been lost and Ifriqiya had received autonomy. The empire, now on the defensive, had been far larger under the Umaiyids

Wealth, industry and commerce, however, had increased out of all proportion since Umaiyid days. Baghdad was the richest city in the world, Constantinople being the only other capital which could aspire to be in the same class for luxury and refinement. Arab merchants did business in China, Indonesia, India and East Africa. Their ships were by far the largest and the best appointed in Chinese

[2] Map 12, page 100.

waters or in the Indian Ocean. Under their highly developed banking system, an Arab businessman could cash a cheque in Canton on his bank account in Baghdad.

In Baghdad, everything was plastered with gold. Not only was it used to adorn the women but also the pillars and the roof-beams of the houses. The buckles of the men's belts were gold, which likewise covered the hilts and scabbards of their swords and daggers, and the saddles and the bridles of their horses. (In Europe, the Emperor Charlemagne, a contemporary of Haroon, was unable to mint a gold currency because the precious metal was unobtainable.)

The beauty of the women, many of them concubines collected from the most distant countries, was enhanced by the lavish use of jewels and pearls, the silks and embroidered fabrics, the priceless carpets and cushions, the sparkling fountains, the soft music and the exotic perfumes of the private apartments.

Yet the Baghdad of Haroon was not characterized by a mere vulgar display of wealth. It was an age in which conversation and culture were considered an art. Intellectual, and even theological, discussions were among the recreations of the educated classes. Poetry was still, as it had been among the nomad tribes before Islam, the most typical Arab art form and was sedulously practised. Not only were there many poets at court but the improvisation of verses in conversation was considered an essential accomplishment in polite society.

In 802, Haroon caused oaths of allegiance to be taken to three of his sons, Ameen, Mamoon and Mutamin. The oaths stated that Ameen was to be the heir of his father but that Mamoon would succeed Ameen and Mutamin would follow Mamoon. Although Ameen was to become khalif, Mamoon was to be governor of Persia and Ameen was not to interfere in that country—an arrangement almost equivalent to a partition of the empire. One is inevitably reminded of the Emperor Theodosius who, in 395, had divided the Roman Empire between his sons, Arcadius and Honorius. Eighty years later, the Roman Empire broke up. The Arab Empire was to collapse sixty years after Haroon's partition.

In 803, the great khalif had ruled for seventeen years, during which the administration of the empire had fallen chiefly on the shoulders of Yahya the Barmecid and his three sons, Jaafar, Fadhl and Musa. Of these, Jaafar was of the same age as Haroon and was for many years his boon companion. The Barmecids appear to have been extremely competent administrators, but they also acquired immense wealth. Jaafar alone was said to have spent more than a million gold pieces to build himself a palace in Baghdad.

The Barmecid family appeared to be as rich as the khalif himself, their palaces were as sumptuous, their slaves, freedmen and retainers as numerous. Lavish patrons of literature and the arts, their hospitality and their generosity were regal. "As generous as Jaafar the Barmecid" became an Arab proverb.

Probably from about 800 onwards, when Haroon had been fourteen years on the throne, he began to tire of the immense power of his supposed servants. An alleged scandal between Jaafar and the khalif's unmarried sister Abbasa, came perhaps as a useful pretext. In a fit of rage, Haroon ordered the instant decapitation of Jaafar, the imprisonment of the whole family and the confiscation of all their vast wealth.

*   *   *

We have already seen that Haroon had led an army to the Bosphorus in 782, during the lifetime of his father Mehedi, and had compelled the Empress Irene to pay tribute. In 802, however, Irene was deposed by a revolution in Constantinople and a member of the aristocracy mounted the throne with the title of Nicephorus I. One of the propaganda points which had enabled the new emperor to overthrow Irene was her subservience to Baghdad. Two years after Nicephorus donned the purple he addressed an ultimatum to the khalif, demanding the instant repayment of all the tribute received over the years from Constantinople.

When he received this letter, Haroon gave way to a furious fit of anger. Turning over the emperor's letter, he wrote on the back:

"From Haroon, the Prince of the Faithful, to Nicephorus, the Roman dog. I have read your letter, you son of a heathen mother. You will see and not hear my reply."

An army, allegedly a hundred and thirty-five thousand strong, was immediately mobilized and swept across Asia Minor unopposed. When within a hundred and fifty miles of Constantinople, Haroon received a humble letter from Nicephorus, begging for peace, on condition of the continued payment of the tribute. Graciously consenting, Haroon withdrew to winter in his palace at Raqqa, now his principal residence.

A few weeks later, however, the approach of winter and the blocking of the Taurus passes with snow emboldened the emperor to denounce the treaty which he had just signed. The khalif immediately recalled the army, passed the Taurus in spite of snow and carried fire and sword over the whole of Asia Minor from the Black Sea to the Mediterranean. The trembling Nicephorus was obliged once more to sue for mercy and to agree to the tribute. In addition, Haroon stipulated that all Muslim prisoners of war be instantly released, while he carried away thousands of Christian boys and girls to be sold into slavery.

The Muslim army was highly professional. The advance guard consisted of light cavalry in chain mail and armed with lances. The main body of the infantry included pikemen, swordsmen and archers. In battle, the pikemen knelt in the front rank, the butts of their pikes stuck into the ground. Behind them stood the swordsmen, while the rear ranks were occupied by the archers.

In contrast to the wild and reckless charges of the first Arab tribes-men, the Muslim armies of Abbasid days moved deliberately, with perfect drill and discipline. In a pitched battle, they preferred to await the enemy's attack. When all his assaults had been repulsed, the Arab army advanced slowly and relentlessly to sweep him from the field.

In the centre of the army rode the Prince of the Faithful, sur-rounded by his royal guards in magnificent uniforms, himself resplendent with gold, jewels and pearls. Over the whole army fluttered a forest of standards, heavily embroidered with gold.

The last years of the great khalif were saddened by the fear of civil war between his sons after his death. In the autumn of 808, he travelled to Khurasan, where he installed his second son, Mamoon, at Merv, as governor of Khurasan.[3] Although he was only forty-five years old, Haroon felt tired and unwell. He moved on to Tus in Khurasan, where he became so ill that he could no longer stand. On 23rd March, 809, Haroon al Rasheed, the mightiest emperor of his day and one of the most famous monarchs in history, died in his tent in a Persian garden outside Tus.

Haroon had been well educated in religion, philosophy and literature, and his reign was marked by a high standard of intellec-tual activity. The energy and vigour of his will are well illustrated by his masterly treatment of Nicephorus. Yet in his reign North Africa was lost, the Maghrib by the independence of Idris, Ifriqiya by the grant of autonomy to the Aghlabids. The strength of his character proves, however, that he could have retained North Africa if he had desired. A loss of interest in empire seems to have been the explanation.

[3] Map 12, page 100.

Like Louis XIV, Haroon raised his country to an unprecedented pinnacle of glory but, like him also, he may have undermined its strength by over-taxation, the unvarying disease of old empires. The deluge was to come fifty-two years after his death.

*   *   *

The family schism which Haroon had feared between his two sons, Ameen and Mamoon, broke out within a year of his death. As we have seen, Mamoon was the governor of Khurasan, while Ameen was acclaimed khalif in Baghdad.

In June 811, the army of Khurasan inflicted a defeat on the khalif's forces near Rei and advanced to Hamadan.[4] On 1st September, 812, the Khurasan army laid siege to Baghdad. The mangonels and catapults were erected and rocks, darts and arrows came hurtling through the air, crashing into the palaces and houses of the magnificent capital of Haroon.

The siege of Baghdad lasted for a whole year. The most splendid and wealthy city in the world lay half in ruins when, on 25th September, 813, the Khalif Ameen was killed and Mamoon's army occupied the capital.

For some reason, Mamoon remained a further four years in Khurasan before he came to Baghdad. The period was marked by a succession of Shiite revolts in Mecca, Medina and Iraq, causing considerable confusion. Some of the discontent may have been due to Mamoon's apparent association with Persians, his mother having been a Persian concubine. Not until 8th September, 819, did Mamoon eventually make his state entry into Baghdad.

The commander who had taken Baghdad and killed Ameen was a certain Tahir al Husain, nicknamed the Ambidextrous. Tahir had grown too powerful and his presence became irksome to Mamoon, as that of Abu Muslim had been to Mansoor. The solution adopted by Mamoon was less brutal than the method employed by Mansoor, but was ultimately to prove more disastrous. Tahir the Ambidextrous was made governor of Khurasan with full delegated powers. When he died soon afterwards, Mamoon was obliged to recognize his son as ruler of Khurasan. By this means, a minor dynasty was established in East Persia which soon became virtually independent.

Mamoon had always been devoted to books and to learned pursuits. His brilliant mind was interested in every form of intellec-

[4] Map 12, page 100.

tual activity. Not only poetry, but also philosophy, theology, astronomy, medicine and law, all occupied his time. His fourteen-year reign in Baghdad saw one of the most brilliant intellectual epochs in history.

In Baghdad he opened an institution which he called the House of Wisdom, the principal object of which was the translation of foreign works. A certain Hunain ibn Ishaq, a Christian, was in charge of translations from the Greek. Aristotle and Plato among the philosophers, Hippocrates and more especially Galen among the physicians, were produced in Arabic. Many of these works, notably the seven volumes of Galen's *Anatomy*, were subsequently to reach western Europe in Arabic, through Sicily and Spain. Hunain himself was a physician and his ten treatises on the eye are the earliest known text-book of opthalmology.

The most outstanding contribution of the Arabs to human knowledge was in the field of mathematics. They introduced the use of zero, which, however, they may have learned from India or China. In contrast to the clumsy method of writing numbers employed by the Romans, the system used by the Arabs, reckoning in units, tens, hundreds and thousands, was to become the very basis of modern mathematics. Indeed we still refer to our method of writing figures as Arabic numerals.

The Arabs themselves invented algebra—itself an Arabic word—and also plane and spherical trigonometry. Al Battani discovered trigonometrical ratios and invented sine and cosine, tangent and cotangent. Logarithms were discovered at the same time, the word being a corruption of the inventor's name, Al Khuwarizmi. An astronomical observatory was also established in the reign of Mamoon, whose astronomers measured the circumference of the earth with remarkable accuracy, six hundred years before Europe admitted that it was not flat. *The Compendium of Astronomy*, an Arabic work, was in use as a text-book in Europe until the sixteenth century.

In the reign of Mamoon, medical schools were opened in Baghdad and doctors, chemists, barbers and orthopaedists were subject to government inspection. No physician could practise until he had successfully completed his training as a medical student and been awarded a diploma. The first free public hospital had been opened in Baghdad in the reign of Haroon al Rasheed.

The Arabs in the ninth century were experts in the art of gracious and refined living. Not only were members of the upper classes cultured, but slaves and concubines were expected to be equally accomplished. A good slave girl spent several years in special schools where she was taught refined manners and was expected to master the Arabic classics and to speak in an educated accent. It was necessary for her also to be able to recite and improvise poetry, to be mistress of a musical instrument and a competent chess-player.

The evening parties in the salons of the wealthy were always of a high standard. After the day's work, people would change into clean clothes of bright and cheerful colours. The guests reclined on low couches, spread with cushions and carpets and scented with musk, myrtle and jasmine. Behind a screen, an orchestra of slave girls sang and played on the violin, the lute or the guitar. The conversation was lively and intellectual and would often include the recitation or the improvisation of poetry.

The historian of the Arab peoples is constantly placed in a dilemma by the problem presented by the word Arab. The original founders of the great empire of the khalifs were the warlike tribesmen of the Arabian peninsula. Some historians, considering these as the real Arabs, have pointed out that the artists, the scientists, the theologians and the philosophers of the Golden Age were individually not Arabs but Persians, Armenians, Syrians or Greeks.

Others allege that the Arab Empire was soon to collapse because the once martial Arabs had lost their military virtues. The fact is that the Syrians and Iraqis of Abbasid times were not the Arabs who had conquered the empire but were new and complex peoples formed by the intermixture of the many races of the empire. As the early historians recognized, these people were not Arabs but arabicized.

While, however, we may minimize the rôle played by the original Arabians in the brilliant, intellectual period of the Abbasids, we may justifiably marvel at the extraordinary diffusion throughout the whole empire of the spirit of the old Arab conquerors. Their code of chivalry, their devotion to poetry, their romantic attitude to sexual love, their princely hospitality and generosity were spread over the whole empire from Spain to India and China. To this day their language is spoken from the Atlantic to Persia, and their religion extends over a great part of Africa and Asia.

But if their splendid qualities were widely diffused, their faults also penetrated the many different races whom they once conquered. Their mutual jealousies, the corollary of their pursuit of private honour, and their anarchic love of personal freedom have resulted ever since in endless internal feuds and rivalries in Muslim countries.

Whether, however, we praise or condemn the qualities of the ancient Arabs of Arabia, it is difficult to deny that there must have been in these men some rugged quality of character which enabled them to impress their virtues and their vices alike on so large a portion of the human race.

*   *   *

There had been no Arab invasions of Byzantine territory since Haroon's defeat of the Emperor Nicephorus in 805. In 830, however, Mamoon crossed the Taurus and destroyed a number of towns. The same procedure was repeated in the summers of 831, 832 and 833, in spite of repeated peace proposals by the Emperor Theophilus. On the return march from the last campaign, however, the khalif fell ill and died on 9th August, 833, near Tarsus.

NOTABLE DATES

Death of the Khalif Mansoor ⎱	
Elevation of Mehedi ⎰	775
Haroon's campaign on the Bosphorus	February 782
Death of Mehedi	785
Elevation of Musa al Hadi ⎱	
Rebellion of Husain ibn Ali in Mecca ⎰	785
Death of Al Hadi ⎱	
Accession of Haroon al Rasheed ⎰	786
Establishment of Idris in the Maghrib	788
Establishment of Aghlabids in Ifriqiya	800
Campaigns of Haroon against Nicephorus	805
Death of Haroon	23rd March, 809
Siege of Baghdad	812–813
Tahir the Ambidextrous made ruler of Khurasan	821
Death of Mamoon	9th August, 833

PERSONALITIES

Abbasid Khalifs

Mehedi	775–785
Hadi	785–786
Haroon al Rasheed	786–809
Ameen	809–813
Mamoon	813–833

Other Personalities

Irene, Byzantine Empress
Nicephorus I, Byzantine Emperor
Idris ibn Abdulla, ruler of the Maghrib
Ibrahim ibn al Aghlab, ruler of Ifriqiya
Tahir the Ambidextrous, ruler of Khurasan

VIII

Disintegration
833–975

MAMOON was succeeded by his brother Mutasim,[1] whose character was in complete contrast to his own. Mamoon's interests had been principally intellectual but Mutasim was indifferent to culture and academic studies, but devoted to practical affairs—gardening, agriculture, architecture and, above all, to soldiering.

Mamoon, it will be remembered, had given autonomy to Khurasan, a country on which the Abbasids had relied for army recruits. To fill the ranks, Mutasim bought large numbers of slave boys from Turkestan, and built up from them the main strength of his army.

The khalif was a man of dominating character and of outstanding personal courage and maintained unquestioned authority over his great mercenary army. His bodyguard of ten thousand Turks, superbly mounted and dressed in splendid uniforms, behaved with arrogant licence towards the people of Baghdad. So bitter was the resentment felt by the public against these pampered troops that Mutasim abandoned the city and built himself a new capital at Samarra on the Tigris, sixty-five miles further north.

In 837, the Byzantine Emperor Theophilus was rash enough to throw down the gauntlet to the martial khalif. Crossing the Taurus, Theophilus captured the town of Zebetra, thirty miles south of Malatia, and razed it to the ground. The Byzantines seem to have behaved with peculiar brutality, more than a thousand Muslim women being driven off as slaves and many men having their eyes put out or their ears and noses cut off.

In June 838, Mutasim, bent on revenge, crossed the Taurus with an immense army. The Arab historian, Masoodi, gives its numbers as two hundred thousand, but this must almost certainly be an exaggeration. Theophilus was completely defeated and withdrew

---

[1] Mutamin, the third son of Haroon al Rasheed, was already dead.

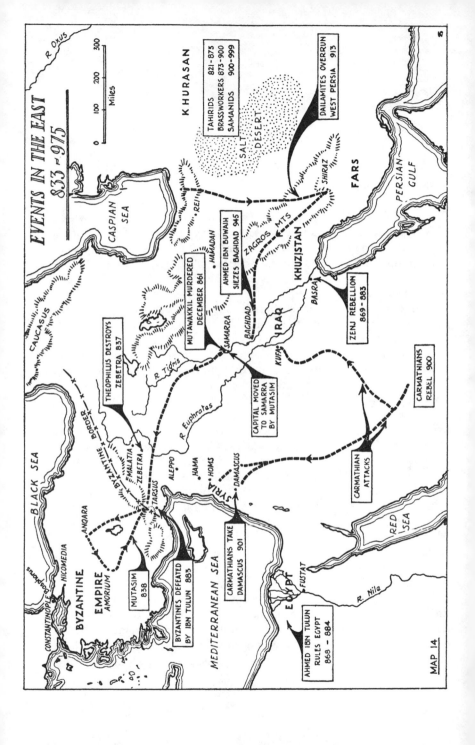

EVENTS IN THE EAST 833 - 975

R. OXUS

KHURASAN

TAHIRIDS   821 - 875
BRASSWORKERS 873 - 900
SAMANIDS   900 - 999

DAILAMITES OVERRUN
WEST PERSIA 913

CASPIAN SEA

SALT DESERT

SHIRAZ

FARS

PERSIAN GULF

REM

HAMADAN

ZAGROS MTS

AHMED IBN BUWAIH
SIEZES BAGHDAD 945

KHUZISTAN

CAUCASUS

THEOPHILUS DESTROYS
ZEBETRA 837

MUTAWAKKIL MURDERED
DECEMBER 861

BASRA

ZENJ REBELLION
869 - 883

SAMARRA

BAGHDAD

IRAQ

R. Tigris

R. Euphrates

KUFA

CAPITAL MOVED
TO SAMARRA
BY MUTASIM

CARMATHIANS
REBEL 900

BYZANTINE BORDER

MALATIA

ZEBETRA

TARSUS

ALEPPO

HAMA

HOMS

DAMASCUS

SYRIA

CARMATHIAN
ATTACKS

ANGARA

BLACK SEA

BYZANTINE
EMPIRE

AMORIUM

MUTASIM
838

BYZANTINES DEFEATED
BY IBN TULUN 883

CARMATHIANS TAKE
DAMASCUS 901

MEDITERRANEAN SEA

RED SEA

CONSTANTINOPLE

BOSPHORUS

NICOMEDIA

AHMED IBN TULUN
RULES EGYPT
868 - 884

EGYPT

FUSTAT

R. Nile

MAP 14

Miles
0   100   200   300

in some disorder to the Bosphorus. Anqara and Amorium were captured, the latter being razed to the ground. Many thousands of
Byzantine citizens were killed and a large number of women and
children were carried off as slaves.

Two hundred years before, when the conquering Arab tribes
emerged from their deserts, no massacres had marked the path of
their triumphant campaigns. It is natural for us to expect the early
emergence of a semi-barbarian race to be characterized by deeds
of massacre, rape and violence but that, two hundred years later,
the character of the early conquerors should have become more
civilized and humane. The fact that the history of the Arabs presents
the exact opposite is a striking tribute to the religious background
of the early Arab conquests, or perhaps to the bedouin idea of chivalrous warfare.

Mutasim died on 5th January, 842, at the age of forty-seven. He
appeared to leave the Arab Empire at the very pinnacle of its
splendour. The treasury contained eight million gold dinars, a very
large sum for those days, and the khalif's army was apparently
invincible. In reality, however, the whole imperial edifice was to
collapse twenty years later and it was Mutasim who had made the
disaster inevitable.

Knowing what was ultimately to occur, it is easy for us to criticize
the course of events, although to contemporaries the empire appeared
to be more glorious than ever before. In Umaiyid times, the state
had been founded on the martial qualities of the tribesmen of
Arabia. But the very hardihood and individualism of these men had
made them troublesome and turbulent subjects. The Abbasids dealt
with their endless seditions by the enlistment of non-Arab troops,
principally Khurasanis. But they made the fundamental error of
relying too greatly on the East Persians and alienating the Arab
tribes. This process was intensified by the gradual increase of
despotism on the Persian model. The Arab tribes were essentially
equalitarian and were no respecters of ranks or titles. They would
loyally follow a real leader but first they must see, know and speak
with their man.

When Mamoon lost Khurasan, his best recruiting ground, by
granting it autonomy in order to get rid of Tahir the Ambidextrous,
he and then Mutasim turned to the Turks for recruits. The Persians
were Muslims and had been closely integrated with the Arabs for
two hundred years. The Turks were mostly heathen, did not even
trouble to learn Arabic, and were hated by the public. By moving

his capital to Samarra, Mutasim openly expressed his preference for the Turks over his Arab subjects and ruled undisguisedly as an inaccessible despot surrounded by foreigners.

Mutasim was succeeded by his son on 5th January, 842. A complete contrast to his fiery and dominating father, Wáthiq was kind, benevolent and fond of eating and drinking. He never travelled, visited the provinces or engaged in a military campaign. Like Mamoon, he enjoyed intellectual pursuits and was well versed in philosophy, in literature and in physical science. The conversation at his receptions was intellectually of a high standard. The khalif himself played on the lute and had composed more than a hundred musical works. However, he took little interest in government, which he left entirely to his wazeers. This good-natured and cultured gentleman died in 847, after a reign of six years.

The next khalif, Mutawakkil, was a younger brother of Wathiq. He had been somewhat bullied as a child and showed his spite by dismissing those who had served under his predecessor and by persecuting the Shiites and the Christians with humiliating vexations. Like Wathiq, he lived in isolation in Samarra, surrounded by his Turkish guards.

He nominated his eldest son Muntasir to succeed him but the irresistible charms of a Greek concubine caused him to revoke the nomination and to appoint her son Mutazz as heir-apparent. Bugha, a Turkish slave promoted to high rank, conspired with the disinherited prince and, on 10th December, 861, Mutawakkil was murdered and Muntasir was declared khalif by the Turkish mercenaries.

The last few years of a great empire seem often to be calm and contented. Life is humane and civilized, the waning empire avoids wars and the public is still sufficiently affluent to afford luxury and leisure. Writing after the murder of Mutawakkil, Arab historians refer nostalgically to the reigns of Wathiq and Mutawakkil during which there were no wars and the economic situation was still satisfactory.

From the death of the Prophet in 632 to the murder of Mutawakkil in 861, the Arab khalifs had enjoyed two hundred and thirty years of extraordinary splendour and power. Not only was their empire the most extensive that had ever existed, but it also enjoyed world leadership in military power, in wealth, culture, science and literature.

The ignorant Turkish soldiers who killed Mutawakkil had not

4. THE PUPPET ABBASID KHALIFS
833—1135

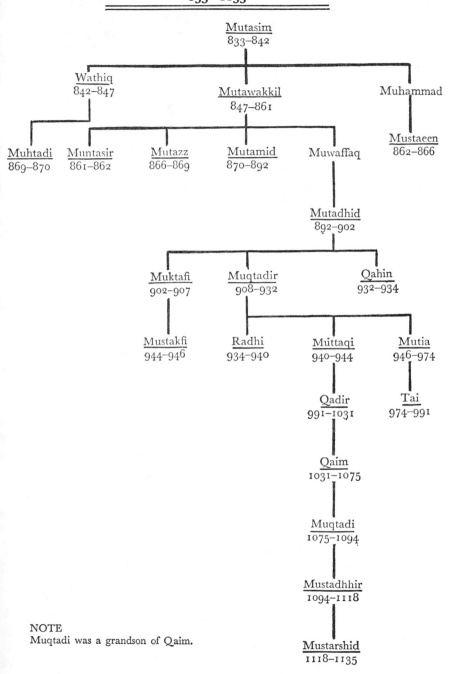

Mutasim
833–842

Wathiq
842–847

Mutawakkil
847–861

Muhammad

Mustaeen
862–866

Muhtadi
869–870

Muntasir
861–862

Mutazz
866–869

Mutamid
870–892

Muwaffaq

Mutadhid
892–902

Muktafi
902–907

Muqtadir
908–932

Qahin
932–934

Mustakfi
944–946

Radhi
934–940

Muttaqi
940–944

Mutia
946–974

Qadir
991–1031

Tai
974–991

Qaim
1031–1075

Muqtadi
1075–1094

Mustadhhir
1094–1118

Mustarshid
1118–1135

NOTE
Muqtadi was a grandson of Qaim.

intended to destroy this dazzling imperial edifice, but had merely become involved in a court intrigue. They acknowledged Muntasir as khalif and expected life to go on as before. But their action had suddenly enabled them to realize their own power. Six months later Muntasir was dead, his murder being also attributed to the troops. The Turkish commanders, who now completely monopolized power, appointed Mustaeen, a grandson of Mutasim, to succeed.

In 865, the army commanders quarrelled among themselves. One faction took Mustaeen and moved to Baghdad. The other party chose Mutazz as khalif and besieged the city. Mustaeen was murdered and Mutazz recognized as khalif but, in 869, the Turks killed Mutazz. He was followed by Muhtadi, a man of courage and character, who tried to end the dictatorship of the army, but was thereupon likewise murdered.

By 881, twenty years after the murder of Mutawakkil, the Turkish commanders had changed and had fallen out among themselves, while some had become Arabicized. From 870 to 892, a kind of *modus vivendi* was gradually established between them and the Khalif Mutamid and, in 892, the capital was moved back from Samarra to Baghdad.

In the interval, however, the Arab Empire had virtually ceased to exist. As long as power had been wielded by a descendant of the Prophet's family, the imperial government enjoyed an aura of sanctity in addition to its military power. But as soon as the provinces realized that the khalif was a helpless prisoner in his own palace and that the government was being exercised by a group of illiterate barbarian soldiers, the provinces fell away.

The soldiers themselves felt no particular loyalty to the empire but were more concerned with plundering the treasury, from which many millions of gold dinars had disappeared after the murder of Mutawakkil. No attempt was made to maintain control over the more distant provinces. From 869 to 883, southern Iraq itself was in the hands of the so-called Zenj rebels, most of whom were revolted negro slaves who worked in the marshes east of Basra.[2] The Zenj rebellion was particularly disastrous, as it put an end to the profitable oriental trade which, coming up the Persian Gulf to Basra, had supplied a great part of the wealth of Baghdad.

From the Arab conquests in 634 and onwards to the Zenj rebellion, a period of two hundred and forty years, Egypt had played a minor rôle in the empire. The Zenj rebellion, however, caused the diversion

[2] Map 14, page 114.

of the oriental trade route up the Red Sea to Egypt, the increasing wealth of which enabled that country henceforward to play a more important rôle.

In 868, Ahmed ibn Tulun, a young Turkish officer, had been sent from Baghdad as governor of Egypt. The improved financial position of the country enabled him to declare himself independent, to occupy Syria and to defeat a Byzantine army near Tarsus. In 884, however, Ibn Tulun died and Egypt and Syria fell into confusion.

In 892, the weak Khalif Mutamid died and was succeeded by his energetic and capable nephew Mutadhid, who set himself to restore the power of the khalifate. If Mutadhid had come to power before the murder of Mutawakkil, he would probably have become one of the greatest of the khalifs but, in 892, it was too late. The Baghdad government was only able to collect taxes from a small area in central Iraq and the revenue obtained was insufficient to maintain an army of mercenaries. An Arab national revival was impossible, the loyalty of the Arabs having already been lost.

Hope, nevertheless, seemed to revive under Mutadhid until, in 900, the Carmathian rebellion broke out in Arabia. The Carmathians were ostensibly Shiites but fundamentally their rising was probably a revolt of the original Arabs of Arabia against Persian despotism and Turkish militarism. Recruited from the same tribes who, two hundred and seventy years before, had formed the spearhead of the great Arab conquests, the Carmathians were puritan and democratic.

In 901, the Carmathians occupied Damascus, Homs and Hama. Then they seized the Yemen and, in 906, captured Kufa and threatened Baghdad. If the khalif could have identified himself with this Arab military revival, a great part of the empire might have been re-established. But the khalifate, largely dominated by Persian and Turkish influence, had lost all sympathy for the tribes of Arabia and indeed regarded them as its bitter enemies.

Mutadhid died in 902 and was succeeded by his son Muktafi, who himself died in 907 at the early age of thirty-two. Their combined reigns, lasting from 892 to 907, had given a gleam of hope which was extinguished by the death of Muktafi.

The years from 907 to 945 were distinguished in Baghdad by an unending succession of riots, rebellions and military seizures of power. One khalif was assassinated, the next was blinded by his own troops, who plundered his palace. One, Radhi, held the throne for six years and succeeded in dying in his bed but his successor was kidnapped and blinded by a Turkish soldier of fortune.

In 913, western Persia had been invaded by the Dailamites, a tribe originating in the mountains at the southern end of the Caspian Sea. Being Shiites, they were extremely hostile to the Abbasid khalifs. Under their tribal chiefs, the Buwaihids, they occupied the whole of West Persia, establishing their capital in Shiraz. Finally, in 945, Ahmed ibn Buwaih marched out of Shiraz and occupied Baghdad unopposed. The Khalif Mustakfi was obliged to recognize his authority and to bestow on him the honorific title of Muizz al Dowla—he who makes the state mighty.

Even such servility as this, however, did not satisfy this tribal barbarian. On 29th January, 946, Ahmed ibn Buwaih—or Muizz al Dowla—broke into the palace with a force of Dailamites. The khalif was dragged from his throne and across the floor of his audience chamber and then driven through the streets of his own capital beneath the blows and jeers of the Dailamite soldiers. His eyes were put out with a red-hot iron and he was thrown into prison, where he died five years later.

Ibn Buwaih then nominated Mutia as khalif, allowing him a mere daily pittance as pocket money. Thenceforward the Buwaihids became the rulers of Baghdad, the khalifs being allowed to retain their title on condition that they remained in the palace and made no attempt to interfere in the government. Muizz al Dowla ibn Buwaih died in 967 and was succeeded by his son.

*   *   *

Unfortunately for the Arabs, the break-up of the Abbasid Empire coincided with a Byzantine military revival. In 867, six years after the murder of Mutawakkil, the Emperor Michael III the Drunkard was assassinated by his groom, who mounted the throne under the name of Basil I, the Macedonian. Although he could neither read nor write, Basil was a man of courage and commonsense.

For more than two centuries, Byzantine Asia Minor had suffered endless disasters from Arab invasions. Basil quickly perceived that the strategic key to the situation was the Taurus Mountains, whose narrow passes were easy to defend. The most important of these passes was that called the Cilician Gates, leading from Heraclea to Tarsus. The next pass on the north negotiable by an army lay to the east of Caesarea. Throughout the long centuries of Arab domination, the Muslims had held these passes from which they debouched

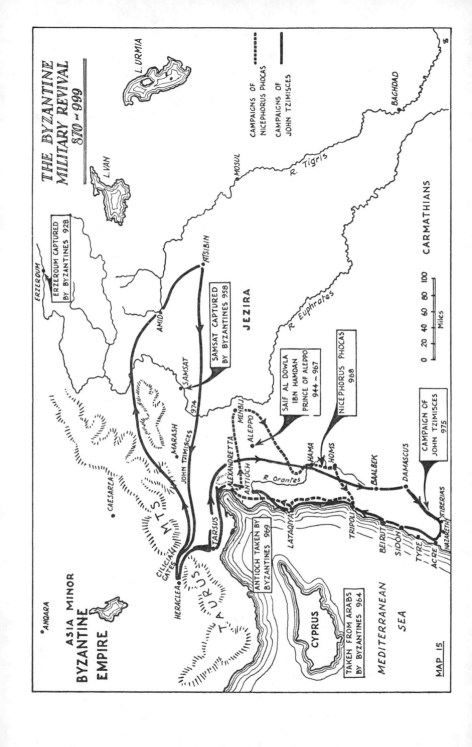

THE BYZANTINE
MILITARY REVIVAL
870–999

CAMPAIGNS OF
NICEPHORUS PHOCAS

CAMPAIGNS OF
JOHN TZIMISCES

L. URMIA

L. VAN

BAGHDAD

R. Tigris

MOSUL

ERZEROUM

ERZEROUM CAPTURED
BY BYZANTINES 928

NISIBIN

AMIDA

SAMSAT

SAMSAT CAPTURED
BY BYZANTINES 958

JEZIRA

R. Euphrates

974

JOHN TZIMISCES

MARASH

MENBIJ

ALEPPO

SAIF AL DOWLA
IBN HAMDAN
PRINCE OF ALEPPO
944 – 967

NICEPHORUS PHOCAS
968

0   20 40 60 80 100
        Miles

CARMATHIANS

ASIA MINOR
BYZANTINE
EMPIRE

ANGORA

CAESAREA

TAURUS MTS

CILICIAN GATES

HERACLEA

TARSUS

ALEXANDRETTA

ANTIOCH

ANTIOCH TAKEN BY
BYZANTINES 969

R. Orontes

HAMA

HOMS

BAALBEK

DAMASCUS

CAMPAIGN OF
JOHN TZIMISCES
975

LATAQIYA

TRIPOLI

BEIRUT

SIDON

TYRE

ACRE

NAZARETH

TIBERIAS

TAKEN FROM ARABS
BY BYZANTINES 964

CYPRUS

MEDITERRANEAN
SEA

MAP 15

whenever they felt so inclined, to ravage the plains and cities of Asia Minor.

In the course of his reign, Basil I occupied and fortified the Taurus passes. In 879, a Byzantine army debouched from the mountains and invaded the Jezira, laying waste the countryside and carrying off the inhabitants to slavery. Basil the Macedonian died in 886 and was succeeded by his son Leo VI, the Wise, a man devoted to book learning and disinterested in war, and the Arabs gained a respite until his death in 912.

Under Constantine VII, surnamed Born-in-the-Purple, the Byzantines again assumed the offensive. Baghdad was in chaos, torn by successive military *coups d'état*. The Carmathians were attacking Syria and lower Iraq, and Egypt was without a government.

The only opposition offered to the Byzantine invasion was that of Saif al Dowla ibn Hamdan, the Arab Ameer of Aleppo, who did not fear to face the Byzantine Emperor himself in battle. The little Hamdanid dynasty of Aleppo presents several points of interest. Not only did it challenge the Byzantine Empire in war, but it was also consciously and proudly Arab. The Abbasid Empire had grown increasingly out of touch with the original Arab spirit which had built the empire—as indeed it was to remain. The Carmathian outbreak in the Arabian peninsula and the establishment of the little Hamdanid dynasty in Aleppo may be seen as deliberate Arab revolts against the process of Persianization and Turkification.

Ibn Hamdan maintained in Aleppo a brilliant little court in traditional Arab style. Saif al Dowla patronized philosophers and men of science and of letters, among whom was Mutanabbi, one of the most famous of Arab poets.

Saif al Dowla died in 967, and thereafter no opposition whatever was offered to the inroads of the Byzantines. In 966, the soldier-emperor Nicephorus Phocas had raided the Jezira. In 968, he entered Syria, sacking Homs and Hama and laying waste the Lebanese coast from Tripoli back to Tarsus. Cyprus was reconquered from the Arabs and, in 969, the great city of Antioch, which, in Greek and Roman days, had for a thousand years been the capital of Syria, was captured by the Byzantines.

In 969, Nicephorus Phocas was murdered by his nephew, John Tzimisces, who was proclaimed emperor the next day. In 974, John Tzimisces invaded the Jezira and in 975 he marched into Syria and took Damascus, Tiberias, Nazareth, Acre, Sidon and Beirut. He had no men to hold the cities he conquered but the whole country was laid waste without mercy, great numbers of young women and children being driven off as slaves.

John Tzimisces died in 976 and for a few years Syria enjoyed a respite from Byzantine invasions.

NOTABLE DATES

Death of the Kahlif Mamoon	9th August, 833
Death of the Khalif Mutasim	5th January, 842
Murder of the Khalif Mutawakkil	10th December, 861
Period of anarchy in Baghdad under military dictators	861–945
Carmathian rebellion in Arabia	900
Seizure of Baghdad by Ahmed ibn Buwaih	945
Byzantine invasions of Syria	966–975
Death of Ahmed ibn Buwaih, Muizz al Dowla	967

PERSONALITIES

Abbasid Khalifs

Mutasim	833–842
Wathiq	842–847
Mutawakkil	847–861

(From 861 to 974, thirteen puppet khalifs were appointed, of whom five were murdered, three were deposed and blinded, and five died a natural death.)

Byzantine Emperors

Basil I, the Macedonian	867–886
Leo VI, the Wise	886–912
Constantine VII, Born-in-the-Purple	912–959
Romanus II	959–963
Nicephorus Phocas	963–969
John Tzimisces	969–976

Other Personalities

Ahmed ibn Tulun, ruler of Egypt	868–884
Muizz al Dowla, Ahmed ibn Buwaih, military dictator	945–967
Saif al Dowla ibn Hamdan, Arab Ameer of Aleppo	944–967

IX

The Seljuq Supremacy

MENTION has already been made of Tahir the Ambidextrous, the army commander of Mamoon, who, in 821,
had founded a virtually independent kingdom in Khura-
san.[1] The dynasty lasted for fifty years until overthrown in 873 by
the rebellion of Yaqoob ibn Leith, commonly called the Brass-
worker. In 876, Yaqoob marched on Baghdad but was defeated
south of the capital. Dying in 879, he was succeeded by his brother
Amr.

The Samanids were an old Persian family of Balkh who, from
Umaiyid days, had always been loyal to the Arabs. Members of the
family had been governors of Samarqand and Herat under the
Abbasids. The Khalif Mutadhid urged the loyal Samanids to sup-
press the Brassworkers' rebellion. In the spring of 900, Ahmed ibn
Ismail the Samanid defeated the rebels and became the ruler of
Trans-Oxiana and Khurasan.

The Samanids were to rule for a hundred years, from 900 to 999.
Centrally placed on the caravan routes from China to Persia, Iraq,
eastern Europe and the Baltic, the country was extremely prosperous.
The Samanids, moreover, were splendid administrators, digging
irrigation canals, repairing roads, encouraging agriculture and
beautifying the cities. Both commerce and industry flourished, textiles, weapons, carpets, furs and many other articles being exported.

Under the Samanids, Bukhara enjoyed an extraordinary flores-
cence of Muslim culture, almost comparable to that of Baghdad
under Mamoon. Now Baghdad, half-ruined, was under the rule of
barbarians, but the brilliant culture of the Abbasids was reproduced
at the two extremities of the former empire, in Bukhara and in
Andalus. Throughout the tenth century, the streets of Bukhara were
crowded with poets, philosophers, historians, scientists, physicians
and doctors. Ibn Sina, known in Europe as Avicenna, worked in
the royal library. Under Samanid patronage, Al Razi wrote his

[1] Map 14, page 114.

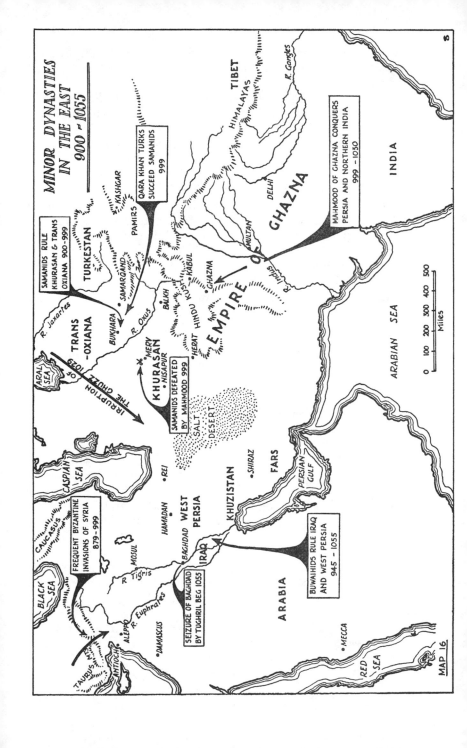

MINOR DYNASTIES
IN THE EAST
900 ~ 1055

TIBET

R. Ganges

HIMALAYAS

INDIA

MAHMOOD OF GHAZNA CONQUERS
PERSIA AND NORTHERN INDIA
999 - 1050

DELHI

KASHGAR

QARA KHAN TURKS
SUCCEED SAMANIDS
999

PAMIRS

GHAZNA

MULTAN

EMPIRE OF

KABUL

R. Indus

SAMANIDS RULE
KHURASAN & TRANS
OXIANA 900-999

TURKESTAN

SAMARQAND

BALKH

HINDU KUSH

HERAT

TRANS
-OXIANA

BUKHARA

R. Oxus

KHURASAN

NISAPUR

MERV

ARABIAN SEA

ARAL
SEA

R. Jaxartes

THE GHUZZ 1029

IRRUPTION OF

SAMANIDS DEFEATED
BY MAHMOOD 999

SALT
DESERT

0   100   200   300   400   500
Miles

CASPIAN
SEA

CAUCASUS

REI

SHIRAZ

FARS

PERSIAN
GULF

BLACK
SEA

FREQUENT BYZANTINE
INVASIONS OF SYRIA
879 - 999

HAMADAN

WEST
PERSIA

KHUZISTAN

MOSUL

R. Tigris

BAGHDAD

IRAQ

BUWAIHIDS RULE IRAQ
AND WEST PERSIA
945 - 1055

TAURUS MTS.

ANTIOCH

ALEPPO

DAMASCUS

R. Euphrates

SEIZURE OF BAGHDAD
BY TUGHRIL BEG 1055

ARABIA

MECCA

RED
SEA

MAP 16

great work on medicine, used for centuries as a text-book in Europe. Firdausi, one of the most famous of Persian poets, lived at the court of Bukhara.

But the Samanids followed the example of other Muslim dynasties and built up their armies with Turkish slaves. On 16th May, 999, the army of the Samanids was completely defeated at Merv by one of their own former Turkish slaves, Mahmood ibn Sabuktakeen, and the dynasty came to an end.

Mahmood established his capital in Ghazna and, in a reign of thirty-two years, conquered almost all Persia and a great part of the plains of India. Although the Samanids were Persians and Mahmood of Ghazna a Turk, the official language of both their empires was Arabic and both paid lip-service to the Abbasid Khalif as their suzerain.

When Mahmood in 999 eliminated the Samanids, the Qara Khans, a family of Turkish chiefs from the steppes, annexed Trans-Oxiana, the Oxus forming the boundary between them and the dynasty of Ghazna.

*   *   *

In Baghdad, as we have seen, Muizz al Dowla ibn Buwaih had died in 967. His son proved to be a failure but in 975 his nephew, Adhud al Dowla, assumed power. In 972, a rival khalif had been established in Cairo,[2] and the Buwaihids were alarmed. As a result, Adhud al Dowla showed more consideration for the Abbasid Khalif than had his predecessor.

Adhud al Dowla was unpopular in Baghdad. He was a strict collector of taxes and invariably spoke Persian, never having troubled to learn Arabic. In his brief reign of eight years, he nevertheless did a notable work of reconstruction. After a century of instability, he imposed law and order over Iraq and West Persia, repaired the roads and bridges, rebuilt ruined cities and encouraged agriculture.

The greatness of the Buwaihids ended with his death in April 983. His three sons and many grandsons fought one another backwards and forwards across Iraq and West Persia, plundering the countryside as they came and went until, in 1055, a new wave of barbarians swept them from the scene.

The Buwaihids never made any attempt to intervene in Syria, which, as we have already seen, had been repeatedly laid waste by

[2] See the next chapter.

the Byzantine emperors, Nicephorus Phocas and John Tzimisces. Tzimisces was succeeded in 976 by the even more capable Basil II, surnamed the Bulgar-Slayer. It was fortunate for Syria that Basil II was involved in long wars with the Bulgarians, though he twice invaded and devastated Syria, in 995 and in 999. Thereafter domestic disturbances in Constantinople gained for Syria a respite from invasions.

The famous Arab writer Muqaddasi published, in 985, his book entitled *A Description of the Muslim Empire*. "The people of Syria," he writes, "live in terror of the Greeks, who have driven many from their homes and devastated the country districts. Iraq is the home of sedition and famine, is daily retrogressing and suffers greatly from oppression and heavy taxes . . . Baghdad was once a magnificent city but is now fast falling into ruin and decay."

The anarchy and indifference of the Buwaihids in Baghdad left a power vacuum in Syria and on the Euphrates,[3] which resulted in the appearance of a number of independent Arab principalities. We have already noticed the Beni Hamdan dynasty in Aleppo. The Euphrates valley from Hit to below Kufa was ruled by the Beni Mizyed, chiefs of the Beni Asad tribe, while Mosul and the southern Jezira were controlled by Ibn Muqallad of the Beni Uqail tribe. In Aleppo, Beni Hamdan were later replaced by Ibn Mirdás, Harran was ruled by Beni Numair, while the northern Jezira obeyed a Kurdish ameer, Ibn Merwán.

These Arab princes should not be thought of as ignorant tribal chiefs. Ibn Mirdas was prepared, like his predecessor Ibn Hamdan, to offer battle to the Byzantine Emperor. Ibn Merwan kept court like a minor king and corresponded with the emperor. Most of these princes were cultured, built up extensive libraries and patronized poetry and literature in the traditional Arab style. Proud of the ancient warlike traditions of the Arabs as much as of their culture, they could truthfully repeat the lines of the contemporary Arab poet, Mutanabbi:

> "I am known to the horse-troop,
> The night and the desert's expanse,
> Not more to the paper and pen
> Than the sword and the lance."

In spite of their jealous quarrels, there is something profoundly attractive about the spirit of the Arabs during their great epoch:

[3] Map 17, page 130.

5. THE SELJUQS

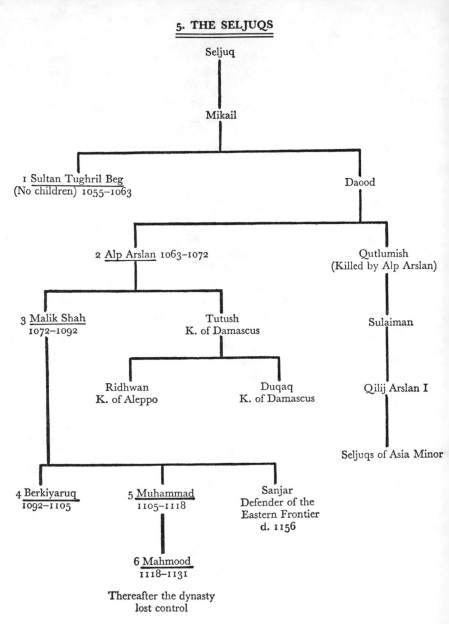

Seljuq

Mikail

1 Sultan Tughril Beg (No children) 1055–1063

Daood

2 Alp Arslan 1063–1072

Qutlumish (Killed by Alp Arslan)

3 Malik Shah 1072–1092

Tutush K. of Damascus

Sulaiman

Ridhwan K. of Aleppo

Duqaq K. of Damascus

Qilij Arslan I

Seljuqs of Asia Minor

4 Berkiyaruq 1092–1105

5 Muhammad 1105–1118

Sanjar Defender of the Eastern Frontier d. 1156

6 Mahmood 1118–1131

Thereafter the dynasty lost control

NOTE
The Sultans are underlined.

their dignified manners, their lavish hospitality, their chivalry in war, their moderation in victory and—for two centuries after the Prophet—their simple religious faith.

* * *

The Ghuzz were a tribe of primitive Turkmans,[4] who grazed on the steppes north of the Aral sea. They were breeders of horses, sheep and camels, and they lived on the milk and meat of their flocks. Their principal occupation was war and their killing weapon was a short bow, which they used on horseback at full gallop.

In 1029, shortly before the death of Mahmood of Ghazna, the Ghuzz burst into northern Khurasan and began to plunder the peaceful countryside.[5] Defeated by the Ghaznevid army, they did not return to the steppes, but, dispersing into small groups, they continued to migrate towards the west. As they went they looted the villages, killing the men and raping the women but, when regular troops arrived, they vanished during the night to reappear in another area.

The chiefs of the Ghuzz were members of the Seljuq family. Two brothers, Tughril Beg and Daood, grandsons of Seljuq, were at the head of the marauders. In 1038, Masood, the incapable son of the great Mahmood, was defeated by the Ghuzz, who thereafter dominated all northern Persia, while the Ghaznevids retired south of the Hindu Kush. In 1040, Tughril Beg took Nisapur by assault, amid terrible scenes of rape and slaughter. The tribes moved on to the west. Hamadan was taken and sacked, then Mosul, the streets of which were left strewn with corpses. In the desert south-west of Mosul, however, they received a severe check in 1042 at the hands of Ibn Muqallad and his Beni Uqail Arabs.

The endless futile family squabbles of the Buwaihid princelings in lower Iraq, Khuzistan and Fars had resulted in a certain rise in prestige on the part of the khalifs. No longer in a position to embark on military conquests, however, they limited themselves to a religious rôle. In 1044, the Khalif Qaim wrote to Tughril Beg, who was in Rei, to arrange a peace between him and the Buwaihid prince of Baghdad. Tughril Beg, who was a Muslim though most of the

---

[4] The difference between Turk and Turkman is not always clear. In general, I have used Turk for individuals who entered the Arab Empire and became Muslims, and Turkmans for whole nomadic tribes.

[5] Map 16, page 125.

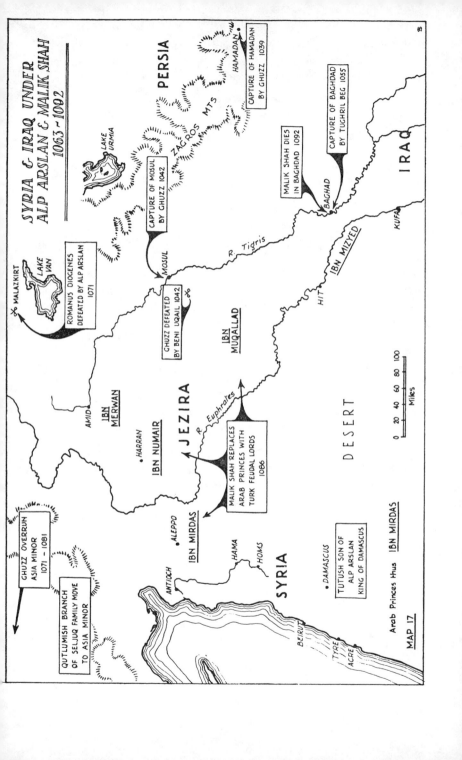

SYRIA & IRAQ UNDER
ALP ARSLAN & MALIK SHAH
1063 ~ 1092

PERSIA

IRAQ

SYRIA

JEZIRA

DESERT

LAKE URMIA

ZAGROS MTS

LAKE VAN

× MALAZKIRT

HAMADAN

BAGHAD

KUFA

HIT

MOSUL

AMID

HARRAN

ALEPPO

ANTIOCH

HAMA

HOMS

DAMASCUS

BEIRUT

TYRE

ACRE

R. Tigris

R. Euphrates

CAPTURE OF HAMADAN BY GHUZZ 1039

CAPTURE OF BAGHDAD BY TUCHRIL BEG 1055

MALIK SHAH DIES IN BAGHDAD 1092

CAPTURE OF MOSUL BY GHUZZ 1042

ROMANUS DIOGENES DEFEATED BY ALP ARSLAN 1071

GHUZZ DEFEATED BY BENI UQAIL 1042

MALIK SHAH REPLACES ARAB PRINCES WITH TURK FEUDAL LORDS 1086

GHUZZ OVERRUN ASIA MINOR 1071 - 1081

QUTLUMISH BRANCH OF SELJUQ FAMILY MOVE TO ASIA MINOR

TUTUSH SON OF ALP ARSLAN KING OF DAMASCUS

IBN MIZYED

IBN MUQALLAD

IBN MERWAN

IBN NUMAIR

IBN MIRDAS

Arab Princes thus   IBN MIRDAS

0   20   40   60   80   100
Miles

MAP 17

Ghuzz were heathen, received the khalif's emissaries with profound respect.

The ruling Buwaihid prince in Baghdad died in October 1048, being succeeded by a young son who took the title of Malik al Raheem, and immediately went off to fight a war with his brother, who had seized the province of Fars. In 1054, the Turkish mercenaries in Baghdad mutinied and the city was in confusion. For a hundred and ten years, since the seizure of Baghdad by Ibn Buwaih, the khalifs had suffered the humiliation of being dominated by Shiites, who refused to recognize their claim to the khalifate. The Seljuqs, however, were Sunnis. In December 1055, the Khalif Qaim decided to send for the Seljuqs.

For a short time the khalif's situation was precarious, for he had invited Tughril Beg to come while the Buwaihid prince, Malik al Raheem, was still in Baghdad. Eventually Tughril Beg and his army arrived on the east bank of the Tigris, while Malik al Raheem confronted him from the west bank. Next morning Ghuzz soldiers entered the city in small parties but were well behaved. The citizens, however, assisted by a few Buwaihid soldiers, attacked them and drove them out.

Tughril Beg was quick to take advantage of the incident. He immediately sent an ultimatum to the khalif, requiring Malik al Raheem to report to him forthwith. The khalif persuaded the young Buwaihid prince to go, whereupon he was arrested and sent to prison in a fortress in Persia. The Khalif Qaim protested in vain for, although it was he who had invited Tughril Beg to come, he had no army at his back to compel attention to his wishes. In Baghdad Tughril Beg moved into the palaces formerly occupied by the Buwaihids, while the Ghuzz scattered over the fertile valley of Iraq, plundering and killing, and carrying off all the young women.

In the summer of 1057, Tughril Beg was received in audience by the Khalif Qaim. He kissed the ground three times before the dais on which the Prince of the Faithful was seated in state, the Prophet's cloak draped over his shoulders. For more than a century, under the Shiite Buwaihid régime, the khalif had taken no part in public affairs, but appears, as a result, to have gained in religious prestige. Tughril Beg, a Sunni and a wild tribesman from the steppes, may have been genuinely impressed by the sophisticated culture of the khalif's court and by the religious aura surrounding a lineal descendant of the Prophet's uncle.

Tughril Beg, the founder of Seljuq greatness, died in August 1063 in Rei, without ever having had any children. He had never learned to read or write but was well gifted with the shrewdness and common sense which often distinguish illiterate old peasants, who rely on their own experience rather than on book learning. He was always patient, prudent and secretive and never relied on his subordinates. He never made any attempt to restrain the Ghuzz from killing or plundering.

Tughril Beg was succeeded by his nephew Alp Arslan whose brother Qutlumish, however, refused to acknowledge his supremacy. A brief civil war ended in a battle at Rei, in December 1063, in which Qutlumish was defeated and killed. This short struggle was to have prolonged political repercussions, for the descendants of Qutlumish, breaking away from the senior branch of the family, were to establish an independent Seljuq sultanate in Asia Minor.

Alp Arslan was young and energetic compared to Tughril Beg, though he also was illiterate. He married his eldest son, Malik Shah, to the daughter of the Qara Khan of Trans-Oxiana and another son to a daughter of the Sultan of Ghazna. Thus the three Turkish dynasties of the time were amicably united. The situation in the east being thus assured, Alp Arslan marched westwards to Armenia and then captured Aleppo, which was ruled by the independent Arab prince, Ibn Mirdas. Meanwhile the Ghuzz carried their plundering raids far into Byzantine territory.

In the spring of 1071, the Byzantine Emperor Romanus Diogenes marched eastwards to Armenia to defend the frontier. Before the arrival of the Seljuqs, the Byzantine Empire had gone through a phase of pacifist politics during which a great part of their armed forces had been disbanded. The appearance of the Ghuzz had resulted in an attempt rapidly to build up the army again but the force thus hastily improvised was ill-trained and badly equipped.

On Friday, 19th August, 1071, a pitched battle was fought at Malazkirt, twenty-five miles north of Lake Van. Romanus had drawn up his army in close order but the Ghuzz, who were all cavalry, adopted their usual tactics of galloping past, shooting arrows into the compact ranks. Unable to close hand-to-hand, the Byzantines were shot to pieces and eventually overrun. The Emperor Romanus, taken prisoner and stripped of the purple, was obliged to kiss the ground before the barbarian conqueror.

After this first humiliation, however, Alp Arslan behaved with magnanimity. A ransom of one million five hundred thousand gold dinars was fixed and, after a brief interval, Romanus Diogenes was released. Meanwhile, however, anarchy had broken out in Constantinople. Michael VII Ducas was raised to the purple and the returning Romanus was arrested and done to death.

The Byzantine army included a contingent of Norman mercenaries under one Roussel de Bailleul, who now turned on his employers and marched on Constantinople. Michael VII Ducas, in despair made a fatal decision—he appealed to the Seljuqs for help against Roussel. Alp Arslan had marched back to Persia but Sulaiman, the son of that Qutlumish who had been killed by Alp Arslan, volunteered his services. With the help of an army of Ghuzz, the Normans were defeated.

In 1078, Nicephorus Botoniates, a provincial governor, rose in rebellion and marched on Constantinople with an army of Ghuzz mercenaries. Then another pretender, supported by yet more Turkmans, appeared on the Bosphorus. At length, in 1081, Alexius Comnenus seized the throne. Meanwhile, however, the Turkmans had overrun all Asia Minor. Sulaiman ibn Qutlumish, placing himself at their head, had established his capital at Nicaea, only eighty miles from Constantinople. The whole of Asia Minor, long the best recruiting ground of Byzantine armies, was lost to the empire.

The new Emperor Alexius Comnenus found himself short of men and sent recruiting agents to western Europe to engage mercenaries. In the spring of 1095, the Byzantine envoys appeared before the pope at Piacenza. On Tuesday, 27th November, 1095, at Clermont in France, Pope Urban II appealed for volunteers to march to the rescue of their Christian brethren in the east.

*   *   *

The year after his victory at Malazkirt, Alp Arslan marched back to Persia where he was killed on 25th November, 1072. Although illiterate, he had been an energetic ruler. He was interested in administration, kind to the poor and dealt vigorously with corrupt officials. Under Malik Shah, the son and successor of Alp Arslan, the Seljuq Empire reached its pinnacle of greatness. Unlike his father and his great-uncle, the young sultan had been educated and was especially interested in astronomy. He established an observatory in Persia, of which Umar Khayyam was in charge and which produced a calendar more accurate than the Gregorian Calendar, which was issued in Europe five hundred years later. Indeed astronomy was not to dawn in western Europe for another four centuries, having been introduced by the Arabs in Spain.

In 1086, Malik Shah visited Mosul, Harran and Aleppo. These places, as already mentioned, had for the previous century been held by independent Arab princes. Malik Shah caused them all to be evicted and gave the cities as fiefs to his Turkman army commanders. Tutush, a brother of the sultan, became King of Damascus, the Fatimids being driven out of Palestine and confined to Egypt.

In April 1087, the Khalif Muqtadi, the grandson of Qaim,[6] married a daughter of Malik Shah in Baghdad. The ceremony was made the occasion of magnificent processions through the streets of the city and a dazzling display of silks, satins, jewels, silver and gold. Malik Shah again visited Baghdad in October and November 1092. One day he returned from a day's gazelle hunting with a high fever and died ten days later at the age of thirty-seven.

He left four sons, all of them still in childhood. Civil war broke out immediately between them, or perhaps between the rival army chiefs, each of whom claimed to be defending the rights of one or other of the children. Like so many of the barbarian dynasties which succeeded the Arabs, the Seljuqs had produced three generations of great rulers, to be followed by an anarchy of minor princes fighting one another for the throne.

*   *   *

The Seljuq conquest put an end to the great age of the Arabs. It is true that, after the murder of Mutawakkil in 861, the political power of the khalifs had disintegrated but, from 861 to 1055, Arab culture was still pre-eminent. The Samanids were Persians and Mahmood of Ghazna was a Turk, but Arabic was the language of their courts, and their poets—including the Sultan Mahmood himself—wrote in Arabic.

But when the Seljuqs established their empire in Persia, Arabic began to lose its position as the language of diplomacy and learning. The Seljuqs at first cared little for culture and Persian became the language of refined society. Even the junior branch of the Seljuqs, who set up an independent state in Asia Minor, used Persian as the speech of the educated classes. We may, therefore, make use of the

---

[6] Genealogical tree 4, page 117.

year 1055, in which Tughril Beg took Baghdad, to look back and assess the results of the four centuries of Arab greatness.

These four hundred years had completely changed the history of the world. The omission of the whole period from our history books has removed a vital link from the history of human development, making the subsequent story of the rise of Europe largely incomprehensible.

From the conquest of Persia by Alexander the Great in 330 B.C. until the Arab conquests in A.D. 634 to 700, Egypt, Syria and North Africa had been "Western" countries. The peoples of North Africa, Syria, Greece, Italy and Spain had been in Roman times fellow-citizens, speaking the same official languages, using the same currency, obeying the same customs and moving from one area to another without restrictions. When the Roman Empire adopted Christianity in the reign of Constantine (emperor 324 to 337), all these countries did the same.

Thus the greater part of the Umaiyid Empire—Syria, Palestine, Egypt, North Africa and Spain—inherited a thousand years of Graeco-Roman culture. Moreover Islam, when it first appeared, was closely connected with Christianity, had originated from nearly the same area and claimed to be based on Judaism and Christianity. The transfer of the capital from Damascus to Baghdad, however, resulted in the gradual orientalization of the empire and of Islam itself.

The economic results of the Arab conquests were as striking as the religious and cultural. Under the Romans, the Mediterranean had been a Roman lake. For seven hundred years, it never saw a naval battle but played the peaceful rôle of a highway for commerce. Egypt and Syria being included in the Roman Empire, the Oriental trade could reach Europe unhindered.

When, however, the Arabs conquered North Africa and Spain, the Mediterranean was divided into two halves by a line running from west to east and North Africa and Syria formed a solid battle front facing France, Italy and Greece. Since then, for thirteen centuries, the Mediterranean has been the scene of endless naval battles.

The extension of the Arab Empire from the Atlantic to China completely cut off western Europe from world trade. In Roman times, Italy, France, Spain and Britain had been a wealthy commercial region but Arab naval command of the Mediterranean destroyed all overseas trade. The cities fell into decay and the West became a purely agricultural region, land replacing cash as the standard of wealth.

These were the Dark Ages—dark only in Europe. In western Asia and North Africa, it was a period of wealth, progress and enlightenment. In the West, land-owning barons replaced bankers and business men as the leaders of the people. With the collapse of the Arab Empire, the trade of the West slowly recovered, but the belief that landowners were a social class superior to traders continued down to our own times. Thus the social development of Europe for more than a thousand years was affected by the four centuries of Arab power.

Finally, the rise, prosperity and decline of the Arabs contain many lessons for us. Politically their power lasted from 634 to 861, two hundred and twenty-seven years. If we assume the British Empire to have started in 1700 and ended between 1930 and 1950, we find that the lives of the two empires were approximately the same. Arab predominance, therefore, was no mere flash in the pan.

The comments of Arab authors living in Baghdad immediately after the collapse of their empire are strikingly relevant to our own situation. Contemporary Arab writers deplore the general indifference to religion, the increase of materialism and the decline of sexual morals. The later Romans complained of the increase of female influence and writers in Baghdad after 861 voice the same grievance. Women, they state, have become clerks, officials, lawyers, doctors and professors.

The loss of empire was followed by a loss of trade but the decline in business did not inspire the people of Baghdad to work harder. On the contrary, they adopted a five day week. Moreover, with the remains of the accumulated wealth of centuries, they introduced the welfare state with which we are familiar. Universities and colleges were built in every city, instruction was free and students received a government grant to cover their expenses. In the larger towns, free hospitals treated patients at government expense and medical students received a four-year course of training free of charge.

The arrogant but superficial spirit of our times scorns to study the history of past civilizations, which did not possess spacecraft or television. But our mechanical achievements have not changed the character of men. Had we been humble enough to learn, the experiences of our predecessors among great nations might have enabled us to avoid many of the errors into which we have fallen.

NOTABLE DATES

Tahir the Ambidextrous becomes ruler of Khurasan	821
Rebellion of the Brassworkers	873–900
Death of Muizz al Dowla ibn Buwaih	967
Rule of Adhud al Dowla ibn Buwaih	975–983
Rule of the Samanids of Bukhara	900–999
Annexation of Trans-Oxiana by the Qara Khans	999
Foundation of the Ghaznevid dynasty by Mahmood	999
Invasions of Syria by Basil II, the Bulgar-Slayer	995 and 999
Rule of Arab princes in Syria and Iraq	945–1086
Seljuq invasion of Khurasan	1029
Capture of Baghdad by Tughril Beg	1055
Destruction of the Byzantine army at Malazkirt	1071
Accession of Alexius Comnenus	1081
Death of Malik Shah } Civil war among the Seljuqs }	1092
The Pope appeals for help for eastern Christendom	1095

PERSONALITIES

The Tahirids, rulers of Khurasan	821–873

The Buwaihids

Muizz al Dowla, ruler of Baghdad	945–967
Adhud al Dowla	975–983
Decline and civil wars of the Buwaihids	983–1055

The Samanids of Bukhara

Nine Samanid Ameers	900–999

The Great Seljuqs

Tughril Beg	1055–1063
Alp Arslan	1063–1072
Malik Shah	1072–1092

X

The Mediterranean
795—1097

HAVING brought Persia, Iraq and Syria up to the brink of the First Crusade in 1097, we must now trace events in North Africa and Andalus up to the same date.

It will be remembered that, while the Abbasid khalifate was still in its golden splendour, Haroon al Rasheed had, in 800, granted autonomy to Ifriqiya under Ibrahim ibn al Aghlab. The concession had not been extorted by "nationalism" or demands for independence, but was due to Haroon's generosity and perhaps also to a lack of interest in these distant provinces.

Ibrahim governed, from 800 to 812, in peace and prosperity. His realm extended from Tripoli to Boujaiya, the Aghlabid capital being in Qairawan. The majority of the people were Berbers, but there was a strong Arab community and also residual groups dating from Roman and Byzantine days, together with many Jews. Further west, the puritan Berber mountaineers maintained their independence. In the Maghrib, the descendants of Idris, the brother of Muhammad, the Pure Soul, still ruled an independent state with its capital at Fez.[1]

It was a period of intense religious devotion. The Arabs and the people of the coast were Sunnis, while the Atlas Berbers were Kharijite puritans. Asceticism was widely practised and many of the pious lived in mortification and seclusion. A remarkable product of this spirit was the *ribat*. Originally frontier fortresses, the *ribats* became centres of intense religious feeling, fasting and prayer. The garrisons of the *ribats* were not vowed to a life of religion, but often consisted of ordinary Muslims, who carried out a religious retreat in a frontier fortress.

The dynasty established by Ibrahim ibn al Aghlab ruled Ifriqiya for one hundred and nine years. These princes, while being careful

[1] Pages 95 and 101.

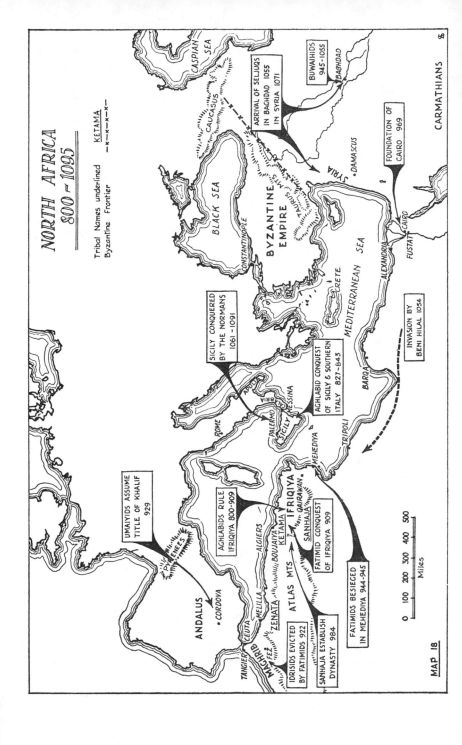

NORTH AFRICA
800 – 1095

Tribal Names underlined ⎯ KETAMA
Byzantine Frontier ⎯ ×—×—×—

UMAIYIDS ASSUME
TITLE OF KHALIF
929

SICILY CONQUERED
BY THE NORMANS
1061 - 1091

AGHLABID CONQUEST
OF SICILY & SOUTHERN
ITALY 827-843

ARRIVAL OF SELJUQS
IN BAGHDAD 1055
IN SYRIA 1071

BUWAIHIDS
945-1055

FOUNDATION OF
CAIRO 969

INVASION BY
BENI HILAL 1054

AGHLABIDS RULE
IFRIQIYA 800-909

FATIMID CONQUEST
OF IFRIQIYA 909

IDRISIDS EVICTED
BY FATIMIDS 922

SANHAJA ESTABLISH
DYNASTY 984

FATIMIDS BESIEGED
IN MEHEDIYA 944-945

CARMATHIANS

CASPIAN SEA
CAUCASUS
BLACK SEA
CONSTANTINOPLE
BYZANTINE EMPIRE
TAURUS MTS
SYRIA
•DAMASCUS
BAGHDAD
CAIRO
FUSTATT
ALEXANDRIA
CRETE
MEDITERRANEAN SEA
BARQA
TRIPOLI
MEHEDIYA•
QAIRAWAN•
IFRIQIYA
SANHAJA
KETAMA
ATLAS MTS
BOUJAIYA
ZENATA
ALGIERS
MELILLA
CEUTA
TANGIER
FEZ
MAGHRIB
PYRENEES
ANDALUS
•CORDOVA
ROME
APULIA
CALABRIA
PALERMO
MESSINA
SICILY

0   100   200   300   400   500
Miles

MAP 1B

65

not to offend the susceptibilities of the pious, were not themselves remarkably religious. Following the tradition set by the Abbasids, the Aghlabids lived in palaces, surrounded by fountains and gardens, and passed their time in music, poetry and horsemanship. Nevertheless, they found time to govern wisely. The country was prosperous, agriculture and irrigation were fostered and many notable public buildings were erected.

The most important exploit carried out by the Aghlabids, however, was the conquest of Sicily. In 827, their army landed on the island, which was still a Byzantine possession. Four years later, they established their capital at Palermo and, in 843, Messina was occupied. Soon they crossed to Italy and occupied Calabria and Apulia. The Arab conquest of Sicily and southern Italy, regarded at the time as a disaster for Christendom, was eventually to provide one of the principal channels for the spread of Arab civilization to Europe.

*   *   *

The Shiites, it will be remembered, were those Muslims who, after the murder of the Khalif Othman in 656, had supported the candidacy of Ali and his descendants. Since those tragic events, desperate Shiite revolts had taken place at intervals but all had been ruthlessly suppressed. The Shiites had also elaborated a number of religious dogmas, which caused them to be denounced by the Sunnis as heretics. One such dogma was the belief that the Divine Spirit which had inspired the Prophet had passed from him to his son-in-law Ali and from him to his descendants, from father to son. The person in whom the Spirit dwelt, at any given moment, was known as the Imam, and was sinless and infallible.

The great-great-grandson of Ali, Jaafar the Truthful, had two sons, Ismail and Musa. Thereupon a schism appeared in the Shiite ranks, some claiming that the Spirit had passed through Ismail to his descendants, while others alleged that it had dwelt in Musa. The descendants of Musa became extinct after the twelfth imam from Ali, and their adherents were consequently known as the Twelvers. Those, on the other hand, who believed the Spirit to have passed through Ismail and his descendants, were known as Ismailis. The Carmathians were of this branch of the Shiites.

In 893, an Ismaili missionary called Abu Abdulla was sent to work among the Berber tribes of Ifriqiya. Settling among the martial Ketama, south of Boujaiya, he converted them and became the

6. QURAISH TO SHOW THE KHALIFS AND IMAMS

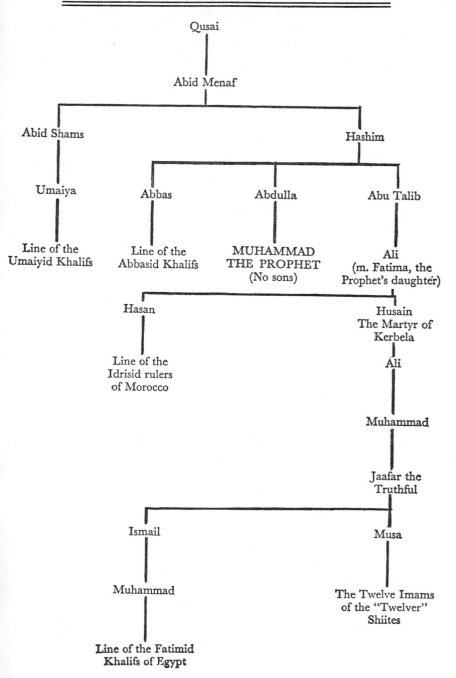

principal man in the tribe. The ruling Aghlabid ameer happened, in 904, to be a drunken degenerate. The Ketama, led by Abu Abdulla, rose in revolt. Promising the early arrival of the true Imam, who would bring in the age of peace and justice, Abu Abdulla captured Qairawan on 27th March, 909, and the Aghlabid dynasty came to an end.

There was living in Syria a claimant to the Shiite imamate, whose name was Saeed ibn Ahmad. Summoned by Abu Abdulla, this man made a triumphal entry into Qairawan, where he assumed the name of Ubaidullah and the titles of khalif, Prince of the Faithful and Mehedi.[2] The new dynasty called itself the Fátimid, claiming descent from Fátima, the Prophet's daughter.

Ubaidullah soon showed himself an energetic autocrat, who regarded Ifriqiya as a mere stepping-stone to the replacement of the Abbasids as sole khalifs of the Muslim world. In 913, he sent his son Qaim with an army to conquer Egypt. Qaim took Alexandria but failed to take the capital, Fustat. In May 915, he was back in Qairawan. In 920, he again invaded Egypt but once more he was not strong enough for the task.

Twice foiled in his attempts on Egypt, Ubaidullah determined to conquer the rest of North Africa. In 922, he sent his army to the west, overran the Berber states and drove the Idrisids from their throne in Fez. Across the straits in Andalus, the great Umaiyid, Abdul Rahman III,[3] was alarmed at the approach of a rival Arab ruler and seized the ports of Melilla and Ceuta, whence he supported Berber resistance to the Fatimids.

In 929, out of jealousy of the Fatimids, Abdul Rahman III also assumed the title of khalif. There were now three rival khalifs, an Umaiyid in Andalus, a Fatimid in Ifriqiya, and an Abbasid in Baghdad. In 934, Ubaidullah died and was succeeded by his son Qaim.

North Africa, meanwhile, was a powder-magazine of religious passions. The Berbers of the Atlas were Kharijite puritans, the people of the coastal plains were orthodox Sunnis, the ruler and the government were Shiites. In 944, Abu Yezeed, a Berber Kharijite ascetic, preached a holy war against the Shiites. Sweeping irresistibly forward at the head of vast numbers of Berbers, he laid siege, in November 944, to the fortress of Mehediya, built on a promontory

[2] This title, sometimes spelt Mahdi, is that given by Muslims to the prophet who will one day establish peace on earth.

[3] See later in this chapter.

7. THE FATIMID KHALIFS OF EGYPT

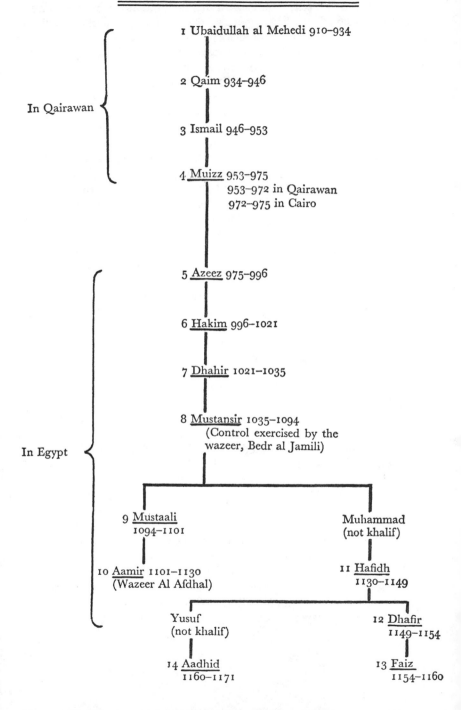

In Qairawan

1 Ubaidullah al Mehedi 910–934

2 Qaim 934–946

3 Ismail 946–953

4 Muizz 953–975
    953–972 in Qairawan
    972–975 in Cairo

In Egypt

5 Azeez 975–996

6 Hakim 996–1021

7 Dhahir 1021–1035

8 Mustansir 1035–1094
(Control exercised by the
wazeer, Bedr al Jamili)

9 Mustaali
1094–1101

Muhammad
(not khalif)

10 Aamir 1101–1130
(Wazeer Al Afdhal)

11 Hafidh
1130–1149

Yusuf
(not khalif)

12 Dhafir
1149–1154

14 Aadhid
1160–1171

13 Faiz
1154–1160

projecting into the sea, where the Fatimids had taken refuge. The dynasty was saved by the support of the Sanhaja, a nomadic tribe of the Sahara, under their chief, Ziri ibn Manad. The Berbers of the Atlas grew tired of the toils of siege warfare and, in September 945, Abu Yezeed was obliged to withdraw after a siege of ten months. In May 946, the Khalif Qaim died and was succeeded by his son Ismail, who drove the remnant of the rebels back into the Atlas. Meanwhile, the Umaiyid Khalif of Andalus had helped the Berbers of the Maghrib to drive out the Fatimid garrisons. From the Atlantic to Algiers, Umaiyid influence reigned supreme.

Ismael died in 953 and was succeeded as Fatimid Khalif by his son, Al Muizz li Deen Allah, "he who makes glorious the religion of God". Muizz at last found himself strong enough to return to the family ambition, the conquest of Egypt. But before marching eastwards, he decided to re-establish Fatimid authority in all North Africa. In 958, a Fatimid army marched out of Qairawan and swept across North Africa to the Atlantic coast, capturing Fez and Tangier. The Umaiyids were obliged to withdraw across the Straits of Gibraltar to Andalus.

The years of chaos which had distracted Baghdad after the murder of Mutawakkil had prevented the Abbasids from controlling Egypt. In August 969, a Fatimid army occupied the country unopposed. It was commanded by Johar, a Sicilian slave of Greek origin converted to Islam. He established his headquarters outside Fustat and marked out in the vicinity the foundations of a new royal palace and city, which he named Al Qahira, the Victorious. In English we call it Cairo.

In July 972, the Kahlif Muizz made his state entry into his new capital where, seated on a golden throne, he received the homage of the notables of Egypt. The indefatigable Johar led the Fatimid armies on to occupy Syria. (In 975, Adhud al Dowla ibn Buwaih assumed power in Bahdad.) For a brief moment, the Fatimids were acknowledged by an immense empire extending from the Maghrib to Syria. When Muizz left Qairawan for Cairo, he had left behind as his viceroy in North Africa the son of Ziri ibn Manad of the Sanhaja Berbers, who had relieved Mehediya during the rebellion of Abu Yezeed. In 984, however, the Sanhaja, under their ameer Mansoor, established an independent dynasty in Qairawan.

Mansoor proved to be a great ruler and a victorious commander, who governed Ifriqiya and Sicily for thirteen years. Both countries were quiet and prosperous and the prince himself became extremely wealthy. Unfortunately, when he died in 996, his son Badces was only twelve years old. Mansoor's brother, Hammád, refused to swear allegiance to a child and the dynasty divided into two parts, Beni Ziri and Beni Hammad. Further west, the Zenata, another Berber group which had replaced the Idrisids, also broke away.[4]

From 996 onwards, therefore, North Africa was divided between three Berber dynasties, the Beni Ziri Sanhaja in Qairawan, the Beni Hammad Sanhaja and the Zenata. Henceforward the authority of the Fatimid khalif extended no further west than Barqa.

*   *   *

The Fatimids, having lost North Africa, were driven likewise from Syria by the invasions of the Byzantine soldier emperors. After the death of Basil II, the Bulgar-Slayer, however, they attempted to reimpose their control on Syria. A contemporary Arab writer remarks pertinently that, of all the Muslim peoples, the Egyptians are the most submissive and the easiest to govern, but those of Damascus are the most turbulent, qualities still unchanged today. The period from 1000 to 1071 witnessed a number of half-hearted Egyptian attempts to conquer Syria.

The Khalif Muizz died in 975 and was succeeded by his son Azeez, a capable and cultured man who gave Egypt twenty-one years of peace, except for occasional attempts to subdue the Syrians. It will be remembered that the disorders in Iraq, after the murder of Mutawakkil in 861, had diverted the oriental trade to the Red Sea and Egypt. As a result, the country was rich and prosperous.

The wealth of the Fatimids in the reign of Azeez (975–996) is almost past belief. The golden thrones covered with precious stones and approached by silver steps, the marble pillars, and the roof-beams covered with gold in their palaces, suggest a fairy story more than the world we know. Azeez was cultured, pleasant and tolerant. His favourite wife was a practising Christian.

The third Fatimid khalif was Hákim, the son of Azeez, who came to the throne at the age of eleven. In 1000, when he was fifteen, he began to show signs of insanity. He delighted to ride round Cairo at night on a donkey and ordered all shops to remain open all night. To prevent women circulating in the streets, he forbade the manu- facture of ladies' shoes. Although his mother had been a Christian, he suddenly gave orders for the destruction of all churches. In 1018, his madness had gone so far that he declared himself to be God. On

[4] Map 18, page 139.

13th February, 1021, he set out at night on one of his accustomed donkey rides and was never seen again.

A notable result of the reign of Hakim was the foundation of the Druze sect in Lebanon. A certain Muhammad al Darazi, who had been one of his adherents, escaped to the Lebanese mountains, where his followers were called Druzes after his name. We shall hear of them again in Syria.

With Egypt rich but militarily ineffective, Baghdad in the throes of civil wars between rival Buwaihid princes and Constantinople weakened by internal dissensions, northern Syria and the Euphrates constituted a power vacuum which was filled, as already related, by a number of Arab princely families.

The mad Khalif Hakim was succeeded by his rather ineffective son, Dhahir, who died in 1035. Nasir i Khusrau, a Persian visitor to Egypt in 1054, gives a glowing account of the wealth of that country. "I could neither limit nor define their wealth," he writes, "and nowhere else have I seen such prosperity."

In 1066 (the year of the Battle of Hastings), Egypt suffered a desperate famine under the Khalif Mustansir, the son of Dhahir.[5] The country fell into confusion, the Turkish and Sudanese mercenaries in the army plundering the inhabitants. In 1074, however, Bedr al Jamali, an Armenian convert to Islam, became wazeer, restored public security and a considerable degree of prosperity. Thereafter, however, the khalifs lost executive power and remained idle in their palaces. Both Bedr and the Khalif Mustansir died in 1094. Bedr was succeeded as wazeer by his son Al Afdhal. Meanwhile, the Seljuq Turks had occupied Syria in 1071.

*   *   *

The establishment of rival khalifates, the Fatimid and the Abbasid, opened a new era. For some three hundred and fifty years, the Arab Empire had formed a monolithic wall, enclosing Europe. But the Fatimids were ambitious to replace the Abbasids, not to fight unbelievers. Soon they were to open diplomatic relations with the Christians of the West and the end of the long blockade of Europe was in sight.

*   *   *

From the departure of the Fatimids to Egypt in 972 until 1054, North Africa enjoyed a period of peace and prosperity. Unfortunately, in 1048 Muizz ibn Badees, the Sanhaja ruler of Ifriqiya,

[5] Genealogical tree 7, page 143.

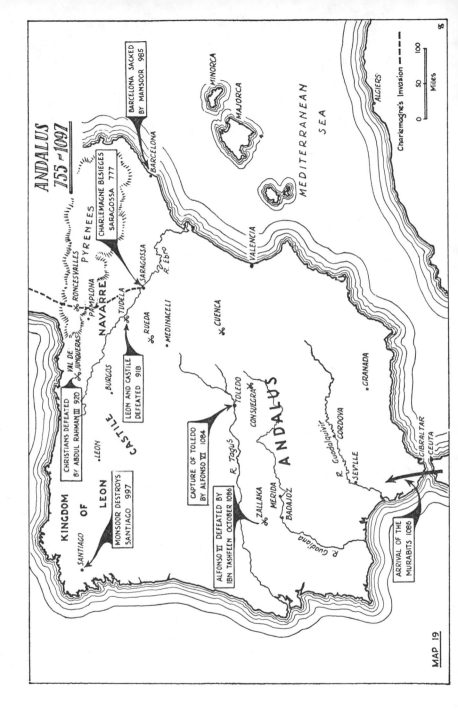

ANDALUS 755–1097

BARCELONA SACKED BY MANSOOR 985

CHARLEMAGNE BESIEGES SARAGOSSA 777

CHRISTIANS DEFEATED BY ABDUL RAHMAN III 920

LEON AND CASTILE DEFEATED 918

MONSOOR DESTROYS SANTIAGO 997

CAPTURE OF TOLEDO BY ALFONSO VI 1084

ALFONSO VI DEFEATED BY IBN TASHFEEN OCTOBER 1086

ARRIVAL OF THE MURABITS 1086

PYRENEES

MINORCA

MAJORCA

MEDITERRANEAN SEA

ALGIERS

Charlemagne's Invasion

0   50   100
Miles

RONCESVALLES

VAL DE JUNQUERAS

PAMPLONA

NAVARRE

SARAGOSSA

TUDELA

R. Ebro

BARCELONA

VALENCIA

RUEDA

MEDINACELI

CUENCA

BURGOS

CASTILE

LEON

KINGDOM OF LEON

SANTIAGO

TOLEDO

CONSUEGRA

R. Tagus

ZALLAKA

MERIDA

BADAJOZ

R. Guadiana

ANDALUS

GRANADA

CORDOVA

Guadalquivir

SEVILLE

GIBRALTAR

CEUTA

MAP 19

decided to show his independence by ordering that public prayers be offered for the Abbasid Khalif in Baghdad, instead of for the Fatimids.

It happened that, at this time, two bedouin tribes from Arabia, Beni Hilal and Beni Sulaim, had migrated across Sinai and camped on the Nile south of Cairo, where their depredations caused anxiety. The Fatimid Khalif, to revenge himself on the Sanhaja and rid Egypt of these marauders, urged them to invade Ifriqiya. In 1054, the bedouins took Tripoli. Beni Sulaim settled in the vicinity, while Beni Hilal went on, taking Qairawan in October 1057. The Sanhaja took refuge in Mehediya, while the nomads spread anarchy over Ifriqiya.

Profiting by the collapse of the Sanhaja, a Norman baron, Roger, the son of Tancred of Hauteville, landed in Sicily in 1061 and, by 1091, had won back Sicily and Malta for Christendom.

*   *   *

Having traced the story of the East and of Ifriqiya down to 1095, it remains for us to bring the history of Andalus down to the same date. We have seen the establishment of an Umaiyid dynasty in Spain under Abdul Rahman ibn Muawiya in 755.[6] In 777, he had been faced with an invasion by Charlemagne, who besieged Saragossa. News of a rising in Saxony, however, obliged the emperor to return to the north. During his retreat through the Pyrenees, his rearguard under Roland was overwhelmed at Roncesvalles, originating the most famous of mediaeval romances.

Dying in 788, Abdul Rahman bequeathed the throne to his son Hisham, who was followed by Hakam. Andalus, with its mixed population, had now become a nation, which regarded the Umaiyids as its legitimate sovereigns. Religious toleration was observed but many Goths and Spaniards had nevertheless been converted to Islam. Abdul Rahman II, who reigned from 822 to 852, ruled over a strong, not to say a glorious kingdom. The succession of two weak rulers, Muhammad and Abdulla, led to rebellions in the ensuing sixty years, until the accession of Abdul Rahman III in 912.

The Arabs had never been as successful in mountains as in plains. The first Muslim conquerors of Spain had pressed on northwards and overrun the south of France, neglecting a remnant of Christians in the mountains of Leon. During the sixty years of weak rule, from the death of Abdul Rahman II to the accession of Abdul Rahman

[6] Page 96.

III in 912, this nucleus of resistance had grown in strength. In 914, indeed, the King of Leon laid waste the district of Merida and advanced to within a hundred miles of Cordova, the Arab capital.

Under Abdul Rahman III, the tide began to turn. In 918, the combined armies of Leon and Castile were defeated at Tudela. In June 920, Abdul Rahman himself routed the Christians at Val de Junqueras, only forty-five miles from the Bay of Biscay. In 924, he captured Pamplona, the capital of Navarre, and carried fire and sword throughout the kingdom. In 934, he took the city of Burgos. In 958, the King and Queen of Navarre and the King of Leon were received by him as suppliants in his palace in Cordova.

The army of Andalus was one of the finest in the world. It consisted of Arabs and Berbers and also of "Slavs", the name given to young boys bought as slaves in France, Germany or Italy, converted to Islam and enlisted as soldiers. This was, of course, the same technique as the Abbasids used for Turkish boys. At this time the Abbasids had already been overthrown by their slave soldiers and it seems curious that Abdul Rahman III should have imitated their methods.

The fact that Arab rulers always used foreign mercenaries seems to need explanation. It was not due to a loss of the Arab military spirit, for we have the example of the fierce Carmathian fighters, and the Muslims of Spain were still excellent soldiers. The turbulent individualism of the Arabs, however, resulted in frequent mutinies and disturbances, and Arab rulers found it necessary to retain a foreign element in the army to ensure stability. The mistake made by the Abbasids was that their armies consisted almost entirely of foreigners, with the result that the Turks ultimately realized their own power. Abdul Rahman III was more prudent and kept his "Slavs" to about one-third of the army, which he found sufficient to ensure stability. His army raised Abdul Rahman III to the position of one of the great rulers of his time. Moreover, it had not been built up by means of heavy taxation. Andalus was extremely prosperous. Industry was active and weapons, wrought iron, enamel, jewellery, goldsmith's work, textiles and pottery were all manufactured. The ships of Andalus were to be seen in every Mediterranean port. Great attention was paid to irrigation and agriculture and the Spanish Muslims were splendid cultivators.

Science and art were fostered no less than commerce and industry. Philosophy, medicine and mathematics were actively studied and the Christians of the north, when in need of medical care, came to consult Arab specialists in Cordova. The Arabs of Andalus were far in advance of western Europe in all forms of knowledge.

Abdul Rahman III was the *roi soleil* of Andalus. Successful in war and a diligent administrator, he was a wise, humane and cultured ruler. He died on 6th October, 961, at the age of seventy, after a reign of forty-nine years.

He was succeeded by his quiet and studious son, Hakam II. When, however, counting on his mild disposition, Leon and Navarre repudiated their treaties with Andalus, he invaded their countries and obliged them to sue for peace.

Hakam II was a passionate lover of books, of which he was believed to have four hundred thousand in his library. The University of Cordova was world famous and many Christians from western Europe resorted there for their studies, as Arab students do now to universities in the West. Free primary schools were opened for poor children and even peasants could read and write, though in Christian Europe kings and nobles were often illiterate.

Hakam II died in 976 after a reign of only fifteen years and was succeeded by his infant son, Hisham. During his minority, a certain Muhammad ibn Abi Aamir became wazeer. In 981, the new wazeer invaded Leon and defeated the Christians at Rueda. On his return, he assumed the name of Al Mansoor, the Victorious, by which title he will be called hereafter.

Throughout the rest of his life, Mansoor invaded the Christian kingdoms every year. On 6th July, 985, he sacked the great city of Barcelona. In 988, he overran Leon, taking the capital by assault. In 997, after a campaign in the wild mountains of Galicia, he destroyed the cathedral of Santiago di Compostela, containing the reputed tomb of Saint James the Apostle.

In 1002, returning from a campaign in Castile, he died on 10th August at Medinaceli. On all his campaigns, he had carefully collected the dust off his armour and had given directions for it to be placed in his coffin, as evidence before the recording angels of his diligence in fighting the Christians.

The great wazeer had ruled Andalus for twenty-five years, during which he had reduced the Christian kingdoms to trembling subservience. His campaigns, however, were marred by excessive ruthlessness. The ultimate Christian *reconquista* in Spain was to be characterized by great cruelty, much of which may well have been revenge for the atrocities of Mansoor.

But while the wazeer was brutal to the Christians of other states, complete religious toleration was practised in Andalus, where Jews and Christians obtained important posts. The same ruthlessness in war and toleration at home had been shown by the great Abbasids.

Mansoor was not only a soldier but was also extremely active in promoting the material welfare of his country. Roads were constructed, irrigation extended and commerce and industry actively fostered. The judicial system was honest and impartial and every effort was made to encourage education.

In one respect, however, Mansoor was responsible for the ruin of Andalus. He had achieved power when the Khalif Hisham was a child, but when he grew up the wazeer showed no sign of allowing him to rule, thereby destroying the prestige of the royal family. As a result, Mansoor was succeeded by his son, Mudhaffar, who, however, died six years later in 1008. The Khalif Hisham, who had lived in seclusion for thirty-two years, was no longer capable of ruling and Andalus fell into anarchy.

From 1009 to 1031, a succession of rival claimants tried to seize the throne. In 1031, the notables of Cordova declared the khalifate to be abolished and the country split up into many small states, which frequently fought one another. By 1055, the smaller princes had been eliminated and the principal surviving kings had established their capitals in Seville, Badajoz, Granada, Valencia and Saragossa.[7]

*   *   *

By a curious coincidence, while the nomadic Beni Hilal were invading Ifriqiya, the nomads of the western Sahara in 1056 invaded the Maghrib. The movement was inspired by an outbreak of religious enthusiasm among the tribes of the western Sahara. The new sect were called the Murabits,[8] because the revival had begun in a *ribat*, one of the religious fortresses already described. Under their great leader, Yusuf ibn Tashfeen, they founded Marákish as their capital. In 1069, they took Fez and, in 1082, Algiers.

Meanwhile, King Alfonso VI of Leon and Castile had taken advantage of the disintegration of Andalus. In 1084, he captured Toledo and obliged the petty Muslim states to pay him tribute. A deputation from Seville, Cordova, Granada and Badajoz crossed to the Maghrib and solicited the aid of Yusuf ibn Tashfeen. The Murabits crossed to Spain and on Friday, 23rd October, 1086, completely defeated Alfonso VI at Zallaka, called in Spanish history

[7] Map 19, page 147.
[8] The Christians transliterated Al Murabit into Almoravid.

Sagrajas. The Murabits removed most of the petty Arab dynasties and added Andalus to their empire. In 1097, Alfonso VI was again defeated by them at Consuegra and at Cuenca.

Thus, when the First Crusade was leaving western Europe for Syria, the Christians in Spain were suffering a series of military defeats at the hands of the Berber Murabits.

NOTABLE DATES

Abdul Rahman ibn Muawiya, Ameer of Andalus	755
Grant of autonomy to Ifriqiya	800
Rule of the Aghlabids in Ifriqiya	800–909
Arab conquest of Sicily and southern Italy	827–843
Establishment of the first Fatimid Khalif in Qairawan	909
Reign of Abdul Rahman III in Andalus	912–961
Establishment of the Fatimid Khalif Muizz in Cairo	972
Rule of the wazeer Mansoor in Andalus	978–1002
Invasion of Ifriqiya by Beni Hilal	1054
Invasion of the Maghrib by the Murabits	1056
Conquest of Sicily by the Norman, Count Roger	1061–1091
Murabit intervention in Spain	1086

PERSONALITIES

Umaiyid Rulers of Andalus

Abdul Rahman ibn Muawiya	755–788
Hisham ibn Abdul Rahman	788–796
Hakam ibn Hisham	796–822
Abdul Rahman II	822–852
Muhammad	852–886
Mundhir	886–888
Abdulla	888–912
Abdul Rahman III	912–961
Hakam II	961–976
Hisham II, the puppet khalif	976–1009
Mansoor the great wazeer	978–1002

Note From 755 to 929, the rulers were called ameers. After 929, they assumed the title of khalifs.

Fatimid Khalifs

Ubaidullah al Mehdi	910–934
Qaim	934–946
Ismail	946–953
Al Muizz li Deen Allah (in Qairawan)	953–972
(in Cairo)	972–975
Azeez	975–996
Hakim	996–1021
Dhahir	1021–1035
Mustansir	1035–1094
Mustaali	1094–1101

Other Personalities

Bedr al Jamali, wazeer of Egypt
His son, Al Afdhal
Yusuf ibn Tashfeen, Prince of the Murabits

XI

The Crusades

AFTER the death of Malik Shah in 1092, three years before Pope Urban II preached the First Crusade, the Seljuq Empire was torn by civil wars. For forty years, the Seljuqs had wielded extraordinary power, due to the overwhelming victories of the Ghuzz, but their empire fell to pieces before it could become civilized, established and administered.

Meanwhile however, the descendants of Qutlumish—the junior branch of the dynasty—had overrun Asia Minor, threatening to destroy the Byzantine Empire, which had appealed desperately to the West for help. For four centuries Islam had been far stronger than Christendom and the fall of Constantinople, had it occurred in 1095, might have allowed the Muslims to overrun the Balkans, as they had previously conquered Spain. The origin of the First Crusade was, therefore, defensive. To imagine that western Europe, barbarous and uncivilized, could conquer the mighty empires of Asia, is to view the eleventh century through the eyes of the twentieth.

The Seljuq occupation of Asia Minor had deprived the Byzantines of their best recruiting ground. The Emperor Alexius Comnenus had asked the pope for help in order to recover it. The leaders of the First Crusade, however, were uneducated, had no maps and probably never grasped this strategic objective. But Jerusalem was a name familiar to Christians, and many pilgrims had been there during the period of rule by the Arabs, who were always tolerant. Since the Seljuq conquest, however, pilgrims had been robbed and murdered. As a result, the whole Byzantine strategic plan was upset by the Crusaders' determination to march on Jerusalem.

When Alexius Comnenus appealed to the West for help, he visualized the arrival of volunteers who would enlist as mercenaries under his command. He had not contemplated the appearance of independent Western armies who would refuse to obey him.

*   *   *

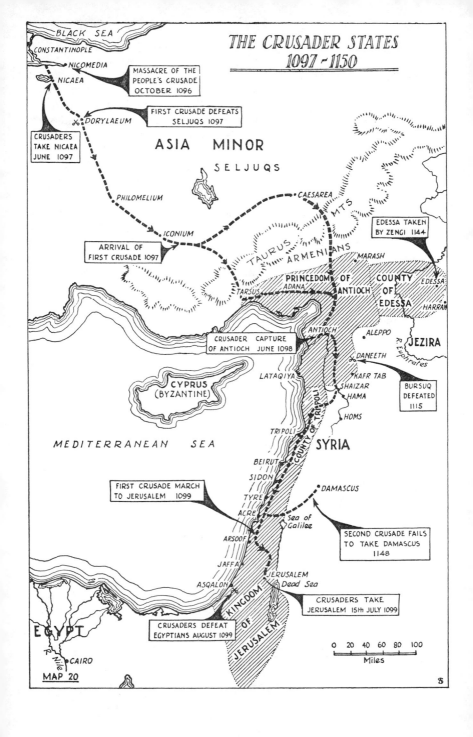

THE CRUSADER STATES
1097~1150

BLACK SEA

CONSTANTINOPLE

NICOMEDIA

NICAEA

MASSACRE OF THE
PEOPLE'S CRUSADE
OCTOBER 1096

DORYLAEUM

FIRST CRUSADE DEFEATS
SELJUQS 1097

CRUSADERS
TAKE NICAEA
JUNE 1097

ASIA MINOR

SELJUQS

PHILOMELIUM

ICONIUM

CAESAREA

TAURUS

MTS

EDESSA TAKEN
BY ZENGI 1144

ARRIVAL OF
FIRST CRUSADE 1097

ARMENIANS

MARASH

PRINCEDOM OF
ANTIOCH

COUNTY
OF
EDESSA

TARSUS

ADANA

EDESSA

HARRAN

ANTIOCH

ALEPPO

JEZIRA

CRUSADER CAPTURE
OF ANTIOCH JUNE 1098

DANEETH

R. Euphrates

CYPRUS
(BYZANTINE)

LATAQIYA

KAFR TAB

SHAIZAR

HAMA

BURSUQ
DEFEATED
1115

HOMS

MEDITERRANEAN SEA

TRIPOLI

SYRIA

BEIRUT

SIDON

COUNTY OF TRIPOLI

DAMASCUS

FIRST CRUSADE MARCH
TO JERUSALEM 1099

TYRE

ACRE

Sea of
Galilee

SECOND CRUSADE FAILS
TO TAKE DAMASCUS
1148

ARSOOF

JAFFA

ASQALON

JERUSALEM

Dead Sea

KINGDOM

CRUSADERS TAKE
JERUSALEM 15th JULY 1099

EGYPT

OF

CRUSADERS DEFEAT
EGYPTIANS AUGUST 1099

CAIRO

Nile

JERUSALEM

0 20 40 60 80 100

Miles

MAP 20

The appeal launched by Urban II was too successful. A number of enthusiasts, of whom the most famous was Peter the Hermit, roused great fervour among the simple peasants of France and Germany. The People's Crusade, a vast rabble, set out immediately and reached Constantinople in August 1096, after much looting and fighting on the way. Probably more than twenty thousand men, women and children were ferried across the Bosphorus. On 21st October, 1096, all were massacred by the Turkmans near Nicomedia.

In 1095, there were no regular national armies in the West. Four great lords, however, took the cross and formed armies from their tenants and feudatories.

(1) The first was Godfrey de Bouillon, who was Duke of Lorraine and of Lower Lotharingia, approximately modern Belgium.

(2) The next was Robert, Duke of Normandy, the eldest son of William the Conqueror.

(3) Raymond de Saint Gilles, Count of Toulouse and Marquis of Provence, led the third contingent.

(4) The fourth division was commanded by Bohemond, Count of Apulia, of the Norman house of Hauteville.

Alexius was taken aback by the news that four armies were on the march. Since the treachery of Roussel de Bailleul, he particularly mistrusted Normans.[1] He decided to insist that the Crusaders swear allegiance to himself before crossing the Bosphorus. Godfrey arrived first on 23rd December, 1096, but refused to swear. In April 1097, however, he finally took the oath and crossed to Asia. Bohemond of Apulia came next and swore without hesitation. Robert of Normandy also made no difficulty but Raymond refused, though he ultimately took a modified oath.

On 14th May, 1097, the Crusaders attacked Nicaea, the capital of the Seljuqs of Asia Minor. After a siege of six weeks, the city surrendered, not to the Crusaders but to Alexius. Thereafter the Frankish[2] army waged its own war, taking no notice whatever of the emperor. Moreover, the Crusaders themselves were four separate armies with no commander-in-chief.

On 1st July, 1097, the Crusaders inflicted a severe defeat on Qilij Arslan I, the Seljuq ruler of Asia Minor,[3] at Dorylaeum. After the Byzantine débâcle at Malazkirt in 1071, many Christian Armenians had fled for refuge to the Taurus Mountains, where they

[1] Page 133.
[2] To the Muslims, all West Europeans were Franks.
[3] Genealogical tree 5, page 128.

had established a number of communities. These groups of Armenians welcomed their fellow-Christian Crusaders when they crossed the Taurus. On 20th October, 1097, the army reached Antioch.

When the Franks invaded Syria, the Seljuqs reoccupied Asia Minor behind them, cutting off their land communications with Europe. Alexius' hope of recovering Asia Minor was disappointed, though he succeeded in pushing his frontier eastwards to Philomelium.

The Crusaders had no siege train with which to attack Antioch and suffered intensely from cold and hunger during their blockade of the city, which they eventually took on 3rd June, 1098. Three days later, they succeeded in defeating a relieving army under Kerboqa, Lord of Mosul, a vassal of the Persian Seljuqs.

On 13th January, 1099, they set out for Jerusalem. The Norman Bohemond, the only leader without any religious motive, stayed in Antioch, of which he declared himself the prince. The remainder marched down the coast past Tripoli, Beirut, Sidon, Tyre and Acre.

At Arsoof they left the coast, and came in sight of Jerusalem on 7th June, 1099, probably at a point just east of the tomb of the Prophet Samuel. "When they heard the name of Jerusalem called," writes William of Tyre, "they began to weep and fell on their knees, giving thanks to our Lord . . . Then they raised their hands in prayer to Heaven and, taking off their shoes, bowed down to the ground and kissed the earth."

There was scarcely any water to be had on the plateau outside Jerusalem, food was extremely scarce and the position of the Franks was precarious. They set to work, however, with enthusiasm, perhaps with desperation. A squadron of Genoese ships had put in to Jaffa and brought up rations, and timber for siege engines.

Jerusalem was surrounded on three sides by ravines and could only be attacked from the north on the narrow front from Herod's Gate to the Damascus Gate. The assault began on 14th July, 1099, but it was not until noon of 15th July that Godfrey gained a footing on the walls. By nightfall the city had been taken and most of its defenders killed. Godfrey was proclaimed king but refused the royal title. "He would not," he said, "wear a crown of gold where his Master had worn a crown of thorns." On 12th August, a relieving army from Egypt was defeated at Asqalon.

No sooner was Jerusalem taken than the great majority of the Crusaders left for Europe by sea. Bohemond had made himself Prince of Antioch and Raymond de Saint Gilles declared himself

Count of Tripoli. Baldwin, the brother of Godfrey, became Count of Edessa, most of his subjects being Armenians. Godfrey was left to defend Jerusalem with only three hundred horsemen and two thousand foot.

Thus, instead of forming one Crusader state, the barons, jealous of one another, had set up four—the Kingdom of Jerusalem, the Counties of Tripoli and Edessa and the Principality of Antioch.

*   *   *

It was fortunate for the Crusaders that the Muslims were even more divided than they were. Malik Shah had died in 1092, leaving four sons, all small children. Each of the boys was supported by a group of warlords and a general civil war broke out immediately. Tutush, the brother of Malik Shah, who had made himself King of Damascus, joined in the mêlée and was killed in Persia in March 1094. His two sons divided Syria between them, Duqaq becoming King of Damascus and Ridhwan King of Aleppo. In Egypt, the government was in the hands of the wazeer, Al Afdhal, the son of the Armenian convert, Bedr al Jamali.

Malik Shah had divided the Seljuq Empire into provinces, ruled by Turkman feudal chiefs, a procedure which changed the nature of the Seljuq armies. The sultans had achieved power as a result of the fighting qualities of the Ghuzz horse-archers. But now the Turkman feudal lords raised armies from the people living on their lands, be they Turks, Arabs, Persians or Kurds.

For twelve years after the death of Malik Shah in 1092, Persia and Iraq were devastated by the Seljuq civil wars. It was during this period, from 1097 to 1099, that the Crusaders established themselves in Syria. Eventually, in January 1105, Malik Shah's second son, Muhammad, became sole ruler of the derelict empire.

The five hundred miles wide Syrian desert divided Jerusalem and Tripoli from the centres of the Seljuq empire in Iraq and Persia. But Antioch and Edessa were engaged in constant hostilities with the Turkish lords of Aleppo, Diyarbekr and Mosul,[4] and their activities drew the attention of the Seljuq Sultan Muhammad. Pressed to act, the sultan appointed Mawdood, his governor of Mosul, to deal with Edessa and Antioch.

Godfrey had died in Jerusalem on 18th July, 1100, and had been succeeded by his brother, Baldwin of Boulogne, as Baldwin I, King of Jerusalem.

4 Map 21, page 162.

8. THE ROYAL HOUSE OF JERUSALEM

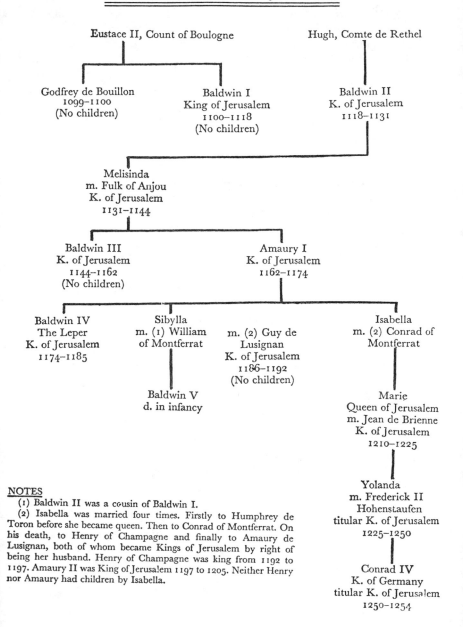

NOTES

(1) Baldwin II was a cousin of Baldwin I.

(2) Isabella was married four times. Firstly to Humphrey de Toron before she became queen. Then to Conrad of Montferrat. On his death, to Henry of Champagne and finally to Amaury de Lusignan, both of whom became Kings of Jerusalem by right of being her husband. Henry of Champagne was king from 1192 to 1197. Amaury II was King of Jerusalem 1197 to 1205. Neither Henry nor Amaury had children by Isabella.

In May 1110, Mawdood laid siege to Edessa, but King Baldwin and the Count of Tripoli arrived and relieved the town. Next year, Mawdood returned with a larger army, and marched to Aleppo, which belonged to Ridhwan ibn Tutush, the nephew of Malik Shah. All the Turkish lords were jealous of one another and Ridhwan closed the gates of Aleppo against Mawdood.

In 1111, Mawdood again invaded Syria and in September reached Shaizar,[5] where he was confronted by King Baldwin I with the combined armies of the Crusader states, sixteen thousand strong. After two weeks of skirmishing, the Muslims withdrew and returned to Mosul. In one of the skirmishes, a Christian knight had single-handed charged a Muslim squadron. His horse being killed, he had defended himself alone on foot until rescued by his comrades.

"Some months later," writes Usama ibn Munqidh, an Arab knight of Shaizar, "we received a letter in Shaizar from the Prince of Antioch, brought by a Frankish knight. The letter said that the knight was shortly returning to his country, but had asked for an introduction to meet some Muslim knights."

"We pressed round the knight," continues Usama, "who was young but disfigured by many scars." He proved to be the man who, single-handed, had charged the army of Mawdood. He was regally entertained by the knights of Shaizar, who, incidentally, were not Turks, but Arabs of Beni Kenana. Usama's memoirs describe many chivalrous acts of this kind between the Muslims and the Crusaders.

In May 1113, Mawdood was back in Syria. Joined by Tughtekeen, the Turkish Lord of Damascus—Duqaq the nephew of Malik Shah was dead—he inflicted a sharp reverse on King Baldwin, south of the Sea of Galilee. In September 1113, however, Mawdood returned to Damascus, where he was assassinated. He was a sincere Muslim and a loyal and simple-minded subject of the sultan. All through the centuries the Turks have periodically produced men of this type, not clever or eloquent (as Arabs are) but simple and devoted to their duty.

In 1115, the sultan sent the Lord of Hamadan, Bursuq ibn Bursuq, to Syria. After taking the Crusader fortress of Kafr Tab, he was completely routed by the army of Antioch at Daneeth.[5] In this campaign, the Muslims of Damascus and Aleppo, anxious to retain their local independence, joined the Crusaders against Bursuq.

In April 1118, the Sultan Muhammad ibn Malik Shah died and

[5] Map 20, page 155.

was succeeded by his eleven-year-old son, Mahmood. During his reign of thirteen years, Muhammad had given West Persia and Iraq a period of relative peace and reconstruction. Persia east of the Salt Desert had been ruled by Sanjar, the sultan's brother. Mosul, the Jezira and Syria had been entrusted to Turkish chiefs who hated one another and rendered only grudging loyalty to the sultan.

King Baldwin I had died in April 1118, the same year as Sultan Muhammad and Alexius Comnenus. He was succeeded by his cousin, Baldwin of Le Bourg, who was crowned Baldwin II. It will be remembered that, when the First Crusade passed through Constantinople, Bohemond had made no objection to swearing allegiance to the Emperor Alexius. The latter claimed that all territory subject to Constantinople before the Battle of Malazkirt in 1071 still belonged to the empire.

The only area in this category conquered by the Crusaders was the province of Antioch. Once Bohemond had made himself Prince of Antioch, however, he rejected all idea of subordination to the Byzantine Empire. Alexius had been greatly incensed against Bohemond and against his nephew, Tancred, who succeeded to the princedom in 1104.

Tancred's perfidy was equalled only by his courage. He had no hesitation in defying the Byzantine Emperor, while at the same time he rejected the claims of suzerainty put forward by the King of Jerusalem and was constantly engaged in attacking his Muslim neighbours.

*   *   *

After the death of Sultan Muhammad in 1118, his four sons became entirely engrossed in civil wars against one another. In East Persia, Sanjar, the only surviving son of Malik Shah, still guarded the eastern frontiers of the empire.

For two hundred years, China had been ruled by the Khitan dynasty. In 1123, however, they were driven out by the Chin Tatars. A member of the fallen dynasty fled westwards and established himself in Turkestan, where he collected about him a number of Turkish tribes. Assuming the title of the Great Khan, he invaded Trans-Oxiana and completely defeated Sanjar at Qutwan, on 12th September, 1141.

For nearly fifty years, Sanjar had ruled East Persia with firmness and justice. He struggled on with unquenchable courage until he died in 1156 at the age of seventy-one. Thereafter East Persia fell

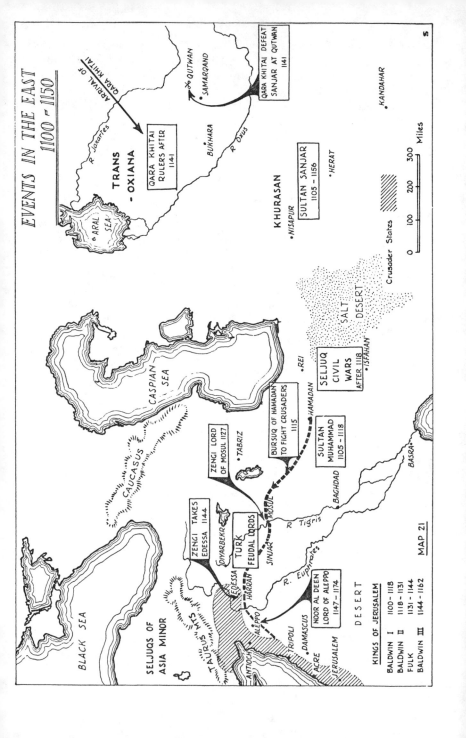

EVENTS IN THE EAST
1100 - 1150

ARRIVAL OF
QARA KHITAI

R. Joxartes

QUTWAN

ARAL
SEA

SAMARQAND

TRANS
- OXIANA

BUKHARA

QARA KHITAI
RULERS AFTER
1141

R. Oxus

QARA KHITAI DEFEAT
SANJAR AT QUTWAN
1141

KHURASAN

KANDAHAR

SULTAN SANJAR
1105 - 1156

•HERAT

•NISAPUR

0   100   200   300
Miles

Crusader States

CASPIAN SEA

SALT
DESERT

•REI

SELJUQ CIVIL
WARS
AFTER 1118

•ISFAHAN

CAUCASUS

SULTAN
MUHAMMAD
1105 - 1118

•TABRIZ

HAMADAN

ZENGI LORD
OF MOSUL 1127

BURSUQ OF HAMADAN
TO FIGHT CRUSADERS
1115

BAGHDAD

BLACK SEA

R. Tigris

BASRA•

ZENGI TAKES
EDESSA 1144

•DIYARBEKR

TURK
FEUDAL LORDS

MOSUL

SINJAR

SELJUQS OF ASIA MINOR

TAURUS MTS.

EDESSA
HARRAN

R. Euphrates

MAP 21

NOOR AL DEEN
LORD OF ALEPPO
1147 - 1174

ANTIOCH

•ALEPPO

DESERT

TRIPOLI

•DAMASCUS

ACRE

JERUSALEM

KINGS OF JERUSALEM

BALDWIN I   1100 - 1118
BALDWIN II   1118 - 1131
FULK   1131 - 1144
BALDWIN III 1144 - 1162

into confusion. The defeat of Sanjar at Qutwan was the first great reverse suffered by Islam in the East. Thereafter, centuries of bloodshed, invasion, massacre, rape and destruction lay before her. The new conquerors called themselves the Qara Khitai. Half Buddhist and half heathen, they annexed Trans-Oxiana, the population of which was Muslim.

Western historians have devoted almost all their labours to the Crusades, which they have termed the Great Debate or the World Conflict. In fact, however, the crumbling of the eastern bulwarks of Islam before the savage nomads of the steppes was to prove both more important and more disastrous than the Crusades. For in the twelfth century Islam, the cousin of Christianity, included the most civilized nations in the world. Thereafter, for five hundred years, Turks and Mongols were to lay waste the Middle East and eastern Europe alike.

*   *   *

The year 1118 had witnessed three royal deaths, Alexius Comnenus, Baldwin I of Jerusalem and Sultan Muhammad, the last of the great Seljuqs of the senior or Persian branch. There were now four contestants on the borders of Syria and Palestine. John Comnenus followed his father Alexius as Byzantine Emperor. The second group were the Turkish warlords of Syria and the Jezira— Damascus, Aleppo, Diyarbekr and Mosul—who rarely co-operated. Thirdly, the rulers of the four Crusader states who, since the death of the aggressive Tancred, had recognized the leadership of Jerusalem in war.

The fourth power in the field was Egypt, which, in 1118, was ruled by the wazeer Al Afdhal, who, however, was assassinated in 1121. Thereafter Egypt experienced a period of weakness and instability. For fifty years, the Fatimid Khalifs had left the task of government to their wazeers. After the murder of Al Afdhal, the Khalif Aamir attempted to resume authority but was himself assassinated in 1130. His successor, Hafidh,[6] lived in seclusion while rival politicians and army commanders struggled for power in a succession of *coups d'état*. This weakness of Egypt relieved the Crusaders of any anxiety on their southern frontier.

Baldwin II, who had married an Armenian, had three daughters but no son.[7] Accordingly, in 1128, the Grand Council in Jerusalem wrote to Louis VI, King of France, asking him to nominate an heir to the throne. Louis sent Fulk, Count of Anjou, who landed at Acre

[6] Genealogical tree 7, page 143.   [7] Genealogical tree 8, page 159.

in 1129 and married Baldwin's eldest daughter, Melisinda. On 21st August, 1131, Baldwin II died and Fulk became king.

Meanwhile, in 1127, a Turkish commander called Zengi had become Lord of Mosul. He immediately seized Nisibin, Sinjar and Harran and then Aleppo. A new and commanding personality had appeared in the field.

It will be remembered that the Byzantine Emperors laid claim to Antioch, as having belonged to them before the Battle of Malazkirt. On 29th August, 1137, John Comnenus appeared with an army beneath the walls. The ruling prince, Raymond of Poitiers,[8] was obliged to acknowledge his suzerainty. The emperor then laid siege to Shaizar but withdrew on payment of an indemnity and a promise of tribute. Zengi, manœuvring in the vicinity, was too weak to offer battle to the emperor. When the Byzantine army left Syria, Zengi endeavoured to seize Damascus, whereupon the city concluded an alliance with Jerusalem.

John Comnenus died in 1143 and Fulk of Jerusalem in 1144. Fulk's twelve-year-old son was crowned King of Jerusalem as Baldwin III. By a previous marriage in France, Fulk had had a son called Geoffrey Plantagenet, who was the father of Henry II, King of England. Thus the royal family of Jerusalem were cousins of the Kings of England.

In the spring of 1144, Zengi's position had been immensely strengthened by the deaths of his two principal enemies, John Comnenus and Fulk of Jerusalem. Zengi's headquarters were in Mosul and the Crusader County of Edessa seemed to threaten his communications with Aleppo. On Christmas Eve, 1144, by a surprise attack, he seized the city of Edessa and that portion of the county which lay east of the Euphrates. He did not long survive his triumph but was assassinated by his own servants on 14th September, 1146.

The loss of Edessa was the first major disaster suffered by the Crusaders, one of their four states being virtually eliminated. The only form of government known to the Franks was the feudal system, under which troops were paid with grants of land. The alleged greed shown by them to acquire estates in the East was due to the fact that land was the only means of maintaining an army. The loss of half the county of Edessa meant a reduction of their military forces by about one-fifth.

[8] Raymond had become Prince of Antioch by marrying the heiress, Constance, the granddaughter of Bohemond I.

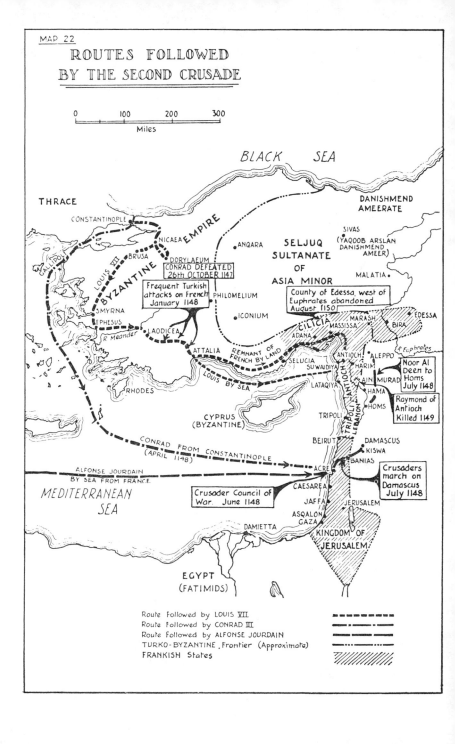

MAP 22

ROUTES FOLLOWED
BY THE SECOND CRUSADE

0   100   200   300
Miles

BLACK SEA

THRACE

DANISHMEND
AMEERATE

CONSTANTINOPLE

NICAEA EMPIRE

GALLIPOLI

BRUSA

BYZANTINE

DORYLAEUM
CONRAD DEFEATED
26th OCTOBER 1147

ANQARA

SIVAS
(YAQOOB ARSLAN
DANISHMEND
AMEER)

SELJUQ
SULTANATE
OF
ASIA MINOR

MALATIA

SMYRNA

EPHESUS

R. Meander

Frequent Turkish
attacks on French
January 1148

PHILOMELIUM

LAODICEA

ICONIUM

County of Edessa, west of
Euphrates abandoned
August 1150

CILICIA

MARASH

EDESSA

MASSISSA

BIRA

ADANA

R. Euphrates

RHODES

ATTALIA

REMNANT OF
FRENCH BY LAND

SELUCIA

ANTIOCH

ALEPPO

SUWAIDIYA

HARIM

Noor Al
Deen to
Homs
July 1148

LOUIS BY SEA

LATAQIYA

AIN
MURAD

HAMA

Raymond of
Antioch
Killed 1149

HOMS

CYPRUS
(BYZANTINE)

TRIPOLI

BEIRUT

DAMASCUS

CONRAD FROM CONSTANTINOPLE
(APRIL 1148)

KISWA

BANIAS

ACRE

Crusaders
march on
Damascus
July 1148

ALFONSE JOURDAIN
BY SEA FROM FRANCE.

MEDITERRANEAN
SEA

CAESAREA

Crusader Council of
War. June 1148

JAFFA

JERUSALEM

DAMIETTA

ASQALON
GAZA

KINGDOM OF
JERUSALEM

EGYPT
(FATIMIDS)

Route Followed by LOUIS VII
Route Followed by CONRAD III
Route Followed by ALFONSE JOURDAIN
TURKO-BYZANTINE Frontier (Approximate)
FRANKISH States

The fall of Edessa produced a deep impression in the West. Louis VII, King of France, and Conrad III Hohenstaufen, King of Germany, both took the cross. Conrad reached Constantinople on 10th September, 1147, and, without waiting for the French, crossed to Asia Minor and continued his march. On 25th October, however, he was completely defeated by Masood, the Seljuq Sultan of Iconium, and arrived back a fugitive at Nicaea, where Louis VII had meanwhile arrived.

Warned by Conrad's disaster, Louis followed the coast through Smyrna and Ephesus, reaching Antioch on 19th March, 1148, after losing most of his infantry on the way. After a bitter quarrel with Raymond of Poitiers, Prince of Antioch, he continued his route, reaching Jerusalem in May 1148, to find that Conrad had already landed in Palestine, having come by sea from Constantinople. Meanwhile a further contingent had arrived from France under Alfonse Jourdain, Count of Toulouse. On 24th June, 1148, a council of war was held in Acre.

When Zengi was murdered in 1146, his eldest son, Saif al Deen Ghazi, had become King of Mosul, while the second, Noor al Deen Mahmood, had made himself King of Aleppo. The strategic situation was perfectly plain. The Crusaders had held their own for fifty years because the various Turkish warlords were at enmity with one another. If, however, the Muslims of Syria and the Jezira were to unite, the Franks would be outnumbered. This had hitherto been avoided because the ruler of Damascus was an ally of the King of Jerusalem.

The only potential leader who might unite all the Muslims was Noor al Deen of Aleppo and the obvious necessity was therefore to eliminate him. Instead of doing so, Louis and Conrad decided to attack Damascus, the only Muslim ally of the Franks. On 24th July, 1148, the Crusader army reached Damascus and nearly took the city in a surprise assault. On 28th July, they abandoned the enterprise and retreated to Acre, suffering heavy losses. As they had no siege train with them, they could not besiege Damascus and their only chance had been to take the city in a sudden unexpected attack.

Such folly and inefficiency seem almost incredible, but in fact no European mediaeval army had an organization capable of fighting a war overseas, nearly a year's march from home. Moreover, without maps a strategic plan is difficult to produce.

From the Frankish point of view, the worst aspect of the débâcle was that it led to bitter recriminations between the French and German crusaders on the one hand and the Franks of the Holy Land on the other. Thereafter, the West was to disassociate itself from the Crusader states for forty years. When eventually another crusade landed in Palestine, Jerusalem had already been lost.

NOTABLE DATES

Death of Malik Shah	1092
Urban II preaches the First Crusade	1095
Arrival of Godfrey de Bouillon in Constantinople	23rd December, 1096
Battle of Dorylaeum	1st July, 1097
Capture of Antioch	3rd June, 1098
Capture of Jerusalem	15th July, 1099
Seljuq civil war in Persia	1092–1105
Death of Alexius Comnenus, Baldwin I and Sultan Muhammad	1118
Campaign of John Comnenus in Syria	1137–1138
Defeat of Sultan Sanjar at Qutwan	12th September, 1141
Death of John Comnenus	1143
Death of Fulk of Jerusalem	1144
Capture of Edessa by Zengi	1144
Assassination of Zengi	1146
Fiasco of the Second Crusade	1148

PERSONALITIES

Byzantine Emperors

Alexius Comnenus	1081–1118
John Comnenus	1118–1143

Crusaders

Godfrey de Bouillon
Robert of Normandy
Raymond de Saint Gilles ⎫ Leaders of the First Crusade
Bohemond of Apulia ⎭

Louis VII, King of France
Conrad III Hohenstaufen ⎫ Leaders of the Second
Baldwin III, King of Jerusalem ⎭ Crusade

Kings of Jerusalem

Godfrey de Bouillon	1099–1100
Baldwin I, brother of Godfrey	1100–1118
Baldwin II, cousin of Godfrey	1118–1131
Fulk of Anjou (married Melisinda)	1131–1144
Baldwin III, son of Fulk	1144–1162

Seljuq Sultans of Persia

Malik Shah	1072–1092
Period of civil wars	1092–1105
Muhammad, son of Malik Shah	1105–1118

Seljuqs of Asia Minor

Sulaiman ibn Qutlumish	1077–1086
Qilij Arslan I, his son	1092–1107
Malik Shah I, son of Qilij Arslan I	1107–1116
Masood, brother of Malik Shah I	1116–1156
Qilij Arslan II, son of Masood	1156–1188

Other personalities

Zengi, Lord of Mosul	1127–1146
Noor al Deen Mahmood, his son	1146–1174

Bedr al Jamali
Al Afdhal, his son } Wazeers of Egypt

XII

The Fall of the Kingdom

FROM their capture of Jerusalem in 1099 until the débâcle of, the Second Crusade in 1148, the Franks of Outremer[1] had relied for support on western Europe, especially France. The Muslims, moreover, had feared to press their attacks for fear of provoking a new Crusade. Now that the Crusade had come and ended in disaster, they felt that they had nothing more to fear.

Left to their own devices, the Crusaders in 1150 abandoned the remnant of the county of Edessa, west of the Euphrates. The Frankish states were thereby reduced to three—Jerusalem, Tripoli and Antioch. Damascus, the Crusaders' only ally, had been alienated by the Second Crusade and, in 1154, was occupied by Noor al Deen, who thereby united under his command the Muslims of Syria and the Jezira.

Meanwhile, on 29th June, 1149, Raymond of Poitiers, Prince of Antioch, had been killed in battle at Ain Murad, near Afamiya, leaving a widow, Constance of Antioch, twenty-two years old, and an infant son, Bohemond III. The re-marriage of Constance to an experienced soldier and statesman might have saved the situation. Rejecting the suit of a near relative of the Byzantine Emperor, however, she fell in love with and married a penniless young knight newly come from France called Renaud de Châtillon.

The new Prince of Antioch was handsome, brave, reckless and completely unscrupulous and was to play a leading part in the destruction of the Crusader states. Although Noor al Deen's border posts were only twenty-five miles from Antioch, Renaud began his career by brutally plundering the Byzantine island of Cyprus.

Deprived of all hope of aid from the West, the youthful Baldwin III, King of Jerusalem, with a wisdom beyond his years, decided to draw nearer to the Byzantines and sent the Constable of the Kingdom of Jerusalem, Humphrey de Toron, to Constantinople. He returned bringing with him the emperor's niece, Theodora Comnena.

[1] Outremer—literally overseas—was the term applied to all Crusader states collectively.

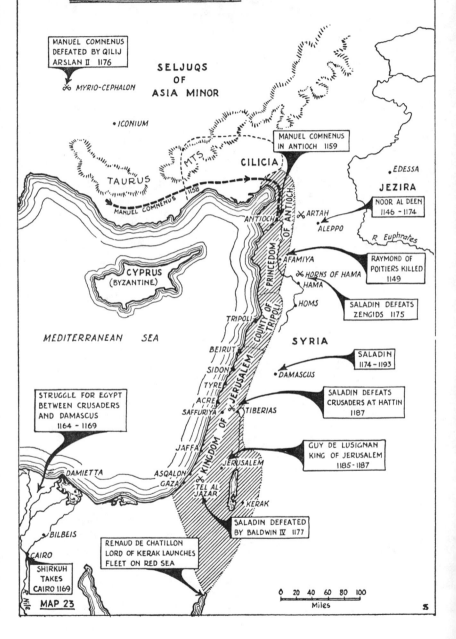

THE CRUSADER STATES
1150 ~ 1187

MANUEL COMNENUS DEFEATED BY QILIJ ARSLAN II 1176

✗ MYRIO-CEPHALON

SELJUQS OF ASIA MINOR

• ICONIUM

TAURUS MTS.

CILICIA

MANUEL COMNENUS 1158

MANUEL COMNENUS IN ANTIOCH 1159

• EDESSA

JEZIRA

NOOR AL DEEN 1146 - 1174

ANTIOCH ✗ ARTAH

• ALEPPO

R. Euphrates

PRINCEDOM OF ANTIOCH

CYPRUS (BYZANTINE)

• AFAMIYA

✗ HORNS OF HAMA

• HAMA

RAYMOND OF POITIERS KILLED 1149

• HOMS

COUNTY OF TRIPOLI

TRIPOLI

SALADIN DEFEATS ZENGIDS 1175

MEDITERRANEAN SEA

BEIRUT

SIDON

TYRE

ACRE

SAFFURIYA •

SYRIA

• DAMASCUS

SALADIN 1174 - 1193

SALADIN DEFEATS CRUSADERS AT HATTIN 1187

✗ TIBERIAS

STRUGGLE FOR EGYPT BETWEEN CRUSADERS AND DAMASCUS 1164 - 1169

KINGDOM OF JERUSALEM

JAFFA

GUY DE LUSIGNAN KING OF JERUSALEM 1185 - 1187

• DAMIETTA

ASQALON GAZA

JERUSALEM

✗ TEL AL JAZAR

• KERAK

SALADIN DEFEATED BY BALDWIN IV 1177

• BILBEIS

CAIRO

SHIRKUH TAKES CAIRO 1169

RENAUD DE CHATILLON LORD OF KERAK LAUNCHES FLEET ON RED SEA

MAP 23

0 20 40 60 80 100

Miles

Baldwin III was twenty-seven and Theodora was only thirteen but already a famous beauty with a fresh pink complexion and a mass of golden hair. Both fell deeply in love and they were married in September 1158.

In October 1158, the Byzantine Emperor, Manuel Comnenus, arrived in Cilicia with a great army. Renaud de Châtillon was obliged to appear barefoot and prostrate himself in the dust before the emperor, to atone for his wanton attack on Cyprus. On 12th April, 1159, the Emperor Manuel, clad in his purple imperial mantle, covered with gold, pearls and precious stones, made a triumphal entry into Antioch, the city which, ever since its seizure by Bohemond of Apulia, had formed a bone of contention between Byzantium and the Crusader states.

Friction had constantly occurred between the Franks and the Byzantines but, in 1159, the growing power of Noor al Deen obliged the former to welcome Manuel Comnenus to Antioch. In May 1159, the combined army marched on Aleppo but, when only twenty-five miles from the city, was met by a deputation from Noor al Deen begging for peace. To the intense indignation of the Crusaders, Manuel immediately agreed, without even consulting his allies.

The astute emperor was perfectly aware that the Franks had only admitted his suzerainty over Antioch out of fear of Noor al Deen and that, if the latter were eliminated, they would once more reject his claims. Nevertheless it is impossible entirely to acquit Manuel of deliberately deceiving his new allies, who he must have known were confidently relying on his armed support. These misunderstandings were to produce disastrous results for the Franks and the Byzantines alike.

The idea of a world government is by no means a modern novelty. Roman Emperors had been inspired by it, in spite of the fact that contemporary Parthian or Persian kings had often been stronger than they were. The early Arab conquerors had confidently anticipated that the khalifs would rule the whole world. Some of this mystique inspired Manuel Comnenus, who seemed to be steadily extending his influence to east and west.

In November 1160, Renaud de Châtillon attempted to raid the flocks of some Armenians with whom he was at peace, but was intercepted by a Muslim force and imprisoned in Aleppo. On 10th February, 1162, Baldwin III, King of Jerusalem, died in Beirut at the age of only thirty-three. Courteous, cultured, wise and brave, he might, if he had lived to old age, have done much to stabilize the precarious Crusader states. He was succeeded on the throne by his brother Amaury,[2] who was twenty-seven years old. With a handsome face and fair hair, he was well-read, particularly in history and law. Unlike the rude warriors of the First Crusade, the Franks of the East had absorbed something of Arab culture and refinement and at times felt more at home with their Muslim neighbours or with the Byzantines than with their rough cousins from north-western Europe.

*   *   *

We left Egypt in 1130, when the Fatimid Khalif Hafidh[3] came to the throne, though deprived of all power. In 1149, he was succeeded by his son Dhafir, who, however, was murdered in April 1154 by his own wazeer, Abbas ibn Temeem. Dhafir's five-year-old son Faiz was proclaimed khalif but the governor of upper Egypt, Talaia ibn Ruzzik, marched on Cairo and made himself wazeer. (This was in the same year that Noor al Deen took Damascus.)

In 1160, the child Khalif Faiz died and was replaced by his cousin Aadhid, a boy of nine. In September 1161, however, the wazeer, Ibn Ruzzik, was assassinated. His son succeeded him but, in December 1162, in a *coup d'état*, Shawar al Saadi seized power. In August 1163, in another military *coup d'état*, Shawar was replaced by Dhirgham al Lakhmi. Caught in this endless succession of revolts, the Egyptian government was in complete confusion. "Scarcely anyone became wazeer of Egypt, except by war, murder or similar means," wrote Ibn al Athir, the Arab historian of the time.

In Syria and Palestine, the Muslims and the Franks were nearly evenly balanced. Egypt was still immensely rich but almost defenceless. If either side were to seize Egypt, it would be able easily to outmatch its rival.

In October 1163, Shawar, the evicted Egyptian wazeer, appealed to Noor al Deen to reinstate him, promising to pay the cost of the campaign. As a result, in April 1164, a column left Damascus commanded by an old Kurdish mercenary officer called Shirkuh, whom Noor al Deen trusted. Shirkuh took with him his nephew Salah al Deen, better known to us as Saladin. Dhirgham was killed and Shawar reinstated. But the Egyptians had no desire for a permanent Turkish occupation and Shawar wrote secretly to invite

---

[2] Amaury is sometimes written Amalric. Genealogical tree 8, page 159.
[3] Genealogical tree 7, page 143.

King Amaury to come and drive Shirkuh out. The Crusaders besieged Shirkuh in Bilbeis, whereupon Noor al Deen created a diversion by attacking and defeating Bohemond III of Antioch at Artah.[4] Eventually Amaury agreed with Shirkuh that both evacuate Egypt.

In January 1167, however, Shirkuh returned to Egypt, whereupon Shawar immediately appealed to Amaury, who left Asqalon with his army on 30th January, 1167. After seven months of campaigning up and down the Nile, Amaury and Shirkuh again agreed to evacuate Egypt. While the terms of the agreement were being executed, Saladin, Shirkuh's nephew, stayed in the Crusader camp and, it is alleged, was knighted by Humphrey de Toron, the Constable. Amaury made arrangements to transport the Muslim wounded in Christian ships to Jaffa.

For the moment, the Franks were popular in Egypt, having saved the country from the Turks. A year later, however, the Grand Council in Jerusalem decided to invade Egypt on its own account, in spite of the king's opposition. Shawar immediately appealed to Noor al Deen, who, this time, sent an army of overwhelming strength. On the previous campaign the Franks had been welcomed as the saviours of Egypt from the Turks. Now Shirkuh was hailed as the protector of the country against the Franks. Shirkuh's army was far too strong for Amaury and was supported by the Egyptians. The Crusaders withdrew and, on 8th January, 1169, Shirkuh entered Cairo in triumph.

Shawar was now anxious only to get rid of the Damascus army, but on 19th January, 1169, when on a visit to Shirkuh, he was seized by Saladin and executed. The young Fatimid Khalif Aadhid found himself defenceless and was obliged to recognize Shirkuh as his wazeer. Shirkuh was sixty years old. A Kurdish mercenary, short, fat, one-eyed and ugly, devotedly loyal to Noor al Deen, he was a splendid fighter and a voracious eater. On 23rd March, 1169, he suddenly died of colic.

After a few tense days of intrigue, Saladin secured control and was appointed wazeer by the Fatimid Khalif, in spite of the opposition of various Turkish officers in the Damascus army. Many Western historians, by calling all Muslims indiscriminately Saracens, have missed the stresses and strains which complicated the situation. Saladin was a Kurd, and the Turks and Kurds eyed one another jealously.

[4] Map 23, page 170.

The supporters of the Fatimids were indignant at the seizure of power by the Turks, who were Sunnis. Saladin, however, replaced all the officials in the khalif's entourage by his own nominees. In August 1169, the Fatimid troops—Sudanese and Armenian mercenaries—were destroyed. Saladin was now in complete control, but was careful to carry out all his actions in the name of Noor al Deen.

On 10th September, 1171, on orders from Noor al Deen, the Fatimid Khalifate was abolished and prayers were read in the name of the Abbasid Khalif in Baghdad. Aadhid, the last Fatimid Khalif, died or was murdered three days later.

Saladin was now virtually King of Egypt and seized the immense accumulated wealth of the Fatimids. Meanwhile, however, his master Noor al Deen was growing jealous and threatened to march on Egypt in person, but, on 15th May, 1174, he died suddenly in Damascus, leaving an eleven-year-old son, Malik al Salih Ismail. Two months later, on 11th July, 1174, King Amaury died also, leaving as heir his nephew, Baldwin IV, who was only thirteen years old. Noor al Deen and Amaury, the two figures dominating the political scene, had both died suddenly, leaving Saladin almost without a competitor.

Marching into Syria, he occupied Damascus on 26th November, 1174. He then took the offensive against the son of his former sovereign, and defeated the Zengids at the Horns of Hama, on 23rd April, 1175. Although Saladin was later to become a Muslim hero, his contemporaries criticized his rebellion against the infant son of his former master.

While Saladin was making himself sole ruler of Syria and Egypt, the Byzantine Emperor Manuel Comnenus suffered a crushing defeat. On 17th September, 1176, at Myrio-cephalon in Asia Minor,[5] the Byzantine army was virtually exterminated by the Seljuq Sultan of Iconium, Qilij Arslan II. Crushed by this disaster, Manuel died four years later, and the Crusaders were deprived of their last external support.

Baldwin IV, the young King of Jerusalem, a handsome and intelligent youth, inflicted a severe defeat on Saladin at Tel al Jazar on 25th November, 1177. But meanwhile, the young king had become a leper. To supply an heir to the throne, William of Montferrat was invited to come from Europe to marry Baldwin's sister, Sibylla, but he died within three months of landing in Palestine.

[5] Map 23, page 170.

In 1180, however, Sibylla declared her intention to marry a young knight newly arrived from France called Guy de Lusignan. Baldwin protested but he was already dying of leprosy, and the young couple were married at Easter 1180. The kingdom was thereby divided into two hostile factions, Guy and Sibylla, the Templars and the knights newly come from France, on the one hand, and the dying Baldwin IV with the native Crusader barons, on the other.

Early in 1185, Baldwin summoned a council to his bedside and declared his heir to be Baldwin V, a posthumous child of William of Montferrat, Sibylla's first husband.[6] The regent during his minority was to be Raymond III, Count of Tripoli. Guy was specifically excluded from the regency and the throne.

In March 1185, the little leper king, already paralysed and blind, was released from his misery. The child Baldwin V succeeded, with Raymond of Tripoli as regent, but, in August 1186, Baldwin V died. Guy immediately secured his own coronation, contrary to the will of Baldwin IV. Weak and frivolous, he soon showed himself incapable of ruling. Renaud de Châtillon, the former bandit Prince of Antioch, had been released from prison in Aleppo and had married the heiress of Kerak. Although a truce had been concluded with Saladin, Renaud launched a fleet of pirate ships on the Red Sea and persisted in plundering Muslim caravans, regardless of the expostulations of King Guy.

Saladin, who was still engaged in periodical hostilities in the Jezira and was anxious to extend his empire to the east, would have been willing to prolong his truce with the Crusaders, had it not been for the outrages committed by Renaud. On 30th June, 1187, Saladin in exasperation crossed the frontier and laid siege to Tiberias.

The Crusaders concentrated at Saffuriya under King Guy. The Templars, Renaud de Châtillon and the knights recently come from France demanded an immediate advance. Raymond of Tripoli and the barons born in the Holy Land pointed out that fifteen miles of bare waterless hills lay between Saffuriya and Tiberias—a distance too great for the infantry to cross beneath the blazing July sun. The council broke up after deciding to remain at Saffuriya. But Gerard de Ridefort, Grand Master of the Templars, returned alone to Guy's tent and persuaded the weak king to order the army to march against Saladin.

All day of 3rd July, 1187, the army plodded over the dusty hills.

[6] Genealogical tree 8, page 159.

In the evening, when it reached Lubiya, the infantry were worn out and mad with thirst. At dawn on 4th July, the Muslims set fire to the dry grass and the flames and smoke blew into the faces of the thirsty Franks. The exhausted infantry were soon overrun, but the knights fought on at Hattin till the afternoon, when the men responsible for the disaster—King Guy, Gerard de Ridefort and Renaud de Châtillon—were taken prisoners. The faithless Renaud was immediately hacked to pieces by Saladin.

Ever since Godfrey de Bouillon had been left in Jerusalem in 1099 with only two thousand three hundred men, the Crusaders had been short of man-power. When the Muslims invaded the Crusader states in strength, the Franks were obliged to mobilize every available man, leaving the countryside, the cities and the castles completely denuded. Realizing that, if they lost their army, it could never be replaced by another, they normally avoided a pitched battle, relying on manœuvre and skirmishing, until the advent of winter compelled the Muslims to withdraw.

Perhaps the new knights from France had not grasped the principle of such Fabian strategy. At Hattin, not only was the field army destroyed, but the countryside, the cities and castles were left without defenders. Saladin, aware of the possibility of a new Crusade from the west, set out immediately to reduce the defended cities.

Acre surrendered without resistance. Saladin failed to take Tyre, but quickly captured Sidon and Beirut. On 20th September, 1187, he laid siege to Jerusalem. The city surrendered on 2nd October, fourteen thousand Christians, mostly women and children, being driven away as slaves. A lesser number were allowed to ransom themselves for cash.

Meanwhile Conrad of Montferrat, brother of that William of Montferrat the first husband of Sibylla, had landed at Tyre and resolutely defended the fortress. Throughout 1188, Saladin continued to reduce, one after another, the Crusader castles and cities. Not until 21st March, 1189, did he return to Damascus for a rest.

*   *   *

The news of the fall of Jerusalem evoked profound emotion in the West. The German Emperor, Frederick Barbarossa, Philippe Auguste, King of France, and Richard I, King of England, all took the cross. Barbarossa, however, was drowned in Cilicia and never reached the Holy Land.

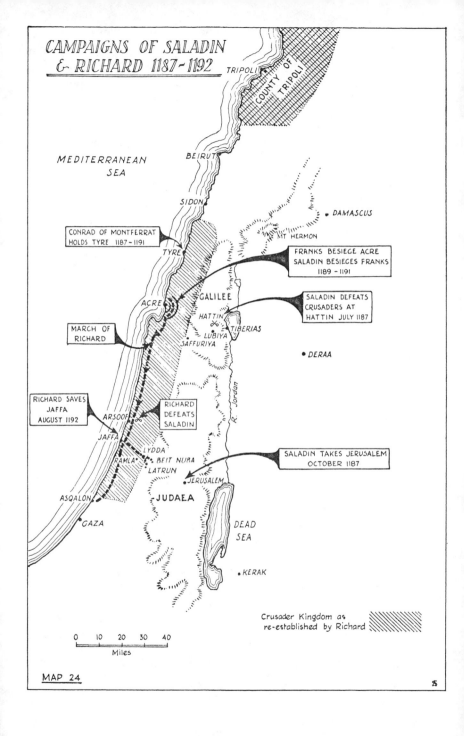

CAMPAIGNS OF SALADIN
& RICHARD 1187-1192

TRIPOLI

COUNTY OF TRIPOLI

MEDITERRANEAN
SEA

BEIRUT

SIDON

• DAMASCUS

MT HERMON

CONRAD OF MONTFERRAT
HOLDS TYRE 1187-1191

TYRE

FRANKS BESIEGE ACRE
SALADIN BESIEGES FRANKS
1189-1191

ACRE

GALILEE

SALADIN DEFEATS
CRUSADERS AT
HATTIN JULY 1187

HATTIN

TIBERIAS

MARCH OF
RICHARD

LUBIYA

SAFFURIYA

• DERAA

R. Jordan

RICHARD SAVES
JAFFA
AUGUST 1192

ARSOOF

RICHARD
DEFEATS
SALADIN

JAFFA

LYDDA

RAMLA

• BEIT NUBA

LATRUN

SALADIN TAKES JERUSALEM
OCTOBER 1187

• JERUSALEM

ASQALON

JUDAEA

• GAZA

DEAD
SEA

• KERAK

Crusader Kingdom as
re-established by Richard

0   10   20   30   40
Miles

MAP 24

Meanwhile, Saladin had released Guy de Lusignan, who had sworn not to fight the Muslims again. In spite of his oath, however, this hitherto vacilllating character now took a desperate resolution. With a few hundred men, he set out to recapture Acre. He just had time to dig himself in on a mound east of the town when Saladin arrived and attacked him, but was repulsed. A few days later, on 1st September, 1189, a fleet arrived bringing ten thousand men, mostly from Flanders and Denmark.

The Franks now besieged Acre, while Saladin took up a position besieging the Franks. Both sides dug themselves in and the winter 1189–1190 was spent in trench warfare. The summer of 1190 dragged on in the same manner, amid heat, flies, dv t, disease, and the stench of unburied corpses, to be followed by yet a second winter of trench warfare amid seas of mud.

On 20th April, 1191, Philippe Auguste, King of France, landed outside Acre and, on 8th June, Richard Cœur de Lion. Finally on 11th July, 1191, Acre surrendered after a siege of nearly two years. The King of France re-embarked on 1st August to return home and Richard, King of England, was left in command. On 25th August, the Crusader army marched southwards down the coast, Saladin and his army keeping level with it and a few miles inland. The Franks marched in close order under constant harassing attacks by Turkman horse-archers and sniping by Arab bedouins, gaunt, nimble men who dodged from rock to rock and tree to tree to shoot at the marching column.

On 7th September, 1191, Saladin, having received large reinforcements of Turkmans, decided to give battle at Arsoof. To the sound of trumpets and rolls of drums, clouds of horse-archers poured down at full gallop on the Frankish column. Richard however, was in his element in battle. The knights charged, swept the light Turkish cavalry from the field and gained a complete victory.

Saladin was deeply distressed, having hoped to win a second Hattin. Afraid to face Richard again in open battle, he adopted a scorched earth policy and destroyed Lydda, Ramla and Asqalon. The Franks reached Jaffa on 10th September. On 8th December, they advanced to Latrun on the road to Jerusalem. The rains, however, had now come and the campaign was postponed.

On 11th June, 1192, the Crusaders again camped at Latrun and Beit Nuba, Saladin being on the Judaean mountains outside Jerusalem. The proposal to climb the mountains and attack Saladin bore a sinister likeness to the campaign of Hattin. Richard would have had to climb the rocky Judaean hills two thousand six hundred feet high. There was no water on the way up or on the plateau above, except behind the army of Saladin. The Crusaders, as at Hattin, would have arrived thirsty and exhausted to face Saladin's army rested and with the water behind them. On 4th July, 1192, Richard withdrew to Ramla.

The coastal plain had been reconquered from Tyre to Asqalon but the Muslims still held Beirut, which divided the southern Crusader territory from Tripoli and Antioch in the north. Richard decided to join up the Crusader states by taking Beirut before he sailed for England. No sooner had he marched away to the north than Saladin, on 27th July, 1192, threw himself on Jaffa with his whole army. Richard had reached Acre when he heard of the attack on Jaffa. Hastily embarking in some galleys with a few men, he arrived off Jaffa on 1st August to find that the town had been captured by the Muslims who were attacking the citadel.

Richard jumped overboard, waded up the beach and drove the surprised Muslims from the town. Then emerging from the gates, he captured Saladin's camp and obliged him to take to flight. On 5th August, the Muslims returned to the attack. Richard had only a few hundred men, drawn up in a solid formation which the Turkmans were unable to break. When their attacks petered out, Richard rode out single-handed and defied the whole Muslim army, but no man dared to take up the challenge. When the battle was over, Saladin sent the king a present of fresh fruit and cold drinks, chilled with snow brought from Mount Hermon.

Peace was signed on 3rd September, 1192. The Third Crusade did not recapture Jerusalem. When it began, however, the Kingdom of Jerusalem consisted only of the fortress of Tyre. When it ended, the whole coastal plain had been recovered as far south as Asqalon, and was to endure for another hundred years.

Courteous and chivalrous relations had been established between Saladin and Richard. As a boy, the latter had been brought up in Aquitaine, in the south of France, where, as we shall see in a later chapter, the influence of Arab culture had been strong. The ease of Richard's relationships with Saladin was doubtless largely due to the growing extension of Arab manners in Western Europe. In the same manner today, a Syrian or Iraqi diplomat would mingle easily with Americans in the United States, if he had been educated in the American University of Beirut.

NOTABLE DATES

Débâcle of the Second Crusade	1148
Succession of *coups d'état* in Egypt	1149–1163
Death of Baldwin III	1162
First struggle for Egypt between Shirkuh and King Amaury	1164
Second struggle between Shirkuh and Amaury	1167
Final conquest of Egypt by Shirkuh	1169
Death of Shirkuh ⎫ Saladin seizes Egypt ⎬	1169
Death of Noor al Deen and Amaury	1174
Seizure of Syria by Saladin	1175
Defeat of Manuel at Myrio-cephalon	1176
Death of Baldwin IV, the Leper	1185
Battle of Hattin ⎫ Fall of Jerusalem ⎬	1187
Siege of Acre	1189–1191
Crusade of King Richard	1191–1192

PERSONALITIES

Kings of Jerusalem

Baldwin III, son of Fulk	1144–1162
Amaury I, his brother	1162–1174
Baldwin IV, the Leper	1174–1185
Baldwin V, died in infancy	1185–1186
Guy de Lusignan	1186–1192

Crusaders

Philippe Auguste, King of France
Richard Cœur de Lion

Muslims

Noor al Deen Mahmood, son of Zengi, Sultan of Syria	1146–1174

Shirkuh, Kurdish mercenary of Noor al Deen
Saladin al Ayoubi, nephew of Shirkuh, Sultan of Syria and Egypt
Aadhid, the last Fatimid Khalif of Egypt

Byzantine Emperors

John Comnenus	1118–1143
Manuel, son of John	1143–1180

XIII

A Berber Empire

IN November 1192, when Richard had sailed for home, Saladin made a state entry into Damascus. He was now the ruler of a great empire, extending from Barqa in North Africa to Mosul and Erbil in Kurdistan. The contemporary Arab historian, Ibn al Athir, states that he was considering the extension of his territory to Iraq and Persia. But on 3rd March, 1193, he died in Damascus at the age of fifty-seven.

Saladin had enjoyed great prestige since his victory of Hattin but he was also loved. He was devoid of arrogance, extremely hospitable and generous and left no money or estates. He was sincerely religious and was always sympathetic to the common people and the poor. He was not a conspicuously great soldier but owed his fame and his power to his wisdom, his patience and the attraction of his personality.

He was, however, no milk and water sentimentalist. He had himself killed Shawar, the Egyptian wazeer, and had gained power in Egypt by massacring, torturing and blinding the supporters of the Fatimids. He matured and became more benign with age, but at the siege of Acre he frequently gave orders for Frankish prisoners-of-war to be killed in cold blood. He became famous in the West for his chivalrous gestures, such as sending presents of fruit to Richard after a battle. When, after Hattin, he captured the Countess of Tripoli in Tiberias, he courteously sent her to rejoin her relatives in Tyre with a suitable escort.

Saladin's *beaux gestes* were learnt, his biographer tells us, from the study of the history of the early Arabs. It is essential to appreciate that the primitive Arab virtues of courage, chivalry, generosity and hospitality had been largely lost in the twelfth century, ownig to the transfer of power to the Turks. As a result, his biographer states, Saladin's chivalrous gestures drew surprise in Syria. When people asked whence he had derived such ideas, it had to be explained to them that these were Arab customs.

9. THE AYOUBIDS
THE FAMILY OF SALADIN

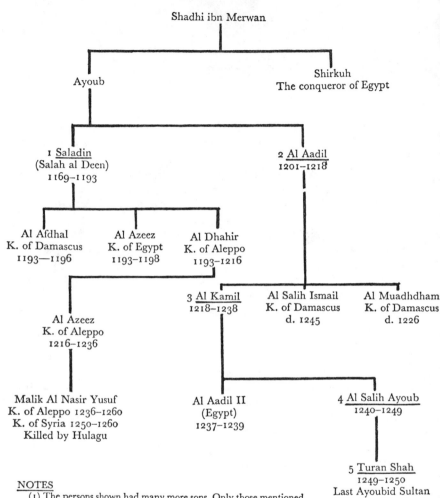

Shadhi ibn Merwan

Ayoub

Shirkuh
The conqueror of Egypt

1 Saladin
(Salah al Deen)
1169–1193

2 Al Aadil
1201–1218

Al Afdhal
K. of Damascus
1193—1196

Al Azeez
K. of Egypt
1193–1198

Al Dhahir
K. of Aleppo
1193–1216

3 Al Kamil
1218–1238

Al Salih Ismail
K. of Damascus
d. 1245

Al Muadhdham
K. of Damascus
d. 1226

Al Azeez
K. of Aleppo
1216–1236

Malik Al Nasir Yusuf
K. of Aleppo 1236–1260
K. of Syria 1250–1260
Killed by Hulagu

Al Aadil II
(Egypt)
1237–1239

4 Al Salih Ayoub
1240–1249

5 Turan Shah
1249–1250
Last Ayoubid Sultan
Killed by Mamlooks

NOTES

(1) The persons shown had many more sons. Only those mentioned in the text are shown.

(2) There were only five Ayoubid Sultans of Egypt and Syria, numbered and underlined: 1 Saladin, 2 Al Aadil, 3 Al Kamil, 4 Al Salih Ayoub, 5 Turan Shah. Other members of the family called themselves "kings" of different cities—Damascus, Aleppo and so on.

Saladin left seventeen sons, not to mention his brothers and their sons.[1] Eight years of family rivalries and battles followed his death. Not until the autumn of 1201 was the empire re-united under his brother, Al Aadil. During the same period, a number of different kings succeeded to the throne of Jerusalem, the capital of the kingdom being Acre. The royal family seemed no longer to produce boys and the crown was conveyed to new kings, who ascended the throne by marrying the heiresses.[2]

On his way to the third Crusade, Richard Cœur de Lion had landed in Cyprus and, in a fourteen-day twelfth-century *blitzkrieg*, had conquered the island. The native Franks of the Holy Land no longer desired Guy de Lusignan as their king, for they rightly attributed the loss of the kingdom to his incapacity. As a result, before returning home, Richard gave Cyprus to Guy. The Lusignan family were to rule the island for three centuries. Guy died in 1192 and was succeeded by his brother Amaury, who took the title of king.

Isabella, the daughter of Amaury I, King of Jerusalem, had been married to Conrad of Montferrat, the defender of Tyre against Saladin, but Conrad was assassinated in 1192. Isabella was then married to Henry of Champagne, who had come out with the Third Crusade but who was killed in 1197. Isabella thereupon married Amaury de Lusignan, who became Amaury II of Jerusalem and I of Cyprus. Amaury signed a new treaty with Sultan Al Aadil on 1st July, 1198, giving the Crusaders Beirut. Meanwhile the Counts of Tripoli had become extinct and Tripoli had become united to Antioch.

Unfortunately Amaury died on 1st April, 1205, followed soon afterwards by his wife Isabella, who left a thirteen-year-old daughter named Marie. A deputation was sent to the King of France to ask him to recommend a suitable husband. Jean de Brienne, a sixty-year-old French noble, was chosen, came to Acre, married the young Marie and was crowned King of Jerusalem.

The great pope Innocent III proclaimed a new Crusade in 1215,[3] and many volunteers reached Acre. On 24th May, 1218, these sailed under the command of Jean de Brienne and landed outside Damietta. The plan was to seize that city and then offer it to the sultan in exchange for Jerusalem. Damietta was taken on 5th November,

---

[1] Genealogical tree 9, opposite.
[2] Genealogical tree 8, page 159.
[3] The so-called Fourth Crusade had attacked Constantinople and did not reach any Muslim country.

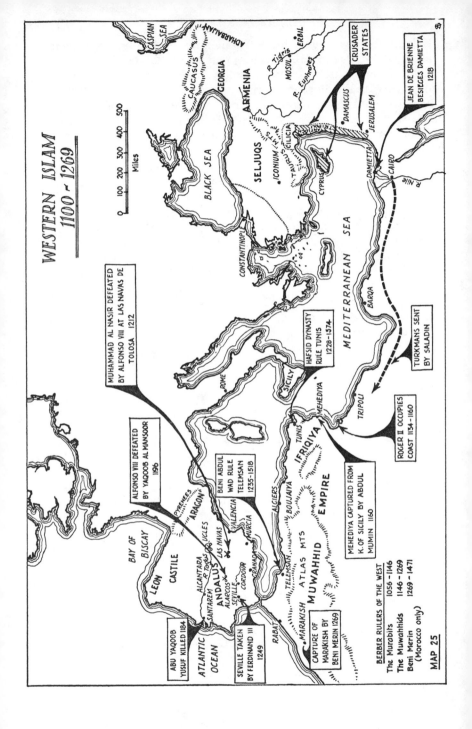

WESTERN ISLAM
1100 ~ 1269

CASPIAN SEA

ADHARBAIJAN

CAUCASUS

GEORGIA

ARMENIA

R. Tigris MOSUL ERBIL

R. Euphrates

CRUSADER STATES

JEAN DE BRIENNE BESIEGES DAMIETTA 1218

BLACK SEA

SELJUQS

0 100 200 300 400 500
Miles

DAMASCUS

ICONIUM

TAURUS CILICIA

JERUSALEM

CYPRUS

DAMIETTA

CAIRO

CONSTANTINOPLE

R. NILE

MEDITERRANEAN SEA

MUHAMMAD AL NASIR DEFEATED BY ALFONSO VIII AT LAS NAVAS DE TOLOSA 1212

BARQA

TURKMANS SENT BY SALADIN

ROME

HAFSID DYNASTY RULE TUNIS 1228-1574

SICILY

TRIPOLI

ROGER II OCCUPIES COAST 1154-1160

ALFONSO VIII DEFEATED BY YAQOOB AL MANSOOR 1196

MEHEDIYA

TUNIS

IFRIQIYA

MEHEDIYA CAPTURED FROM K. OF SICILY BY ABDUL MUMIN 1160

BENI ABDUL WAD RULE TELEMSAN 1255-1518

BAY OF BISCAY

PYRENEES

ARAGON

LEON

CASTILE

ALCANTARA SANTAREM R. TAGUS UCLES

ANDALUS ALARCOS

SEVILLE CORDOVA

GRANADA

VALENCIA

MURCIA

ALGIERS

BOUJAIYA

TELEMSAN

ATLAS MTS

MUWAHHID EMPIRE

ATLANTIC OCEAN

ABU YAQOOB YUSUF KILLED 1184

RABAT

MARAKISH

SEVILLE TAKEN BY FERDINAND III 1249

CAPTURE OF MARAKISH BY BENI MERIN 1269

BERBER RULERS OF THE WEST
The Murabits   1056 - 1146
The Muwahhids   1146 - 1269
Beni Merin   1269 - 1471
(Morocco only)

MAP 25

1219, but meanwhile the Papal Legate, Cardinal Pelagius, had arrived and claimed the supreme command.

The old Sultan Al Aadil[4] had died on 31st August, 1218, and had been succeeded by his son, Al Kamil, who now offered to exchange Damietta for Jerusalem, the original object of the Crusade. But Pelagius, a hard and arrogant prelate, had set his heart on capturing Cairo and rejected the offer. In July 1221, Pelagius and his army advanced southwards into the Egyptian delta, but the season of the annual rise of the Nile had come. The Muslims cut the dykes and the Crusaders found themselves surrounded by swirling waters.

With extraordinary magnanimity, Sultan Al Kamil rescued the Franks and provided them with food and neccessaries, on the sole condition that they peacefully evacuate the country. Thus ended the Fifth Crusade in a fiasco which served only to illustrate the generosity of Saladin's nephew, Al Kamil.

*   *   *

The year 1220 was to usher in a new era in the history of the Muslim world. We must, therefore, leave the Ayoubid Empire with Al Kamil as sultan after the débâcle of the Fifth Crusade and bring the story of a number of other countries up to the fateful year of 1220.

We have seen how, after the Battle of Malazkirt in 1071, many Armenians had fled to the Taurus. These refugees had now established a stable government in Cilicia. Leo II, the Armenian ruler, assumed the title of king in 1196. Leo had shown himself a great ruler but died in 1219 at the height of his glory, leaving no son. He was succeeded by his son-in-law with the title of Haithum I, King of Cilicia.

North of Cilicia, the Seljuqs of Iconium reached their golden age from 1175 to 1240. Under them Asia Minor enjoyed a period of peace and prosperity. The ruling classes were originally Turkmans from the east, but after a century of rule they had become wealthy and cultured. Their civilization, however, was not inherited from the Arabs but from Persia. The upper classes spoke Persian and the titles of their sultans were copied from pre-Islamic Persian heroes.

With the death of the great Sultan Sanjar in 1156, Seljuq rule in Persia had given place to confusion. In 1194, the last Seljuq claimant, Tughril III, was killed by a certain Tukush, a former Seljuq slave, appointed governor of Khuwarizm. Beyond the Oxus, the Qara

[4] Genealogical tree 9, page 182.

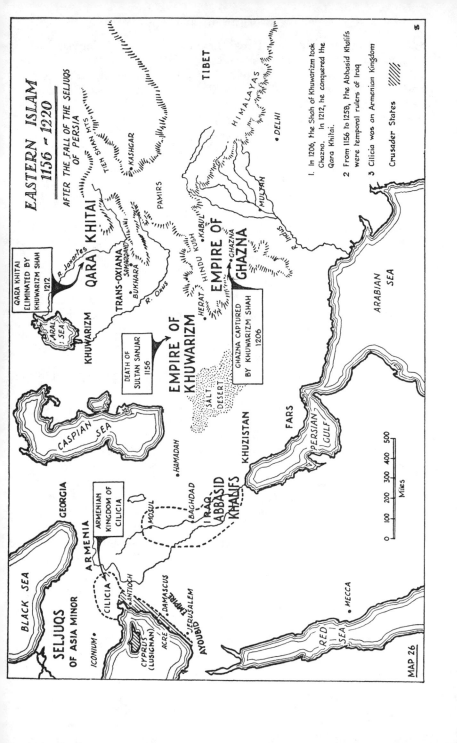

EASTERN ISLAM
1156 - 1220

AFTER THE FALL OF THE SELJUQS
OF PERSIA

1. In 1206, the Shah of Khuwarizm took Ghazna. In 1212, he conquered the Qara Khitai.

2. From 1156 to 1258, the Abbasid Khalifs were temporal rulers of Iraq

3. Cilicia was an Armenian Kingdom

Crusader States ///////

QARA KHITAI ELIMINATED BY KHUWARIZM SHAH 1212

DEATH OF SULTAN SANJAR 1156

GHAZNA CAPTURED BY KHUWARIZM SHAH 1206

ARMENIAN KINGDOM OF CILICIA

TIBET

• DELHI

HIMALAYAS

TIEN SHAN MTS

• KASHGAR

PAMIRS

QARA KHITAI

R. Jaxartes

TRANS-OXIANA

SAMARQAND•
BUKHARA•

KHUWARIZM

ARAL SEA

R. Oxus

HINDU KUSH

• KABUL

HERAT•

EMPIRE OF KHUWARIZM

SALT DESERT

EMPIRE OF GHAZNA

GHAZNA•

R. Indus

• MULTAN

CASPIAN SEA

• HAMADAN

KHUZISTAN

FARS

PERSIAN GULF

ARABIAN SEA

GEORGIA

ARMENIA

MOSUL•

• BAGHDAD

IRAQ
ABBASID KHALIFS

CILICIA

BLACK SEA

SELJUQS
OF ASIA MINOR

ICONIUM•

ANTIOCH•

• DAMASCUS

ACRE•

JERUSALEM•

AYOUBID EMPIRE

CYPRUS (LUSIGNAN)

• MECCA

RED SEA

0   100   200   300   400   500
Miles

MAP 26

Khitai Buddhists still held sway. In 1200, Tukush died and was succeeded by his son, Ala al Deen Muhammad, who, in 1206, conquered Ghazna and annexed it. In 1212, he attacked and eliminated the Qara Khitai and extended his frontier to the Jaxartes. Thus, almost overnight, a family of former Seljuq slaves had conquered a great empire including all modern Persia and Afghanistan.

* * *

Until the end of the ninth century, the Arab Abbasid Khalifs of Baghdad had been the world's greatest emperors. Then for a century they had been bullied and tortured by the Buwaihids. From 1055 to 1156, they had been mere puppets of the Seljuqs, treated with formal veneration but playing no part in the affairs of state. With the collapse of the Seljuqs, however, the khalifs once again became the actual executive rulers of Iraq and Khuzistan.

Their power, moreover, was not limited to the small kingdom which they ruled. The upstart dynasties of Turks, Kurds, Mamlooks or mercenaries, who rose and fell in the east, regarded with profound veneration the ancient family whose lineage descended through six centuries from the uncle of the Apostle of God.

When one of these petty Turkish princes mounted his throne, he hastened to write to the khalif to consecrate his accession. If he approved, the Prince of the Faithful would despatch a representative, accompanied by a suitable retinue, to present the new ruler with a sword, a ring, a banner and a diploma. The prince would ride out in state to meet the khalif's emissary, dismount and kiss his hand and escort him to his capital with due pomp and ceremony.

Particularly from 1179 to 1225, the great Khalif Al Nasir li Deen Allah was not only a strong ruler but the moral arbiter of eastern Islam. His son ruled for only nine months but was succeeded, in 1226, by another great and enlightened ruler, the Khalif Mustansir. Thus, for a century after the disappearance of the Seljuqs, the Abbasids enjoyed an Indian summer of prosperity and veneration.

* * *

We left the Maghrib in 1097,[5] when it was ruled by the Murabits, the Berber revivalist sect who had built for themselves a great empire. The cultured Muslims of Andalus resigned themselves to the rule of the puritan Murabits as long as they continued to drive back the Christians. Yusuf ibn Tashfeen died in 1106 and in 1108,

[5] Page 152.

the Murabits again defeated the King of Castile at Ucles but thereafter the Berbers themselves became enervated by the luxurious
living standards of Andalus.[6]

Meanwhile, however, another Berber sect had appeared, this
time in a village of the High Atlas. Muhammad ibn Toumert was
the son of a village headman of the Musamda Berbers, but he had
studied in Baghdad. Returning to the Maghrib, he saw the daughter
of Yusuf ibn Tashfeen riding through Marakish with a party of girls,
all with their faces unveiled. Such had always been the custom of
the Sahara tribes—the men went veiled but not the women. But
the sight was too much for the new reformer, Ibn Toumert. In
Baghdad, in his student days, the women had always been strictly
veiled. Our young theologian was shocked and beat their mules so
violently that the young ladies fell off. Ibn Toumert fled to his
mountain village in the Atlas, where he preached a new puritan
revival, banning music and intoxicating drinks and insisting on the
rigid veiling of women. Assuming the title of the Mehedi, the
Muslim saviour who was to come in the last days to establish peace
on earth, he rose in rebellion against the Murabits.

In 1129, however, the new Mehedi died and was succeeded by
Abdul Mumin ibn Ali, his first associate and convert. The origin of
Abdul Mumin is not known, the Berbers claiming him as one of
themselves, while the Arab historian, Ibn al Athir, calls him an
Arab of Beni Sulaim. The new sect assumed the name of the Muwah-
hids, which may be translated "Those who say God is One."

Seventeen years of civil war in the Maghrib followed. Eventually,
in 1146, Marakish was taken and Murabit rule was replaced by
that of the Muwahhids. In 1151, Abdul Mumin surprised and captured both Algiers and Boujaiya.

The defeat of the Beni Ziri Sanhaja by Beni Hilal in 1057 had
destroyed the power of Ifriqiya. In 1134, King Roger II, the Norman
King of Sicily, had landed in North Africa and, by 1148, had occupied the whole coastline from Tunis to Tripoli. The people of
Ifriqiya, however, bore with indignation the rule of a Christian
prince and, in 1156, they invited Abdul Mumin to free them. In
1159, he marched out of Marakish. The campaign had been
thoroughly well prepared and the Muwahhids occupied the whole
of Ifriqiya, the Normans withdrawing to Sicily. For the first and
last time, a Berber dynasty had established a North African empire
extending from southern Morocco to Tripoli.

[6] Map 25, page 184.

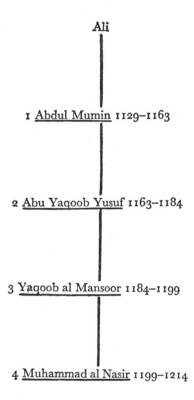

Ali

1 Abdul Mumin 1129–1163

2 Abu Yaqoob Yusuf 1163–1184

3 Yaqoob al Mansoor 1184–1199

4 Muhammad al Nasir 1199–1214

Thereafter the dynasty declined
until its final collapse 1269

As soon as Abdul Mumin had consolidated his authority over all North Africa, he crossed the Straits of Gibraltar to Andalus. In the great mosque of Cordova, which still stands today, he was proclaimed the ruler of Andalus. In May 1163, however, while raising a fresh army in the Maghrib, he died in Rabat, a city largely built by himself and which is the capital of Morocco today. Abdul Mumin had been a statesman and an administrator as well as a great fighter. In addition to his land victories, his fleet enjoyed undisputed command of the western Mediterranean.

Abdul Mumin was succeeded by his son, Abu Yaqoob Yusuf. At the head of the army which his father had collected, he crossed to Andalus, captured Alcántara, ravaged the valley of the Tagus, and consolidated Muwahhid rule over all Andalus. Most of the remainder of his reign was spent in Africa, but, in 1184, he returned to Spain and was killed in a Christian sortie while besieging Santarem. Tall, of majestic mien, but courteous and cultured, he was a student of science and medicine. His favourite subject, however, was philosophy and he delighted in learned discussions on the relative merits of Plato, Aristotle and the Arab philosophers. The learned Ibn Bajja, long famous in Europe as Avempace, lived at his court.

It was during the reign of Abu Yaqoob Yusuf that Saladin seized power in Egypt in 1169. Alarmed at the splendid prestige enjoyed by the Muwahhid Sultan (who also called himself khalif), Saladin sent a force of Turkmans to make trouble in Tripoli.

The Khalif Yusuf was succeeded by his son Yaqoob, who assumed the title of Mansoor. On 18th July, 1196, he inflicted a crushing defeat on Alfonso VIII of Castile at Alarcos, the Christian army being virtually exterminated. Twenty thousand Christian prisoners were released by Yaqoob without ransom. All Spain was at his mercy but he was obliged to cut short his operations to return to Africa, where a Murabit rebellion had broken out, supported by Saladin's Turkmans from Egypt.

The Muwahhid movement, which had begun as a severe puritan sect, became liberalized under Yaqoob al Mansoor. Beautiful mosques and palaces were erected, and the ruling classes were cultured, educated and artistic. Ibn Rushd, the famous Averroes, flourished in the reign of Yaqoob. Abdul Mumin, Abu Yaqoob Yusuf and Yaqoob al Mansoor had all three been great, victorious and cultured rulers, worthy of an imperial throne.

Yaqoob died in 1199 and was succeeded by his son Muhammad al

Nasir, a shy and timid boy of eighteen years of age. Encouraged by the death of the great sultan, Alfonso VIII broke his truce with the Muslims and began to raid Andalus. Not until 1211 did Muhammad al Nasir retaliate. On 16th July, 1212, however, he was completely defeated at Las Nevas de Tolosa by Alfonso VIII of Castile. A Berber tribe, Beni Merin,[7] rebelled in the Maghrib and in 1269 captured Marakish. The Muwahhid dynasty came to an end, and Beni Merin thereafter ruled in their stead.

In Andalus, the Christians continued to press their advantage and, in 1236, Cordova, once the Umaiyid capital, was captured. In 1238, Valencia was taken by the King of Aragon and in 1246, Ferdinand III, the Saint, King of Castile, occupied Murcia and invaded the territory of Granada. The Ameer of Granada, Muhammad ibn Nasr, thereupon took a bold step, rode into the camp of Ferdinand III and offered to become his vassal. The offer was accepted and the Kingdom of Granada became a tributary of Spain. As such, it was to endure for another two hundred and fifty-three years. In 1249, however, Ferdinand took Seville and Granada remained the only Arab kingdom in Spain. Of the citizens of Seville, some sailed for North Africa, while others migrated to the Kingdom of Granada.

The weakness of Beni Merin, in comparison with the great Muwahhids, deprived the Arab Kingdom of Granada of effective support from Africa. Under its dynasty of Beni Nasr, however, the Arab Kingdom was to survive until 1492, sometimes professing allegiance to Castile, sometimes declaring war. Granada was eventually overcome when Ferdinand and Isabella at last succeeded in uniting Spain.

The Arabs of Granada, though in many ways decadent, maintained for two hundred years an Indian summer of refined and luxurious Muslim culture in Europe. In their fairy castle of the Alhambra, the Nasrid Kings held gorgeous tournaments of chivalry, composed poetry and music, and revived, on a miniature scale, the glories of Abbasid Baghdad or of their own Umaiyid Khalifs in Cordova. The Beni Nasr Kings claimed descent from the Khazraj tribe, which had given sanctuary to the Prophet in Medina, 800 years before.

In spite of their religious differences, the Christians and the Muslims of Spain were closely integrated in their customs and culture. Before the ultimate disappearance of Granada, Arab chivalry, science

[7] Pronounced Mereen.

and literature had deeply impregnated the culture of Spain. Carried by the Conquistadors to America in the sixteenth century, its traces are still obvious in Central and South America, where Arab immigrants still find themselves almost at home.

NOTABLE DATES

Death of Yusuf ibn Tashfeen, the Murabit ruler	1106
Rise of the Muwahhids in the Maghrib	1111
Replacement of the Murabits by the Muwahhids	1146
Occupation of the Tunisian coast by Roger II, King of Sicily	1134–1160
Death of Sultan Sanjar / Collapse of Seljuqs of Persia	1156
Abdul Mumin ruler of North Africa	1160
Death of Saladin the Ayoubid	3rd March, 1193
Confusion in the Ayoubid family	1193–1201
Defeat of Alfonso VIII by Yaqoob al Mansoor at Alarcos	1196
Coronation of Jean de P. 'enne, King of Jerusalem	1210
Defeat of the Muwahhids .. Las Navas de Tolosa	1212
Death of Sultan Al Aadil / Accession of his son, Al Kamil	1218
Crusade of Jean de Brienne	1218–1221
Death of Leo II, Armenian King of Cilicia / Accession of Haithum I	1219
Reign of Ala al Deen, Khuwarizm Shah	1200–1220
Indian summer of the Abbasids of Baghdad	1156–1258
Extinction of the Muwahhids / Rise of Beni Merin	1269

PERSONALITIES

The Ayoubids

Saladin	1169–1193
Al Aadil, his brother	1201–1218
Al Kamil, the son of Al Aadil	1218–1238

Kings of Jerusalem

Guy de Lusignan	1186–1192
Conrad of Montferrat	1192
Henry of Champagne	1192–1197
Amaury de Lusignan	1197–1205
Jean de Brienne	1210–1225

Shah of Khuwarizm

Ala al Deen Muhammad	1200–1220

Abbasid Khalifs (after the fall of the Seljuqs)

Al Muqtafi	1135–1160
Al Mustadhi	1160–1179
Al Nasir li Deen Allah	1179–1225
Al Dhahir	1225–1226
Al Mustansir	1226–1242
Al Mustasim	1242–1258

The Muwahhids

Muhammad ibn Toumert	1121–1129
Abdul Mumin ibn Ali	1129–1163
Abu Yaqoob Yusuf	1163–1184
Yaqoob al Mansoor	1184–1199
Muhammad al Nasir	1199–1213

OTHER PERSONALITIES

Haithum I, Armenian King of Cilicia
Yusuf ibn Tashfeen, leader of the Murabits
Roger II, Norman King of Sicily
Alfonso VIII, King of Castile
Ferdinand III, King of Castile
Muhammad ibn Nasr, King of Granada

XIV

The Mongol Catastrophe

IN the twelfth century, Central Asia from the Jaxartes to Lake Baikal was inhabited by wild nomadic tribes. Those from the Altai Mountains westwards we classify as Turks, while those further east we call Mongols. The tribes themselves, however, were ignorant of these classifications.

The Turkish tribes were in general less savage than the Mongols, while many Turks had entered the Muslim empire and become civilized. In 1206 a tribal council, assembled near Lake Baikal, chose a certain Temujin to be chief of all the Mongols, with the title of Jenghis Khan. From 1211 to 1216, he consolidated his power by invading China. In 1219, he set out on a campaign in the West.

We have already seen that, in 1220, Sultan Al Kamil, the nephew of Saladin, ruled the Ayoubid Empire. In Iraq, the Abbasid Khalif Al Nasir was enjoying an Indian summer of peace and prestige. Persia had fallen under the sway of a family of former slaves of the Seljuqs, known as Khuwarizm Shahs, but their rise had been so rapid that their new subjects had had no time to acquire a sense of loyalty. The ruler in 1220 was Ala al Deen Muhammad, Khuwarizm Shah.

In February 1220, Jenghis Khan and his Mongols crossed the Jaxartes and stormed Bukhara and Samarqand, two of the richest cities in the world, on the caravan route from China to the West. Ala al Deen, the Khuwarizm Shah, offered no resistance but died a few weeks later, a fugitive on the shores of the Caspian.

The Mongols worked according to a carefully organized drill. As they marched, they carried off the young men from the countryside as labour gangs. On reaching a walled city, they immediately surrounded it with a rampart and ditch, using their gangs of slave prisoners. Then mangonels were erected to bombard the walls. When a breach was effected, the prisoners were obliged to fill in the moat and to lead the assault. The Mongols were thus able to capture fortified cities without suffering many casualties, the prisoners being obliged to execute the dangerous tasks.

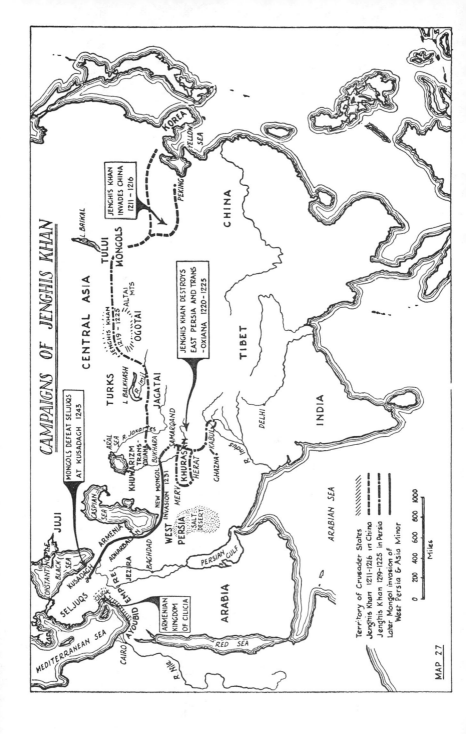

CAMPAIGNS OF JENGHIS KHAN

JENGHIS KHAN
INVADES CHINA
1211 - 1216

KOREA

YELLOW
SEA

PEKING

L. BAIKAL

CHINA

TULUI

ALTAI
MTS

MONGOLS

CENTRAL ASIA

JENGHIS KHAN
1219 - 1225

OGOTAI

TIBET

TURKS

L. BALKHASH

JAGATAI

R. Ili

INDIA

DELHI

JENGHIS KHAN DESTROYS
EAST PERSIA AND TRANS
-OXIANA 1220 - 1225

ARAL
SEA

R. Joxartes

KHUWARIZM

TRANS-
OXIANA

SAMARQAND

BUKHARA

KHURASAN

MERV

HERAT

GHAZNA

KABUL

R. Indus

MONGOLS DEFEAT SELJUQS
AT KUSADAGH 1243

JUJI

CASPIAN
SEA

ARMENIA

NEW MONGOL
INVASION 1251

WEST
PERSIA

SALT
DESERT

ARABIAN SEA

ADHARBAIJAN

BLACK SEA

CONSTANTINOPLE

KUSADAGH

SELJUQS

JEZIRA

EMPIRE

BAGHDAD

PERSIAN GULF

ARMENIAN
KINGDOM
OF CILICIA

CILICIA

AYOUBID EMPIRE

CAIRO

R. Nile

MEDITERRANEAN SEA

ARABIA

RED SEA

Territory of Crusader States
Jenghis Khan 1211-1216 in China
Jenghis Khan 1219-1225 in Persia
Later Mongol invasion of
West Persia & Asia Minor

0   200   400   600   800 1000
Miles

MAP 27

11. THE MONGOL KHAKANS OR SUPREME KHANS

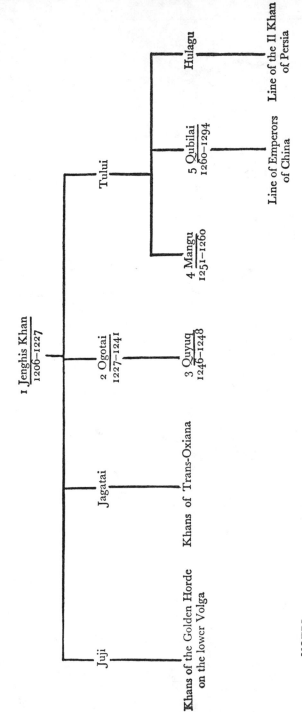

1 Jenghis Khan
1206–1227

Juji — Jagatai — **2 Ogotai** 1227–1241 — Tului

Khans of the Golden Horde on the lower Volga

Khans of Trans-Oxiana

2 Ogotai 1227–1241

3 Quyuq 1246–1248

4 Mangu 1251–1260

5 Qubilai 1260–1294

Hulagu

Line of Emperors of China

Line of the Il Khan of Persia

NOTES

(1) Jenghis Khan bequeathed the post of Supreme Khan to Ogotai but it was later usurped by the sons of Tului.

(2) Persons who became Supreme Khan are numbered and underlined.

When the city was taken, all the inhabitants were marshalled on an open space outside the walls. The women were then raped, after which all were butchered, regardless of age or sex. The town was then plundered, demolished and burned. Jenghis Khan spent the years 1220 to 1225 in reducing East Persia to an uninhabited desert in this manner. Khurasan and Trans-Oxiana had for centuries been two of the most wealthy and cultured countries in the world. The Persians had already enjoyed a thousand years of civilization before they were conquered by the Arabs in the seventh century. After the Arab conquest, they had shared for six centuries in that brilliant Perso-Arab culture, which extended from the Atlantic to India and Turkestan. Now all this wealth, art and civilization—libraries, palaces, irrigation systems, gardens and cities—was reduced to heaps of rubble, covered with weeds and scrub.

"In the Muslim countries devastated by Jenghis Khan," wrote the Persian historian,[1] "not one in a thousand of the inhabitants survived . . . If from now until the day of the Resurrection, nothing hindered the natural increase of the population, it could never reach one-tenth of its density before the Mongol conquest."

On the 18th August, 1227, the World Conqueror died at the age of sixty-six, after an illness of only eight days. On his deathbed, Jenghis Khan divided his steppe empire between his four sons. Juji, the eldest, received the country north of the Caspian, Jagatai that east of the Jaxartes, Ogotai was given the Imil valley, and Tului the Mongol homeland round Lake Baikal. The conquered lands of Persia and China were not divided, but were to be the perquisite of the Supreme Khan, a post to which he nominated Ogotai.

In 1231, a Mongol army appeared in West Persia, overran Adharbaijan and Armenia and, in 1243, defeated the Seljuq Sultan of Iconium at Kusadagh. Adharbaijan was annexed but the Seljuq Sultan and the Armenian King of Cilicia were accepted as feudatories on payment of tribute. West Persia was likewise annexed up to the Zagros Mountains. Both on the east and the north, the Mongols had reached the border of the Arab countries.

*   *   *

While the eastern lands of Islam were suffering these terrible disasters, two more crusades had come from the West.

The island of Sicily, it will be remembered, had been held by the

[1] Ala al Deen al Juwaini, *History of the Conqueror of the World.*

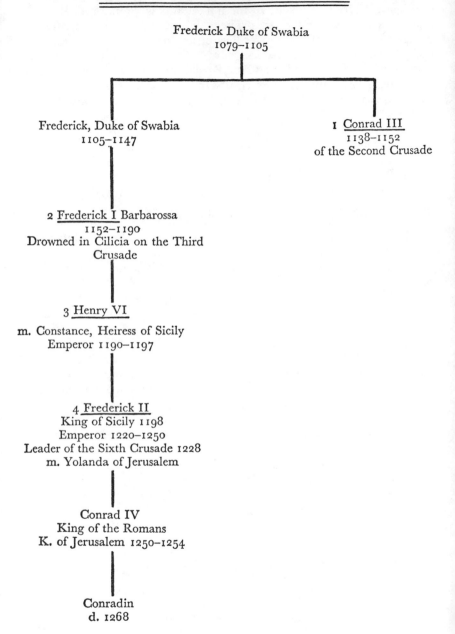

Frederick Duke of Swabia
1079–1105

Frederick, Duke of Swabia
1105–1147

1 Conrad III
1138–1152
of the Second Crusade

2 Frederick I Barbarossa
1152–1190
Drowned in Cilicia on the Third
Crusade

3 Henry VI
m. Constance, Heiress of Sicily
Emperor 1190–1197

4 Frederick II
King of Sicily 1198
Emperor 1220–1250
Leader of the Sixth Crusade 1228
m. Yolanda of Jerusalem

Conrad IV
King of the Romans
K. of Jerusalem 1250–1254

Conradin
d. 1268

Arabs from 827 to 1061, when it had been conquered by the Normans, who had ruled it until 1189, when King William II died childless. The heiress was his aunt Constance, married to the Emperor of Germany, Henry VI Hohenstaufen, who thereby became King of Sicily. The emperor, however, died in 1197, leaving an infant son called Frederick, who grew up as an orphan in Sicily.

During the hundred years of their rule, the Normans had instituted in Sicily an extraordinary system of toleration. Arabs, Greeks, Italians and Normans lived cheek by jowl, churches and mosques stood side by side, and Arabic, Italian, Greek and French were spoken with equal facility. Frederick II had grown up in Sicily, spoke Arabic fluently and received a good education from Arab tutors.

In 1225, Frederick married Yolanda, the daughter of Jean de Brienne and of Marie, Queen of Jerusalem, and assumed the title of King of Jerusalem. He was also Emperor of Germany and King of Sicily. His chief preoccupation was his struggle with the pope for supreme power in Europe.

*   *   *

In spite of his triumphant victory over Jean de Brienne, the Ayoubid Sultan Al Kamil was harassed by the rebellion of his brother, Al Muadhdham, who declared his independence in Damascus. Aware of his predilection for Arabs, Al Kamil invited Frederick to come to his aid.

The emperor landed at Acre on 7th September, 1228. Meanwhile, however, Al Muadhdham had died and Al Kamil was no longer in need of help. Indeed the presence of the emperor was now an embarrassment. Al Kamil camped at Gaza, while Frederick was at Acre. Having come at the sultan's invitation, he had with him only a small force, inadequate for a war with the Muslims. In fact the emperor was indifferent to religion but hoped that his crusade would strengthen his hand against the pope.

After five months of bargaining, an agreement was signed on 18th February, 1229. Jerusalem was to be handed over to the Franks, on condition that they did not rebuild the walls. They also received a corridor leading from Jaffa to Jerusalem. The temple area and the villages surrounding the city were to be retained by the Muslims. Further north, the Franks also recovered Nazareth.

Frederick was fired by the old dream of universal empire. He already ruled Germany, Italy and Sicily and, owing to his marriage to Yolanda, called himself King of Jerusalem and suzerain of Cyprus,

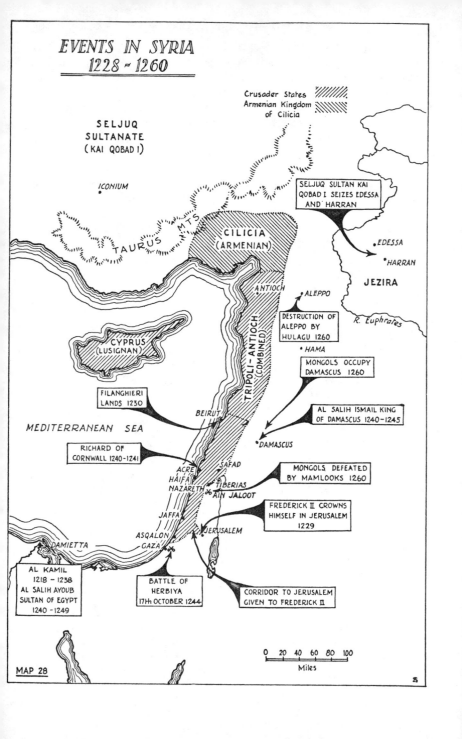

EVENTS IN SYRIA
1228 ~ 1260

Crusader States ///////
Armenian Kingdom
of Cilicia \\\\\\\\

SELJUQ
SULTANATE
(KAI QOBAD I)

•ICONIUM

TAURUS MTS.

CILICIA
(ARMENIAN)

SELJUQ SULTAN KAI
QOBAD I SEIZES EDESSA
AND HARRAN

•EDESSA

•HARRAN

JEZIRA

ANTIOCH

•ALEPPO

R. Euphrates

CYPRUS
(LUSIGNAN)

TRIPOLI-ANTIOCH
(COMBINED)

DESTRUCTION OF
ALEPPO BY
HULAGU 1260

•HAMA

MONGOLS OCCUPY
DAMASCUS 1260

FILANGHIERI
LANDS 1230

BEIRUT

AL SALIH ISMAIL KING
OF DAMASCUS 1240-1245

MEDITERRANEAN SEA

•DAMASCUS

RICHARD OF
CORNWALL 1240-1241

ACRE
HAIFA
NAZARETH

SAFAD

TIBERIAS
✳AIN JALOOT

MONGOLS DEFEATED
BY MAMLOOKS 1260

JAFFA

ASQALON
GAZA

•JERUSALEM

FREDERICK II CROWNS
HIMSELF IN JERUSALEM
1229

•DAMIETTA

AL KAMIL
1218 – 1238
AL SALIH AYOUB
SULTAN OF EGYPT
1240 -1249

BATTLE OF
HERBIYA
17th OCTOBER 1244

CORRIDOR TO JERUSALEM
GIVEN TO FREDERICK II

0   20 40 60 80 100
Miles

MAP 28

5

Antioch and Cilicia. The Franks born in Outremer, however, were aware that his motives were purely selfish and were bitterly opposed to him. On 17th March, 1229, Frederick visited Jerusalem to be crowned. As he had been excommunicated by the pope, no priests were willing to recognize him, and he crowned himself King of Jerusalem with his own hands, in the Church of the Holy Sepulchre.

The emperor had been educated by Arab professors and possessed a good knowledge of mathematics, physics and engineering, subjects at the time almost completely unknown in Europe. His appearance, however, was not impressive, for he was small in stature, short-sighted, had red hair and was clean shaven. He re-embarked at Acre on 1st May, 1229, amid the jeers of the Frankish inhabitants. Returning to Italy, he sent an army under Marshal Filanghieri, not to fight the Muslims, but to compel the Crusader states to submit to his rule. Thirteen years of civil war resulted between the supporters and the opponents of the emperor, thereby reducing the Frankish states to even greater anarchy and weakness than before.

Fortunately for the Crusaders, the Muslims, during the years from 1230 to 1243, were also in confusion. The Sultan Al Kamil was again in difficulties with family revolts in Syria. The Sultan of Iconium, Kai Qobad I, seized Edessa and Harran. In 1236, Al Kamil retook them but in 1237 his brother, Al Salih Ismail, rebelled in Damascus. These endless rivalries between petty Muslim princes fill us with amazement for, as we know, the savage and merciless Mongols were already at the gates. Yet all history, even in our own times, is full of such jealous and petty follies.

On 8th March, 1238, the Sultan Al Kamil died at the age of sixty. A man of peace by inclination, he had been a great ruler and an enlightened administrator, though constantly harassed by the revolts and jealousies of his Ayoubid brothers and cousins. After two years of seditions and rivalries between members of the Ayoubid family, Al Kamil's son, Malik Al Salih Ayoub, was proclaimed sultan in Cairo on 19th June, 1240. His uncle, Al Salih Ismail, declared himself independent in Damascus.[2]

On 11th October, 1240, Richard, Earl of Cornwall, the brother of Henry III, King of England, landed at Acre. "In the Holy Land," he wrote bitterly, "peace has been replaced by discord, unity by division." Nevertheless, the presence of Richard, a reasonable and moderate man, did much to quieten the internal feuds of the Franks. In March 1241, he signed an agreement with the Sultan Al Salih

[2] Genealogical tree 9, page 182.

Ayoub, which resulted in the surrender of Tiberias to the Franks and the release of all prisoners-of-war. Richard sailed for England on 3rd May, 1241, and chaos broke out once more.

In 1244, Al Salih Ismail, the rebel Ayoubid, made an agreement with the Frankish government in Acre to march against the Sultan Al Salih Ayoub, who was in Egypt. On 17th October, 1244, a pitched battle was fought at Herbiya, north of Gaza,[3] in which the Damascus army was completely defeated and its Crusader allies virtually exterminated. The Sultan Al Salih Ayoub was able to march on to Damascus and to reunite the Ayoubid Empire. The Franks of Acre and Cyprus had joined in this campaign, but Bohemond V, Prince of Antioch and Count of Tripoli, had held aloof.

In 1247, the Ayoubid princes of Aleppo and Hama rebelled again and the Sultan Al Salih Ayoub marched back once more to Damascus. He was seriously ill, perhaps with tuberculosis, and was carried in a litter with the army. In May 1249, however, information reached him which caused him to patch up a hasty peace with the rebels and to hurry back to Egypt.

*   *   *

The news which caused Al Salih Ayoub to hasten back to Egypt was that of the landing of Louis IX, King of France, near Damietta. Louis IX, better known as Saint Louis, was a true Christian hero. Of a pure and simple piety, he was brave, unselfish and courteous.

The Crusaders landed on 5th June, 1249, and took Damietta the next morning. The annual rise of the Nile, which had drowned the Crusade of Jean de Brienne, was due to begin and it was necessary to wait for five months until the floods had subsided, before operations could be resumed. Meanwhile Al Salih Ayoub had camped at Mansoora, the site occupied by Al Kamil during Jean de Brienne's invasion. The sultan, however, was dying slowly in his tent, nursed only by his devoted wife, Shajar al Durr or Spray of Pearls. In spite of all her devotion, he died in her arms on 23rd November, 1249. Meanwhile, the floods had gone down and the Crusaders were about to advance.

In this crisis, the sultan's death was kept secret. Spray of Pearls daily issued orders to the army under the sultan's forged signature and assured the officers who reported to headquarters that the sultan was much better. Faced with a major battle, this extraordinary woman commanded the army and ruled Egypt.

[3] Map 28, page 200.

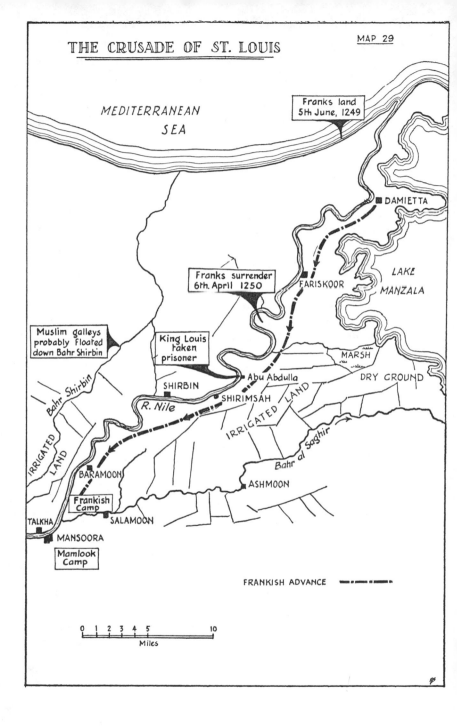

MAP 29

THE CRUSADE OF ST. LOUIS

MEDITERRANEAN
SEA

Franks land
5th June, 1249

■ DAMIETTA

LAKE
MANZALA

FARISKOOR

Franks surrender
6th. April 1250

MARSH

DRY GROUND

Muslim galleys
probably floated
down Bahr Shirbin

King Louis
taken
prisoner

Abu Abdulla

SHIRBIN

Bahr Shirbin

SHIRIMSAH

R. Nile

IRRIGATED LAND

IRRIGATED
LAND

Bahr al Saghir

BARAMOON

ASHMOON

Frankish
Camp

TALKHA

SALAMOON

MANSOORA

Mamlook
Camp

FRANKISH ADVANCE ━ ━ ━ ━

0 1 2 3 4 5   10
Miles

On 25th November, the Crusaders moved southwards. On 8th February, 1250, a battle was fought outside Mansoora, but Louis' careful plans were spoiled by the indiscipline of his brother, the Comte d'Artois. A four months' deadlock ensued, the two armies digging in close to one another, neither strong enough to attack. Soon dysentery and then typhus appeared in the Frankish camp. The ground was strewn with rotting corpses and the water supply was infected. Then, by floating their galleys down to near Shirbin, the Muslims cut the Crusader communications with Damietta and starvation was added to sickness.

On 5th April, 1250, Louis IX, himself so weak from dysentery that he could not stand, gave the order for retreat but the next day, when half way back to Damietta, the Crusaders were overwhelmed and obliged to surrender, the king being taken prisoner.

Meanwhile, on 28th February, 1250, Turan Shah, the eldest son of Al Salih Ayoub, had arrived from Syria and had been accepted as sultan. Although, since the accession of Al Kamil in 1218, the head-quarters of the Ayoubid Sultanate had moved from Damascus to Cairo, the army consisted almost entirely of Turkish soldier slaves, commonly called Mamlooks.[4] Saladin, his brother Al Aadil, and his nephew Al Kamil, had all been great rulers and the dynasty had enjoyed overwhelming prestige and the unquestioning loyalty of its Mamlooks. But with the long illness of Al Salih Ayoub and the endless rebellions of the junior members of the family, the Ayoubids had lost the public respect, and the discipline of the Mamlooks had been relaxed.

Just as the long reign of the Abbasids in Baghdad had been terminated in 861 by the murder of the Khalif Mutawakkil by his Turkish soldiers, so, on 1st May, 1250, the Mamlooks murdered Turan Shah and the Ayoubid sultanate collapsed. The Mamlook leaders accepted an immense ransom in gold from Louis IX, who sailed from Damietta on 7th May, 1250, with the remnant of his army. Spray of Pearls, to whom the Mamlooks were devoted, was greeted as Queen of Egypt.

Shortly afterwards, however, a letter was received from the Abbasid Khalif, quoting a traditional saying of the Prophet, "Unhappy is the nation which is governed by a woman." "If you have no men," added the khalif, "I will send you one." As a result, Spray of Pearls married Aibek, the commander-in-chief, a Mamlook of her late husband. The marriage, however, was not a success. In 1257

[4] Pronounced as in the name Luke.

Spray of Pearls arranged the murder of her husband and was herself murdered a few days later. One of the most remarkable women in history, her body, almost naked, was thrown from the battlements of the citadel of Cairo into the ditch, where it lay for several days before burial.

Syria had refused to recognize the accession of Spray of Pearls and Aibek and had proclaimed Malik al Nasir Yusuf, a great-grandson of Saladin,[5] as King of Syria. The former Ayoubid Empire was thus divided in half.

*　　　*　　　*

After the death of Jenghis Khan, the Mongols continued their conquests in China, in Russia, in Hungary and in Asia Minor. In Iraq, however, the great Abbasid Khalif Mustansir (1226–1242) maintained an efficient and active army and, on two or three occasions, repulsed the Mongol invaders. Jenghis Khan's third son, Ogotai, nominated as Supreme Khan, died in 1241, and was succeeded after a five-year interregnum by his son Quyuq, who died of drink in 1248.

The descendants of the other sons of Jenghis Khan had always been resentful at the selection of Ogotai as supreme khan. On 1st July, 1251, Mangu, the son of Tului,[6] was chosen as supreme khan by the tribal council. Thereafter the Mongols were divided by perpetual civil wars, the families of Jagatai and Ogotai being allied against the descendants of Tului.

The tribal council which elected Mangu authorized the despatch of an army under his brother Hulagu to conquer Iraq, Syria and Egypt. In January 1256, Hulagu crossed the Oxus and pursued his leisurely campaign, camping for the summer on the slopes of Demavend, at the southern end of the Caspian Sea. Many Ismaili castles, occupying the mountainous districts at the southern end of the Caspian, were taken and demolished.[7]

In March 1257, Hulagu moved to Hamadan, whence he sent an ultimatum to the Khalif Mustasim in Baghdad, demanding that he come and do homage. The capable and energetic Khalif Mustansir had died in 1242 and had been succeeded by his frivolous son, Mustasim. The Christian religion does not promise worldly power

---

[5] Genealogical tree 9, page 182.

[6] Genealogical tree 11, page 196.

[7] The Fatimid Khalifs of Egypt, it will be remembered, had been Ismailis. As a result of a dispute regarding the succession in 1094, however, a large group of Ismailis had seceded from the Fatimids and established themselves in northern Persia.

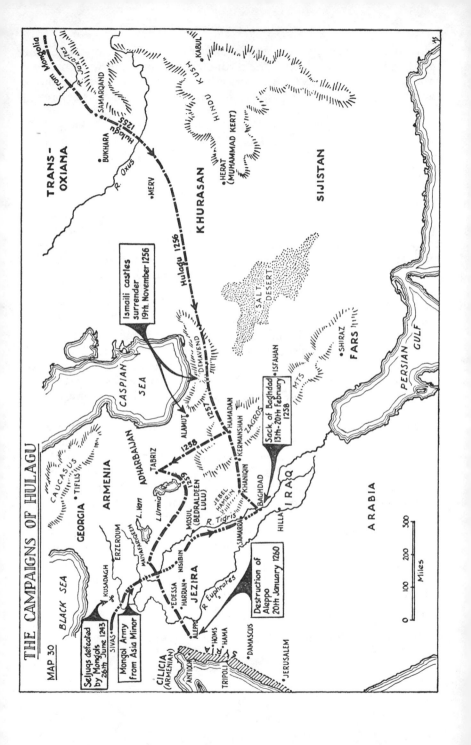

THE CAMPAIGNS OF HULAGU

MAP 30

Seljuqs defeated by Mongols 26th June 1243

Mongol Army from Asia Minor

Destruction of Aleppo 20th January 1260

Sack of Baghdad 13th-20th February 1258

Ismaili castles surrender 19th November 1256

From Mongolia

TRANS-OXIANA

KHURASAN

SIJISTAN

Hulagu 1255

R. Oxus

BUKHARA

SAMARQAND

MERV

HERAT (MUHAMMAD KERT)

KUSH

KABUL

Hulagu 1256

SALT DESERT

DEMAVEND

ALAMUT

1257

HAMADAN

KERMANSHAH

ISFAHAN

SHIRAZ

FARS

PERSIAN GULF

CASPIAN SEA

ADHARBAIJAN

TABRIZ

1258

L. Urmia

MOSUL (BEDRALDEEN LULU)

1259

JEBEL HAMRIN

KHANIQIN

ZAGROS MTS.

R. Tigris

SAMARRA

BAGHDAD

HILLA

IRAQ

ARMENIA

ARABIA

GEORGIA

TIFLIS

CAUCASUS

BLACK SEA

KUSADAGH

ERZEROUM

SIVAS

MIYAFARIQEEN

L. Van

EDESSA

NSIBIN

HARRAN

JEZIRA

R. Euphrates

ALEPPO

HOMS

HAMA

DAMASCUS

TRIPOLI

ANTIOCH

CILICIA (ARMENIAN)

JERUSALEM

0   100   200   500
Miles

to its adherents, but in Islam, politics are closely connected with religion. The khalif should be the ruler of the world. It was impossible for the khalif to do homage to a heathen, and the Mongols were animists.

On 18th January, 1258, Hulagu's army arrived outside Baghdad, where it was joined by the Mongol garrison of Asia Minor. Using large gangs of slave prisoners, the Mongols quickly surrounded the city with a continuous breastwork and ditch. On 30th January, 1258, Hulagu opened a massive bombardment with his mangonels. Within three days, the defences were in ruins. On 5th February, the Mongols mounted a long stretch of the walls.

Hulagu, thereupon, ordered the khalif's army to assemble on the plain outside the walls, where all were massacred. On 10th February, the Khalif Mustasim gave himself up. Hulagu ordered him to instruct the whole civil population to gather on the plain outside the walls, where they also were shot, slashed and hacked to death in heaps, regardless of age or sex.

Not until 13th February did the Mongols enter the city. For a week, they had been waiting on the walls, not a man daring to leave his unit to plunder. Such iron discipline, unknown in the Middle Ages, goes far to account for their invincibility. The city was then systematically looted, destroyed and burnt. Eight hundred thousand persons are said to have been killed. The Khalif Mustasim was sewn up in a sack and trampled to death under the feet of Mongol horses.

For five hundred years, Baghdad had been a city of palaces, mosques, libraries and colleges. Its universities and hospitals were the most up-to-date in the world. Nothing now remained but heaps of rubble and a stench of decaying human flesh.

The Muslim world was thunderstruck at the news of the destruction of Baghdad and the murder of the khalif. Hulagu, laden with incredible quantities of treasure, the wealth accumulated by the Abbasids over five centuries, marched away to Adharbaijan to rest and graze his horses.

*   *   *

We left Egypt in 1257, on the occasion of the murders of Aibek and Spray of Pearls. After a brief struggle for power, Qutuz, an army officer, became sultan of the Mamlook state. In Damascus, Malik al Nasir Yusuf, the great-grandson of Saladin, was King of Syria. Hulagu marched out of Tabriz on 12th September, 1259, and quickly overran the Jezira. An Ayoubid princeling, taken prisoner, was put to death by cutting pieces of flesh off his body and stuffing them in his mouth. The Mongols then established themselves in Edessa.[8]

On 20th January, 1260, they took Aleppo by assault. One hundred thousand young women and children were driven off as slaves, the remainder of the inhabitants being systematically exterminated. Malik al Nasir Yusuf abandoned Damascus and fled, but was subsequently captured by the Mongols and executed. When all Syria and Egypt seemed to be about to meet the fate of Persia and Iraq, news reached Hulagu of the death of his elder brother, the Great Khan Mangu. Perhaps hoping himself to succeed, he marched back with his army towards Mongolia and the remnant of Muslim civilization was saved.

The Mamlook Sultan Qutuz, receiving from Hulagu a summons to surrender, had admitted to his officers that the Mamlooks were no match for the Mongols. But when they heard that Hulagu had gone, the Mamlooks decided to fight. Hulagu had left a force in Syria which, on 1st March, 1260, had occupied Damascus without opposition and without any massacring or looting.

On the 3rd September, 1260, a pitched battle occurred at Ain Jaloot,[9] or Goliath's Spring, eleven miles south-east of Nazareth, between the Mamlook army under Sultan Qutuz and the Mongol forces left behind by Hulagu. The Crusaders of Acre assisted the Mamlooks with food and other facilities, but did not take part in the battle.

After a desperate struggle the Mamlooks were completely victorious and the Mongols were obliged hastily to evacuate Syria. Sultan Qutuz made a state entry into Damascus and announced the union of Syria and Egypt under the Mamlooks. On the return march, however, Qutuz was murdered in the Sinai desert by another Mamlook commander, Baybers the Bunduqdari, who made a triumphal entry into Cairo and was immediately proclaimed sultan.

*   *   *

Baybers the Bunduqdari was the real founder of the Mamlook Empire, which was to endure for three centuries. The word Mamlook means owned—by someone else. It was originally applied to boys from the tribes of Central Asia, who were bought by the Abbasid Khalifs for use as soldiers. Ordinary domestic slaves were in an

[8] Map 30, page 206.
[9] For Ain Jaloot, see Map 28, page 200.

entirely different category. The use of the word slaves for both is misleading.

Mamlook boys, after their purchase, were subjected to several years of vigorous training. The Turkish tribes of the steppes lived almost entirely on horseback and their weapon was the bow, which they used at full gallop. Doubtless Mamlook boys were already splendid horsemen and during their training they spent endless hours —all day and every day—in mounted exercises with sword, lance and bow.

The régime established by the Mamlooks was not based on heredity, for every Mamlook arrived in Syria or Egypt as a slave of unknown genealogy. Compulsorily converted to Islam, he worked his way up from recruit by merit alone. The commanders of the army, who held the rank of ameer, had all risen from the rank of slave-recruit. The result was to produce, in the highest ranks, a succession of leaders of unrivalled personality, courage and ruthlessness.

When the Mamlooks became masters of Egypt and Syria, they continued the same methods. They themselves employed agents to buy and import boys from Central Asia for their armies. Their own sons born to them in Egypt were considered by them to be socially inferior and were not recruited into regular Mamlook units, which only admitted boys born on the steppes. Syrians and Egyptians were not accepted in the army.

This constant supply of new blood from some of the hardiest and most warlike tribes in the world saved the Mamlooks from degeneracy when they became the possessors of wealth and power. An autocratic military caste, they ruled with considerable harshness, taxation was heavy and the Egyptian peasants suffered much oppression.

On the other hand, the Mamlooks made great use of Syrians and Egyptians in civilian posts. They were promoted to high rank in the civil administration and were received and honoured by the sultan. The Mamlook ameers kept great state, were dressed in gorgeous robes of silk and satin, and not only their persons but their weapons, their saddles and their bridles were covered with gold, silver and jewels.

When criticizing the harshness of Mamlook rule, we must remember that they saved Egypt from the total devastation which the Mongols had inflicted on Persia. Egypt and Syria were great and wealthy under their régime and the Mamlook Empire was one of the most powerful in the world.

NOTABLE DATES

Mongols elect Jenghis Khan as their chief	1206
Jenghis Khan devastates East Persia	1220–1225
Death of Jenghis Khan	1227
Crusade of Frederick II	1228–1229
Mongol conquest of Adharbaijan, Armenia and Asia Minor	1231–1243
Death of Sultan Al Kamil	1238
Defeat of Al Salih Ismail and the Franks at Herbiya	1244
Crusade of Louis IX	1249–1250
Murder of Turan Shah End of the dynasty of Saladin	1250
Destruction of Baghdad by Hulagu	1258
Destruction of Aleppo by Hulagu	1260
Battle of Ain Jaloot Mongols evacuate Syria	1260

PERSONALITIES

Mongols

Jenghis Khan	1206–1227
Hulagu, his grandson	1256–1265

Mamlook Sultans of Egypt

Aibek and Spray of Pearls	1250–1257
Qutuz	1259–1260
Baybers the Bunduqdari	1260–1277

Ayoubid Sultans

Saladin	1169–1193
Al Aadil	1201–1218
Al Kamil	1218–1238
Al Salih Ayoub	1240–1249
Turan Shah	1249–1250

Note Interregna were periods when the throne was in dispute

Crusaders

Frederick II Hohenstaufen	Crusade: 1228–1229
Louis IX of France (Saint Louis)	Crusade: 1249–1250

XV

The Mamlooks

IN the previous chapter, we left Baybers the Bunduqdari as sultan in Cairo of the new Mamlook Empire, formed by the union of Egypt and Syria. Meanwhile Hulagu, the grandson of Jenghis Khan, had established his capital in Tabriz, and, assuming the title of Il Khan, consolidated an empire which included all Persia up to the Oxus. On the west, the Seljuqs of Asia Minor, now in rapid decline, had become his tributaries, as also was the Armenian King of Cilicia.

Fortunately for the Mamlooks, the Mongols were divided against one another. Hulagu's brother, Qubilai, had become Great Khan in 1260, and had established himself as Emperor of China. Qubilai and Hulagu were sons of Tului, the fourth son of Jenghis Khan.[1] The descendants of his three elder sons, Juji, Jagatai and Ogotai, were bitterly resentful at the elevation of the sons of Tului, and declared war. Hulagu was unable again to invade Syria, because he was engaged in hostilities with the family of Jagatai in Trans-Oxiana and with that of Juji in the Caucasus.[2]

The coming of the Mongols had divided the Frankish states into two camps. The Counts of Tripoli were extinct and in 1187, Bohemond IV had united the two states becoming himself Prince of Antioch and Count of Tripoli. His grandson Bohemond VI, had, in 1260, become an ally of the Mongols, while the Kingdoms of Jerusalem and Cyprus had favoured Egypt.

The Crusaders were now too weak and too divided to constitute any danger to the Mamlook Empire, unless the Mongols were to return to Syria. In such an event, however, if the Franks joined the Mongols, their alliance would be too strong for the Mamlooks. Baybers accordingly decided that it would be wise to eliminate the Crusaders before the Mongols could again invade Syria.

In a series of swift and dynamic campaigns, from 1265 to 1268, he captured Jaffa, Safad and the great city of Antioch. Bohemond VI

[1] Genealogical tree 11, page 196. [2] Map 27, page 195.

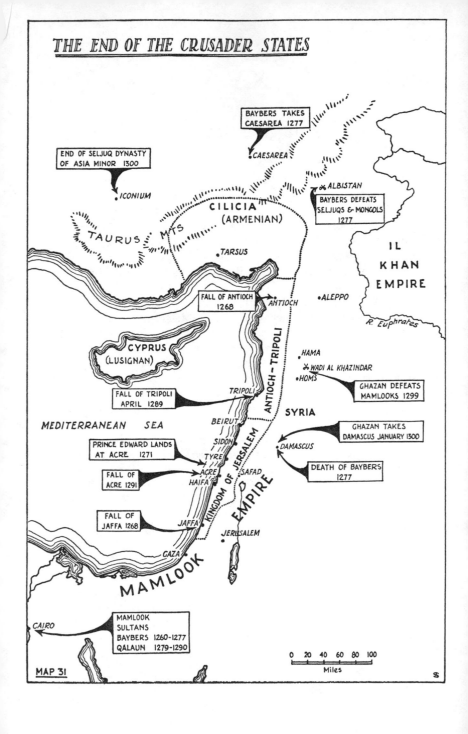

THE END OF THE CRUSADER STATES

BAYBERS TAKES
CAESAREA 1277

• CAESAREA

END OF SELJUQ DYNASTY
OF ASIA MINOR 1300

• ICONIUM

✗ ALBISTAN

BAYBERS DEFEATS
SELJUQS & MONGOLS
1277

CILICIA
(ARMENIAN)

TAURUS MTS

• TARSUS

IL
KHAN
EMPIRE

• ALEPPO

R. Euphrates

CYPRUS
(LUSIGNAN)

FALL OF ANTIOCH
1268

→ ANTIOCH

• HAMA
✗ WADI AL KHAZINDAR
• HOMS

GHAZAN DEFEATS
MAMLOOKS 1299

FALL OF TRIPOLI
APRIL 1289

TRIPOLI

BEIRUT

SYRIA

GHAZAN TAKES
DAMASCUS JANUARY 1300

MEDITERRANEAN   SEA

SIDON

• DAMASCUS

PRINCE EDWARD LANDS
AT ACRE 1271

TYRE

DEATH OF BAYBERS
1277

FALL OF
ACRE 1291

ACRE
HAIFA

SAFAD

FALL OF
JAFFA 1268

JAFFA

• JERUSALEM

GAZA

MAMLOOK

CAIRO

MAMLOOK
SULTANS
BAYBERS 1260-1277
QALAUN 1279-1290

0 20 40 60 80 100
Miles

MAP 31

ANTIOCH-TRIPOLI

KINGDOM OF JERSALEM   EMPIRE

was left with Tripoli alone. The so-called Kingdom of Jerusalem was
reduced to a tiny state consisting only of Haifa, Acre, Tyre, Sidon
and Beirut.

In 1271, when Baybers seemed to be about to take Tripoli,
Prince Edward of Cornwall—later Edward I of England—landed at
Acre. The force which he commanded was too weak to enable him to
attack the Mamlooks, but he communicated with Abagha, the son
and successor of Hulagu, to arrange co-operation. The threat was
enough to persuade Baybers to sign a ten-year truce with Tripoli. On
16th June, 1272, Prince Edward was stabbed by an assassin, possibly
sent by Baybers. His life was saved by his wife, Eleanor, who sucked
the poison from the wound into her own mouth.

In 1277, Baybers carried his arms northwards to Caesarea in
Asia Minor, defeating a Mongol army at Albistan. Shortly afterwards, the Seljuqs of Asia Minor ceased to exist and, for a time, were
succeeded by a Mongol governor. On his return from this campaign,
Baybers was present at a reception in Damascus on 17th June, 1277.
Another of the guests was an Ayoubid prince of whom Baybers was
jealous, and whom he invited to join him for a drink. Baybers had
put poison in the prince's cup but inadvertently drank its contents
himself and died three days later.

The death of Baybers was followed by two years of uncertainty.
Hereditary succession was foreign to the Mamlook system, which was
based on capability alone. All started as slaves and the best man was
free to fight his way to the top. The death of a sultan was often followed by a period of internal struggle between rival commanders
until one succeeded in defeating his competitors. On 9th December,
1279, the Ameer Qalaun was acclaimed as sultan. Like Baybers, he
was a Qipchaq Turk, who had been brought to Egypt as a slave boy
and sold to the Sultan Malik al Salih Ayoub.

In 1281, a Mongol army invaded Syria but was defeated after
desperate fighting on 30th October, 1281, near Homs. It is remarkable that, in the days of Jenghis Khan, the Turks had been utterly
unable to stand up to the Mongols but that, after the death of
Hulagu, the Mamlooks were nearly always victorious. The reason
was perhaps as much administrative as tactical. The Mongols had
reduced Persia to a wilderness and continued to treat the surviving
inhabitants with extreme brutality. They themselves, however, were
incapable of administering the country which they could only
plunder and reduce to penury. As a result, the Il Khans were always
short of money and their army was never paid.

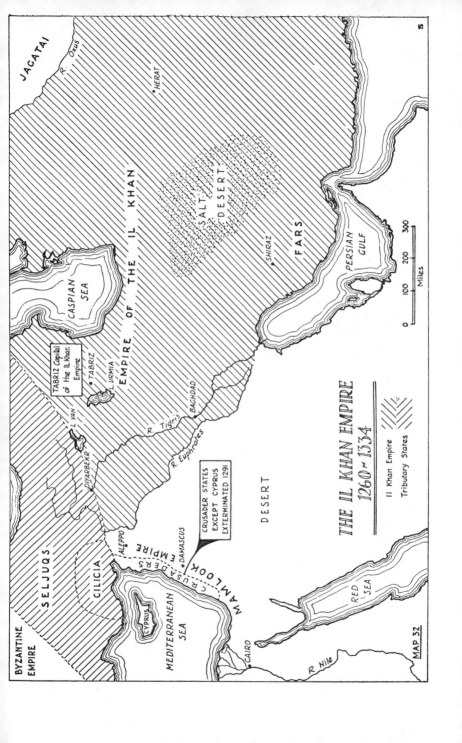

BYZANTINE
EMPIRE

JAGATAI

R. Oxus

• HERAT

SELJUQS

L. VAN

DIYARBEKR

CASPIAN
SEA

URMIA

• TABRIZ

TABRIZ Capital
of the IL Khan.
Empire

EMPIRE OF THE IL KHAN

SALT DESERT

• SHIRAZ

FARS

PERSIAN
GULF

0   100   200   300
Miles

R. Tigris

BAGHDAD

R. Euphrates

CILICIA

• ALEPPO

• DAMASCUS

CRUSADERS

MAMLOOK EMPIRE

CRUSADER STATES
EXCEPT CYPRUS
EXTERMINATED 1291

DESERT

MEDITERRANEAN
SEA

CYPRUS

• CAIRO

R. Nile

RED
SEA

THE IL KHAN EMPIRE
1260–1334

Il Khan Empire

Tributary States

MAP 32

13. THE IL KHANS OF PERSIA

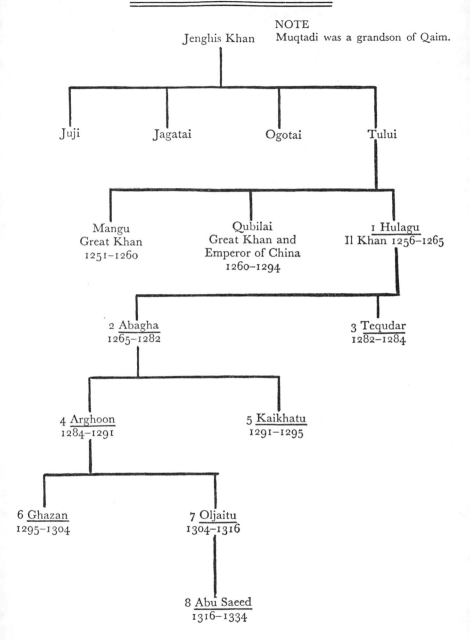

Jenghis Khan

NOTE
Muqtadi was a grandson of Qaim.

Juji

Jagatai

Ogotai

Tului

Mangu
Great Khan
1251–1260

Qubilai
Great Khan and
Emperor of China
1260–1294

1 Hulagu
Il Khan 1256–1265

2 Abagha
1265–1282

3 Tequdar
1282–1284

4 Arghoon
1284–1291

5 Kaikhatu
1291–1295

6 Ghazan
1295–1304

7 Oljaitu
1304–1316

8 Abu Saeed
1316–1334

The Mamlooks were almost as ignorant and as ruthless as the Mongols but they made use of the highly competent Egyptian and Syrian civil service to administer their empire, which was consequently extremely wealthy and prosperous. The Mamlook army was, therefore, well paid and lavishly equipped.

Having defeated the Mongols in 1281, Qalaun decided to complete the extermination of the Franks. In violation of the ten-year truce, he carried Tripoli by assault on 26th April, 1289. All the male inhabitants were massacred, the women being carried into slavery. The remnant of the Crusaders now held only a tiny strip of coast from Acre to Beirut. Early in 1290, Venice, which derived large commercial profits from trade with Acre, sent out a rabble of ill-trained volunteers to defend the city. These, being unpaid and undisciplined, broke out in August 1290 and massacred large numbers of Muslim Arabs.

Using this outrage as a *casus belli*, Qalaun decided to make an end of the Franks, but died on 10th November, 1290, while preparing for the campaign. His son, Khalil, however, led his army to attack Acre. The Mamlooks were ten times as numerous as the garrison and possessed the most powerful siege train ever used in war. On 18th May, 1291, after desperate fighting, the city was carried, all the defenders being killed. The remaining fortresses on the coast were abandoned and the Crusades came to an end after one hundred and ninety-four years of war. The Lusignan Kingdom of Cyprus, however, was to survive for another two centuries.

The death of Sultan Qalaun in 1290 was followed in Egypt by thirteen years of unstable government during which six successive sultans or regents held power. In 1299, a new Mongol invasion occurred under the Il Khan Ghazán, the Mamlooks were defeated at the Battle of Wadi al Khazindar and the Mongols took Damascus. Two months later, however, an army of Jagatai Mongols invaded Persia from the east and the Il Khan was obliged to leave Syria to repel it. The Mamlooks were thus able to reoccupy Damascus unopposed.

*   *   *

As already explained, the Mongols had made the mistake of reducing Persia to an almost uninhabited desert, and continued to plunder and oppress the survivors of its once teeming population. The land went out of cultivation, the cities were destroyed and many of the people took to begging or banditry in order to survive.

Arghoon, the grandson of Hulagu, reigned from 1284 to 1291 and was slightly more enlightened. His wazeer was a Jew and attempted to introduce a regular system of taxation instead of uncontrolled looting. He wrote to Philippe le Bel, King of France, and to Edward I of England, suggesting a new crusade with which he promised to co-operate. The Christian kings, however, replied only with polite excuses.

Ghazan, the son of Arghoon, ruled from 1295 to 1304. His reign was the Golden Age of the Il Khanate. He took Damascus, as we have seen, in 1300, but was obliged to retire from Syria to meet an attack by his Jagatai cousins. Ghazan was a man of quite extraordinary powers. He carried out a survey of the empire, and drew up an assessment of the taxes due from every holding, allowing a period for appeals against the amounts assessed.

For the first time since Jenghis Khan, the government repaired irrigation works and encouraged agriculture. Ghazan was a man of exceptionally versatile genius, a soldier, a lawyer, a financier, an astronomer, a chemist and a botanist. Most of the Mongols were still animists but Ghazan was converted to Islam when he came to the throne.

The reign of this great man seemed to give hope that the Il Khan Empire was about to become a civilized state but, with his death in 1304, the Mongol Empire in Persia declined rapidly. His nephew, Abu Saeed, ruled until 1334, but his reign was punctuated by frequent rebellions and disorders. Anarchy followed his death in 1334 and the Il Khan Empire was divided up between a number of rival chiefs, with their respective capitals in Baghdad, Shiraz, Herat, Diyarbekr and Van.[3]

*   *   *

The Mamlooks reached the pinnacle of their glory at the time when the Il Khans were in decline. The greatest of the Mamlook Sultans was Malik al Nasir Muhammad who, after many early vicissitudes, ruled autocratically from 1310 to 1341. A small, insignificant-looking man, lame in one foot, he possessed a will of iron and the Mamlook ameers—an unscrupulous and ruthless crew—went in terror of his anger.

The Il Khans being in decline, Egypt was left without a serious enemy and grew extremely wealthy from the profits of the trade which flowed through the country from India and the Far East on the

[3] Map 32, page 214.

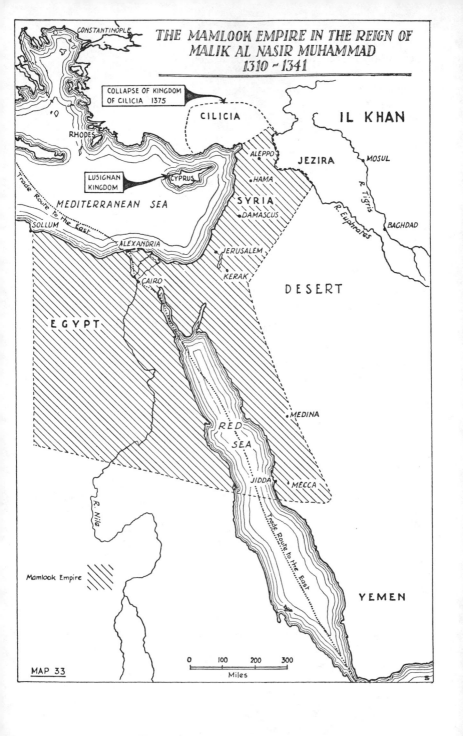

THE MAMLOOK EMPIRE IN THE REIGN OF
MALIK AL NASIR MUHAMMAD
1310 ~ 1341

CONSTANTINOPLE

COLLAPSE OF KINGDOM
OF CILICIA 1375

CILICIA

IL KHAN

RHODES

ALEPPO

JEZIRA

MOSUL

HAMA

LUSIGNAN
KINGDOM

CYPRUS

SYRIA

R. Tigris

Trade Route to the East

MEDITERRANEAN SEA

DAMASCUS

R. Euphrates

BAGHDAD

SOLLUM

ALEXANDRIA

JERUSALEM

CAIRO

KERAK

DESERT

EGYPT

RED
SEA

MEDINA

R. Nile

JIDDA

MECCA

Trade Route to the East

Mamlook Empire

YEMEN

0   100   200   300
Miles

MAP 33

way to Europe. Unlike most Mamlook sultans, Al Nasir was the son of his predecessor, the Sultan Qalaun. As a child he had been exiled to Kerak, east of the Dead Sea, where he had mixed with the Arabs on the verge of the desert. He was the only Mamlook Sultan hitherto who spoke Arabic fluently; most of them had used only Turkish.

Like the Il Khan Ghazan, Al Nasir was thoroughly conversant with every branch of the administration. He watched the government's revenue and expenditure personally, checking the financial statements submitted to him. He was sincerely religious, made several pilgrimages to Mecca, and was extremely severe in punishing bribery, drunkenness and sexual licence. On the other hand, he was not fanatical and was incensed at the persecution of his Christian subjects.

He himself dressed in plain cotton clothing, but he liked magnificence at court and in the army. The Mamlook ameers went gorgeously clad in cloth of gold, silks and satins of all the rainbow colours, and their weapons, saddles and bridles were plastered with gold. The Syrians and Egyptians were not eligible for service in the army but they supplied the civil officials, judges and professors. They also wore robes of honour at court but of a more sombre hue than those of the soldiers.

All this magnificence, and the lavish equipment of the army, called for a great deal of money and the tax collectors often pressed hard on the poor Egyptians, flogging and torture being freely used to extract more cash from the people. Al Nasir was also passionately fond of horses and bought thoroughbred Arab mares for very large sums, thereby enriching the bedouin tribes who bred them.

Great activity was evident during his reign in the building of splendid mosques, palaces and colleges. It was also a period famous for silver, gold filigree, beautiful textiles, artistic furniture and works of art in general. Egypt was one of the Great Powers of the fourteenth century world and Al Nasir was her *roi soleil*. Unlike Louis XIV, however, his reign was followed immediately by the deluge.

*   *   *

With the death of Al Nasir in 1341, the glory departed from Egypt. In the ensuing forty years, twelve of his descendants mounted the unstable throne. Frequent epidemics of bubonic plague, known in contemporary Europe as the Black Death, added to the country's misfortunes.

In 1365, Peter I de Lusignan, King of Cyprus, led a crusade which captured Alexandria. The king was inspired by sincere religious motives and hoped to hold the city as a bargaining counter for the return of Jerusalem to the Christians. His followers, however, consisted of large numbers of adventurers and soldiers of fortune from different European countries. Refusing to obey his orders, they plundered and burned the city and re-embarked with the loot. This piratical operation was disastrous—it exacerbated the hatreds between Muslims and Christians, brought trade to a standstill and ultimately caused the ruin of Cyprus.

On 26th November, 1382, the last of Al Nasir's feeble descendants was dethroned. His successor, Malik al Dhahir Barqooq, was a Circassian, born in the Caucasus and sold as a slave boy into Egypt. The Circassians were a mountain people from the Caucasus, in no way related to the Turkish tribes of the steppes, who had hitherto supplied all the Mamlook sultans. Thenceforward nearly all the sultans were to be Circassians.

The change of race introduced many modifications in the nature of the Mamlook régime. The Circassians were less ruthless and less martial than the Turks. Under them, the discipline of the army was gradually relaxed and its efficiency deteriorated. In Egypt, the régime became more humane, the Mamlooks learned Arabic, were well educated, cultured and polite. Unfortunately the greatness of Egypt had been maintained precisely by the fierce combativeness of the Turks. Under the Circassians, the country was gradually to weaken and then to collapse. Barqooq died on 20th June, 1399, after a prosperous reign of nearly seventeen years.

*   *   *

A hundred and eighty years before the death of Barqooq, during Jenghis Khan's invasion of Persia in 1220, a small Turkman tribe had fled from Khurasan to Asia Minor to escape the Mongol conqueror. A little group of perhaps some four hundred Turkman families settled at Sugut, on the Seljuq-Byzantine frontier, under the suzerainty of the Seljuq sultan.

The chief of the Turkman immigrants was a heathen but his son, Othman, became a Muslim. Curiously enough, Othman was born in 1258, the year of the destruction of Baghdad by Hulagu. The descendants of Othman were to found a mighty Muslim empire and themselves to lay claim to be the successors of the Abbasid khalifs. They assumed the name of the Othmanlis, a word corrupted in Europe to Ottoman.

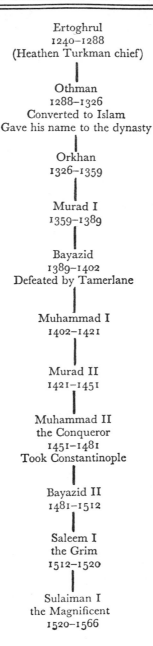

Ertoghrul
1240–1288
(Heathen Turkman chief)

Othman
1288–1326
Converted to Islam
Gave his name to the dynasty

Orkhan
1326–1359

Murad I
1359–1389

Bayazid
1389–1402
Defeated by Tamerlane

Muhammad I
1402–1421

Murad II
1421–1451

Muhammad II
the Conqueror
1451–1481
Took Constantinople

Bayazid II
1481–1512

Saleem I
the Grim
1512–1520

Sulaiman I
the Magnificent
1520–1566

Thereafter the dynasty
degenerated

In 1300, the Seljuq dynasty of Asia Minor came to an end and Othman found himself an independent chief. With the enthusiasm of the convert, he began to prey upon his Christian Byzantine neighbours. The government in Constantinople was completely decadent and the ruling family, the Palaeologi, engaged in endless civil wars. The Othmanlis fought as mercenaries on one side or the other and, in return, obtained lands and settlements.

There were no great battles. The Byzantines were disintegrating and the Othmanlis cautiously and patiently infiltrated into Thrace, then into Macedonia. Murad I (1359–1389) defeated the Bulgarians, the Serbians and the Hungarians, and moved his capital to Adrianople in Thrace. The Othmanlis had become a European power.

Murad was murdered in 1389 by a Serbian and was succeeded by his son Bayazid. Hitherto the Ottomans had dedicated themselves to the holy war against the Christians of Europe. Bayazid, however, turned back to Asia. The collapse of the Seljuqs had been followed by anarchy and more than twenty little Turkish ameerates had divided up their empire between them. By 1393, Bayazid had occupied the whole of Asia Minor. A great new Muslim empire had appeared, extending from the Danube to the Taurus Mountains.

The family of Othman was of Turkman origin but the majority of the inhabitants of their empire were Greeks, Bulgarians, Serbs or of other European nations. Moreover the Turks themselves made lavish use of concubines from many races. As a result, the Ottomans soon constituted a new nation, probably more than half European in origin.

In 1395, the King of Hungary appealed to France for a crusade to drive the Muslims from Europe. In the spring of 1396, the Crusaders left Buda, the western European contingent being commanded by Jean de Nevers, the eldest son of the Duke of Burgundy. On 26th September, 1396, however, they were completely defeated by Bayazid at Nicopolis on the Danube.

*   *   *

Sixty years before, on 8th April, 1336, a boy called Timur had been born in a small Turkish tribe in Trans-Oxiana. The Mongol Jagatai Khans claimed suzerainty over the area but the country was in fact in a state of semi-anarchy. Timur began life as a bandit leader. During this period, he received an arrow-wound in the leg, as a result of which he was nicknamed Timur i Lenk or Timur the Lame, corrupted in the West to Tamerlane.

THE OTTOMAN EMPIRE

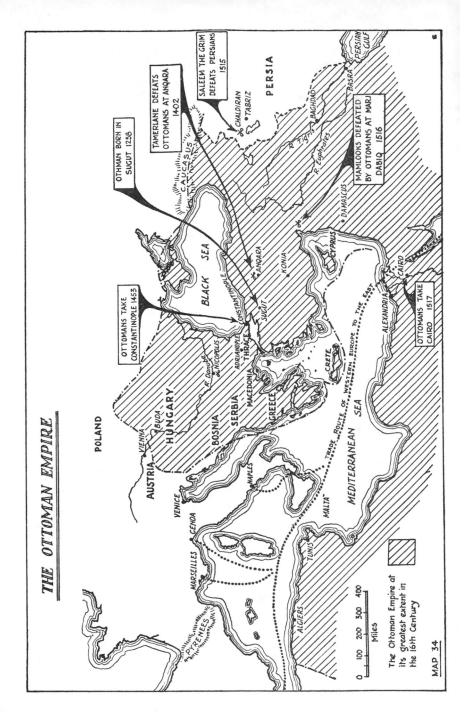

POLAND

AUSTRIA
VIENNA
BUDA
HUNGARY
BOSNIA
SERBIA
GREECE
MACEDONIA
THRACE
ADRIANOPLE
NICOPOLIS
R. Danube

VENICE
GENOA
MARSEILLES
NAPLES

BLACK SEA

CONSTANTINOPLE
SUGUT
KONIA
ANQARA

CAUCASUS

CHALDIRAN
TABRIZ

PERSIA

PERSIAN
GULF

BASRA
BAGHDAD
R. Tigris
R. Euphrates
DAMASCUS
CYPRUS
CRETE

MEDITERRANEAN SEA
TRADE ROUTE OF WESTERN EUROPE TO THE EAST
ALEXANDRIA
CAIRO

ALGIERS
TUNIS
MALTA
PYRENEES

OTHMAN BORN IN SUGUT 1258

TAMERLANE DEFEATS OTTOMANS AT ANQARA 1402

SALEEM THE GRIM DEFEATS PERSIANS 1515

OTTOMANS TAKE CONSTANTINOPLE 1453

MAMLOOKS DEFEATED BY OTTOMANS AT MARJ DABIQ 1516

OTTOMANS TAKE CAIRO 1517

The Ottoman Empire at its greatest extent in the 16th Century

Miles
0   100   200   300   400

MAP 34

By 1370, he had made himself the dictator of Trans-Oxiana. Thence he seized Khuwarizm and, in 1375, he defeated the nominal suzerain of the country, the Jagatai Khan. In the years from 1381 to 1385, he overran the whole of Persia and, in 1386, he took Tabriz and ravaged the Christian Kingdom of Georgia.

It will be remembered that the descendants of Juji, the eldest son of Jenghis Khan, had established themselves on the steppes north of the Caspian, where they were known as the Golden Horde. In 1391, and again in 1395 and 1396, Tamerlane invaded what is now the Ukraine, reaching a point only a little over two hundred miles from Moscow. The Golden Horde was utterly defeated.

In 1398, the conqueror invaded India and sacked Delhi. He recrossed the Indus in March 1399, leaving behind him a trail of smoking ruins and a country strewn with rotting corpses. Everything Tamerlane did was in the tradition of Jenghis Khan, whose name still dominated Central Asia, as that of Napoleon was later for a hundred years to overshadow Europe.

Like Jenghis Khan, Tamerlane massacred every living human being in the cities he captured and then looted and burned them. Perhaps he was more sadistic than Jenghis Khan, for sometimes several days were spent torturing the civilian population and raping the women, before all were killed. The heads of those killed were cut off and built into towers commemorating his victories. In one place, the living bodies of his victims were used as bricks and were built with mortar into a tower. He made no attempt to set up administrations in the countries he conquered. After killing all the inhabitants whom he could catch and burning all the towns and villages, he moved on to seek fresh fields to conquer.

It will be remembered that Sultan Barqooq had ruled the Mamlook Empire from 1382 until 1399. When he returned from Delhi, Tamerlane heard of the death of Barqooq and of the succession of his son, Faraj, who was still a child. After resting for only four months in his capital, Samarqand, he set out again in October 1399, and laid waste the Kingdom of Georgia.

On the west, Tamerlane was faced by two military empires, the Ottomans and the Mamlooks. In August 1400, he took Sivas, which belonged to the Ottoman Sultan Bayazid. In Cairo, Sultan Faraj, the son of Barqooq, was only ten years old and the government was in a ferment of personal intrigues. In October 1400, Tamerlane took Aleppo by storm. The sack of the city lasted four days; all the men and children were killed immediately, but the women were retained

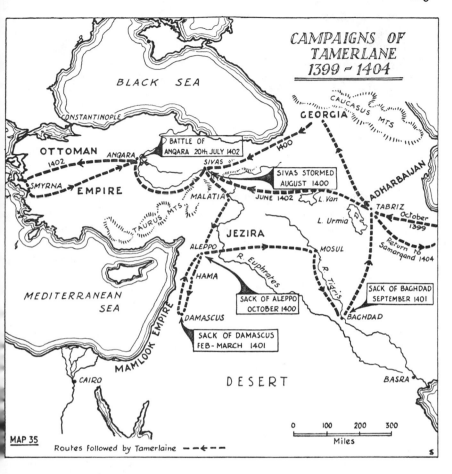

CAMPAIGNS OF
TAMERLANE
1399 ~ 1404

BLACK SEA

CONSTANTINOPLE

CAUCASUS MTS

GEORGIA

OTTOMAN   ANQARA   BATTLE OF
1402   ANQARA 20th JULY 1402

SMYRNA   EMPIRE   SIVAS   1400

MALATIA   SIVAS STORMED
AUGUST 1400

TAURUS MTS   JUNE 1402   L. Van

ADHARBAIJAN

L. Urmia   TABRIZ   October
1399

JEZIRA

ALEPPO   R. Euphrates   MOSUL   Return to
Samarqand 1404

MEDITERRANEAN
SEA

HAMA   R. Tigris

SACK OF ALEPPO
OCTOBER 1400   SACK OF BAGHDAD
SEPTEMBER 1401

DAMASCUS   BAGHDAD

SACK OF DAMASCUS
FEB - MARCH 1401

CAIRO   DESERT   BASRA

MAP 35   Routes followed by Tamerlaine — — ← — —

0   100   200   300

Miles

for some days for the amusement of the troops. A few days later, the
same scenes were repeated in Hama.

Although Aleppo was sacked on 30th October, the Mamlook army
did not leave Cairo until 8th December. On 26th December, an
indecisive action between the two armies took place outside Damascus. On 8th January, 1401, a rumour reached the Mamlook camp
that a rival group of ameers was planning a *coup d'état* in Cairo.
Incredible as it may appear, the sultan and the senior officers
deserted the army during the night and rode for Cairo. In the
morning the troops, finding that the senior officers had vanished,

themselves followed their example, leaving Tamerlane in possession of the field.

Damascus, however, was a walled city and Tamerlane, not wishing to undertake a siege, sent for a deputation of the notables and told them benevolently that he would spare Damascus "for the sake of the Companions of the Prophet who had dwelt there". The citizens, immensely relieved, threw open the gates. No sooner, however, was Tamerlane's army inside than the sack began. All the women were herded together to be raped, while the men were tortured in public with every form of sadistic refinement. This orgy of brutality lasted for nineteen days. Before leaving, Tamerlane gave orders for the city to be burnt to the ground.

From Damascus, the conqueror returned to Aleppo, and then marched on Baghdad, which he reached in July 1401. The people of Baghdad, warned by the fate of Damascus, put up a desperate resistance for six weeks. When the city was eventually taken by storm, a hundred thousand people were massacred. One hundred and twenty towers were built with the severed heads.

From Baghdad Tamerlane marched to Adharbaijan. In June 1402, he invaded Asia Minor and utterly defeated the Ottomans at Anqara on 20th July. Sultan Bayazid was taken prisoner and died in captivity seven months later. All Asia Minor was laid waste with fire and sword, and the Ottoman Empire seemed to have ceased to exist. Tamerlane returned to Samarqand and died on 18th February, 1405.

*   *   *

Tamerlane's ultimate heir, his fourth son, Shah Rukh (1409–1447) proved to be a man of peace. He made his capital in Herat and the mangled remains of the Ottoman and Mamlook Empires enjoyed a breathing space. Iraq and Baghdad, however, continued to be over-run and plundered by Turkman tribes. In the days of the Abbasids, Iraq had been one of the richest countries in the world. Then the Ghuzz Turkmans in the eleventh century, Hulagu in the thirteenth and Tamerlane, followed by more Turkmans, reduced its wealth, culture and beauty to heaps of dusty rubble. "The very word civilization is no longer applied to Baghdad," laments a contemporary Egyptian historian.

*   *   *

The Mamlook Empire recovered some of its prosperity in the century following the death of Tamerlane. The Circassian Sultans were, on the whole, peaceable, pious and conscientious but the discipline of the army continued to deteriorate. The Mamlooks had owed their military triumphs entirely to their cavalry which, in the thirteenth and fourteenth centuries, had been unrivalled anywhere in the world with sword, lance and bow.

The Ottoman Empire remained in weakness and confusion until 1413. Thereafter it began slowly to recover. In 1453, the Sultan Muhammad II, the Conqueror, took Constantinople and the last poor remnants of the Byzantine Empire disappeared from the map. Muhammad the Conqueror had taken the city by the use of great masses of the new artillery, but the Mamlooks regarded the use of firearms as dishonourable. In military tactics, the Ottomans were ahead of any army in Europe. The use of gunpowder as a propellent had indeed been invented in the West but the Ottomans were in advance of their competitors in its tactical employment.

At the beginning of the sixteenth century, the position of the Ottoman Empire was not unlike that of the United States today. Armed with all the most modern weapons, virile, energetic and powerful, it was expanding in every direction. In Persia, a national revival was also in progress under the new dynasty of the Safavids. Of the old régimes, the Mongols and the Seljuqs had vanished. Only the Mamlook Empire, now two hundred and thirty-six years old, still survived.

In 1512, Saleem I, nicknamed the Grim, became Ottoman Sultan. Marching first against Persia, Saleem I completely defeated Shah Ismail the Safavid at Chaldiran.[4] The victory was gained by the Ottoman artillery, the Persians having virtually no firearms.

Saleem the Grim then turned on the Mamlooks. The two armies met at Marj Dabiq, north of Aleppo, on 24th August, 1516. The Ottomans brought a large mass of artillery and the Janissary infantry were armed with handguns. The Mamlook cavalry, clad in splendid uniforms and superbly mounted but armed only with sword, lance and bow, were shot to pieces. The Mamlook Sultan Qansuh al Ghori was killed in action and the army destroyed. In October 1516, the Ottomans occupied Damascus unopposed and marched on to Egypt. On 22nd January, 1517, the Mamlooks were again defeated outside Cairo and Saleem the Grim entered the city.

Syria and Palestine were to remain under Ottoman rule for four hundred years. Not until 1917 did the British army advancing from Egypt and the Arabs from the Hejaz commence the task of their eviction.

[4] Map 34, page 223.

NOTABLE DATES

Accession of Baybers the Bunduqdari	1260
Fall of Antioch	1268
Death of Baybers	1277
Fall of Tripoli	1289
Fall of Acre	1291
Capture of Damascus by Il Khan Ghazan	1300
End of the Seljuqs of Asia Minor	1300
Collapse of the Il Khan Empire	1334
Reign of the Mamlook Sultan Al Nasir	1310–1341
Accession of the first Circassian, Sultan Barqooq	1382
Defeat of the Crusade at Nicopolis	1396
Capture of Aleppo by Tamerlane	1400
Sack of Damascus	1401
Destruction of Baghdad by Tamerlane	1401
Conquest of Syria and Egypt by the Ottomans	1517

PERSONALITIES

Great Mamlook Sultans

Baybers the Bunduqdari	1260–1277
Qalaun	1279–1290
Malik al Nasir Muhammad	1310–1341
(He had previously been twice appointed and dethroned as a child)	
Malik al Dhahir Barqooq	1382–1399

Famous Mongol Khans

Jenghis Khan	1206–1227
Qubilai, Emperor of China	1260–1294
Hulagu, Il Khan of Persia	1256–1265
Abagha	1265–1282
Arghoon	1284–1291
Ghazan	1295–1304
Abu Saeed	1316–1334
End of the dynasty (Only famous or successful khans are mentioned)	

Famous Othmanlis

    Othman, founder of the dynasty   1288–1326
    Murad I, his grandson   1359–1389
    Bayazid   1389–1402
    Muhammad the Conqueror   1451–1481
    Saleem the Grim   1512–1520

Other Personalities

    Tamerlane   1370–1405

XVI

The Ottoman Period

THE conquest of Syria, Palestine and Egypt by the Ottomans resulted in an immediate deterioration in the administration and wealth of those countries. At first sight this may seem surprising. The Mamlooks had consisted of a ruling class continually recruited from the wild nomads of Central Asia. The Othmanlis were a mixed race, composed partly of Turks but, to at least an equal degree, of Muslim converts who were racially Greeks, Serbs, Bosnians, Albanians, Bulgarians and other peoples. Moreover they had been established for two centuries on the territories of the former Byzantine Empire, one of the most civilized governments then in existence. It would have been natural to expect the Othmanlis to be a great improvement on the Mamlooks.

The cause may perhaps best be found in the problem of distance. The Mamlooks had lived in Cairo and Damascus. Themselves no more than a military ruling class, they had left administration, justice, revenue collection, religion, education and commerce to the Syrians and the Egyptians. The Othmanli capital, on the other hand, was in Constantinople—henceforward called Istanbul[1]—several weeks' journey from Damascus.

Moreover the origin of the Othmanli state had been a community of Muslim warriors on the borders of Christendom, whose task in life was holy war. This outlook coloured the whole of their mentality for the many centuries of existence of their empire. Religion and war were their guiding stars. Culture, science, commerce and industry were contemptuously abandoned by them to the subject races. The Mamlooks, on the other hand, were nearly all born heathen and converted to Islam on arrival in Syria or Egypt where, in their own interests, they carefully fostered commerce and agriculture.

Like the Mamlooks, the Ottoman government relied largely on boys recruited as slaves. Some of these were bought, but many were the sons of Christian families, taken as children, converted to Islam and

[1] It has been suggested that Istanbul was a Turkish mispronunciation of Constantinople.

rigorously trained and educated in special schools in Istanbul. The intellectually brilliant were used as clerks and civil officials. The strong and courageous were drafted into the Janissaries, the finest infantry in the world. The whole framework of the imperial government consisted of such men who could rise, as a result of their own efforts, from slaves to wazeers, pashas and army commanders.

Returning from his conquest of Egypt in 1517, Saleem the Grim appointed Fakhr al Deen Mani to be the ruler of Lebanon. The mountains made military operations difficult and it was to the advantage of the distant imperial government to delegate control of the area to a local dynasty. Lebanon was to enjoy some form of local autonomy throughout the whole Ottoman period. The open plains east of the mountains, extending from Aleppo and the Jezira to Damascus, afforded fewer obstacles to military operations and large garrisons in Damascus, Aleppo and Diyarbekr sufficed to maintain a moderate degree of control.

When Saleem died in 1520, the Ottoman Empire was at the very height of its glory, perhaps the greatest military power in the world. The very *raison d'être* of the empire was to fight the Christians of Europe and, although Saleem the Grim had devoted several years to wars against the Persians and the Mamlooks, his son, Sulaiman the Magnificent, returned to the traditional preoccupations of his forbears. He completely defeated the Hungarians at Mohaç in 1526 and annexed nearly all Hungary. The Ottomans were to remain in Budapest for two hundred and fifty years.

The principal enemy of Sulaiman the Magnificent in Europe was the Holy Roman Emperor, Charles V. Against him, the sultan concluded a treaty with François I, King of France, which included the grant of special facilities to French nationals in the Ottoman Empire. This favour granted by the magnificent sultan to his weaker ally, the King of France, was to develop into the system of capitulations, used by the European Powers to interfere, three hundred years later, in Ottoman internal affairs. Sulaiman's two abortive attempts to take Vienna constituted the high water mark of Ottoman conquest in Europe.

*   *   *

In the East, as we have seen, Baghdad had been destroyed by Hulagu in 1258 and again by Tamerlane in 1401. Thereafter, the once glorious capital of the khalifs was held, first by the Jalair Mongols, then the Black Sheep tribe and subsequently the White

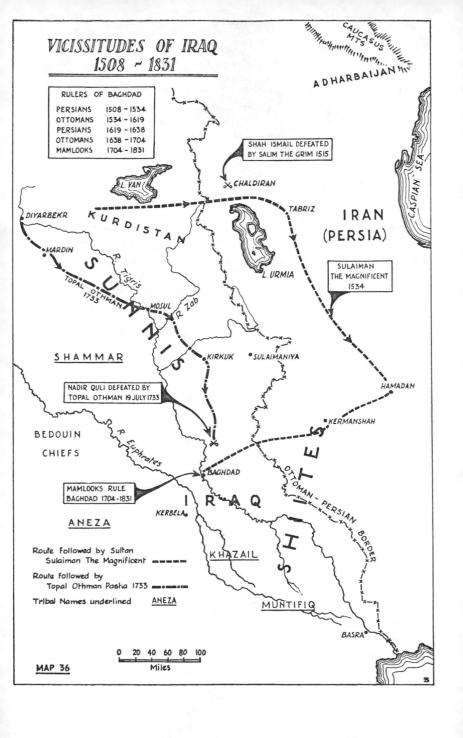

VICISSITUDES OF IRAQ
1508 ~ 1831

RULERS OF BAGHDAD

PERSIANS	1508 ~ 1534
OTTOMANS	1534 ~ 1619
PERSIANS	1619 ~ 1638
OTTOMANS	1638 ~ 1704
MAMLOOKS	1704 ~ 1831

CAUCASUS MTS

ADHARBAIJAN

SHAH ISMAIL DEFEATED
BY SALIM THE GRIM 1515

× CHALDIRAN

CASPIAN SEA

L. VAN

DIYARBEKR

K U R D I S T A N

TABRIZ

IRAN
(PERSIA)

MARDIN

TOPAL OTHMAN 1733

S U N I S

R. Tigris

L. URMIA

SULAIMAN
THE MAGNIFICENT
1534

MOSUL

R. Zab

SHAMMAR

KIRKUK   • SULAIMANIYA

HAMADAN

NADIR QULI DEFEATED BY
TOPAL OTHMAN 19 JULY 1733

×

• KERMANSHAH

BEDOUIN

CHIEFS

R. Euphrates

BAGHDAD

S H I I T E S

OTTOMAN ~ PERSIAN BORDER

MAMLOOKS RULE
BAGHDAD 1704~1831

ANEZA

KERBELA

I R A Q

Route followed by Sultan
Sulaiman The Magnificent ‒ ‒ ‒ ‒

KHAZAIL

S H I

Route followed by
Topal Othman Pasha 1733 ‒·‒·‒·

Tribal Names underlined   ANEZA

MUNTIFIQ

BASRA•

0 20 40 60 80 100

Miles

MAP 36

Sheep Turkmans. A shabby provincial town, it consisted of mudbrick buildings amid mounds of the rubble of its former palaces.

But in 1500 began the Persian national revival under the Safavids. In 1508, Shah Ismail took Baghdad and then Mosul and the whole of Iraq was incorporated in Persia. In 1515, the Persian revival received a severe check when Shah Ismail was defeated by Saleem the Grim at Chaldiran. But Saleem did not march southward into Iraq. Leaving garrisons in Mosul, Mardin and Diyarbekr, he returned to confront the Mamlooks.

In 1534, however, Sultan Sulaiman, at the very pinnacle of his magnificence, decided once more to chastise the Shiites. In April of that year, the Grand Wazeer, Ibrahim Pasha, marched out of Aleppo and occupied Tabriz. Here the sultan joined the army and assumed command. In November, the Ottomans marched through the mountains to Hamadan and Kermanshah, suffering intensely from the cold, which caused the death of many men and horses and the loss of guns and waggons. At length the exhausted army reached Baghdad unopposed, and Sulaiman made a state entry into what was left of the once glorious city of the Abbasids. Leaving a garrison of two thousand men, the sultan returned to Tabriz.

Incorporation in a mighty empire might well have brought peace and recovery to unhappy Iraq, which had suffered three centuries of ruin, chaos, plunder and devastation at the hands of the Turks, Mongols and her own lawless tribes. Her fate was in fact to be sadly different. Her situation, almost infinitely remote from Istanbul, made supervision from the capital impossible. The governors sent to rule her were anxious only to amass fortunes and recoup themselves for the bribes which they had paid in order to secure their appointments.

Wars with Persia were henceforward to be endemic, aggravated by the fact that the inhabitants of Iraq south of Baghdad were Shiites and thus more favourable to the shah than to the sultan. In 1587, a furious battle was fought just outside the city with a column of invading Persians. In 1604 they were back again and, in 1605, they blockaded the city.

In general, large Ottoman garrisons held Mosul and Baghdad but over Kurdistan and Basra scarcely any control was exercised. The local Arab and Kurdish princes and chiefs found ample scope for intrigue in simultaneous professions of devotion to shah and sultan, while offering violent opposition to the troops of either, should they enter their territory.

The Syrian desert from Aleppo to Kerbela was in the hands of the great bedouin tribes, who exacted transit dues from travellers and merchants and tribute from the towns and villages on the fringes of the desert. The bedouin princes went clad in satin and cloth of gold, rode on the purest of thoroughbreds and affected the manners of haughty aristocrats when dealing with members of such lesser breeds as townsmen or villagers.

Yet town life in the early Ottoman days was very similar to that of contemporary Europe. The Qoran, reading and writing were taught in the mosque schools. Merchants paid their own watchmen to guard their property. The Qadhi judged lawsuits according to Muslim religious law, which they believed to have been dictated by God himself. Some officials were honest and efficient, others took bribes. Travellers between one town and the next were well advised to pay tolls to the chiefs of the tribes through whose territory they wished to pass, but, if they did so, they were normally safe from interference. Life might have been much worse.

From the death of Sulaiman the Magnificent in 1566 to the reign of Murad IV (1623–1640), the Ottoman Empire went through a period of weakness and confusion under a succession of vicious or incapable sultans. In 1619, during this period, Bekr the Su Bashi, a captain of Janissaries in Baghdad, in a military *coup d'état* made himself master of the city. When an Ottoman army was sent to chastise him, Bekr invited Shah Abbas of Persia to take over.

Alarmed at the possibility of Baghdad reverting to the Persians, the sultan agreed to appoint the mutinous captain as governor. As a result, when the shah arrived, Bekr declared himself a loyal Ottoman and refused to admit him. But the Janissary who had betrayed his sultan was himself betrayed by his own son, Muhammad. The latter secretly opened the gates to the shah, in return for his own appointment as governor in lieu of his father, who was tortured to death. The Ottoman relief army was defeated by Shah Abbas the Great and Baghdad remained Persian. In 1629, however, Abbas the Great died after a reign of forty-two years. His grandson and successor, Shah Safi, proved unequal to the task of maintaining the military conquests of his mighty grandfather.

In the Ottoman Empire, by contrast, Murad IV had ascended the throne in 1623, after sixty years of confusion under seven weak sultans. Murad IV was the last sultan to lead his armies in person. On 15th November, 1638, he appeared beneath the walls of Baghdad with a great army. On Christmas Day the Persian governor surrendered and a general massacre of Persians ensued. Peace was concluded in 1639, the Persian frontier being fixed on approximately its present alignment. For the ensuing eighty years, Iraq was quieter than Syria and very much quieter than Istanbul.

This does not, of course, mean that the government was in control, but only that no major international disturbances occurred. The Ottoman administration held Baghdad, Mosul and Kirkuk in general but Basra only fitfully. The tribes, however, were almost completely out of control, notably such powerful groups as Shammar (who arrived from Central Arabia in the 1640s), Aneza, Khazail and the Muntifiq in the south.[2]

The appointment of Hasan Pasha[3] Mustafa to be governor of Baghdad in 1704 opened a new era in Iraq. Mustafa Beg, his father, had been a cavalry officer under Murad IV and Hasan was brought up in the palace school in Istanbul. In 1683, at the age of twenty-five, Hasan began a series of palace appointments, culminating in the governorships of Konia, Aleppo and Urfa (the ancient Edessa). In 1704, at the age of forty-seven, he became Pasha of Baghdad. For nineteen years, his endless campaigns against insurgent tribes from Kurdistan to the Persian Gulf maintained the prestige of the sultan without contributing to the peace or progress of Iraq.

In 1723, however, Mahmood Khan Ghilzai, an Afghan chief, marched on Isfahan, dethroned the last shah of the Safavid dynasty, and proclaimed himself Shah of Persia. Hoping to profit by the ensuing confusion, the Porte[4] in 1723 declared war on Persia. Hasan Pasha, with the Baghdad army, occupied Kermanshah but died in the middle of the campaign. His son, Ahmad Pasha, replaced him and captured Hamadan. After four years of useless and costly war, peace was concluded on the basis of the pre-war frontier.

Meanwhile, however, the Ghilzai usurper had been overthrown and Nadir Quli Khan, a great conqueror in the old style, had seized power in Isfahan. In January 1733, he invaded Iraq and laid siege to Baghdad. The Persians, weak in artillery, were unable to breach the walls but their blockade was so close that, by July 1733, the city was starving. Not only was there no sign of a relieving army but Baghdad itself contained many Shiites, some of them Persians, who

[2] Map 36, page 232.
[3] The title of Pasha was awarded in the Ottoman Empire to cabinet ministers, generals commanding divisions or provincial governors. It was not hereditary and corresponded approximately to knighthood in Britain.
[4] The Sublime Porte, or the Exalted Gate, was a synonym for the Ottoman government as the Court of St. James' was for that of England

sympathized with the enemy. Only the dominating personality of Ahmad Pasha made continued resistance possible.

But help was on the way. Topal Othman Pasha, or Othman the Lame, had been educated in the palace schools of Istanbul and had served a long career, rising to be commander-in-chief in Greece and governor of Roumelia. Old, lame and crippled with wounds, he was called back to the colours by the crisis in Baghdad, though he had to be carried in a litter on the long march from Istanbul to Kirkuk, a distance of more than a thousand miles. Simple, loyal and brave, a personal friend of every private soldier in the army, he was gentle, humble, generous and pious. The magnificent, boastful and ruthless Nadir Quli Khan impatiently awaited the arrival of the old pasha on the plain north-east of Baghdad.

Topal Othman rose on the morning of 19th July, 1733, said his prayers and mounted his horse, for the first time in the whole campaign. "I saw him riding along like a young man, sword in hand, with animated countenance and sparkling eyes," wrote his French doctor, Jean Nicodème.[5]

A terrific pitched battle lasted all day long on 19th July. The Persian cavalry, fifty thousand horsemen, led in person by the dashing, fearless Nadir Quli Khan, drove the Turkish cavalry from the field, but the infantry stood firm. Two thousand Kurds, deserting the Ottoman army in the middle of the battle, opened a gap in the line but old Othman, cool and determined, called up his reserves and restored the situation. Not until a little before sunset did the Janissaries advance and sweep the broken Persian army from the field. Nadir Quli Khan, who had had two horses shot under him, recrossed the frontier, and Baghdad was saved. More than a hundred thousand persons are said to have died of starvation in the city.

Both sides had lost half their effectives in the battle. Nadir halted in Hamadan for three months, during which he summoned contingents from all parts of the Persian empire, until he found himself at the head of a new army as powerful as that which he had lost. But Topal Othman's desperate appeals to Istanbul produced no reinforcements or stores. On 26th October, 1733, the two armies met once again. Topal Othman was shot dead and his army virtually exterminated.

Nevertheless Baghdad was saved. Nadir, receiving reports of a rising in Fars, was obliged to return to Persia, where, in 1736, he was

[5] S. H. Longrigg, *Four Centuries of Modern Iraq*.

proclaimed Nadir Shah and became one of the great conquerors of history.

Ahmad Pasha continued to govern Iraq until his death in 1747. The Ottoman Empire was in weakness and confusion and Ahmad Pasha reigned as an almost independent prince. His father and he himself had been products of the "slave" schools of Istanbul and had built up around themselves a similar court and army of "slaves", most of whom they recruited from Georgia and Caucasia.

In these circumstances, the Sublime Porte welcomed the death of Ahmad Pasha as an opportunity to appoint a governor of their own choice. The officials and the troops in Baghdad, however, were nearly all the slaves or the freedmen of Ahmad Pasha or of his father. Four Istanbul nominees having failed to exercise any control, the sultan was obliged to recognize Sulaiman Pasha, the son-in-law of Ahmad Pasha, as governor of Iraq.

Thereafter the "Mamlook" régime was to rule Iraq until 1831, a total period of one hundred and twenty-five years. During the winter of 1830–31, a terrible visitation of bubonic plague reduced Baghdad to helplessness. In April 1831, two to three thousand persons are said to have died in the city every day. All those able to do so fled from Baghdad. Military discipline vanished, whole regiments were exterminated, robbers ranged the streets unchecked, communications had broken down and there was no food to be bought.

In April 1831, the Tigris burst its banks, the city was flooded, the citadel collapsed and hundreds of houses fell in ruins. The stars in their courses seemed to be intent on the ruin of the Mamlooks. Their palaces, their jewels, their silks and their satins, their handsome courtiers and their splendid regiments had vanished.

In June 1831, Ali Ridha Pasha arrived with an army outside Baghdad, bearing an imperial decree deposing Daud, the Mamlook ruler. After some procrastination, looting and misery, Daud rode out to the camp of Ali Ridha, and gave himself up, expecting instant death. Ali Ridha Pasha, however, was a gentleman, greeted the fallen prince with dignity and a cup of coffee and secured his pardon by the sultan. Daud Pasha, at first exiled to Brusa, was later employed in high office and died in 1851.

Thus ended the one hundred and twenty-seven years of Mamlook rule in Baghdad, during which a succession of Caucasian slaves, many of them originally Christian boys from Georgia, had ruled Iraq, in the midst of a brilliant court and in well-nigh regal splendour. Thereafter Iraq, as we shall see in a later chapter, was to become an

Ottoman province and to be subjected to those unhappy reforms which did little to improve the lot of the people.

*   *   *

In Syria and Palestine, the termination of the Mamlook régime in 1517 had, as we have seen, led to a deterioration of the standard of administration. The Ottoman governors secured their appointments through bribery or favouritism at court, and were so frequently changed that no continuity was possible. In the Arab countries, personal government has always been the rule and everything depends on the establishment of a sympathetic and loyal relationship between the ruler and the people. In its first one hundred and eighty years under Ottoman rule, however, Damascus suffered no less than a hundred and thirty-three governors.

Ever since the dawn of history, three thousand years before Christ, Syria had been at the centre of the world. The cockpit between the Pharaohs and the Assyrians, the Persians and the Greeks, the Persians and the Romans, then the capital of the Arab Empire, she had been the perpetual victim of foreign conquest. This constant subjection to foreign rule had in Syria assumed a pattern, endlessly repeated for four thousand years.

After each conquest, the foreigners garrisoned the great cities, Tyre, Sidon, Beirut, Antioch, Aleppo, Hama, Damascus, all of which rapidly adopted the outward appearance of the new culture, Greek, Latin, Arab or Turk. To some extent, the foreign rulers intermarried with the people of the cities, so that the racial composition of the town-dwellers was changed. But beneath this surface conformity with successive foreign cultures, a deep conservatism dwelt in the souls of the people, particularly of the rural and tribal populations, who rarely mixed with, or even encountered, the foreign rulers.

This isolation of the rural and desert populations, on the one hand, from the city-dwellers on the other, became increasingly emphasized in Ottoman times, owing to the failure of the government to maintain public security. The tribes were constantly out of control and the merchants and townsmen, living in perpetual fear, rallied to the authorities, such as they were, as their only protection. Thus the population was divided into two mutually suspicious groups, townspeople and countrymen, a breach not healed to this day.

The Ottomans had early abandoned any attempt to control Trans-Jordan, which, for nearly four hundred years, remained under Arab tribal chiefs. Lebanon also was virtually independent, the mountainous country being too costly to conquer. From the Ottoman conquest

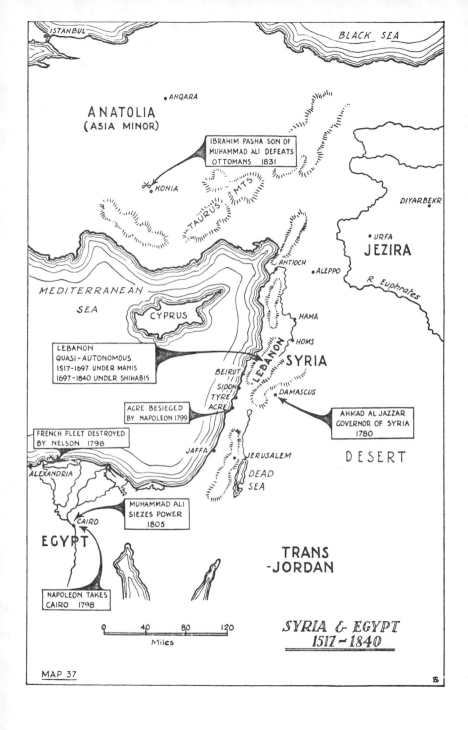

ISTANBUL

BLACK SEA

ANATOLIA
(ASIA MINOR)

• ANQARA

IBRAHIM PASHA SON OF
MUHAMMAD ALI DEFEATS
OTTOMANS 1831

✂ KONIA

TAURUS MTS

DIYARBEKR

• URFA

JEZIRA

MEDITERRANEAN

SEA

CYPRUS

ANTIOCH

• ALEPPO

R. Euphrates

HAMA

HOMS

LEBANON
QUASI-AUTONOMOUS
1517-1697 UNDER MANIS
1697-1840 UNDER SHIHABIS

BEIRUT

LEBANON

SYRIA

SIDON
TYRE
ACRE

• DAMASCUS

ACRE BESIEGED
BY NAPOLEON 1799

FRENCH FLEET DESTROYED
BY NELSON 1798

AHMAD AL JAZZAR
GOVERNOR OF SYRIA
1780

JAFFA

✂

ALEXANDRIA

DESERT

• JERUSALEM

DEAD
SEA

MUHAMMAD ALI
SIEZES POWER
1805

CAIRO

EGYPT

TRANS
-JORDAN

NAPOLEON TAKES
CAIRO 1798

0   40   80   120

Miles

SYRIA & EGYPT
1517 – 1840

MAP 37

in 1517 until 1697, Lebanon was ruled by the Manis. The greatest of this line of princes was Fakhr al Deen II, who governed from 1590 to 1635, and who, without the cognizance of the Ottoman Sultan, concluded a treaty with the Medici, the then rulers of Florence.

In 1625, the first Jesuit missionaries arrived in Lebanon and a Maronite[6] college was established in Rome, drawing Lebanese students to be educated in Italy. Thus did Lebanon renew its contacts with Europe, severed more than three centuries earlier after the fall of Acre in 1291.

When the Manis became extinct in 1697, their place as princes of Lebanon was taken by the Shihabis, who were to survive until 1840. The greatest of the dynasty was Basheer II al Shihabi, who ruled from 1788 to 1840. His palace at Bait al Deen above Beirut, a little Lebanese Versailles, is still worthy of a visit.

The inaccessible mountain fastnesses of Lebanon had always been the refuge of persecuted sects and its population included not only Maronite, Orthodox and Roman Catholic Christians, but also Sunni and Shiite Muslims and Druzes. The great Basheer al Shihabi is reputed to have demonstrated his religious neutrality by keeping three wives, a Muslim, a Christian and a Druze. All three religions claimed the prince as a member of their community but Basheer himself, like Brer Rabbit, just lay low and said nothing.

In 1772, the Ottoman Empire being at war with Russia, a Russian fleet bombarded Sidon and Beirut. At the same time, Ottoman control being at a low ebb, Dhahir al Umar, an Arab chief, made himself ruler of northern Palestine with his capital at Acre, and is said to have governed better than did the sultan's officers, doubtless because he was known to the people.

A more picturesque adventurer was Ahmad al Jazzár, or the Butcher, a Christian Bosnian boy, sold as a slave in Egypt. Escaping from his master, he succeeded Dhahir al Umar in Acre, whence he embarked on a career of conquest culminating in the seizure of Damascus. Unable to evict him, the sultan appointed him governor of Syria in 1780. In 1799, Napoleon, having conquered Egypt, laid siege to Acre, which was heroically defended by Ahmad the Butcher, assisted by the British fleet under Sir Sidney Smith.

*   *   *

[6] The Maronites were a Christian Church, pronounced heretical by the Byzantines in 680, who took refuge in the Lebanese mountains. In 1736, the Maronites acknowledged the authority of the pope, while retaining certain local peculiarities. The great majority of Lebanese Christians are Maronites today.

When Saleem the Grim returned from Egypt in 1517, he left behind him an Ottoman governor and a garrison of five thousand Janissaries. But the whole ruling class of Egypt consisted of Mamlooks, who also owned the greater part of the land. Already in the seventeenth century, the governors sent by the Sublime Porte were frequently resisted or assassinated. As a military expedition to Egypt was beyond Ottoman resources, the sultan was unable to retaliate.

By 1700, all power in Egypt was once again in the hands of the Mamlooks, the pasha, or Ottoman governor, being little more than the ambassador of a foreign government. In 1770, Ali Bey, a Mamlook, even declared Egyptian independence. The Mamlooks, however, were not united and Ali was overthrown by a rival.

On 1st July, 1798, Napoleon Bonaparte landed near Alexandria, defeated the Mamlooks and took Cairo, though his fleet was destroyed on 1st August by Nelson. He invaded Syria but his failure to take Acre and his own return to France resulted in the evacuation of Egypt.

The whole of this campaign is of great historical significance. From perhaps 3000 B.C. to the end of the fifteenth century A.D., Egypt and Syria had been at the very centre of human progress. Then, in 1498, Vasco da Gama had discovered the Cape of Good Hope, and the expanding fleets and commerce of Europe had by-passed the Middle East and had reached India and China round the Cape. To the world at large, Egypt and Syria became a forgotten backwater. The mind of Napoleon, however, grasped the significance of their geographical position at the crossroads of the three continents of Europe, Asia and Africa.

Napoleon's plan was to establish a French military base in Egypt, with French fleets commanding the Mediterranean and the Red Sea. This, he believed, would enable him to secure naval command of the Indian Ocean, and to defeat the British fleet which was maintained in those waters at the end of a long line of communications round the Cape.

The destruction of the French fleet at the Battle of the Nile destroyed these hopes, but, in the last years of his life on St. Helena, Napoleon expressed the opinion that it was his failure to hold Egypt which had spoiled his destiny.

There is food for thought in the realization that every great empire in history, from the Assyrians and the Babylonians to the Ottomans and the British, have made a point of holding Egypt. Such attempted empires as failed to secure Egypt—those of Napoleon, Kaiser

Wilhelm II and Hitler—failed to secure the domination of Europe.

After the Napoleonic débâcle, the British government assisted the Ottomans to instal a governor in Egypt. This officer attempted a treacherous massacre of the leading Mamlooks, whom he had invited to a reception. Shortly afterwards, a force of Albanian troops in Ottoman service mutinied and drove out the Turkish governor. Egypt was now torn between three rival parties, the Ottomans, the Mamlooks and the Albanians. All three groups were foreigners, the people of Egypt being passive spectators of their battles.

In 1805, as a result of bloody street fighting in Cairo, Muhammad Ali, the commander of the Albanians, seized power and drove out the Ottomans. In 1811, Muhammad Ali invited the principal Mamlooks to a ceremony in the citadel at which they were treacherously massacred, leaving him as the undisputed ruler of Egypt.

While these events had been in progress, a fanatical puritan revival, known as Wahhabi-ism had taken place in Central Arabia. Under the leadership of a minor chief of the Aneza tribe, Muhammad ibn Saud, the tribes of Central Arabia had swept northwards, massacring and plundering, alike in Iraq and in Syria. In 1802, they had captured the Holy Cities of Islam, Mecca and Medina. Unable to send an expedition to Arabia, the Ottoman Sultan Mahmood II commissioned his nominal feudatory, Muhammad Ali, to do so. Fighting lasted from 1812 to 1818, when the Wahhabis were, at least temporarily, suppressed.

In 1831, however, Muhammad Ali rebelled and an army under his son, Ibrahim Pasha, marched triumphantly through Syria and defeated the Ottomans at Konia in Asia Minor. The war was stopped by the intervention of the Powers of Europe, Muhammad Ali being allowed to annex Syria to Egypt. Fighting was resumed in 1840 but the Powers again intervened; Muhammad Ali was obliged to abandon Syria but was recognized as the hereditary ruler of Egypt, under purely nominal Ottoman suzerainty.

Muhammad Ali's military successes had been partly due to his employment of European officers, doctors and other officials. By this means, he started Egypt on the path of westernization, long before Syria, Iraq or Arabia, which were to remain under Ottoman rule until 1918.

Many people in the West today believe Egypt to have been the traditional leader of the Arabs in history. The present narrative has already shown the falsity of this impression. In the great days of the Arabs, from 634 to 900 let us say, the capital was first in Medina, then in Damascus and ultimately in Baghdad. Egypt reached its greatest power and extension under the Mamlooks, who were neither Arabs nor Egyptians but Turks.

Historical precedent would certainly suggest that Egypt cannot be, and never has been, the leader of the Arabs. This fact may be attributed to a number of reasons. Firstly, Egypt is geographically situated in a position which makes her the key to the domination of Europe, Western Asia and North Africa. As a result, she is always seized by the great nation which, at any given moment, aspires to dominate the Old World. When the Arabs were in this position, they held Egypt, as the Greeks and the Romans had done before them and as the Ottomans and the British did after them. Egypt, therefore, endlessly conquered and garrisoned by successive empires, has never been free to associate herself with her Arabic-speaking neighbours.

Secondly, the Egyptians are a race ethnically unconnected with the Arabs east of Sinai. Their characteristics are not only different but often diametrically opposed to those of the Arabs further east. Thirdly, the various Arabic-speaking countries have never been united except by force and the people of Egypt have never been successful soldiers. Courteous, cultured, humorous, lovable as they are, they have never formed good military material.

If only some element of Middle East history were included in our educational system, our statesmen might have been aware of these factors, so readily deducible from history. Such knowledge might have enabled the nations of the West to avoid some of the cruder misconceptions which have led them, in the years since the First World War, into so many disastrous errors of policy.

Muhammad Ali and his descendants conferred many benefits on Egypt by introducing European methods and knowledge. His military campaigns, however, resulted in ever-increasing taxes and in terrible oppression of the fellaheen. He did not succeed in making Egypt a Great Power, as the Mamlooks had done.

NOTABLE DATES

Ottoman conquest of Syria and Egypt	1517
Ottoman conquest of Baghdad	1534
Death of Sulaiman the Magnificent	1566
Commencement of Ottoman decline	1566
Occupation of Baghdad by Shah Abbas of Persia	1619–1638

Rule of the Mani princes in Lebanon	1517–1697
Campaign of Nadir Quli Khan and Topal Othman	1733
Rule of the Mamlooks of Baghdad	1704–1831
Rise and decline of the Wahhabis under Ibn Saud	1750–1818
Campaign of Napoleon Bonaparte in Egypt and Palestine	1798–1799
Muhammad Ali Pasha sole ruler of Egypt	1811
Campaign of Muhammad Ali against the Ottomans	1831–1840

PERSONALITIES

Saleem the Grim	1512–1520
Sulaiman the Magnificent	1520–1566
Murad IV	1623–1640

(The innumerable undistinguished sultans have been omitted)

Lebanon

Basheer II al Shihabi	1788–1840

Syria

Ahmad Pasha al Jazzar, who defeated
   Napoleon at Acre in 1799

Egypt

Muhammad Ali Pasha	1811–1849

XVII

The Age of Reforms

FROM the death of Sulaiman the Magnificent in 1566 to that of Abdul Hameed I in 1789, the Ottoman Empire had suffered a succession of largely incompetent sultans. Their ineffectiveness had been only partly atoned for by a number of capable wazeers. In 1774, however, after a humiliating defeat at the hands of Russia, Abdul Hameed I (1773–1789) engaged a number of European experts.

His son, Saleen III, attempted to introduce reforms in imitation of Europe but was murdered by the Janissaries, who had now become the principal opponents of change in the army. Quietly improving the training and discipline of army units other than the Janissaries, Sultan Mahmood II (1808–1839) was able, in 1826, to use them to destroy the Janissaries—in the usual Ottoman manner—by means of a general massacre.

The well-meaning reforms of Mahmood II, however, were rendered inoperative by successive disasters, by the constant attacks of Russia, by a Greek rebellion in 1821 and by the revolt of Muhammad Ali of Egypt in 1831. Mahmood II died in 1839 and was succeeded by the young and energetic Abdul Majeed I (1839–1861). The new sultan issued the famous Gulhana decrees, which introduced the programme of reforms known as the *tandhimat*. These, among other changes, introduced state schools, financial reforms and many other attempts to "modernize" the administration.

One of the chief advocates of the reforms was Midhat Pasha, the son of a minor government official. After serving as an official in the Balkans, Midhat became governor, first of Damascus and then, in 1869, of Baghdad. Hitherto the theoretical reforms decreed in Istanbul had produced little or no effect in the distant Arab provinces.

Midhat's three years of office in Iraq were characterized by an imposing list of reforms, almost all of them directly imitated from Europe, some useful, others unwise and hasty. The patron of reform, the Sultan Abdul Majeed, died in 1861 and was followed by Abdul

Azeez (1861–1876). Midhat Pasha, the father of the Westernization movement, succeeded in deposing Abdul Azeez in 1876. His successor, Murad V, reigned only three months and was likewise deposed.

Abdul Hameed II (1876–1909), the next sultan, was obliged by Midhat to sign a constitution. In 1877, however, Russia declared war and the sultan, using the crisis as a pretext, dissolved the National Assembly and Midhat Pasha went into exile. From 1877 to 1908, Abdul Hameed ruled despotically.

*   *   *

So much for the vicissitudes of Istanbul. Let us now consider what had become of the Arab provinces of the empire.

In 1830, the French had landed in Algeria. In 1840, as already related, Muhammad Ali had become virtually independent in Egypt. In the Persian Gulf, piracy had long been a menace to shipping. In 1853, following operations by the Royal Navy, a treaty was signed between Britain and the Arab chiefs on the coast, providing for the cessation of Arab piracy. Indirectly, the treaty gave Britain predominant influence in the Gulf. The Ottomans maintained a precarious hold in the Yemen and the Hejaz. The only Arabic-speaking provinces, however, still actually under Ottoman administration after 1840 were Iraq, Syria, Palestine and Tripoli in Africa.

In Syria and Iraq superficial changes had been made. The Janissaries had been replaced by "regulars" in slovenly European uniforms. The silks and the satins, the snowy white turbans and the flowing beards had been discarded for shabby European clothes, stubbly, one-shave-a-week-on-Friday chins and that most ridiculous of hats, the red fez or tarboosh. But, in the provinces at least, to scratch a new Turk was to find an old Ottoman.

From first to last, from 1517 to 1917, the Ottomans, who possessed many sterling virtues, had never been able to feel much sympathy for their Arabic-speaking subjects. The imperial officers were often hardy and brave, their minds were simple and direct, but they seemed to be incapable of understanding the Arabs. Like many people who fail to understand, their only remedy in every difficulty was the use of force. To them, any Arabs who met force with force were just traitors.

The Ottoman system of government was to maintain large garrisons in the great provincial cities, Aleppo, Damascus, Mosul and Baghdad. Cultivators within twenty or thirty miles of the cities were

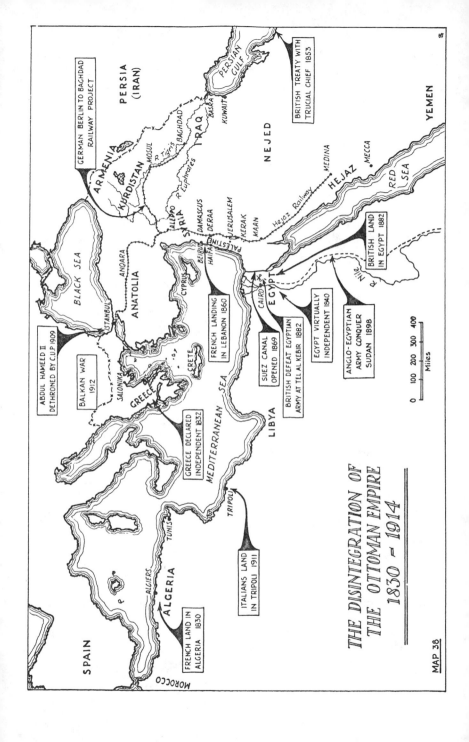

THE DISINTEGRATION OF
THE OTTOMAN EMPIRE
1830 - 1914

MAP 38

0   100 200 300 400
Miles

SPAIN

MOROCCO

ALGERIA

FRENCH LAND IN ALGERIA 1830

ALGIERS

TUNIS

TRIPOLI

ITALIANS LAND IN TRIPOLI 1911

LIBYA

MEDITERRANEAN SEA

GREECE

GREECE DECLARED INDEPENDENT 1832

SALONIKA

BALKAN WAR 1912

ABDUL HAMEED II DETHRONED BY C.U.P. 1909

BLACK SEA

ISTANBUL

ANATOLIA

ANGARA

CRETE

CYPRUS

FRENCH LANDING IN LEBANON 1860

BEIRUT

HAIFA

SUEZ CANAL OPENED 1869

CAIRO

EGYPT

BRITISH DEFEAT EGYPTIAN ARMY AT TEL AL KEBIR 1882

EGYPT VIRTUALLY INDEPENDENT 1840

ANGLO-EGYPTIAN ARMY CONQUER SUDAN 1898

R. Nile

BRITISH LAND IN EGYPT 1882

SYRIA

ALEPPO

DAMASCUS

DERAA

JERUSALEM

PALESTINE

KERAK

MAAN

HEJAZ

Hejaz Railway

MEDINA

MECCA

RED SEA

ARMENIA

KURDISTAN

GERMAN BERLIN TO BAGHDAD RAILWAY PROJECT

MOSUL

R. Tigris

R. Euphrates

BAGHDAD

IRAQ

BASRA

KUWAIT

PERSIAN GULF

PERSIA (IRAN)

NEJED

BRITISH TREATY WITH TRUCIAL CHIEF 1853

YEMEN

5

bullied, oppressed and squeezed for exorbitant taxes. Further afield, the tribes were out of control, no taxes could be collected and the roads were unsafe, except to such as paid toll to the tribal chiefs for safe conduct.

Every few years, the governor of the province would collect a large force of troops and march into the territory of some contumacious tribe. Villages would be burnt, tribesmen killed, the crops trampled and the livestock driven off. Sometimes these columns would be ambushed and defeated, at others the tribe, familiar with this type of diplomacy, would send messages of loyalty. A local notable or the chief of another tribe would act as mediator. A few well placed bribes would induce the authorities to take a more lenient view, the troops would be withdrawn with their loot and peace would be established for a few months, after which the process would recommence.

Where the subjection of the tribes was beyond the capacity of the government forces, the Ottomans had other methods. The first of these was to provoke a war between two tribes. Alternatively, if any tribal chief became powerful, a junior member of his family was given a sum of money and "acknowledged" by the authorities as head of the tribe. The Arabs have always been a jealous people and such intrigues often resulted in an internal struggle, in which the Arabs killed one another instead of the government troops.

The last resort of the Ottoman governors was treachery. Tribal leaders would be invited to conferences, entertained to banquets, sometimes even given safe conduct. When their suspicions had been thus allayed, the tribal shaikhs would be suddenly loaded with chains and sent to Istanbul, where they would be put to death. The Turkish rulers were convinced that the use of such methods was the only way to deal with the endemic "disloyalty" of Arab tribesmen.

The peoples of the West will naturally attribute Arab turbulence to the foreign rule of the Turks or to the despotism of the sultans. These explanations, so satisfying to us today, are nevertheless almost entirely erroneous. The Arabs in the nineteenth century were without "national" feeling. Their loyalty was basically religious and the Ottomans enjoyed the priceless advantage of professing the same faith as their subjects. In so far as despotism was concerned, almost all Arabs were, in principle, loyal to the sultan, whom they regarded as the leader and defender of their faith.

Yet the rural Arabs regarded the government as their worst enemy and resisted it, by diplomacy or by force, whenever they could. Perhaps if they had troubled to analyse their motives, the tribesmen would have said that their only object was to resist the oppression and the rapacity of the local officials, while acknowledging the supremacy of the mighty, but distant, sultan. In fact, however, the Arabs, like ourselves, accepted the conditions under which they lived as being natural and inevitable. The local government was their principal enemy, the sultan was so far away that he scarcely ever entered their thoughts. Certainly none of them dreamed of overthrowing him or of ridding themselves of Turkish rule and replacing it by "Arab" governments.

The fate of those rural areas near the big cities which were directly administered did not encourage more distant tribes and villages to submit. The Turkish security forces were divided into two branches—the city police and the rural gendarmerie. The latter, who were mounted, accompanied tax collectors and dealt with breaches of the peace in administered rural areas. Although most of the men were Arabs with Turkish or Turkified-Arab officers, they had absorbed the official attitude that Arabs could only be ruled with a big stick.

When an official or tax collector entered an Arab village with his gendarmerie escort, the community was thrown into confusion. The great man, possibly the lowest grade of minor tax collector, assumed the airs of a mighty lord. The best carpets and cushions must be laid out for him in the guest room of the village headman, who would hasten to kiss his hand and stand humbly awaiting His Excellency's orders.

Meanwhile the gendarmerie sergeant and his troopers would have commenced their "duties". If, for example, a crime were to be investigated, a selected number of villagers would be beaten or bastinadoed to encourage them to give information regarding the whereabouts of the offenders.

Meanwhile everyone was working to prepare a banquet for the unwelcome guests. Sheep, lambs and chickens must be killed, quantities of rice or bread, stews, gravy, oil, butter and fruit must be prepared. If the meal failed to come up to the expectations of the visitors, the police sergeant might order the host to take it out and tip it into the nearest ditch and to start again on a more lavish scale.

To the poor villager in Ottoman-administered territory, the police sergeant, rather than the sultan, was the lord of all he surveyed. The story is well known of a new governor of Baghdad, who, with a vast retinue and a regiment of cavalry as escort, was travelling across country to take up his post. One evening, when camp was pitched, the pasha looked out of his tent, saw a soldier beating a peasant and sent an officer to rescue the victim. When the soldier had been reprimanded, the officer whispered to the Arab, "Go and kiss the pasha's hand, you son of an immoral mother." The fellah fell at the governor's feet and, embracing his knees, called loudly to heaven, "May God prolong your life, O pasha! May you rise, to yet higher rank! Some day, if God wills, may you become a sergeant in the police!"

*   *   *

The relations between the city-dwellers and the Ottomans were more complicated. On the one hand, in cities which had large garrisons, officers and men mixed socially with the citizens and, being of the same religion, frequently inter-married with them. For political reasons, state schools taught in Turkish, not in Arabic, with the result that educated "Arabs" often spoke and wrote Turkish more easily than their own language.

Cities necessarily subsist on trade and commerce, which require safe communications from one city to the next. Thus the merchant class was on the side of strong government. No more than the tribesmen did the merchants regard the Ottomans as foreign oppressors. To them, the Arabs were not a nation to which they themselves belonged but lawless tribesmen, who committed acts of highway robbery and interfered with trade.

Such were the dangers and difficulties of travel (from Jerusalem to Baghdad was a month's journey) that transfers of soldiers and officials were comparatively rare and many Ottomans—natives of Greece, Anatolia, Albania or Kurdistan—served all their lives in some Arab city, where they married, had children and died. Thus, to some extent, the ethnic composition of the cities became different from that of the countryside.

These phenomena were not new. During the one thousand years of Graeco-Roman rule of Syria, Greek became the language of the cities of Syria and Lebanon where great numbers of Greeks came to live. Conversely, many Syrian intellectuals migrated to Rome and became leading philosophers, professors and even tutors of Roman princes. Several emperors of Rome were natives of Syria.

Similarly, during the centuries of British rule in southern Ireland, many of the upper class Irish became anglicized and provided distinguished statesmen and soldiers to the British Empire. A similar development took place in Austria-Hungary.

*   *   *

Modern writers in the West have been lavish of criticisms of the Ottoman Empire, normally basing their remarks on its condition in the nineteenth and twentieth centuries. It is only just to record, however, that until the seventeenth century at least, it was probably in advance of the administrative standards of most European governments. During the reign of Sulaiman the Magnificent, the Christian villagers of southern Greece preferred Turkish rule to that of the Venetians. Some Christian villages in Hungary voluntarily chose Turkish government in preference to that of their fellow-countrymen.

In the matter of religious toleration, the Arab Empire in the seventh century had abstained from persecution and had permitted Jews and Christians to practise their own laws and to elect their own judges. Nearly a thousand years later, people in Europe were still being tortured and burned alive for their faith. Military service, it is true, was limited to Muslims and, in a community which venerated soldiers, this fact carried a certain social stigma. In general, however, the Ottomans continued the policy of religious toleration which they had inherited from the Arabs.

Certain European Powers, however, notably Russia, did not want the Ottoman Empire to be reformed but to be destroyed. Concessions made to the Balkan Christians and to the Armenians were, therefore, rejected and demands for independence were pressed at the instigation of Russia. Under Catherine the Great (1762–1796) Russia had begun her attempts to break through to the Mediterranean. In pursuit of this objective, Russia fought no less than ten wars against the declining Ottoman Empire, from the reign of Catherine the Great to the First World War.

Britain regarded the Mediterranean, Egypt and the Red Sea as essential to her line of communications to the East, both from a commercial and a strategic point of view. The British government, therefore, had no wish to see Russia established in the eastern Mediterranean, where she would be in a position to cut Britain's life-line to Asia and Australia. Britain accordingly supported the Ottoman Empire, in order to keep Russia out of the strategic Middle East area.

This struggle, which lasted for two centuries, is relevant to our present narrative because the vital strategic areas at which Russia was aiming were the Arab countries, Syria, Egypt and North Africa. The general public, who saw the battles fought in the Balkans or the Caucasus, failed to appreciate that the neglected Arab provinces were the long-term objective of the Russian programme. Once established in the eastern Mediterranean, she would be in a position increasingly to dominate Europe and to cut Britain's trade route to the East.

The declining years of great empires seem to present an inevitability reminiscent of the last years of old people. Every nation rises to greatness through its "personality", a complicated structure of mental and spiritual qualities which are exactly appropriate for that moment in history. But two or three centuries later, these characteristics are no longer suitable for a changing world. It is vain, however, at this stage, to recommend the weakening empire to abandon its own character in favour of that of another entirely different civilization. The Ottomans, once the most up-to-date nation in Europe, were senile. They could not be rejuvenated by abandoning their own ethos and adopting the "personality" of other and utterly different peoples. The prescription offered was the complete transformation of the empire into a European state. The medicine, however, killed the patient before curing any of his diseases—the result, for that matter, for which the "doctors" were hoping.

*   *   *

The abandonment of political reform imitated from Europe and the return to autocracy under Abdul Hameed II (1876–1909) may, therefore, be partly explained by the fact that some at least of the Powers advocated a liberal constitution and then took advantage of the relaxation of authority to foment rebellion.

With the Balkan provinces in constant sedition as a result of these activities, Abdul Hameed turned his attention to the Arabs, the largest racial group in the empire and one hitherto completely neglected. Harassed by the rise of nationalism in the Balkans, the sultan endeavoured to rally the Arab provinces by religious propaganda. The great majority of Arabs even today are, in their heart of hearts, more emotionally loyal to Islam than to any national feeling. The result of this policy, therefore, was to render Abdul Hameed II not unpopular with many Arabs.

We have already noted the arrival of Christian missionaries in Lebanon. In 1734, the Jesuits had opened the first modern school in any Arab country. American Presbyterian missionaries landed in Beirut in 1820 and, in 1866, opened the Syrian Protestant College, later to become the American University of Beirut. British and Prussian missionaries soon followed suit.

Government schools in the Ottoman Empire taught in Turkish; Arabic, for political reasons, was deliberately neglected. The missionaries, however, taught in Arabic, especially the Americans. The teaching of Arabic led to a revival of interest in Arabic literature. The study of the old Arab historians resulted in the rediscovery of the forgotten glories of Arab civilization, which in its turn sowed the seed of the later demands for emancipation from Ottoman rule.

These influences, however, were as yet restricted to a very small group of intellectuals, principally in Beirut, but later spreading to a limited extent to Damascus. The immense majority of Arabs were unaware of the very existence of such a movement.

*　　　*　　　*

Not only had the Sultan Abdul Hameed II become interested in the long-neglected Arab provinces; so had certain European Powers.

In April 1860, the Druzes in Lebanon began to massacre the local Christians, partly, at least, at the instigation of the Ottoman authorities, who always practised the policy of divide and rule. On 9th July, the attacks spread to Damascus, resulting in ten days of rioting.

Thereupon the Great Powers intervened and Napoleon III sent a French army to Beirut. The outcome was the signature of a special charter for Lebanon, under which that territory was always to be governed by a Christian approved by the Great Powers. Revised in 1864, this charter lasted until the First World War.

*　　　*　　　*

Mention has already been made of the rise of the Muslim Wahhabi sect in Central Arabia in the 1750s and their subsequent military repression in 1818 by Muhammad Ali of Egypt. Nejed, the provincial name of Central Arabia, remained in confusion from 1818 to 1834. In 1834, however, a certain Feisal ibn Saud seized power and, by 1843, had succeeded in freeing his country from the Egyptian army.

Feisal ruled Nejed successfully until his death in 1867, after which a civil war broke out between his sons. In 1871, however, an Ottoman military force landed in the Hasa and occupied the whole province. In 1887, a certain Muhammad ibn Rasheed, whose father had previously been a retainer of Feisal ibn Saud, seized power in Nejed. The Sauds were imprisoned in Hail,[1] which Ibn Rasheed had made his capital.

Muhammad ibn Rasheed proved to be a great ruler and was the undisputed despot of Nejed until 1897. He was succeeded by Abdul Aziz ibn Rasheed, a famous raider and a romantic figure but lacking

[1] Pronounced Hile, as in file.

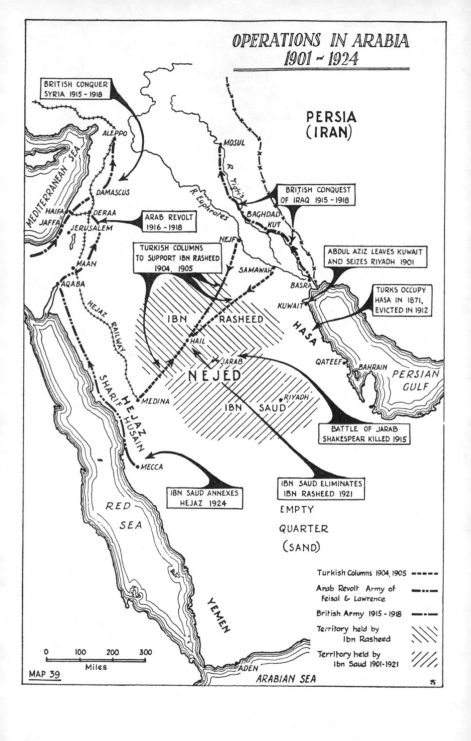

OPERATIONS IN ARABIA
1901 ~ 1924

BRITISH CONQUER
SYRIA 1915 - 1918

PERSIA
(IRAN)

ALEPPO

MOSUL

R. Tigris

DAMASCUS

BRITISH CONQUEST
OF IRAQ 1915 - 1918

HAIFA
JAFFA

DERAA

R. Euphrates

BAGHDAD
KUT

ARAB REVOLT
1916 - 1918

JERUSALEM

NEJF

ABDUL AZIZ LEAVES KUWAIT
AND SEIZES RIYADH 1901

TURKISH COLUMNS
TO SUPPORT IBN RASHEED
1904, 1905

SAMAWAH

BASRA

MAAN

KUWAIT

TURKS OCCUPY
HASA IN 1871,
EVICTED IN 1912

AQABA

HEJAZ RAILWAY

IBN   RASHEED

HASA

HAIL

QATEEF

BAHRAIN

PERSIAN
GULF

JARAB

NEJED

SHARIF HUSAIN

MEDINA

RIYADH

IBN   SAUD

BATTLE OF JARAB
SHAKESPEAR KILLED 1915

HEJAZ

MECCA

IBN SAUD ANNEXES
HEJAZ 1924

IBN SAUD ELIMINATES
IBN RASHEED 1921

EMPTY

RED
SEA

QUARTER

(SAND)

Turkish Columns 1904, 1905 -----

Arab Revolt Army of
Feisal & Lawrence -·-·-

British Army 1915 - 1918 -··-··

Territory held by
Ibn Rasheed ///

Territory held by
Ibn Saud 1901-1921 ///

YEMEN

0   100   200   300
Miles

MAP 39

ADEN

ARABIAN SEA

in political skill. In 1901, Abdul Aziz ibn Saud, a grandson of the great Feisal, left Kuwait, where he had been in exile, with a party of forty camel-riders and, by a sudden *coup de main* seized the former Saudi capital, Riyadh. The southern half of Nejed rallied to his side, the northern half remaining loyal to Ibn Rasheed. Nejed was thus divided between two rival states.

In January 1904, Ibn Rasheed appealed for help to the Ottoman Government, claiming that Ibn Saud was receiving support from the British. The Sublime Porte had recently concluded an agreement with Germany, and work had begun on the Hejaz Railway.[2] Abdul Hameed had decided on a forward policy in Arabia. In May 1904, a Turkish force of two thousand men left Samawah in Iraq to support Ibn Rasheed against Ibn Saud. In 1905, a second column three thousand strong left Iraq for Hail while another force advanced from Medina. But the Turkish army, always brave and stubborn in battle, was badly administered. In the desert, without clothing or rations, the troops melted away. In 1912, Ibn Saud took the offensive, driving the Ottoman garrison from the Hasa.

*   *   *

Throughout the Middle Ages and until the end of the Mamlook régime in 1517, Egypt had been the depot and half-way house for the commerce between India and the Far East on the one hand and Europe on the other. The sea route round the Cape of Good Hope, however, had been discovered by Vasco da Gama in 1498 and, as a result, Egypt had suddenly become a commercial backwater.

Muhammad Ali, the founder of Egyptian independence, had died in 1849. He had started Egypt on the road to Westernization, but at the price of oppressive taxation, particularly of the peasants. The crash came under his grandson, Ismail, who reigned from 1863 to 1879. Ismail was a passionate Westernizer. He borrowed vast sums in Europe and spent them on railways, telegraphs, harbour works and finally on the Suez Canal, which was opened in 1869.

Eventually Egypt became bankrupt and was obliged to accept the dual financial control of France and Britain. As the result of a military revolt against the khedive in 1882, Britain intervened, inviting France and Italy to co-operate. The two countries having declined, a British force landed, under Sir Garnet Wolseley, and defeated the rebels under Arabi Pasha at Tel al Kebir, on 13th September, 1882.

In January 1884, Sir Evelyn Baring, later Lord Cromer, was

[2] See below, page 257.

appointed British Consul-General in Cairo. With this modest title, but supported by a British army of occupation, Cromer reformed the finances, repaired and extended the irrigation system and brought solvency and prosperity to Egypt. In 1898, the Sudan, annexed by Muhammad Ali but lost in the revolt of the Mahdi,[3] was reoccupied by an Anglo-Egyptian army, commanded by General (later Lord) Kitchener. In 1900, Egypt was quiet and prosperous, public security firmly established, slavery and forced labour abolished and the living conditions of the fellaheen immensely improved.

All this had been achieved without any change of the constitution. Egypt was still ruled by a descendant of Muhammad Ali with the title of khedive, with a prime minister and cabinet. Thus far Britain had brought Egypt nothing but benefits. The tragic misunderstandings of the future were still unforeseen.

*   *   *

In writing history, the most difficult task is not to ascertain facts but to understand the mentality of the people of an earlier age. Perhaps the most striking example is the utter transformation of British thought since the 1880s. In the nineteenth century, the general tone of opinion was religious, even if wealth and success had made it self-satisfied.

One form the British conscience took was the feeling that it was her duty to interfere in every ill-governed country and to insist on higher standards of justice and the end of oppression. Today such interventions are denounced as wicked. An often ill-informed idea of nationality seems to be our sole concern. However unjust and oppressive a government may be, we proclaim ourselves satisfied if we believe the oppressed to be of the same "nation" as the oppressors.

British officials who worked in Egypt under Lord Cromer, alleviating the oppression of the fellaheen, were convinced that they were carrying out a great work of humanity. So complete a change has taken place in the fashions in idealism that we refuse to believe in the altruism of our grandfathers and condemn them out of hand as "imperialists".

*   *   *

Germany, a late comer among the Powers of Europe, aspired to find her own outlet to the East and contracted with the Ottoman Government to build a railway from Istanbul to Baghdad and Basra,

[3] Earlier in this book, this word was spelt Mehedi, which is nearer to its pronunciation. Mahdi, however, is the spelling used in English concerning the Sudan.

at the head of the Persian Gulf. Abdul Hameed II conceived the idea of building a similar railway through Aleppo and Damascus to Medina and Mecca.

In pursuance of his pan-Islamic policy, the sultan claimed that the object of the enterprise was to facilitate the travel of pilgrims to the Muslim Holy Cities. Inevitably, however, it would also strengthen the hold of the empire on Syria, Palestine, Trans-Jordan and the Hejaz. A branch line from Deraa was to be constructed to the port of Haifa. Such a development of railway services would undoubtedly also benefit the countries concerned economically. On 12th April, 1900, work began on the Hejaz Railway from the Damascus end.

The Ottoman authorities had not attempted to administer the country east of the Jordan from the time of their first conquest. In the 1880s, half-hearted efforts were made to collect taxes from tribes east of the Jordan, although there was little attempt to enforce law and order. On the contrary, the Ottoman authorities, as usual, encouraged inter-tribal wars.

The construction of the railway, however, made the establishment of control essential and a governor and staff were appointed to Kerak. In 1910, a tribal rebellion in the area was crushed but government control in Trans-Jordan remained precarious until the First World War.

*   *   *

After the suppression of the constitution in 1877, the reformers or Young Turks made Paris a centre for revolutionary activities. Beset on all sides by foreign enemies, the sultan had entrusted the training of his army to a German military mission. In order to modernize their methods, the Germans had established military colleges for the education of officers, with the result that the latter were soon better educated and more permeated with Western ideas than were their civilian contemporaries. The garrison of Salonika, at the heart of the Balkan troubles, was soon "infected" by young officers bent on political reforms. In the summer of 1908, revolt broke out in the name of the Committee of Union and Progress. Abdul Hameed gave way and on 24th July, 1908, granted a constitution.

A tremendous wave of enthusiasm swept the empire, including even the Arab provinces. *Hurriya*, freedom, was the cry and men wept and embraced one another in the streets, although few can have had much idea of what freedom would involve. In April 1909, as the result of an attempted counter-revolution, Abdul Hameed was dethroned and his brother Muhammad Rashád was proclaimed a constitutional sultan, the real power remaining in the hands of the Committee of Union and Progress.

The C.U.P. commenced by adhering to Abdul Hameed's policies of Ottomanism and pan-Islamism. But, overwhelmed by the Italian invasion of Tripoli and the Balkan wars, the party turned to Turkish nationalism, thereby estranging the Arabs. In 1912, a political party was formed in Egypt, consisting of Syrians, Lebanese and Palestinians, who were unable to carry out political propaganda in their own countries. The object of the party was to secure autonomous governments in the Arab countries, but within the empire. The C.U.P. retorted by doing the opposite—increasing the centralization of power in Istanbul.

Meanwhile a political secret society, called Al Fatat, the Young Arabs and consisting mostly of students, was formed in Beirut and Damascus. Its members were sworn to work for complete Arab independence. In 1914, a secret association called Al Ahad or the Covenant was formed among Arab officers serving in the Turkish army. The existence of these little secret societies was unknown to the Arab peoples, the majority of whom remained loyal to the Ottoman connection throughout the First World War.

NOTABLE DATES

Massacre of the Janissaries	1826
French landing in Algeria	1830
Rebellion of Muhammad Ali in Egypt	1831
Inauguration of *tandhimat* reforms	1840
Opening of the Suez Canal	1869
Signature of a constitution by Abdul Hameed II	1876
Repudiation of the constitution	1877
Battle of Tel al Kebir	1882
Anglo-Egyptian conquest of the Sudan	1898
Commencement of construction of the Hejaz Railway	1900
Revolt of the Committee of Union and Progress	1908
Deposition of Abdul Hameed II	1909

PERSONALITIES

Ottoman Sultans

Abdul Hameed I	1773–1789
Saleem III (murdered by the Janissaries)	1789–1807
Mustafa IV	1807–1808
Mahmood II (massacred the Janissaries)	1808–1839
Abdul Majeed I, the Reformer	1839–1861
Abdul Azeez (deposed by Midhat Pasha)	1861–1876
Abdul Hameed II (returned to despotism)	1876–1909

OTHER PERSONALITIES

Midhat Pasha, Turkish reformer

Muhammad Ali, the founder of Egyptian independence

Ismail Pasha, the spendthrift khedive

Lord Cromer, administrator, British Consul-General in Cairo

XVIII

North Africa down to our own Times

WE left North Africa in 1269. The great Berber Empire of
the Muwahhids, extending from the Atlantic to Tripoli,
had collapsed, and three states had risen on its ruins. In
the Maghrib, Beni Merin won control but failed to reconstitute the
empire. In Telemsan, the Beni Abdul Wad Berbers struggled to
maintain a precarious independence, while in Tunis the Hafsids
ruled an often powerful and prosperous kingdom.[1]

The brilliant Berber civilization of North Africa had originated
with the Arab conquest from 640 to 712, and had reached its apogee
under the Muwahhids from 1146 to 1269. Ironically enough, one of
the chief causes of the collapse of this Arab-Berber culture was the
second Arab invasion of 1054, when the Fatimid Khalifs of Egypt,
piqued at the denunciation of their suzerainty, had encouraged the
Arab tribes of Beni Hilal and Beni Sulaim to invade the Berber
countries.

Abdul Mumin, the Muwahhid unifier of North Africa, conceived
the idea of using these Arab bedouins in his army and encouraged
them to migrate to the Maghrib, where he treated them with
marked favouritism. Beni Hilal settled on and dominated the plains
of Morocco, while the Berbers remained supreme in the Atlas.

Beni Merin never achieved the power, civilization or prestige of
the Muwahhids. Their weakness obliged them to rely more on these
Arab tribes, to whom they granted great areas of land in the plains
in return for hereditary military service. The dominant position thus
granted to the Arab bedouins in the plains of Morocco resulted in the
estrangément of the mountain Berbers, who for many centuries were
to remain virtually independent of the governments in the Maghrib.

Perhaps under the influence of a parochialism caused by the weakness of Beni Merin, the divisions between Berbers and Arabs, and the
impassability of the immense mountain block of the Atlas, North
African Islam developed a peculiar tendency of its own. Devotion to

[1] Map 25, page 184.

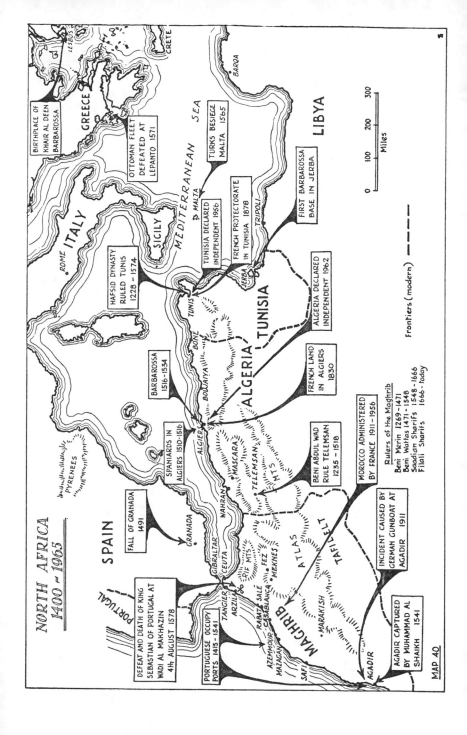

NORTH AFRICA
1400 – 1965

SPAIN

PORTUGAL

BIRTHPLACE OF
KHAIR AL DEEN
BARBAROSSA

LESBOS

GREECE

CRETE

OTTOMAN FLEET
DEFEATED AT
LEPANTO 1571

ITALY

ROME

SICILY

MEDITERRANEAN SEA

MALTA

TURKS BESIEGE
MALTA 1565

HAFSID DYNASTY
RULED TUNIS
1228 – 1574

TUNISIA DECLARED
INDEPENDENT 1956

FRENCH PROTECTORATE
IN TUNISIA 1878

TRIPOLI

FIRST BARBAROSSA
BASE IN JERBA

LIBYA

BARQA

BARBAROSSA
1516–1534

ALGERIA DECLARED
INDEPENDENT 1962

TUNIS

BONE

BOUJAIA

TUNISIA

ALGERIA

SPANIARDS IN
ALGIERS 1510–1516

ALGIERS

MASCARA

TELEMSAN
MTS

FRENCH LAND
IN ALGIERS
1830

PYRENEES

FALL OF GRANADA
1491

GRANADA

GIBRALTAR

CEUTA

WAHRAN

MAHRAN

BENI ABDUL WAD
RULE TELEMSAN
1235 – 1518

MOROCCO ADMINISTERED
BY FRANCE 1911–1956

Rulers of the Maghrib
Beni Merin 1269 –1471
Beni Wattas 1471 – 1548
Saadian Sharifs 1548–1666
Filali Sharifs 1666 – today

DEFEAT AND DEATH OF KING
SEBASTIAN OF PORTUGAL AT
WADI AL MAKHAZIN
4th AUGUST 1578

TANGIER

ARZILA

RIF MTS

FEZ

MEKNES

PORTUGUESE OCCUPY
PORTS 1415 –1541

RABAT

SALÉ

AZEMMOUR

CASABLANCA

MAZAGAN

SAFI

MARAKISH

ATLAS

MAGHRIB

TAFILELT

INCIDENT CAUSED BY
GERMAN GUNBOAT AT
AGADIR 1911

AGADIR CAPTURED
BY MUHAMMAD AL
SHAIKH 1541

AGADIR

Frontiers (modern) – – – –

0   100   200   300
Miles

MAP 40

the memory and the tombs of local saints, a multiplication of alleged sharifs or descendants of the Prophet, and the formation of brotherhoods of holy men in various districts, served both to intensify and to break into local fragments the enthusiastic piety of the Berbers.

This revival of religious enthusiasm was partly due to the action of the Christian governments. No sooner had the Spanish and the Portuguese governments evicted the Muslims and the Jews from the peninsula, than they continued the offensive by invading North Africa. The action of the Portuguese will be described later in this chapter, in connection with the history of Morocco. For the moment, events in Algeria and Tunis will be recounted.

In 1509, the Spanish seized Wahran (Oran) and in 1510 Algiers. They built a massive fort, the Peñon, on an island in Algiers harbour, from which the town could be bombarded at a range of only three hundred yards. The danger of a Christian conquest of North Africa was averted by the arrival of two adventurers, the so-called Barbarossa brothers, sons of a coasting trader of Mitylene on the Island of Lesbos, but possibly of Albanian origin. At one time they established their headquarters on the Island of Jerba. In 1516, the elder brother, Arooj, recaptured Algiers from the Spaniards. In 1518, he intervened in a civil war among Beni Abdul Wad in Telemsan, as a result of which that dynasty was exterminated, but shortly afterwards Arooj was himself killed.

His younger brother, Khair al Deen, succeeded him in Algiers and made profession of loyalty to the Ottoman Sultan, Saleem the Grim. In return he received the titles of pasha and bey of beys and an army of six thousand men. Khair al Deen at first co-operated with the many Muslims evicted from Spain, who raided the Spanish coast and Spanish shipping in the name of the holy war against Christians. Khair al Deen's activities gradually became more and more acts of piracy, the religious motive with him being secondary. Algiers, situated half way between Gibraltar and Sicily, was ideally situated for a pirate base. In 1529, Khair al Deen at last succeeded in taking the Peñon, the guns of which commanded the city of Algiers.

In 1534, the decadence of the Hafsids enabled Khair al Deen, on 18th August, to capture Tunis, which he did in the name of Sulaiman the Magnificent. Soon afterwards, however, the Emperor Charles V intervened and retook the town, on 20th July, 1535, after landing an army of thirty thousand men. In 1541, Charles V attacked Algiers also but the expedition ended in fiasco.

Khair al Deen Barbarossa was one of the most astounding adventurers in history. Not only was he intrepid, ruthless and determined but he was also a gifted diplomat and politician. In 1533 and 1534, he commanded an Ottoman fleet off the coast of Provence, with the title of kapitan pasha, or admiral of the fleet. Thereafter he was established in Istanbul as commander-in-chief of the Ottoman navy, the friend and counsellor of Sulaiman the Magnificent. Here, living in a sumptuous palace, he remained one of the greatest figures in the capital until his death in 1546.

The departure of Barbarossa was followed by one of those extraordinary Mamlook or Janissary régimes which kept appearing in Muslim countires. The Janissaries had originally been sent by the sultan but, with the departure of Barbarossa, they formed themselves into an extraordinary equalitarian brotherhood, in which promotion, and even the supreme command, was awarded on seniority alone.

The pirate captains formed a community engaged in constant rivalry with the Janissaries of the land army. The corsair galleys were extremely efficient and kept the sea all through the winter when, according to a contemporary authority, the Christians were feasting on shore. The Muslim galleys were always faster than the Christian ships, perhaps because they were better designed for speed or because the crews were better trained. Many of the corsairs were themselves Christian renegades who, having been captured by the pirates, preferred conversion to Islam and membership of the crew to adherence to the Christian faith and slavery at the oars beneath the supervisor's whip.

Spanish ships, and towns and villages on the coast of Spain were, in the sixteenth century, the principal objectives of the Barbary Corsairs. These hostilities could scarcely be described as wars of religion, the Most Christian King of France being the active ally of the Muslims against His Catholic Majesty of Spain. In 1558, the pirates were operating a fleet of thirty-five galleys and twenty-five brigantines. It must be remembered, however, that privateering was a regular feature of naval war at the time. Under Queen Elizabeth, English privateers frequently attacked and plundered Spanish ships.

The Ottoman Empire at this period commanded the eastern half of the Mediterranean and was engaged in a struggle with Spain for naval command of the western Mediterranean also. In 1530, the Knights of St. John, evicted from Rhodes by the Ottomans, had taken charge of Malta. The failure of the Ottomans to take Malta in 1565 was the turning point of the struggle for command of the western Mediterranean. Hasan Pasha, the son of Khair al Deen Barbarossa, took part in the siege.

On 9th October, 1571, the defeat of the Ottoman fleet at Lepanto, at the entrance to the Gulf of Corinth, finally decided the issue. It also ushered in the decline of the Ottoman Empire, which ceased any longer to threaten to dominate Europe. As both Napoleon I, Kaiser Wilhelm II and Hitler were subsequently to discover, Europe cannot be conquered without naval command of the Mediterranean.

The last bey of beys died in 1587, whereupon the sultan seized the opportunity to declare Algiers a regular province of the empire, governed by a pasha to be relieved every three years. Only anarchy ensued, however, from the appointment of officials from Istanbul, who found themselves helpless figureheads between the rival factions of the Janissaries and the sea-captains. After 1659, the emissaries of the sultan retained no power at all. In 1671, the executive power was vested in a locally elected officer, who held the title of dey.[2]

The seventeenth century was the Golden Age of the Barbary Corsairs who now terrorized the Mediterranean in their own interest, regardless of the Ottoman Empire. In the second half of the seventeenth century, the population of Algiers had risen to a hundred thousand, not including twenty-five thousand Christian slaves. The endless wars of the Christian Powers of Europe against one another provided ample opportunity for piracy.

The pirate captains of Algiers accumulated immense fortunes, built themselves palaces, luxuriously furnished with priceless oriental carpets, silk tapestries and marble colonnades, while they themselves went bravely clad in silks and satins. The sale of Christian slaves was one of their principal sources of income, persons of wealth being released on the payment of ransom, while others were sold locally as servants, concubines or labourers, or employed as rowers on the pirate galleys.

The corsair captains and the Janissaries in Algiers were, like the Phoenicians and the Romans before them, principally interested in the Mediterranean cities and the coastal plain, but made little attempt to extend their power to the Atlas. Like the Ottomans, their tribal policy was to set one tribe to fight another and thus to neutralize their powers. The coastal plain of Algiers was divided into three provinces, each governed by a bey, whose loyalty at times caused anxiety to the dey himself.

The deys continued to rule Algiers until the French landed, on 14th

---

[2] The titles of dey and bey seem to have been peculiar to the janissary-cum-corsair régimes of Algeria and Tunis. In the Ottoman Empire proper, the title of beg was employed.

June, 1830, with a force of thirty-seven thousand men, and took the town. Until 1840, they attempted to limit their occupation to a few coastal towns, Algiers, Wahran (Oran), Boujaiya (Bougie) and Bone. In 1840, however, a forward policy was decided upon, their principal opponent being Abdul Qadir, originally a religious leader in the district of Mascara, fifty miles south-east of Wahran. He proved, however, to be a man of splendid military and diplomatic gifts, who prolonged the war for no less than eighteen years, although the French had, at the end, a hundred thousand men in the field. The conquest of all Algeria was completed in 1848.

The policy of settling Frenchmen in Algeria was thereafter steadily pursued, although the country suffered various periods of instability, originating from revolutionary movements in metropolitan France and from the French defeat in 1871. After 1871, however, Algeria received a civil administration with the status of a department of France. Many Algerians fought in the French army in the First World War, after which increasing numbers of Algerian Muslims went to France for their education.

In the 1930s, the French government prepared a plan to give increased political power to the Algerian Muslims, but the proposals were later dropped, in consideration of the bitter opposition of the French settlers. The country, which had, before the French came, been torn for many centuries by disturbances and civil wars, was peaceful and prosperous, but the Muslims felt that the principal benefit from these improvements had been reaped by the French settlers.

The fall of France in 1940 and the landing of the American and British armies in North Africa in 1942, provided an opportunity for Algerian nationalists to press their claims. After the Second World War, however, both the nationalists and the French settlers increased their demands. Armed rebellion made its appearance at the end of 1954 and, by the end of 1956, nearly all areas in Algeria were in revolt.

In June 1958, General de Gaulle took office in Paris. After numerous tentative efforts at negotiation, during which military operations continued, a ceasefire was signed at Evian on 18th March, 1962. On 3rd July, 1962, Algeria was declared an independent state.

*   *   *

As had occurred in Algiers, Tunis had become an Ottoman province in 1574, but, in 1591, a military mutiny took all real power from the Ottoman governor. Control passed to the councils of army officers and corsair captains, in the same manner as in Algiers. For a few years, the power was held by army officers with the title of deys. These in turn were replaced by beys, of whom the second, Murad Bey (1612–1631), secured the hereditary right of succession of his family. The Murad family ruled until 1702, when they were overthrown, but in 1710, Husain ibn Ali, a native of Crete, seized power, and his family remained rulers of Tunis until our own times. They maintained a fair degree of control and the country was relatively prosperous.

After the Napoleonic wars, piracy ceased and the Beys of Tunis made several attempts to modernize their administration. In 1878, however, France declared a protectorate over Tunisia. In April 1881, she invaded the country and the ruling bey, Muhammad VI, was obliged to submit on 8th June, 1883. The bey remained the nominal ruler but the administration was, in fact, entirely controlled by the French.

Curiously enough, nationalist sentiment became active in Tunisia earlier than in Algeria. In the Second World War, however, the country suffered a German occupation. In August 1946, the "National Congress" demanded complete independence. As in Algeria, the peaceful transfer of authority to a Tunisian government was violently opposed by the French settlers, and later was delayed by a split among the Tunisian nationalists themselves. On 20th March, 1956, a protocol was signed in Paris, recognizing the independence of Tunisia. On 25th July, 1957, the Constituent Assembly abolished the rule of the bey, and invested President Bourguiba with the powers of head of state of the Tunisian Republic.

*   *   *

We must now return to the sixteenth century to recount the history of the Maghrib. The Portuguese were more active than the Spaniards in Africa. In 1415, they had seized Ceuta. In 1471 they took Arzila and Tangier, in 1505 Agadir, in 1508 Safi, in 1513 Azemmour and in 1514 Mazagan. Meanwhile, in 1509, Wahran (Oran) was captured by Spain and, in 1510, Algiers met the same fate. These conquests, however, were not pursued with any energy by either Portugal or Spain. Both these countries had developed far wider interests, the Spanish in their American empire, the Portuguese in the Indian Ocean.

From 1471 to 1548, the Maghrib was nominally ruled by Beni

Wattás, a Berber dynasty which had replaced Beni Merin but which was never able to obtain undisputed power. The reaction to the Spanish and Portuguese attacks could not be controlled by so weak a government and passed into the hands of religious leaders. In 1541, an alleged descendant of the Prophet, the Saadian Sharif[3] Muhammad al Shaikh, captured Agadir from the Portuguese. Safi, Azemmour, Arzila and Qasr al Saghir were abandoned soon afterwards.

With the prestige gained in their holy war against the Portuguese, the Saadian Sharifs succeeded in replacing Beni Wattas and, in 1550, they took Fez, the Wattasid capital. The Beni Saad Sharifs, however, established their capital in Marakish.

On 4th August, 1578, a Portuguese army commanded by the King of Portugal, Dom Sebastian, in person, was completely destroyed by the Beni Saad Sharif Abdul Malik at Wadi al Makhazin. The King of Portugal was killed, and Abdul Malik, already ill, died during the battle. The Golden Age of the Beni Saad Sharifs was from 1578 to 1603, the reign of the Sultan Ahmad al Mansoor. In 1585, a Barbary Company had been established in London for trade with the Maghrib and in 1588, when the Spanish Armada was sent to conquer England, the sultan was the ally of Queen Elizabeth I.

Ahmad al Mansoor sent a military expedition of four thousand men across the desert to black Africa, establishing a colonial government there with its capital at Timbuctoo, from whence he obtained immense wealth in gold, slaves, civet and ebony. The first convoy brought also thirteen virgin daughters of the King of Gao, a slight overdose of princesses, perhaps, even for a sultan. Ahmad al Mansoor was not only a great ruler but a cultured man of letters. He embellished Marakish with buildings and palaces and maintained a splendid and luxurious court.

The death of Sultan Ahmad al Mansoor was followed by civil war between his sons and the rapid decline of the Beni Saad sharifs. In 1662, incidentally, England came into possession of Tangier, as the dowry of the Portuguese princess, Catherine of Braganza, married to Charles II. It was evacuated, however, twenty-two years later, in 1684.

Other new arrivals in the Maghrib were several successive waves of Muslims from Spain, evicted between 1609 and 1614. Many of these established themselves at Salé, near Rabat, where they fitted

[3] The title of sharif, pronounced shareef, is held by all alleged descendants of the Prophet.

out a fleet of privateers. Filled with rancour against Spain, they plundered Christian shipping and even raided towns on the south coast of England, where they were known as the Sallee Rovers. On a contemporary English map, Salé is charmingly designated Old Sally.

The collapse of the Beni Saad was followed by the rise of another family of sharifs, this time genuinely descended from Fatima and Ali ibn abi Talib.[4] On 6th June, 1666, Maulay al Rashid, of the so-called Filali or Alawi Sharifs, was proclaimed sultan in Fez. By 1671, he had brought all the Maghrib under his control. His brother Maulay Ismail, however, who reigned from 1672 to 1727, became even more famous.

Ismail was a fiery, dominating personality, brave, enterprising and energetic. Indifferent to luxury or even comfort, he was nevertheless extremely fond of women. His army, allegedly a hundred and fifty thousand strong, consisted partly of negro slaves and partly of *mujahideen*, or volunteers for holy war. He fought with equal vigour against the rulers of Algeria, the Spanish and the Portuguese. But in spite of his untiring energy and strong will, he failed to pacify the country completely and his reign was punctuated by tribal rebellions. He moved his capital to Meknes, where he erected many buildings, palaces and mosques. On his death, this extraordinary man left a library of two thousand volumes.

The death of Sultan Ismail was followed by fifty years of instability, but thereafter the dynasty was firmly established and is still on the throne today. The long reigns of Muhammad III (1757–1790) and of Sulaiman (1792–1822) passed peacefully. The European Powers, engrossed in colonial enterprises further afield or in the Napoleonic wars, had lost interest in Morocco. The country itself, freed from the incentive of foreign competition, fell increasingly behind the times. Maulay Abdul Rahman ruled from 1822 to 1859, Muhammad IV 1859 to 1873 and Al Hasan I from 1873 to 1894. The long reigns of the sultans is an indication of the quiet stability of the country.

Throughout the eighteenth and nineteenth centuries, the sultans were only in complete control of the coastal plains. The Berber tribes of the Atlas were virtually independent and paid no taxes to the state. The sultans, however, succeeded in surviving, partly by negotiation and diplomacy with the tribes, partly by periodic military expeditions

---

[4] The enemies of the Beni Saad claimed that they were not descended from Ali but from the Prophet's wet nurse, who was of a tribe called Beni Saad outside Mecca. See page 28.

and partly because the Berbers, invincible in their mountains, were unable to defeat the sultan's army in the coastal plain. Such was the situation in the Maghrib at the end of the nineteenth century.

*   *   *

France had long been firmly established in Algeria but did not extend her power to Morocco until the twentieth century. In 1904, Britain and Spain recognized the special position of France in the Maghrib, Spain receiving in return zones of influence in the north and south of the country. In 1911, an international crisis was provoked by the appearance of a German gunboat at Agadir, but the result was the German recognition of Morocco as a French sphere of influence.

From 1912 to 1925, the famous Marshal Lyautey was French Resident General in Morocco, and succeeded in establishing authority over the greater part of the country. From 1921 to 1926, the French assisted the Spanish forces in suppressing the formidable rebellion of Abdul Karim in the Rif mountains. Government authority was not, however, completely established all over the Atlas and the Tafilelt until 1934.

After the Second World War, an independence party was formed in the cities of the Maghrib, and received the support of the Sultan Muhammad V ibn Yusuf. The Berber tribes, however, led by the chief Thami al Glawi and encouraged by the French, opposed modernization and, in August 1953, the sultan agreed to go into exile. Disturbances continued and, on 5th November, 1955, Sultan Muhammad returned to the throne. France recognized the independence of the Maghrib and, on 12th November, 1956, Morocco became a member of the United Nations. In 1957, the title of sultan was abolished and that of king substituted.

On the death of King Muhammad in 1961, he was succeeded by his son, Hasan II. In November 1962, a new constitution was promulgated, involving universal suffrage and a parliament consisting of two houses. In October 1963, however, fighting broke out between Morocco and Algeria, on the subject of the undemarcated frontier east of the Atlas. A cease fire was signed on 30th October and most of the difficulties between the two countries were solved before the end of 1964.

The establishment of a constitution on Western democratic lines did not, however, prove an unqualified success in the Maghrib and, as in most Asian and African countries, a need was felt for a more authoritative system. As a result, on 7th June, 1965, King Hasan took over executive power.

The population of Morocco is a little over thirteen millions. There is some industry, chiefly in the Casablanca area but many Moroccans go to France to earn higher wages, some of which they remit to their homes.

The French protectorate over Morocco lasted forty-five years, during which the whole country was brought under government control, for the first time since Beni Merin, perhaps since the Muwah-hids. In addition, the country was equipped with good roads, with excellent ports, a railway system and an efficient administration.

Much of the success of the French in Morocco was due to the personality of Lyautey. After the Second World War, the situation deteriorated rapidly.

NOTABLE DATES

Collapse of the Muwahhid Empire	1269
Collapse of Beni Merin	1465
Portuguese conquests in Morocco	1415–1541
Spanish capture of Algiers	1510
Recapture of Algiers by Arooj	1516
Career of Khair al Deen Barbarossa	1518–1546
Battle of Lepanto	1571
Rule of the Beni Saad Sharifs in the Maghrib	1548–1666
Rule of the Murad family in Tunis	1612–1702
Proclamation of the first Filali Sharif in the Maghrib	1666
Proclamation of Husain ibn Ali as Bey of Tunis	1710
French landing in Algiers	1830
French invasion of Tunisia	1881
French penetration of Morocco	1904
Tunisian Independence	1956
Moroccan Independence	1956
Algerian Independence	1962

PERSONALITIES

Khair al Deen Barbarossa	1518–1546
Sultan Ahmad al Mansoor, of the Beni Saad Sharifs of Morocco	1578–1603

Maulay Ismail, Sultan of Morocco	1672–1727
Abdul Qadir, Algerian, who opposed the French	1830–1848
Marshal Lyautey, French Administrator of Morocco	1912–1925
Abdul Karim, the Rif rebel leader	1921–1926
Muhammad V ibn Yusuf, Sultan of Morocco	1927–1961
Hasan II, King of Morocco	1961 (still reigning)

XIX

The Twentieth Century

DURING the six years which divided the Young Turk revolution of 1908 from the First World War, the Ottomans suffered an endless succession of disasters. In the Balkans they met with many reverses until their territory in Europe was reduced to Thrace alone. In 1912, Tripoli became an Italian colony. In the same year, Ibn Saud occupied the Hasa province on the Persian Gulf, driving out the Ottoman garrison. In Syria, the pan-Turkish policy of the Committee of Union and Progress had alienated Arab intellectuals and two secret societies had come into existence, pledged to work for Arab independence.

When war began in Europe in August 1914, the Committee of Union and Progress were divided, the civilian members favouring neutrality, the military members wishing to enter the war on the German side. In September, however, war was declared.

The governors of Mecca and Medina had been chosen from the decendants of the Prophet, ever since the seventh century. The Ottomans had inherited the suzerainty over the Holy Cities from the Mamlooks in 1517. For centuries Ottoman overlordship had been little more than nominal, but during the nineteenth century, control was strengthened. The Porte tried to achieve greater authority by its normal practice of divide and rule—in this instance by sowing discord between the members of the Prophet's family. When a clash occurred between rival sharifs, the government supported one of the weaker candidates, who was obliged to rely on Ottoman assistance in order to resist his opponents.

In 1892, a certain Sharif Husain ibn Ali was "invited" by Sultan Abdul Hameed II to come to Istanbul, where he was received with veneration, made a member of the Council of State and kept under strict observation. In 1903, however, the Committee of Union and Progress dismissed the then Sharif of Mecca and sent Sharif Husain in his place, contrary to the advice of Abdul Hameed II, who was in some ways a more acute politician than the young reformers.

When the National Assembly was constituted in Istanbul, Sharif Abdulla, the second son of Husain, sat as the member for the Hejaz. In February 1914, Abdulla, on his way from Mecca to Istanbul, called on Lord Kitchener in Cairo to enquire what would be the attitude of Britain to an Arab revolt in the Hejaz. Lord Kitchener's reply was non-committal.

In November 1914, the Sultan of Turkey, in his capacity of khalif, declared a *jihad* or holy war, calling upon all the Muslims in the world to fight against France, Britain and Russia. To Britain in India and Egypt, and to France in North Africa, a universal rising of Muslims would have been extremely embarrassing. British contacts with the Sharif of Mecca were renewed and, on 5th June, 1916, Sharif Husain rebelled against the Turks.

In January 1917, it was agreed that an Arab force commanded by Husain's third son, the Ameer Feisal, should advance northwards and operate on the eastern flank of a British army which was invading Palestine from Egypt. On 6th July, 1917, an Arab tribal force, accompanied by T. E. Lawrence, captured Aqaba. On 9th December, 1917, the British army under General Allenby took Jerusalem.

A Turkish garrison of some ten thousand men remained blockaded by the Arabs in Medina throughout the war. The Arabs cut the railway north of Medina, while the Turks used several thousand men trying to repair it. When the front moved northwards to Jerusalem, the Arabs likewise destroyed the railway north of Maan, where they cut off another seven thousand Turks.

On the whole, it has been estimated that the Arab revolt diverted between twenty and thirty thousand Turkish troops from the Palestine front. In the final British offensive, on 19th September, 1918, the Arabs seized the railway junction at Deraa behind the Turkish lines, thereby ensuring the almost complete destruction of the 4th, 7th and 8th Turkish armies.

The most active part of the Arab forces consisted of bedouin tribesmen who, being able to move freely in the desert, were in a position continually to turn the Turkish eastern flank. The result was a striking example of guerilla tactics. The Arabs, who could scarcely have defeated a Turkish brigade in battle, were able by guerilla methods to divert thirty thousand men from the main battle front. The Arab effort was, of course, only maintained by the aid of British money and weapons, but their performance was nevertheless remarkable.

In addition to this actual contribution to the fighting, the revolt of the Sharif of Mecca against Turkey helped to counteract the effect

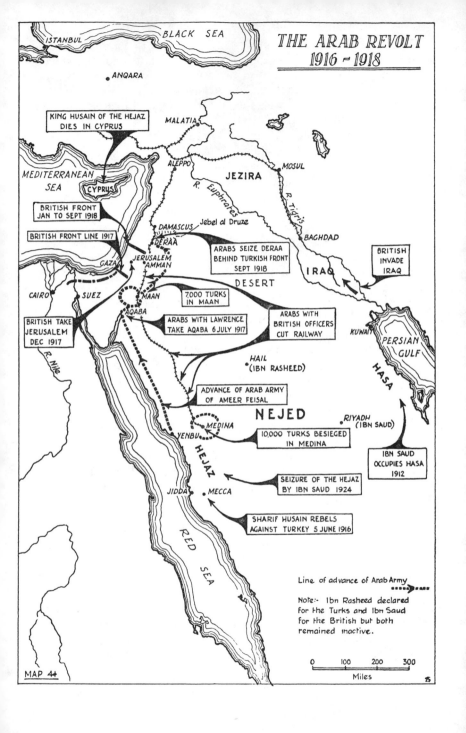

THE ARAB REVOLT
1916 ~ 1918

ISTANBUL

BLACK SEA

ANQARA

KING HUSAIN OF THE HEJAZ
DIES IN CYPRUS

MALATIA

MEDITERRANEAN
SEA

CYPRUS

ALEPPO

JEZIRA

MOSUL

R. Euphrates

R. Tigris

BAGHDAD

BRITISH
INVADE
IRAQ

BRITISH FRONT
JAN TO SEPT 1918

BRITISH FRONT LINE 1917

DAMASCUS

DERAA

Jebel al Druze

JERUSALEM

AMMAN

ARABS SEIZE DERAA
BEHIND TURKISH FRONT
SEPT 1918

IRAQ

GAZA

CAIRO

SUEZ

MAAN

DESERT

7,000 TURKS
IN MAAN

BRITISH TAKE
JERUSALEM
DEC 1917

AQABA

ARABS WITH LAWRENCE
TAKE AQABA 6 JULY 1917

ARABS WITH
BRITISH OFFICERS
CUT RAILWAY

KUWAIT

PERSIAN
GULF

R. Nile

HAIL
(IBN RASHEED)

HASA

ADVANCE OF ARAB ARMY
OF AMEER FEISAL

NEJED

RIYADH
(IBN SAUD)

MEDINA

YENBU

10,000 TURKS BESIEGED
IN MEDINA

IBN SAUD
OCCUPIES HASA
1912

HEJAZ

SEIZURE OF THE HEJAZ
BY IBN SAUD 1924

JIDDA

MECCA

SHARIF HUSAIN REBELS
AGAINST TURKEY 5 JUNE 1916

RED
SEA

Line of advance of Arab Army
••••▶••••

Note:- Ibn Rasheed declared
for the Turks and Ibn Saud
for the British but both
remained inactive.

MAP 44

0   100   200   300

Miles

of the holy war declared by the sultan, for the sharif was a descendant of the Prophet Muhammad himself.

Moreover, the news of the Hejaz rising resulted in the spread of anti-Turkish feeling in Syria and Lebanon. The military governor, Jamal Pasha the Less, added fuel to the fire by the severity of his repression of pro-Arab sentiment.

*   *   *

When the Turkish Empire entered the First World War, Ibn Rasheed declared his support for the sultan, while Ibn Saud asked for help from the British government in India. Captain W. H. I. Shakespear, then British agent in Kuwait, was sent to Ibn Saud.[1] This gallant officer persuaded Ibn Saud to attack Ibn Rasheed, who threatened to interfere with the British invasion of Iraq. In January 1915, an indecisive battle was fought between the two Arab princes at Jaráb, in the course of which Shakespear was killed.

Ibn Saud did not move again until 1921, when he finally defeated Ibn Rasheed and became sole ruler of Nejed and the Hasa, and the neighbour of King Husain of the Hejaz.

*   *   *

The Arab revolt in the Hejaz had been preceded by an exchange of letters between Sir Henry McMahon, the British High Commissioner in Egypt, and Sharif Husain, in which the former had agreed in general to the grant of independence to the Arabs after the war. (Egypt and North Africa were not then included in the Arab independence movement.) Sir Henry McMahon excluded from this pledge an undefined area "west of Damascus". The correspondence was terminated by the outbreak of the Arab revolt and never reached the stage of a formal agreement.

From the beginning of the war, however, Russia, Britain and France had signed a secret agreement on the subject of the dismemberment of the Turkish Empire. Russia, which coveted Istanbul, seems to have been the original prime mover. In May 1916, Britain and France signed the so-called Sykes–Picot Agreement, in which they agreed to establish spheres of influence in the Arab State to be set up after the war.

The establishment of spheres of influence was a common practice before 1914. Russia and Britain had signed an agreement in 1907, defining their spheres of influence in Persia. Immediately before the

[1] Map 39, page 254.

First World War, France, Germany and Britain had initialled an agreement regarding their economic concessions in the Turkish Empire. Looked at from an economic angle, the Powers agreed not to interfere with one another. If, for example, Ruritania required a railway in its northern province, Russia (let us say) would offer to build it, France and Britain remaining aloof. If, however, a railway was needed in the south, Britain (for example) would offer.

Agreements of this nature have since been stigmatized as economic imperialism but, in 1914, this sharing of economic benefits was not considered incompatible with the political independence of the country concerned. Sir Mark Sykes, who signed the agreement on behalf of Britain, was an enthusiastic orientalist and a strong advocate of Arab independence.

For Britain to assist the Arab countries to form a large independent state was not merely a piece of sentimental idealism but was also a wise and statesmanlike policy. It will be remembered that the Mediterranean, Egypt and the Red Sea constituted Britain's main trade and strategic route to India and Australia. It was her constant fear that some potentially hostile Great Power, like Russia or Germany, might place itself astride this commercial highway and strangle British commerce. In 1915, the Turks and the Germans had actually reached the banks of the Suez Canal.

For more than a hundred years, Britain had protected her lifeline by supporting the Ottomans to keep the Russians out. The Ottomans had now become enemies, so why not support an Arab state in the rôle formerly played by the Ottomans? The Arabs would be too weak to defend their independence alone, but, with British assistance, might form a stable government which would resist any advance by Germany or Russia. Thus an Anglo-Arab alliance seemed to present the ideal solution for both peoples.

No sooner did the British take Damascus in September 1918 than they set up an Arab government under the Ameer Faisal. In July 1919, the self-appointed General Syrian Congress assembled in Damascus, claiming to represent Syria, Palestine, Lebanon and Trans-Jordan, which had not as yet been divided into separate countries. It passed a number of resolutions of which the gist was that Syria, including Palestine, should be an Arab state with the Ameer Faisal as king, and that foreign tutelage should be rejected but foreign assistance accepted. If possible, the assistance should be provided by the United States. If that were impossible, Britain would be accepted but French aid would be refused.

In September 1919, President Woodrow Wilson sent Dr. King and Mr. Crane to report on the situation. Their recommendations were to the effect that a mandatory power was necessary, preferably the United States or, failing her, Britain, and that Syria, Lebanon, Palestine and Trans-Jordan should be one country with one mandatory. There can be no doubt that the resolutions of the Syrian Congress and the recommendations of the King–Crane Commission provided a just and wise solution.

A French army had meanwhile landed in Lebanon. On 20th July, 1920, General Gouraud's army marched on Damascus, which it occupied on the 25th, and the Arab state ceased to exist. In the Sykes–Picot Agreement, the only privileges awarded to France in Syria were "a right of priority in enterprises and local loans" and that she "shall alone supply foreign advisers or officials *on the request of the Arab state*".[2] The uninitiated have sometimes denounced the "iniquitous" Sykes–Picot Agreement as the cause of the French occupation of Syria. Not only is this incorrect but Sir Mark Sykes, when he signed it, was under the impression that he was promoting Arab independence.

* * *

The situation had been further confused meanwhile by the issue of the Balfour Declaration on 2nd November, 1917. This document stated that the British government viewed with favour "the establishment of a national home for the Jewish people in Palestine". The second part of the declaration stated, "it being clearly understood that nothing shall be done which may prejudice the civil and religious rights of existing non-Jewish communities in Palestine".

The phrase "a national home for the Jewish people in Palestine" has often been pointed to as a typical piece of political chicanery. "How," it has been asked, "could a national home exist *in* Palestine, except under a Jewish government?" In fact, however, such was all that the Jews had ever enjoyed in history. Palestine had all through history been inhabited by a mixture of races.

The second provision in the Balfour Declaration, protecting the rights of non-Jewish communities in Palestine, seems to suggest that the British government believed that the majority of the inhabitants of Palestine were already Jews, this sentence being the usual reservation to protect the rights of minorities. In fact, when the Balfour Declaration was issued, Jews formed only seven per cent of the

[2] The italics are mine.

population of Palestine, "non-Jewish communities" constituting ninety-three per cent.

When considering the slovenly wording and careless diplomacy of the Sykes–Picot Agreement and the Balfour Declaration, it is necessary to remember the war situation in 1917. Russia had ceased to fight and the whole strength of Germany, Austria and Turkey was turned against the Allies. When the Balfour Declaration was issued, the continued independence of Britain and France themselves hung in the balance. The best, perhaps the only hope of being able to repulse the expected German offensive in the spring of 1918, was to secure the entry of the United States into the war. The British government was advised that this could most easily be achieved by conciliating Jewish opinion, in view of the powerful influence exerted by leading Jews in America.

The Balfour Declaration would appear therefore to have been an emergency measure to meet the war crisis which had arisen as a result of the defection of Russia. It need not be assumed, however, that the British government was aware that the promise made to the Jews would ruin their plans for long term co-operation with the Arabs. The fact that Israeli–Arab hostility has since then achieved world-wide publicity should not cause us to imagine that, when the Balfour Declaration was issued, the matter appeared in Britain to be of much importance.

Zionist policy throughout showed a remarkable contrast to that followed by the Arabs in one respect. The Zionists always accepted whatever concessions they could get and, having consolidated the ground won, immediately began to work for more. The Arabs repeatedly rejected compromise solutions and insisted on all or nothing. The Balfour Declaration was so vaguely worded that it could mean everything or nothing. The Zionists nevertheless accepted it and immediately began to use it as a lever to get more.

The Mandate for Palestine, allotted by the League of Nations, consisted principally of provisions in favour of the Jews. Although Jews only constituted seven per cent of the population, the word Jews or Zionist appears twelve times in the Mandate. The Arabs, who formed ninety-three per cent of the population, were not once mentioned.

*   *   *

The French seizure of Syria provoked at first more indignation than the Jewish National Home, because it took place immediately and by force. The implications of the Palestine Mandate were not fully appreciated for some time. On 20th July, 1925, the Druzes of Syria, living in the area south-east of Damascus known as the Druze Mountain or Jebel al Druze, rose in rebellion against the French. The remainder of Syria gave them little military support, but fighting continued against the Druzes until the summer of 1926.

The years 1926 to 1939 passed somewhat uneasily in Syria. Opposition to France, however, was almost entirely political and there were no further military operations. Lebanon also remained under direct French administration during the same period. The Lebanese, however, had throughout history looked westward across the Mediterranean rather than eastward towards Arabia. Many of their leaders had been educated in France or in French schools in Lebanon, and opposition to the mandate was never acute, as it was in Syria.

Iraq had been occupied by the British army during the course of the First World War, but here no Arabs had fought on the side of the allies. After the end of the war, the future of Iraq, unlike that of Syria and Palestine, was not of interest to other Great Powers or to strong political groups capable of bringing pressure on the League of Nations or lobbying the members. Harassed by the more urgent problems of Germany, Russia, Austria and Turkey, the British government shelved the question of Iraq, leaving that country under an improvised military administration.

In June 1920, the Iraq tribes rose in revolt. The principal military officers in the army of the Ameer Feisal had been Iraqis, who had previously been serving in the Turkish army. They had witnessed the French seizure of Damascus and had returned to Iraq, stating that Britain had betrayed her pledges. The arrival of these officers caused an outburst of resentment in Baghdad. The actual fighting, however, was done entirely by the tribes, who were not inspired by nationalist ambitions, but by opposition to government control in any form. The British administration had attempted to govern the whole country, but the tribes were determined to retain their independence, as they had done for four centuries under the Ottomans. The military operations involved were not extensive, but they were an unhappy prelude to Anglo-Iraqi relations.

The imposition of a mandate by the League of Nations was, however, resented. A system of dyarchy, under which Iraqi executive officials were "doubled" by British advisers, inevitably produced some personal friction. The mandate, however, was terminated in October 1932 and Iraq became a member of the League of Nations.

In the 1920s, Iraq had been surrounded by enemies. The French and the Turks wished to annex Mosul, the Kurds were often hostile, and a new revival of Wahhabi fanaticism in Central Arabia led to bloodthirsty raids from the desert against the tribes on the Euphrates. Moreover, the Iraqi tribes themselves were by no means reconciled to control by any government. Britain freely used her armed forces and her international prestige to defend Iraq and to subject the tribes to control. Without such help, it is doubtful whether Iraq would have survived.

Amid all the impassioned political propaganda of the past fifty years, the actual administration of the Arab countries after the First World War is often forgotten. The fact remains, however, that until the end of the war, almost all senior government posts had been held by Turks. For four hundred years, the Arabs had enjoyed no opportunity to produce statesmen, administrators, technicians or soldiers. Thus the task which faced them, when the Turks suddenly disappeared in 1918, was one of immense difficulty.

For twenty years, between the two World Wars, many British officials worked with untiring zeal and devotion to build up every department of modern government. The methods of taxation, the preparation of annual budgets, the legal system, irrigation, public works, roads and railways, education, police and the build-up of armies from nothing—all these varied and essential services were the work of mandatory officials, many of whom were inspired by a deeply loyal devotion to the Arab countries in which they worked. It is not right that such patient and devoted service be entirely forgotten.

*   *   *

At the end of the First World War, Sharif Husain of Mecca had assumed the title of king. Central Arabia, then known as Nejed, was ruled by the Saud family, which for a hundred and fifty years had provided the leaders of the Wahhabi religious movement. In 1924, the Wahhabis invaded the Hejaz and drove King Husain from his throne.[3] Abdul Azeez ibn Saud assumed the title of King of the Hejaz and Nejed, later changed to that of King of Saudi Arabia. King Husain died, an exile from his country, in Cyprus.

*   *   *

Egypt, which had been in chaos and misery in 1882 when the British army occupied Cairo, had become rich, strong, and well-governed in the ensuing thirty years. But, as always occurs in such

[3] Map 41, page 274.

cases, benefits soon came to be accepted as a matter of course, while grievances rankled. The situation was mishandled by the British government, partly owing to the deterioration in the quality of British officials in Egypt, and to their frequent transfer and replacement. Lord Cromer had spent twenty-four years in Egypt, but during the war years, most of his staff had left.

The peoples of Asia and Africa differ profoundly from those of north-west Europe. Their personal relationships are warmer and they do not expect their governments to be impersonal machines. The modern Western practice of moving officials to other appointments every three years renders extremely difficult the maintenance of those close and amicable personal relations on which in Asia almost everything depends.

Disturbances occurred in Egypt in March 1919, but, on 28th February, 1921, the country was declared independent and, on 19th April, 1923, a constitution was promulgated. On 19th November, 1924, however, the assassination of Sir Lee Stack jeopardized all the progress achieved. On several occasions when a complete understanding was nearly reached, terrorist actions made progress impossible. King Fuad, moreover, was himself alarmed by the demagogy of Zaghlul Pasha, the Egyptian nationalist leader.

*   *   *

At the commencement of the Second World War, a large French army was in occupation of Syria and Lebanon. With the fall of France, however, an Italo-German armistice commission arrived. In April 1941, a military *coup d'état* took place in Baghdad, and the regent was obliged to escape to Jordan. The military government declared war on Britain and appealed to Germany for help. On 30th April, the Iraqi army attacked the British Air Force Station at Habbaniya. In May, a column of British troops from Palestine, accompanied by the Jordan Arab Legion, crossed the desert and retook Baghdad, replacing the regent and his ministers in office.

On 8th June, 1941, British and Free French troops and the Arab Legion invaded Syria and Lebanon, the occupation of which was completed on 11th July. The civil administration was then handed over to the Free French. On the occasion of this invasion of Syria, the Free French had issued a promise of independence to that country. In May 1945, however, when the war came to an end, the French showed no readiness to withdraw and fighting broke out in the streets of Damascus.

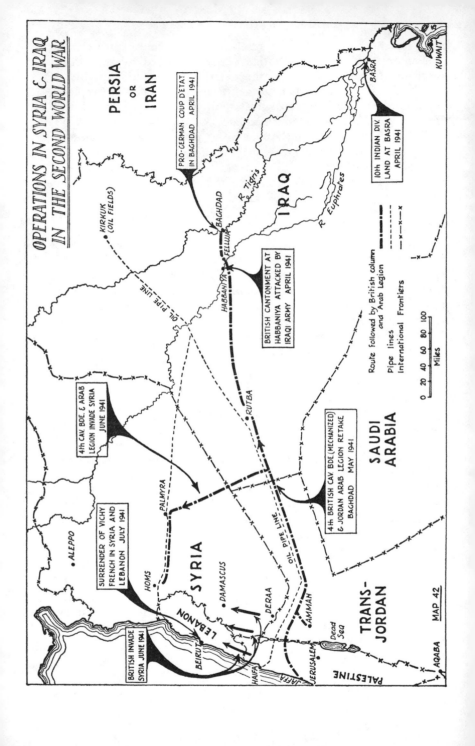

OPERATIONS IN SYRIA & IRAQ
IN THE SECOND WORLD WAR

PERSIA
OR
IRAN

PRO-GERMAN COUP D'ETAT
IN BAGHDAD APRIL 1941

10th INDIAN DIV.
LAND AT BASRA
APRIL 1941

KIRKUK
(OIL FIELDS)

IRAQ

R. Tigris

BAGHDAD

FELLUJA

BASRA

KUWAIT

OIL PIPE LINE

HABBANIYA

BRITISH CANTONMENT AT
HABBANIYA ATTACKED BY
IRAQI ARMY APRIL 1941

RUTBA

4th CAV. BDE & ARAB
LEGION INVADE SYRIA
JUNE 1941

SAUDI
ARABIA

SURRENDER OF VICHY
FRENCH IN SYRIA AND
LEBANON JULY 1941

PALMYRA

4th BRITISH CAV. BDE (MECHANIZED)
& JORDAN ARAB LEGION RETAKE
BAGHDAD MAY 1941

Route followed by British column
and Arab Legion
Pipe lines
International Frontiers

0 20 40 60 80 100
Miles

ALEPPO

HOMS

SYRIA

DAMASCUS

DERAA

OIL PIPE LINE

BRITISH INVADE
SYRIA JUNE 1941

LEBANON

BEIRUT

AMMAN

TRANS-
JORDAN

Dead
Sea

HAIFA

JAFFA

JERUSALEM

PALESTINE

AQABA

MAP 42

The British government, which for twenty-five years had smarted under taunts of having betrayed Syrian independence in 1920, ordered British troops to assume control and, in 1946, both the French and British armies were withdrawn. Thirty years after the exchange of letters between Sharif Husain and Sir Henry McMahon, Syria and Lebanon became independent. For a short time, Britain was the heroine of the Syrians but, alas, political memories are all too short.

* * *

In Palestine, Jews and Arabs ceased fighting one another when the Second World War broke out, and a number of both enlisted in the British Army. But when the tide of victory turned against Germany, Jewish underground organizations commenced terrorist attacks on British soldiers and base installations. As soon as hostilities were over, the United States and Russia, in almost identical words, attacked the presence of British forces in Palestine as did also Jews and Arabs alike. Britain, as a result, notified the United Nations of her intention to surrender the mandate. If British troops had remained in Palestine and supervised the execution of the partition plan, the operation might have been carried out without fighting. Pressure brought to bear on Britain by the United States and Russia, demanding the immediate withdrawal of British troops, was partly responsible for the subsequent disasters.

In November 1947, a resolution dividing Palestine into Jewish and Arab areas was passed with some difficulty by the United Nations General Assembly. Unfortunately the assembly made no provision for the enforcement of its resolution. When the British mandate ended on 15th May, 1948, the state of Israel was declared and the Arabs and Jews began to fight one another. Eventually, on 24th February, 1949, Egypt signed an armistice with Israel. Lebanon concluded a similar armistice on 23rd March, and Jordan on 3rd April, 1949.

When the fighting came to an end, the only portion of Palestine retained by the Arabs was that which had been defended by the Arab Legion, the army of Jordan. The Iraqi army, which had defended the Nablus area, withdrew without concluding an armistice with Israel. This remnant of Palestine was united to Trans-Jordan to constitute the Kingdom of Jordan.

* * *

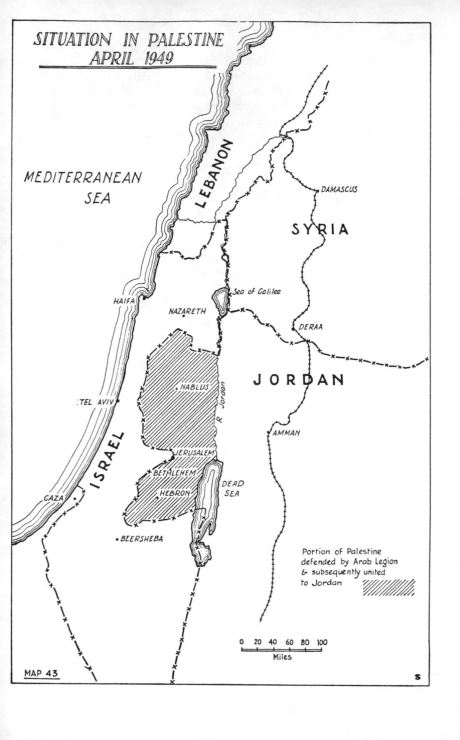

SITUATION IN PALESTINE
APRIL 1949

MEDITERRANEAN
SEA

LEBANON

SYRIA

DAMASCUS

Sea of Galilee

HAIFA

NAZARETH

DERAA

JORDAN

NABLUS

R. Jordan

TEL AVIV

ISRAEL

AMMAN

JERUSALEM

BETHLEHEM

HEBRON

DEAD
SEA

GAZA

BEERSHEBA

Portion of Palestine
defended by Arab Legion
& subsequently united
to Jordan

0 20 40 60 80 100

Miles

MAP 43

At the end of the Second World War, Britain had conceived the idea that a federation or alliance of all the Arab countries would ensure stability in the Middle East. From the point of view of British interests such Arab strength and stability was desirable, in order to ensure the security of the trade route to the Indian Ocean.

It is interesting to notice that subsequent Arab propaganda has always insisted that Britain and the United States created the state of Israel in order to weaken and divide the Arabs, and the vast majority of people in the Middle East believe this to have been the case. In fact, however, Britain's principal interest in the area was to protect the passage to the Indian Ocean from Russian or German control, an objective which might have been achieved by a strong Arab empire replacing the Ottoman Empire.

As a result, Britain encouraged the formation of the Arab League, the Charter of which was signed on 22nd March, 1945. Egypt, who had never before identified herself with the Arabs, claimed leadership of the League. The signatories of the Charter were Egypt, Syria, Lebanon, Jordan, Iraq, Saudi Arabia and the Yemen.

The possibility of fruitful co-operation between Britain and the Arab League was destroyed by the tragedy of Palestine. The Arab League, which Britain had hoped would form a power bloc sufficient to thrust back attempts at Russian infiltration, threw all its energies into the struggle against Israel.

*   *   *

A notable feature of Middle East politics since 1950 has been the rapid development of radio broadcasting for political propaganda. The almost unrestrained use of violent polemics and bitter vituperation has done much to cause unrest and even to provoke outbreaks of violence. Broadcasting is a peculiarly powerful weapon in the Middle East because it can reach many communities who did not previously read the press, and also because it can be heard in their homes by women who would not attend political meetings.

Perhaps, like other weapons, it will become blunted with use, the very violence of the language used contributing eventually to deaden the effect.

*   *   *

Psychologists, professional and amateur, have devoted a good deal of paper to the study of the mental and emotional stresses produced in the younger generations in the Middle East, as the result of the impact of Western civilization. It is interesting to note that such a situation is not new in Syria and Egypt which, throughout their history, have been conquered alternately by the East and the West. The Syrians and the Lebanese have always been extremely quick in adapting themselves to such cultural changes.

Those peoples whom today we call Arabs form, as we have already seen, a linguistic and cultural group composed of many races of differing ethnological origin. It is not, therefore, possible to say that "the Arabs" possess or lack this quality or that. In general, the Syrians, Lebanese, and the former inhabitants of Palestine are prob-ably considerably mixed with Greek and other European strains. The adaptability and intelligence of these people, however, will doubtless convince the world and themselves of their ability to com-pete intellectually with any nation on earth.

Every race, however, has the faults of its virtues, and the Syrians, Lebanese and Palestinians have never been successful as soldiers. In Roman as much as in Turkish times, they reached the highest positions in the intellectual world, but rarely, if ever, served in the armed forces. If the Syrians have been psychologically disturbed by contact with the West, therefore, the trouble has arisen from their military incapacity to oppose the West—whether in the form of France or of Israel—rather than from any lack of intellectual ability.

The Saudi Arabians, on the other hand, are excellent military material, though still handicapped by lack of education. Their minds are essentially practical rather than academic—a complete contrast to the Syrians, to whom they are racially unrelated.

It is an unfortunate feature of the press in Western countries today that only unpleasant things are believed to possess news value. Thus a bitter attack on our country by a foreign politician is front page news, but if a friendly statesman expresses his appreciation, his remarks are not reported. This system does very great harm to international relations.

It is not possible, as a result, for persons living far from the Arab countries to form any idea of these peoples. Only those who have lived among them can know their irresistible charm, their warm-hearted kindness, their tender pity for the weak, their fantastic hospitality or their extravagant generosity. As one who has spent the best part of his life among them, it is a pleasure to be able to pay my humble tribute to their gifts. And these, after all, not money, oil, comfort or a high standard of living, are the ingredients of human happiness.

NOTABLE DATES

Young Turk revolution in Istanbul	1908
Balkan War	1912
Annexation of Tripoli by Italy	1912
Turkish entry into the First World War	1914
Arab revolt against the Turks	1916
Balfour Declaration	1917
Seizure of Damascus by the French	1920
Declaration of Independence of Egypt	1921
Druze rebellion in Syria	1925–1926
Declaration of Independence of Iraq	1932
Outbreak of the Second World War	1939
Coup d'état in Baghdad	1941
British occupation of Syria	1941
Signature of the Arab League Charter	1945
Anglo-French evacuation of Syria	1946
End of the Palestine Mandate	1948

PERSONALITIES

Husain ibn Ali, Sharif of Mecca (later King of the Hejaz)
Abdulla, his second son (later King of Jordan)
Feisal, his third son (later King of Iraq)
Sir Henry McMahon, British High Commissioner in Egypt
Abdul Azeez ibn Saud, King of Saudi Arabia

XX

The Value of History

SOME knowledge of Arab history should undoubtedly form part of every educational syllabus. The principal reasons for this statement, opposed as it is to present practice among Western nations, will be set out in this chapter.

The first reason may be described as continuity. History is a continuous process and to read extracts from it, taken from here and there and separated by long periods of silence, destroys the interest of the story. The Arab Empire which dominated the Western world for six centuries, was itself founded on its mighty predecessors, Rome and Persia. The rise, the greatness and the civilization of the Arab Empire are incomprehensible without some knowledge of Greek, Persian and Roman culture, on which they were largely built. In the same manner, the rise of Christian Europe cannot be explained without some understanding of the accomplishments of Arab civilization, from which Western culture largely derived its knowledge and its early ways of thought. Thus some acquaintance with Arab history is necessary to the comprehension of our own beginnings.

Arab control of what we call the Middle East and their naval command of the Mediterranean imposed a blockade on Europe, which destroyed the commercial and urban society left behind by the Romans. During five centuries, from the seventh to the twelfth, Europe was deprived of all overseas commerce by the long Arab barrier extending from the Atlantic to Central Asia north of Tibet.

The Roman commercial connections with India and the Far East were taken over in their entirety by the Arab Empire, the ships of which plied to India, East Africa, Indonesia and China. As a result, the Muslim countries became immensely wealthy, and their standard of living was as much in advance of that of Europe as the wealth of the West today exceeds that of the Arabs.

Europe, shut off from the rest of the world, was obliged to become self-supporting, and produced only its own food and home-made clothing. Cash, the product of commerce, was scarce and gold almost unobtainable. Land became the normal form of wealth and the barons, not the businessmen or the bankers, were the leading citizens. For more than a thousand years after the Arab conquests of the seventh century, families which owned land were considered in Western Europe to be socially superior to persons engaged in commerce. Thus the social consequences of the Arab blockade of Europe lasted far longer than the commercial. Even when Europe had already outstripped the Arabs economically, the social superiority of the landed gentry in the West still remained. This example gives ample proof of the necessity of continuity, if the meaning of historical and social changes is to be understood.

In spite, however, of the Muslim blockade, a trickle of commerce still reached Constantinople, either from Arab territory in periods of truce, or by caravans passing north of the Caspian and Black Seas, or by means of Jewish merchants, who were able to operate in both Christian and Muslim countries. These surviving channels of trade, however slender, were sufficient to allow the Byzantines to maintain a limited urban and commercial civilization and to enable them to escape the feudal system and the Dark Ages, which had settled upon Western Europe.

If knowledge of the history of the period from the seventh to the twelfth centuries is vital to the comprehension of the development of Europe, why, it may be asked, has it never been taught? Throughout these five hundred years, Christendom lived in constant fear of Muslim conquest. From the twelfth to the fifteenth centuries, Islam and Christendom were equally balanced. The West was overtaking and gradually surpassing the Muslim countries in power, principally owing to its technical improvements in firearms and ship building. Not until 1498 did Vasco da Gama, by discovering the Cape route, enable Europe once again to trade with India and the Far East.

But throughout the Renaissance period in Europe, fear of the Muslims was still strong and hostility, political and commercial as much as religious, was intense. Doubtless as a result of these factors, the indebtedness of Western Christendom to Arab civilization was systematically played down, if not completely denied. A tradition was built up, by censorship and propaganda, that the Muslim imperialists had been mere barbarians and that the rebirth of learning in the West was derived directly from Roman and Greek sources alone, without any Arab intervention.

Modern Oriental studies have proved the falsity of this historical propaganda, although the latter is still widely believed by the general public. Unfortunately, a great part of the educational world still adheres to these ancient taboos and the period of some five or six centuries which separates the decline of Rome from the Norman invasion of England is omitted from school curricula and from public examinations. As is always the case, this falsification of history for propaganda purposes has injured ourselves more than anyone else, and has been largely responsible for the many political errors which our governments have committed in the Middle East in the last sixty years.

The history of "progress", the rise of man from a primitive state to his modern condition, is a fascinating story. The interest is lost, however, when the continuity is concealed by the omission of periods of several centuries and the presentation of bits and pieces of history, gathered from here and there, in accordance with our own emotional prejudices or our national vanity.

*   *   *

The Arab blockade not only destroyed the material prosperity but also the culture and learning of the West, which was reduced to poverty and ignorance, while the Arabs themselves continued to advance in knowledge and wealth. When the Muslims conquered Spain, Sicily and southern Italy, they established in those countries their own high standards of refined living and profound scholarship.

When the tide turned and Christendom reconquered Spain, the Balearics, Sicily, Italy and Crete, these Muslim communities were the means of once more spreading science, scholarship and culture to the West. Thus the Arabs first destroyed the civilization of the West and then replenished it.

Were the Arabs then mere carriers, who inherited the culture of Greece and Rome and then gave it back to Europe? Only partially so. They did indeed preserve the writings of the ancient Greeks and pass them on to Europe in Arabic, to be translated into Latin. In addition, however, they added a greater or a lesser contribution to every form of knowledge which passed through their hands.

Their most outstanding performance was probably in the field of mathematics, in which they introduced our present system of writing units, tens, hundreds and thousands and so on. Modern mathematics, and thus modern science, could never have been discovered if the cumbrous Roman way of writing numbers had remained in use. Having introduced those numerals which we still call Arabic, the Arabs went on to invent logarithms, algebra and trigonometry.

In the same manner, they studied the medical writings of the Greeks and improved upon their knowledge and their methods. Arab medical treatises remained standard textbooks for students in Europe for centuries. In botany, geography, natural history, zoology and other minor sciences, they were centuries ahead of Europe.

Their manufactures were far in advance of those of the West. Their textiles, silk, embroideries, glassware, weapons and metalwork were immensely superior to anything Europe could produce. They introduced the use and manufacture of paper to the West.

Yet, in all their arts, sciences and manufacturing skills, they inherited their knowledge. It is true that if they received ten talents they added to them ten talents more. Nevertheless these branches of knowledge had originated elsewhere and were to be inherited and yet further improved upon in Europe after the Arab decline. They ran but one lap in the relay race of knowledge—they snatched the torch of learning from their predecessors and when they fell, they passed it on to those who followed them.

But in one direction, the Arabs made an entirely original and unique contribution to thought—they introduced Europe to romance. The fact that the word "Arab" covers a great many different races has already been explained.[1] Western historians, while at times obliged to admit the extraordinary contributions to science and the arts which we owe to the Arab imperial age, sometimes point out that the intellectuals concerned were not of Arabian origin. This statement is, at least partly, true. The brilliant intellects were Syrians (perhaps of Greek descent), Persians, Indians or Spaniards, though it is only just to give some credit to the Arabians, who had built the splendid imperial structure which housed the authors, the doctors and the scientists.

In the field of poetry and romance, however, it was the people of the Arabian peninsula who were the innovators. The tribesmen of Arabia had always been passionate devotees of poetry, even though most of them were illiterate. Rhyming verse, unknown to the Greeks and Latins, was brought by them to Europe.

More important, however, than poetical forms was the Arabian idea of honour. The desert peninsula had always been too poor to support a government and each tribe enjoyed independence. Inevitably the interests of different tribes sometimes clashed, giving rise to wars. But nomadic tribes had no cities, lands or houses to be conquered. Their only property was their flocks, which could be raided,

[1] Introduction, page 13.

but which the owners could always raid back. Such circumstances did not make for "total war". No Arab tribe wished to destroy its rivals. Waged under such conditions, wars became little more than a dangerous sport.

Apart from human enemies, the great open spaces of the desert made survival difficult. The sparsity of the population meant that men were often obliged to cross wide tracts of desert alone, threatened by tribal enemies, wild beasts, hunger and thirst. Only men of outstanding character and individuality could survive.

In the crowded delta of Egypt or the streets of a modern city, men are constantly surrounded by thousands of human beings and rarely have to act for themselves. The bedouin, on the other hand, was completely self-reliant and ready to take a personal initiative. His principal object in war was to win honour for himself by personal acts of heroism.

This ideal of personal honour had its advantages and its drawbacks but it was entirely distinctive and peculiar to the nomads of Arabia. On the one hand, it prevented dishonourable actions, treachery and ruthlessness. It would cause modern war, with its bombing of open cities, its poison gas and its liquid fire and napalm, to be regarded with intense horror and disgust. But it made the bedouin headstrong, hard to discipline and lacking in communal spirit.

While the Syrian, conquered by the Arabs, settled down to intellectual pursuits, the Arabian tribesmen swept on to Spain on the wave of conquest. In Andalus, he established a régime which incorporated his intense sensitivity to personal honour, his jealousy of rivals leading to frequent challenges and civil wars, and his flamboyant love of glory, romance and poetry.

His code of chivalry, retained by the Spaniards for centuries after the fall of Granada, passed over into France and to England, where it ultimately formed the basis of our codes of sport and fair play. It crossed the Atlantic with the *conquistadors* and permeated the thinking of New Spain.

The extraordinary variety of races which constituted the Arab Empire thus enabled one group to bequeath to humanity many brilliant legacies of the intellect, while another branch spread the quixotic and romantic ideas of chivalrous love and the generous rivalry of honourable enemies. Had such ideas survived to our own times, they might have done something to refine and elevate the savage and primitive brutality of modern war.

*   *   *

The study, even if brief and superficial, of long periods of history has also a philosophical value. The peoples of Europe and North America today believe themselves to be immensely superior to all previous nations recorded in history. This supercilious attitude inspires them with the belief that the history of the past has no lessons for them and that a knowledge of physics or mechanics is of more "practical use" than a study of the vicissitudes of mankind.

Physical science itself has achieved its modern spectacular advances by a basically simple method, namely the execution of a great number of experiments and the careful observation and tabulation of the results observed. When a sufficient number of accurate records has been accumulated, a theory can be formulated and eventually a law deduced.

But while, by these methods, we have transformed the material conditions of our lives, we have made no progress whatever in the art of human government. Treatises on the subject written more than two thousand years ago are in advance of many of the systems still employed today. The indifference we show towards the art of government is increasingly dangerous in proportion to the advance of physical science, which provides the discontented with ever more lethal instruments wherewith to vent their resentment on their fellow-men. Perhaps never before in human history has so large a proportion of mankind been fired with so much indignation against the governments which control their own or other countries.

It is remarkable that in an age claiming to be scientific, we never think of investigating the experiments in government carried out by our predecessors or the results which they obtained. In politics we prefer to adhere to our narrow, individual prejudices rather than to study the recorded conclusions of those who have done similar experiments in the past.

*   *   *

It so happens that the Arab Empire (all knowledge of which has been systematically concealed from us) carried out a considerable number of experiments which are extremely relevant to our own situation today. It lasted at its greatest political strength for some two hundred and thirty years, almost exactly the length of the life of the British Empire. It enjoyed complete command of the sea and it earned its wealth by commerce with India and the Far East.

After two hundred years of power, when it appeared to be at the pinnacle of its glory, it tired of ruling distant peoples. Haroon al

Rasheed voluntarily gave dominion status to Ifriqiya and his son, Mamoon, did the same for Khurasan.

When the empire commenced to break up and economic decline set in, the people did not work harder to atone for the loss of trade— on the contrary, in Baghdad they introduced a five-day week. A welfare state was inaugurated similar to our own, with free medical treatment, free hospitals, free university education and government grants to students. It would appear as if, at the beginning of its period of power, an imperial race scatters all over the world, full of initiative and the love of adventure. In its later life, however, a reaction sets in and the pendulum swings to the opposite extreme.

At this stage, the people become purely inward-looking. All interest in the empire is lost and the nation's attention is focussed only on its own domestic affairs. As there are still reserves of wealth which have survived from the great days, lavish expenditure is incurred on social services, on education and on humanitarian projects. But with the decline in the national status, the accumulated wealth of the past is soon dissipated. At first, an attempt is made to maintain social expenditure by increasing taxes and devaluing the currency. But these subterfuges only increase the disease, the welfare state has to be abandoned and an increasingly low standard of living must be accepted. Far from being a wonderful modern concept, the welfare state may well be a regular and recurrent feature of great nations in decline.

Another interesting phenomenon of the Muslim Empire was the emergence of women into public life. Tenth-century writers in Baghdad state that women in their time had become lawyers, doctors, officials and university professors. This also seems to have been a temporary phase, for the next stage in the national decline was a breakdown in law and order, accompanied by an increase of banditry, rioting, and political *coups d'état*. Possibly the multiplication of acts of violence made it inadvisable for women any longer to go out to work unescorted and obliged them to remain at home.

While the life history of the Arab Empire seems thus to bear an extraordinary resemblance to our own, the same factors are perceptible to a greater or a lesser degree in all the empires recorded in history. Our ignorance alone allows us not only to repeat the identical errors committed by our predecessors, but also loudly to proclaim as innovations the same ideas that have so often been tried out by other nations in the past.

History, thoughtfully studied, can provide a touchstone which can be used to test the validity of the beliefs and the prejudices of our times. It is the fashion today, for example, to state that all races are "equal". It would certainly be blasphemy for us to claim that they are not equal before God, but our ideas of equality in other respects are extremely confused. They lead us, for example, to prescribe our own political institutions, as they are today, as a panacea for the poverty of some distant nation, largely illiterate, living in the jungle thousands of miles away. To criticize such a suggestion is to draw down on oneself the supercilious remark, "I believe all nations to be equal, even if you do not."

Many of these errors are due to neglect of the element of time, which is revealed by the study of history. Nations can, in many respects, be compared to individuals, who begin their lives in ignorance and in innocence, without strength and without possessions. Gradually they grow in experience, in knowledge and in wealth, until, in the prime of life, they may win the loyalty and the admiration of all who know them.

But all too soon they pass their peak. Physical effort becomes exhausting, mental concentration grows difficult, receptivity to new ideas is lost and the memory begins to fail. Yet we cannot say that, as a human being, a child or an old man is of less value than a young man. In most respects, however, they cannot be said to be equal. An old man is inferior to a youth at physical exertion, but superior to him in experience or in wealth.

The application of the historical time element to the different branches of the human race gives us a more realistic pattern than either the claim that all nations are equal or the converse belief that our own is superior to all others. Races, like people, are born, grow up, become strong and powerful, then weaken and waste away.

The Assyrians, the Persians, the Greeks, the Romans and the Arabs, each in their turn grew strong, wise, brave and cultured. Then, one after another, they became old and weak and decayed. The Greeks, the Romans and the Arabs were, at one time, as rich, as enterprising and as civilized as Victorian Britain. Today they are leaders no longer. Britain herself, in her turn, has fallen from the high estate she but recently enjoyed. We are no more entitled today to regard the Persians, the Greeks or the Arabs as "inferior", than the Americans or the Russians are to say the same of the British. Our varying capabilities are largely a matter of age.

It is a sobering thought to realize that when a great nation loses its pre-eminence, it does not merely drop back into second or third place. In most cases, it ceases to exist as a political entity. The Greeks, for example, who led the world for some three centuries, lost their independence for the ensuing two thousand years. After the fall of Rome, Italy remained only a geographical expression for fifteen centuries.

There may here be some factor of exhaustion. To be a leading nation for three or four centuries is no sinecure. The effort needed, the heavy drain imposed on the best types of citizens and the loss of the most devoted and courageous in wars or in pioneering, leave the master race permanently impoverished. These losses may become increasingly damaging as the national decline continues and many citizens, impatient at the humiliation of their country, migrate to other states.

Apart from the casualties caused by wars, pioneering and emigration, national decadence is probably largely attributable to too long a duration of wealth and power. The nation gradually, but unconsciously, assumes that pre-eminence is automatically its due, without any obligation to toil or struggle.

A surprising number of empires have endured for some two hundred to two hundred and fifty years. The Assyrians lasted from 860 B.C. to 626 B.C., two hundred and thirty years. The Persians from 538 B.C. to 330 B.C., or two hundred and eight years. The Greeks, Alexander and his successors, from 330 B.C. to about 100 B.C., two hundred and thirty years. The Arabs from A.D. 634 to A.D. 861, or two hundred and twenty-seven years. The Spaniards from 1556 to 1800, two hundred and forty-four years. The Ottomans were a great and virile empire from the accession of Murad I in 1359 to the death of Sulaiman the Magnificent in 1566, two hundred and seven years. The British Empire may be said to have endured from 1700 to 1930, two hundred and thirty years.

It is not desired to insist on rigid numbers, for many outside factors influence the fates of great nations. Nevertheless, the resemblance between the lives of so many and such varied empires is extremely striking, and is obviously entirely unconnected with the development of those mechanical devices of which we are so proud.

The explanation of this uniformity would appear to lie in the field of human psychology rather than of electronics. Eight or nine generations seem to be sufficient to change the hardy and enterprising pioneers into the idle and querulous citizens of the welfare state.

A further point of interest arising from the study of Arab history is the similarity between the periods of survival of the successor dynasties. The Samanids in East Persia lasted from 875 to 999, or one hundred and twenty-four years. The Buwaihids from 945 to 1055, one hundred and ten years. The Seljuqs of Persia from 1055 to 1156 (the death of Sultan Sanjar), one hundred and one years. The Ayoubids from 1169 to 1250, or eighty-one years. The Muwahhids from 1129 to 1214, or eighty-five years.

In brief, the life of a dynasty, the rise of which was due to the outstanding personality of its founder—not to a national expansion—is in the vicinity of a hundred years, or four generations. This period is about one half that required for the rise and decline of a whole nation.

Interesting results might be obtained from research into the family histories of the descendants of great industrialists, merchants and millionaires. In some cases, at least, the third generation from the builder of the family fortunes seems to show the first signs of idleness and incompetence. In their case, as in that of minor oriental dynasties, four generations transform the vigorous and enterprising founder of the business into the languid and frivolous—or at least unenterprising—heir.

These considerations should broaden our views and replace our arrogance by humility. How wrong we are to sneer at the Persians, the Greeks, the Italians or the Arabs, who, one after the other, built up the structure of civilization which we inherited. Soon we ourselves will have joined them in retirement and will have become an object of contempt to our younger successors.

A further comparison with human life may be seen in the fact that, as far as our historical records go, no nation has ever been young twice. All those peoples which, throughout history, have for a time been the leaders of mankind, are now in comparative weakness. We should regard them with gratitude and veneration, as we do the great men of the past, who once formed the glory of our respective countries.

It may be objected, perhaps, that, if no nation can be great twice, the time will come when all the races of the world are old and decadent and incapable of leadership. A closer scrutiny, however, will show us that, in fact, nations, like individuals, continually combine together to give birth to new generations of peoples. Conquests and migrations produce new mixtures and compounds, which often rapidly take the lead and present to the world fresh and original national personalities.

The Arabs were themselves, in their day, an example of this process. The warlike, romantic and poetic tribesmen of Arabia mingled with the pseudo-Greek intellectuals of Syria, the sturdy Berbers of the Atlas and the Romans and Goths of Spain, to produce original and fertile combinations. Today, the United States is the most prominent example of a new national personality, born as the child of older races.

Yet it would be an over-simplification to visualize the nations of the world as all alike, save that some are old and some are young. For every race, like every human being, has original and distinct characteristics and possesses a number of peculiar qualities, not quite identical with any other. One may be supreme in the field of art, another may have taught mankind respect for law and order, a third is pre-eminently gifted with romance and imagination, or with mathematical skill or business acumen.

This factor explains the necessity for regular changes of leadership, for, if one race were to remain too long in supreme power, the particular qualities which it happened to possess would become over-emphasized throughout humanity. Thus, for example, a paramount race which has laid particular emphasis on personal freedom may need to be followed by one which is peculiar for its insistence on authority and discipline, in order that the general balance of human growth may be preserved.

*   *   *

Reference has already been made to those persons who claim that history has no lessons for us because former empires did not possess spacecraft, jet fighters or other such mechanical or electronic devices. There is here a considerable confusion of thought. History teaches us lessons in human nature, which has not changed. The inhabitants of the world today are moved by the same passions of greed, cruelty, love of power, self-sacrifice, heroism and fanaticism as were the Romans and the Arabs. It is the manner of operation of these emotions which we learn from history.

The ancient Assyrian Empire lasted the same number of years as the British Empire, although the Assyrians travelled on foot and fought with spears and bows and arrows. Yet the Assyrians began as aggressive fighters and went on to acquire great wealth. The last King of Assyria was more interested in his library than in his army. Thus the psychological and moral rise and decline of nations is the same, regardless of weapons, means of transport or material surroundings.

Later empires, owing to improvements in navigation, extended beyond the seas, but the effect of wealth and power on the thoughts and characters of the "imperialists" remained the same. Today the word "empire" has an unpopular and old-fashioned sound. We may, therefore, refer to the same phenomenon as "paramount nations". Subject to this change of name, the process of rise and decline seems to be unaltered.

In recent times, it is true, new methods of achieving power have begun to emerge. The first of these is the power of high finance. When we are told, for example, that in the First World War, the same group of financiers was providing funds for the war efforts of the United States, Britain, Germany and revolutionary Russia, we inevitably begin to wonder. The power wielded by a small number of financiers, however, must necessarily be secret for if the peoples knew of it, they could destroy the money-manipulators.

A more obvious modern development is the power of the mass media of publicity, such as the press, television, broadcasting, the cinema and book publishing. If a number of these media come under the influence of any group, whole nations can be "brain-washed" in the direction desired by the manipulators. In former ages, governments kept order by the use of armed force, with which they applied coercion to the discontented. To control the opinions of the public by influencing the media of publicity is both a less painful and (to the future of humanity) a more dangerous method. It is useless to say that intelligent people will think for themselves. Nobody can, in fact, remain unaffected by the mass information directed at them by modern publicity.

But if governments can "brain-wash" their citizens by these means, in "free" countries the same influence can be brought to bear secretly by large financial interests, who exercise a controlling influence over the press, the television and the cinema. Elected governments can become helpless puppets in the hands of such concealed, but powerful forces. The same secret groups can undermine the morals, destroy the patriotism or ridicule the religion of any nation, the moral fibre of which may resist their ambitions.

None of these manœuvres are really new. We have already seen that the Abbasids destroyed the Umaiyids by subversive propaganda in the modern style. But, if the idea of subversion is old, the modern expansion of the press, broadcasting, the cinema and publishing have immensely increased the power of subversion and indoctrination.

In brief, the motives and the psychology of mankind are unchanged and can be observed again and again in history. The heads of modern governments and the magnates of high finance are driven onwards by the same lust for power as inspired the Roman Emperors or the Mongol Khakans. And once that power is achieved, it corrupts those who wield it until they weaken and collapse and are replaced by new and more energetic seekers after wealth and domination.

We are terrified, in our moments of weakness, at the possibility of extermination in a nuclear war. Yet the prospect of the destruction of our minds and our morals by mass brain-washing media is in a way even more alarming. Yet there are reserves of spiritual strength available to men, sufficient to enable them to resist. Only by a real revival of spiritual life can these subversive machinations be defeated.

*   *   *

These brief and inadequate remarks may have suggested something of the fascination of the study of human history if we can so far transcend our narrow prejudices as to view these great processes impartially and as a continuous whole. To be able to consider these mighty movements as part of a vast and benevolent plan to carry forward the whole human race may even do something to ease the fear, the pain and the despair which we tend to feel in our personal or our national humiliations.

"We are so busy rushing about," writes Evelyn Underhill,[2] "so immersed in what we call practical things, that we seldom pause to realize the mysterious truth of our situation: how little we know that really matters, how completely our modern knowledge leaves the deeps of our existence unexplored."

To some, the majesty and the harmony of these movements, like many other natural processes which we so easily take for granted, may suggest the masterly planning of the Mind of God, for the manifestation of which the whole creation still groans and suffers in pain, awaiting its perfection and its deliverance from this earthly bondage,

[2] Evelyn Underhill, *The School of Charity.*

A Short Bibliography

NOTE Only works in English or French are shown. For Arabic works of reference, see *The Lost Centuries* by J. B. Glubb.

Ambroise *Histoire de la Guerre Sainte* (Eng. trans. M. J. Hubert "The Crusade of Richard Lion Heart")
Arabshah, Ahmad ibn *Tamerlane* (Eng. trans. J. H. Sanders)
Arberry, A. J. *The Holy Qoran*
Atiya, A. S. *Crusade, Commerce and Culture*
— *The Crusade in the Later Middle Ages*
Battuta, ibn *Travels* (Eng. trans. H. A. R. Gibb)
Bell, G. *Amurath to Amurath*
— *The Desert and the Sown*
Benjamin of Tudela *Early Travels in Palestine* (ed. T. Wright)
Berard, V. *Le Sultan, L'Islam et les Puissances*
— *La Revolution Turque*
Boyle, J. A. *History of the World Conqueror* by Ala al Deen al Juwaini
Bréhier, Louis *Vie et Mort de Byzance*
Brion, Marcel *Tamerlan*
Brockelmann, C. *A History of the Islamic Peoples*
Browne, E. G. *A Literary History of Persia*
Bury, J. B. *A History of the Eastern Roman Empire*
Butler, A. J. *The Arab Conquest of Egypt*
Cambridge Mediaeval History
Conder, C. R. *The Latin Kingdom of Jerusalem*
Creasy, S. E. S. *History of the Ottoman Turks*
Davis, E. J. *The Invasion of Egypt by Louis IX*
Dermenghen, E. *The Life of Muhammad*
De Slane *Résumé de l'Histoire des Croisades* (Fr. trans. of Arabic of Abulfeda)
Devizes, Richard of *Concerning the Deeds of Richard I, King of England*
Dozy, R. *The Moslems in Spain*
Encyclopedia of Islam

Fagnan, E. *Histoire des Almohades* (Fr. trans. of Arabic of Marakishi)

Finlay, G. *History of the Byzantine Empire*

Gaudefroye-Demombynes *La Syrie à l'Epoque des Mamelouks* (Fr. trans. of Arabic of Al Qalqashandi)

Gaudefroye-Demombynes et Platonov *Le Monde Musulman et Byzantin jusqu'aux Croisades*

Gibb, H. A. R. *The Arabs*

— *The Damascus Chronicle* (Trans. of Al Qalanisi)

Gibbon, E. *Decline and Fall of the Roman Empire*

Gibbon, H. A. *The Foundation of the Ottoman Empire*

Gilman, A. *The Saracens*

Glubb, J. B. *The Great Arab Conquests*

— *The Empire of the Arabs*

— *The Course of Empire*

— *The Lost Centuries*

— *Britain and the Arabs*

Grousset, René *Histoire des Croisades* (3 volumes)

Grunebaum, von *Mediaeval Islam*

Guillaume, A. *A Life of Muhammad* (Trans. of Ibn Ishaq)

Hell, Joseph *The Arab Civilization* (Eng. trans. S. Khuda Bukhsh)

Hitti, P. K. *A History of the Arabs*

Houdas et Marçais *Les Traditions Islamiques*

Howorth, Sir Henry *A History of the Mongols*

Huart *Histoire des Arabes*

Hughes *A Dictionary of Islam*

Jubair, ibn *Travels* (Eng. trans. R. J. C. Broadhurst)

Julien, C. A. *Histoire de l'Afrique du Nord*

Kirk, G. E. *A Short History of the Middle East*

Kremer, von *The Orient under the Caliphs*

Lane-Poole, S. *The Story of Cairo*

— *A History of Egypt in the Middle Ages*

— *The Moors in Spain*

— *The Muhammadan Dynasties*

— *Saladin*

Lawrence, T. E. *Revolt in the Desert*

Lévi-Provençal, E. *Islam d'Occident*

— *La Civilization Arabe en Espagne*

Lewis, Bernard *The Arabs in History*

Margoliouth *Muhammad and the Rise of Islam*

Mazahéri, Aly *La Vie Quotidienne des Musulmans au Moyen Age*

Mez, Adam *The Renaissance of Islam*

Montgomery-Watt, W. *Muhammad at Mecca*
Muir, Sir William *The Caliphate, Its Rise, Decline and Fall*
— *Annals of The Early Caliphate*
— *Life of Muhammad*
— *The Mameluke Slave Dynasty of Egypt*
Nabih Amin Faris (Editor) *The Arab Heritage*
Nasir i Khusrau *Diary of a Journey through Syria and Palestine* (Eng. trans. Guy le Strange)
Nicholson, R. A. *A Literary History of the Arabs*
Ockley, Simon *History of the Saracens*
Ohsson, Baron d' *Histoire des Mongols*
O'Leary, de Lacy *Arabia before Muhammad*
Osborn, R. D. *Islam under the Arabs*
Pirenne, Henri *Muhammad and Charlemagne*
Popper, William *A History of Egypt 1382–1469* (Eng. trans. of Ibn Taghri Birdi)
Quatremère *Histoire des Mongols de Perse* (Fr. trans. of Rasheed al Deen)
— *Histoire des Sultans Mamlouks de l'Egypte* (Fr. trans. of Maqrizi, Kitab al Suluk)
Revue de l'Orient Latin *Collection of Historians of the Crusades*
Runciman, Steven *A History of the Crusades* (3 volumes)
Scott, S. P. *The Moorish Empire in Europe*
Setton, K. M. (Editor) *History of the Crusades*
Smail, R. C. *Crusading Warfare*
Strange, Guy le *Baghdad during the Abbasid Caliphate*
— *Palestine under the Moslems*
— *Lands of the Eastern Caliphate*
Sykes, P. M. *A History of Persia*
Toynbee, A. S. and Kirkwood, K. P. *Turkey*
Tyre, William of *A History of Deeds done beyond the Seas* (Eng. trans. Babcock and Krey)
Usama ibn Munqidh *An Arab Gentleman in the Period of the Crusade* (Eng. trans. P. K. Hitti)
Wellhausen, J. *The Arab Kingdom and its Fall*
— *Muhammad in Medina*
Wittek, P. *The Rise of the Ottoman Empire*

NOTE The bibliography is chiefly historical, this book being a history. Since 1945, innumerable books have been written about Arabs, Zionism, Oil and other such subjects.

Index

Index

Aadhid, Khalif (Fatimid, of Egypt), 143, 172, 173–4, 180
Aadil, Al, Sultan (Ayoubid, of Egypt), 182–3, 185, 192, 204, 210
Aadil II, Al, King (Ayoubid, of Egypt), 182
Aamir, Abdulla ibn, 65
Aamir, Khalif (Fatimid, of Egypt), 143, 163
Aamir, Muhammad ibn abi, *see* Mansoor, Wazeer
Aasi, Amr ibn al, 56–60, 62, 64, 68–9, 72
Aasi, Saad ibn al, 64, 65
Abagha, Il Khan (Mongol, of Persia), 213, 215, 228
Abbas, Uncle of Muhammad, 27, 74, 91, 92, 141; *See also* Abbasids
Abbas, Muhammad ibn Ali ibn Abdulla ibn, Khalif, *see* Saffah, Khalif
Abbasa, Sister of Haroon al Rasheed, 106
Abbasids, 92, 97, 138, 140–2, 144, 299
rise of, 91–9, 101
orientalization of, 93–4, 96
in Baghdad, 94, 97, 103–6, 226
and Spain, 96
army of, 99, 103, 107, 113, 115–23, 149, 208
administration of, 99
and Byzantium, 101, 104, 106–7, 111, 112–13, 115
culture of, 109–11, 124
decline of, 115–23, 204
Turks control, 118–23, 149, 187, 204
Buwaihids control, 120, 126, 187
and Samanids, 124, 126
and Ghazharids, 126
and Fatimids, 138, 140, 142, 144, 146, 148
Indian Summer of, 187, 192–3, 194
See also Baghdad
Abbas ibn Temeem, 172
Abbas the Great, Shah (Safavid, of Persia), 234, 243
Abdul Azeez, Sultan (Ottoman), 245–6, 259
Abdul Azeez, Umar ibn, Khalif, *see* Umar ibn Abdul Azeez, Khalif
Abdul Aziz ibn Saud, King (of Saudi Arabia), 255, 272, 275, 280, 287
Abdul Hameed I, Sultan (Ottoman), 245, 259
Abdul Hameed II, Sultan (Ottoman), 246, 252–3, 255, 257, 258, 259, 273
Abdul Karim, 269, 271
Abdulla, son of Abu Bekr, 33
Abdulla, Ameer (Umaiyid, of Spain), 148, 152
Abdulla, King (of Jordan), 273, 287
Abdulla al Saffah, Khalif (Abbasid, of Kufa), 91, 92, 93, 97, 98
Abdulla ibn Umar ibn al Khattab, 43
Abdulla ibn Zubair, Khalif (in Mecca), 77, 78, 79, 82, 83
Abdul Majeed I, Sultan (Ottoman), 245, 259
Abdul Malik at Wadi Makhazin, Sultan (of Morocco), 267
Abdul Malik, Hisham ibn, Khalif, *see* Hisham ibn Abdul Malik, Khalif
Abdul Malik ibn Merwan, Khalif (Umaiyid, of Damascus), 74, 77–80, 82, 83, 87, 88
Abdul Malik, Maslama ibn, 81
Abdul Malik, Sulaiman ibn, Khalif, *see* Sulaiman ibn Abdul Malik, Khalif
Abdul Malik, Waleed I ibn, Khalif, *see* Waleed I ibn Abdul Malik, Khalif

Abdul Malik, Yezeed II ibn, Khalif, *see* Yezeed II ibn Abdul Malik, Khalif
Abdul Mumin ibn Ali, 188–90, 192, 193, 260
Abdul Muttalib, 27, 28, 74, 92
Abdul Qadir, 265, 271
Abdul Rahman I, Ameer (Umaiyid, of Spain), 74, 96–7, 103, 148, 152
Abdul Rahman II, Ameer (Umaiyid, of Spain), 148, 152
Abdul Rahman III, Khalif (Umaiyid, of Spain), 142, 148–50, 152
Abdul Rahman ibn Auf, 63–4
Abdul Wad, Beni, tribe, 260, 262
Abid Menaf, 27, 74, 92, 141
Abid Shams, 27, 74, 92, 141
Abs tribe, 43
Abu Abdulla, 140, 142
Abu Bekr, Khalif (First), 30, 33–4, 36, 40, 42–3, 45–8, 50, 54, 62–3
Abu Lulu, 63
Abu Muslim, 91, 93–4, 96, 97, 109
Abu Saeed, Il Khan (Mongol, of Persia), 215, 217, 228
Abu Sofian, 27, 34–5, 39, 41, 64, 69, 70, 74
Abu Sukhair, 52
Abu Talib, 27, 28–9, 30, 33, 41, 74, 92, 141
Abu Ubaid, 50, 51
Abu Ubaida, 42
Abu Yaqoob Yusuf, Khalif (Muwahhideen, of North Africa), 189–90, 193
Abu Yezeed, 142, 144
Abyssinia, 33
Acquitaine, 179
Acre, 122, 157, 163, 166, 176, 178–9, 180, 181, 183, 199, 201, 202, 208, 213, 216, 228, 240, 241, 244
Aden, 18
Adharbaijan, 90, 197, 207, 210, 226
Adhud al Dowla, 126, 137, 144
Adrianople, 222
Afamiya, 169
Afdhal, Al, King (Ayoubid, of Damascus), 182
Afdhal, Al, Wazeer (of Egypt), 143, 146, 153, 158, 163, 168
Affan, Othman ibn, Khalif, *see* Othman ibn Affan, Khalif
Afghanistan, 187
people of, 235
Africa, 16
Central, 17
East, 24, 104, 288
North, *see* North Africa
Agadir, 266, 267, 269
Aghlab, Ibrahim ibn al, *see* Ibrahim ibn al Aghlab
Aghlabids:
rule Ifriqiya, 104, 107, 111, 138–40, 152
conquer Sicily, 140
fall of, 142
Ahad, Al, 258
Ahmad al Mansoor, Sultan, *see* Mansoor, Ahmad al, Sultan
Ahmad Pasha, 235–6, 237
Ahmed ibn Ismail, 124
Ahmed ibn Tulun, 119, 123
Ahmed Pasha al Jazzár, 240, 244

Aibek, 204–5, 207, 210
Ain al Tamr, 46
Ain Jaloot, Battle of, 208, 210
Ain Murad, Battle of, 169
Aisha, wife of Muhammad, 36, 40, 41, 68
Ajnadain, Battle of, 47, 54
Ala al Deen Muhammad, Shah (of Khuwarizm),
    187, 192, 193, 194
Ala ibn Mughith, 96
Alarcos, Battle of, 190, 192
Albania, 250
Albanians, 230, 242
Albistan, 213
Alcantara, 190
Aleppo, 16, 23, 238
    Hamdanids in, 122, 127
    Ibn Mirdas in, 127, 132
    Seljuqs rule, 132, 134, 158, 160, 163, 164, 166,
        171, 175
    Ayoubids in, 182, 202
    Mongols destroy, 208, 210
    Tamerlane sacks, 224–6, 228
    Ottoman Turks and, 227, 231, 233, 234, 235, 246,
        257
    railway and, 257
Alexander the Great, 16, 46, 135, 296
Alexandria, 59, 142, 220, 241
Alexius Commenus, Emperor (of Byzantium), 133,
    137, 154, 156, 157, 161, 163, 167
Alfonso VI, King (of Leon and Castile), 151, 152
Alfonso VIII, King (of Castile), 190–3
Algeria, 72, 246, 258, 262, 265, 266, 268, 270, 271
    See also Algiers, North Africa
Algiers, 144, 151, 188, 262–5, 266, 270
    See also Algeria, North Africa
Alhambra, 191
Ali, Abdul Mumin ibn, 188–90, 192, 193, 260
Ali, Abu Jafar ibn Muhammad ibn, Khalif, see
    Mansoor, Khalif
Ali Bey, 241
Ali, Hasan ibn, see Hasan ibn Ali
Ali, Husain ibn, Bey (of Tunisia), 266, 270
Ali ibn abi Talib, Khalif (Umaiyid, of Damascus),
    27, 30, 33–4, 41–3, 63–70, 73, 74, 75, 77, 90, 92,
    93, 94
    descendants of, 92, 93, 101, 103, 140, 141, 268
Aliids, 91, 92
Ali Ridha Pasha, 237
Allenby, General, 273
Alp Arslan, Sultan (Seljuq, of Persia), 128, 132–3,
    137
Altai Mountains, 194
Amalric, see Amaury
Amaury I, King (of Jerusalem), 159, 172–4, 180, 183
Amaury II, King (of Cyprus and Jerusalem), 159,
    183, 193
Ameen ibn Haroon Al Rasheed, Khalif (Abbasid, in
    Baghdad), 92, 105, 108, 111
America, Central, 192
    South, 18, 192, 292
    See also United States of America
American University of Beirut, 252–3
Ammar ibn Yasir, 62–3
Amorium, 115
Amr ibn al Aasi, 56–60, 62, 64, 68–9, 72
Amr ibn Leith, 124
Anatolia, 251
Anbar, 45–6
Andalus, see Spain
Aneza tribe, 45, 235, 242
Anqara, 115, 226
    Battle of, 226
Antioch, 48–9, 122, 171, 211, 228, 238
    Crusaders and, 157–8, 160, 161, 164, 166, 167,
        169, 171, 175, 179, 183, 201, 202, 211
Apostasy, the, 43, 45, 54
Apulia, 140
Aqaba, 273
Arab Empire,
    its extent, 13, 288

its disintegration, 13, 64, 105, 115, 118–19, 120,
    134–6, 163, 294–300
poetry in, 35–6, 105, 109–10, 291
early conquests of, 42–64, 135
orientalization of, 105, 135
culture of, 109–10, 134–6, 140, 190–2, 288–92
learning and science of, 108–10, 136, 288–92
brought Dark Ages to Europe, 135–6, 288–9
trade of, 135–6, 288
civilization reached Europe from, 109, 140, 179,
    288–92
chivalry and, 291–2
women in, 294
Arabia, 15–18, 21, 23–6, 30–45, 94, 119, 242, 253,
    280; see also Saudi Arabia
Arabi Pasha, 255
Arab League, 285, 287
Arab Legion of Jordan, 281, 283
Arab Peoples:
    who they are, 13–19, 55, 104, 243, 285–6
    chivalry of, 181, 286, 291–2
Aral Sea, 129
Arcadius, Emperor (of Byzantium), 21, 105
Arghoon, Il Khan (Mongol, of Persia), 215, 217, 228
Arish, Al, 57
Arles, 88
Armenia, 21, 49, 132, 197, 210; see also Armenians;
    Cilicia
Armenians, 156–7, 158, 163, 171, 185, 192, 197, 210,
    251; see also Armenia; Cilicia
Arsoof, 157
    Battle of, 178
Artah, 173
Artois, Comte d', 204
Arzila, 266, 267
Asad, Beni, tribe, 43, 127
Asia, 16
    Central, 81, 87, 194, 208–9, 224, 230, 288
    See also Asia Minor; China; Far East; India
Asia Minor, 15, 21, 55, 120, 122
    Persians in, 23, 29
    Abbasids and, 101, 107
    Seljuqs in, 128, 132–3, 134, 154, 156–7, 166, 168,
        174, 185, 211, 213, 222, 228
    Mongols and, 205, 210, 211, 213
    Ottoman Turks in, 220, 222, 242
    Tamerlane in, 226
    See also Iconium
Asim, 52
Asma, 33
Asqalon, 157, 173, 178, 179
Assyrian Empire, 295–6, 298
Astronomy, 133–4
Athir, ibn al, 172, 181, 188
Atlantic Ocean, 13, 72, 73, 85, 90, 110, 135, 144, 197,
    260, 288
Atlas Mountains, 18, 72, 95, 96, 138, 144, 188, 260,
    262, 264, 268–9, 298
Auf, Abdul Rahman ibn, 63–4
Australasia, 21, 251, 276
Austria, 250, 278, 279; see also Hungary
Autun, 88
Avempace, 190
Averroes, 190
Avicenna, 124
Awwam, Zubair ibn al, 59, 63, 66–7, 77
Ayoubids, 182, 185, 192, 194, 199, 201–2, 204–5,
    207–8, 210, 213, 297; see also Egypt; Saladin
Azeez, Khalif (Fatimid, of Egypt), 143, 145, 153
Azeez, Al, King (Ayoubid, of Aleppo), 182
Azeez, Al, King (Ayoubid, of Egypt), 182
Azemmour, 266, 267
Aziz ibn Rasheed, ruler (of Nejed), 253, 255, 275

Baalbek, 48
Babylon (Egypt), 57–9, 63
Babylon (Iraq), Battle of, 54
Badajoz, 151
Badees, Muizz ibn, 145–6, 148
Baghdad, 94, 97, 123, 131, 135, 144, 294
    Abbasids in, 94, 97, 103–6, 109, 113, 115–16,
        118–20, 142, 148, 187, 191–3, 204, 243

Baghdad—*cont.*
  culture and learning in, 109–10, 124, 136
  Mamoon's siege of, 108, 111
  Turks control, 118–23, 187, 204
  Buwaihids rule, 120, 123, 124, 126–7, 129, 131, 144, 146, 187, 297
  Seljuqs capture, 131–2, 135, 187, 226
  Mongols destroy, 205–7, 210, 217, 220, 226, 231
  Tamerlane sacks, 226, 228, 231
  Black Sheep tribe in, 231
  White Sheep tribe in, 231, 233
  Safavids and, 233–7, 243
  Ottoman Turks and, 233–7, 243, 245–6, 249–50
  "Mamlook" rule in, 237, 244
  railway and, 256
  British in, 279, 281
  coup d'état, 1941, 281, 287
Baikal, Lake, 194, 197
Bait al Deen, 240
Bajja, ibn, 190
Baldwin I, King (of Jerusalem), 158, 159, 160, 161, 163, 167, 168
Baldwin II, King (of Jerusalem), 159, 161, 163–4, 168
Baldwin III, King (of Jerusalem), 159, 164, 167, 168, 169, 171–2, 180
Baldwin IV, King (of Jerusalem), 159, 174–5, 180
Baldwin V, King (of Jerusalem), 159, 175, 180
Balearic Islands, 291
Balfour Declaration, 277–8, 287
Balkans, 245, 251, 252, 257, 258, 272, 287
Balkh, 65, 94, 124
Baltic Sea, 124
Barbarossa, Arooj, 262, 270
Barbarossa, Khair al Deen, Pasha, 262–3, 270
Barbary pirates, 263–4
Baring, Sir Evelyn, *see* Cromer, Lord
Barmecids, 103–6
Barqa, 72, 73, 79, 96, 145, 181
Barqooq, Malik al Dhahir, Sultan (Mamlook, of Egypt), 220, 224, 228
Basheer II al Shihabi, Prince (of Lebanon), 240, 244
Basil I, Emperor (of Byzantium), 120, 122–3
Basil II, Emperor (of Byzantium), 127, 137, 145
Basra, 55, 64–5, 66, 68, 70, 73, 78, 118, 233, 235, 256
Bayazid, Sultan (Ottoman), 221–2, 224, 226
Baybers the Bunduqdari, Sultan (Mamlook, of Egypt), 208, 210, 211, 213, 228
Bedr, Battle of, 35, 38, 39, 40, 51, 64
Bedr al Jamali, Wazeer (of Egypt), 143, 146, 153, 158, 168
Beersheba, 46
Beirut, 122, 157, 171, 176, 179, 183, 213, 238, 240, 252–3, 258
Beit Nuba, 178
Bekr ibn Wail, Beni, tribe, 45, 46, 47, 54
Bekr, the Su Bashi, 234
Belgium, 156
Belisarius, 21
Belqa, 46–7, 48
Berbers, 18, 72–3, 79, 80, 87–8, 90, 95–7, 103, 138, 140, 142, 144–5, 149, 151–3, 187–8, 192–3, 260, 262, 266–9, 298; *see also* North Africa
Bilbeis, 57, 173
Black Death, 219, 237
Black Sea, 107, 289
Black Sheep tribe, 231
Bohemond I, Prince (of Antioch), 156–7, 161, 167, 171
Bohemond III, Prince (of Antioch), 169, 173
Bohemond IV, Prince (of Antioch), and Count (of Tripoli), 211
Bohemond V, Prince (of Antioch), and Count (of Tripoli), 202
Bohemond VI, Prince (of Antioch), and Count (of Tripoli), 211, 213
Bone, 265
Bordeaux, 88
Bosnians, 230, 240
Bosphorus, 101, 106, 115, 133, 156
Bougie, *see* Boujaiya
Boujaiya, 138, 140, 148, 188, 265

Bourguiba, President (of Tunisia), 266
Bridge, Battle of the, 50–1, 54
Britain, 21, 135, 299
  Empire of, 136, 250, 293, 295–6, 298–9
  Middle East and, 227, 240–4, 246, 255–6, 258–9, 273, 275–9, 280–1, 283, 285, 287
  and Ireland, 250
  and Russia, 251–2
  and Ottoman Turks, 251–2, 275
  and Australia, 251, 276
  and Mediterranean, 251, 276
  in North Africa, 265, 269
  and India, 273, 276
  and World War II, 281
  and Arab League, 285
  See also England
Brusa, 237
Buda, 222
Budapest, 231
Buddhists, 163, 187
Bugha, 116
Bukhara, 72, 78, 94, 124, 126, 137, 194
Bulgarians, 187, 222, 230
Bulgars, 82
Burgos, 149
Burgundy, Duke of, 222
Bursuq, Bursuq ibn, 160
Busir, 93
Buwaib, Battle of, 51, 54
Buwaih, Ahmed ibn, 120, 123, 126, 137
Buwaihids, 120, 123, 124, 126–7, 129, 131, 137, 144, 146, 187, 297
Byzantine Empire, 18, 21–6, 28, 29, 54, 64
  and Persia, 39, 40, 46
  Moslems attack, 39, 45, 46–9, 63
  administration of, 56
  in Egypt, 57–9, 62, 119
  in North Africa, 72–3
  riches of, 84
  and Crusades, 154, 156, 161, 164, 169, 171
  Umaiyids and, 101
  Abbasids and, 101, 104, 106–7, 111–15, 120–3
  Military revival in 10th Century, 120, 122–3, 126–7
  and Syria, 122–3, 126–7, 145
  and Ghuzz, 132–3
  army of, 133
  and Sicily, 140
  and Asia Minor, 174
  and Ottoman Turks, 220, 222, 227, 230
  See also Constantinople
Byzantium, *see* Constantinople

Cadiz, 80
Caesarea, 57, 120, 213
Cairo, 126, 144
  Fatimids in, 126, 144–5, 148, 152–3
  Ayoubids in, 185, 201, 204–5
  Fifth Crusade and, 185
  Mamlooks in, 208, 211, 224–5, 230
  Ottoman Turks and, 227, 242
  Napoleon and, 241
  Albanians take, 242
  British in, 256, 259, 273, 280
  See also Egypt
Calabria, 140
Camel, Battle of the, 68–9
Camels, 23, 24
Canton, 105
Cape of Good Hope, 241, 255, 289
Carcasonne, 88
Carmathians, 119, 140, 149
  revolt of, 119, 122–3
Carthage, 72, 73, 79
Casablanca, 270
Caspian Sea, 120, 194, 197, 205, 224, 289
Castile, 149, 150, 151, 188, 190–1, 193
Catherine of Braganza, Queen (of England), 267
Catherine the Great, Empress (of Russia), 251
Caucasus, 23, 90, 211, 220, 237, 251
Central Asia, 81, 87, 194, 208–9, 224, 230, 288
Ceuta, 96, 142, 266

Chaldiran, Battle of, 227, 233
Charlemagne, Emperor (of Franks), 105, 148
Charles II, King (of England), 267
Charles V, Emperor (Holy Roman), 231, 262
China, 13, 21, 24, 85, 90, 109, 110, 135, 194
    Qutaiba ibn Muslim and, 81
    Emperor of, 81
    trade, 104–5, 124, 241, 288
    Khitan rule, 161
    Chin Tatars rule, 161
    Mongols and, 196, 197, 205, 211, 228
Chin Tatars, 161
Chosroes Parwiz, King (of Persia), 23, 29, 46
Christianity, 32
    Orthodox, 24, 26, 48, 57
    Monophysite, 24, 48, 57
    Nestorians, 269
    in Abyssinia, 33
    Attitude to war of, 36
    in Damascus, 48
    in Jerusalem, 49
    Arab attitude to, 56, 84–5, 135, 251
    in Egypt, 57, 59, 158, 219
    in Spain, 80–1, 148–52, 190–2, 260, 262, 268, 290
    persecuted, 116
    in Roman Empire, 135
    in Georgia, 224
    Ottomans and, 230–1, 237, 251–3
    in Lebanon, 240, 253
    in Greece, 251
    in Hungary, 251
    Presbyterians, 252
    in North Africa, 262–4
    Attitude to Moslem history of, 289–90
    See also Armenians; Crusades
Cilicia, 171, 176, 185, 192, 193, 197, 198, 201, 211;
    see also Taurus Mountains
Cilician Gates, 120
Circassians, 220, 226, 228
Clermont, 133
Committee of Union and Progress, 257–8, 272
Conrad III, King (of Germany), 166, 167, 198
Conrad IV, King (of Germany), 159, 198
Conradin, 198
Conrad of Montferrat, King (of Jerusalem), 159,
    176, 183, 193
Constance, Princess (of Antioch), 164, 169
Constance of Sicily, Empress (of Germany), 198–9
Constantine V, Emperor (of Byzantium), 101
Constantine VII, Emperor (of Byzantium), 122–3
Constantinople, 21, 24, 59, 63, 72, 81–2, 101, 104,
    106, 127, 133, 146, 156, 161, 166, 169, 171, 183,
    222, 227, 230, 289; see also Byzantine Empire;
    Istanbul
Consuegra, Battle of, 152
Cordova, 96, 149–51, 190–1
Corsairs, 263–4
Crete, 266, 290
Cromer, Lord, 255–6, 259, 281
Cromwell, Oliver, 50, 68
Crusades, 163
    Pope calls, 133, 137
    First, 138, 152, 154, 156–65, 167, 172
    People's, 156
    Second, 166–7, 169, 180, 198
    Third, 176–81, 183, 198
    Fourth, 183, 202
    Fifth, 183–5
    Sixth, 198–201, 210
    Seventh, 202–4, 210
    end of, 216–17
    See also Acre; Antioch; Edessa; Jerusalem;
    Tripoli
Ctesiphon, see Medain
Cuenca, Battle of, 152
Cyprus, 202, 280
    Moslems conquer, 64
    Byzantines reconquer, 122
    Renaud de Châtillon and, 169, 171
    Lusignans rule, 183, 216
    Frederick II and, 199
    and Egypt, 211, 219–20

Cyrencaia, 72
Cyrus, Patriarch, 57, 59

Dailamites, 120
Damanhur, 59
Damascus, 23, 26, 29, 34, 46–8, 51, 54, 55, 66, 68, 88
    Umaiyid capital, 73–5, 77–9, 81–2, 84–5, 87, 90,
    93, 98, 135, 243
    Carmathians occupy, 119
    Byzantines capture, 122
    Seljuqs in, 128, 134, 158, 160, 163, 164, 172, 173–4
    Fatimids and, 145
    Crusaders attack, 166
    Ayoubids and, 172–6, 181, 182, 199, 201–2, 204,
    207
    Mongols and, 207–8, 216, 217, 228
    Mamlooks and, 208, 213, 216, 230
    Tamerlane sacks, 225–6, 228
    Ottoman Turks rule, 227, 231, 238, 240, 245–6,
    258, 275
    Ahmad al Jazzar governs, 240
    railway and, 257
    British and, 276
    French in, 276, 279, 281, 287
    See also Syria
Damietta, 183–5, 202–4
Daneeth, Battle of, 160
Danube, River, 222
Daood, 128, 129
Darazi, Muhammad al, 146
Dardanelles, 72
Dark Ages, 136, 288–9
Daud Pasha, 237
Deen II, Fakhr al, Prince (of Lebanon), 240
Deen Mahmood, Noor al, King (of Aleppo), 166
    168, 169, 171, 172–4, 180
Deen Mani, Fakhr al, 231
Deen Muhammad, Ala al, Shah (of Khuwarizm),
    187, 192, 193, 194
de Gaulle, General, 265
Demavend, 205
Denmark, 178
Deraa, 47–9, 257, 273
Dhafir, Khalif (Fatimi, of Egypt), 143, 172
Dhahir, Khalif (Fatimi, of Egypt), 143, 146, 153
Dhahir, Al, Khalif (Abbasid, in Baghdad), 193
Dhahir, Al, King (Fatimi, of Aleppo), 182
Dhahir al Umar, 240
Dhirgam al Lakhmi, 172
Dhobian, tribe, 43
Diyarbekr, 158, 163, 217, 231, 233
Don Sebastian, King (of Portugal), 267
Dorylaeum, Battle of, 156, 167
Dowla, Adhud al, 126, 137, 144
Dowla, Ahmed ibn Buwaih, Muizz al, 120, 123, 126
    137
Dowla, Saif al, ibn Hamdan, 122, 123
Druzes, 146, 240, 253, 279
Duma, 47
Duqaq, King (of Damascus), 128, 158, 160
Dura Europus, 21

Edessa, 158, 160, 164–7, 169, 201, 208, 235
Edward I, King (of England), 213, 217
Egypt, 13, 15, 17–18, 21, 23, 24, 26, 28, 29, 93, 94,
    96, 241–3, 255, 286, 292
    Moslems conquer and rule, 57–62, 64–6, 68–9,
    72–3, 77, 85, 119, 122–3, 135, 243
    Christians in, 57, 59, 158, 219
    trade of, 118–19, 255
    Fatimids in, 134, 141–6, 148, 153, 158, 163–4,
    180–1, 205
    Abbasids in, 144, 172–3, 174
    Crusades and, 157, 163, 173, 185
    Ayoubids in, 172–85, 192, 201–2
    Mongols and, 205, 208, 210, 211
    Mamlooks and, 204–5, 208–11, 216–20, 224–8,
    230, 241–3, 255
    Tamerlane and, 224
    Ottoman Turks conquer, 227–8, 230–1, 241, 243
    Napoleon conquers, 240–2, 244
    Britain and, 241–4, 255–6, 258–9, 273, 275, 276,
    280–1, 287

Egypt—*cont.*
 Muhammad Ali of, 242–6, 253, 255–6, 258–9
 Europeans in, 241–3, 255, 258, 259
 Russia and, 251
 France and, 255
 Independent, 281, 287
 and Israel, 283, 285
 and Arab League, 283, 285
 See also Cairo
Eleanor, Queen (of England), 213
Elephants, 50, 51–3
Elizabeth I, Queen (of England), 263
Empty Quarter, 18
England, 98, 135, 164, 176, 201, 202, 267, 268, 290, 292; *see also* Britain
Ephesus, 167
Erbil, 181
Euphrates, River, 15, 21, 23, 24, 26, 45–7, 50–4, 55, 68, 94, 127, 146, 169, 280
Europe, 16, 48, 72, 105, 133, 163
 trade with East, 124, 219, 255, 288–9
 Arab culture reaches, 109, 140, 288–92
 Dark Ages in, 135–6, 288–9
 Ottoman Turks and, 222, 231, 245, 250–3, 265
 and Egypt, 241–2, 255, 258, 259
 Russia and, 251–2
 and Lebanon, 253
 and North Africa, 262–71
 chivalry and, 292–3
 Arab Empire and, 288–300
 romance reaches, 291
 See also Britain; Crusades; France; Germany
Eustace II, Count (of Boulogne), 159
Evian, 265

Fadhl ibn Yahya, 105
Faiyum, 57, 93
Faiz, Khalif (Fatimid, of Egypt), 143, 172
Fakhr al Deen II, Prince (of Lebanon), 240
Fakhr al Deen Mani, 231
Faraj, Sultan (Mamlook, of Egypt), 224
Farama, 57
Far East trade, 217, 288–9, 293
Fars, 129, 131, 236
Fatat, Al, 258
Fatima, daughter of Muhammad, 27, 75, 92, 103, 141, 142, 268
Fatimids, 134, 142, 144, 260
 in Egypt, 134, 141–6, 148, 152, 153, 158, 163–4, 180, 181, 205
Feisal, King (of Iraq), 273, 276, 279, 287
Feisal ibn Saud, ruler (of Nejed), 253, 255
Ferdinand III, King (of Castile), 191, 193
Feudal system, 164
Fez, 103, 138, 142, 144, 151, 267, 268
Filali Sharifs, 268, 270
Filanghieri, Marshal, 201
Firdausi, 126
Flanders, 178
Florence, 240
France, 18, 88, 97, 135, 149, 280
 Crusaders from, 133, 156, 166–7, 175, 176, 202–4, 210, 222
 and Ottoman Turks, 231, 240–1, 273, 275–6
 and Egypt, 240–2, 244, 255–6
 and Algeria, 246, 264–5, 269–70, 273
 and Tunisia, 266, 270, 273
 and Morocco, 269–71, 273
 and Syria, 276–7, 278–9, 281, 283, 287
 and World War I, 278
 and Lebanon, 279, 281
 fall of, 281
 chivalry in, 292
François I, King (of France), 231
Franks, *see* Crusades
Frederick I Barbarossa, Emperor (of Germany), 176, 198
Frederick II, Emperor (of Germany), 159, 198–201, 210
Fuad, King (of Egypt), 281
Fulk, King (of Jerusalem), 159, 163–4, 167, 168, 180
Fustat, 66, 142, 144

Galicia, 81, 150
Galilee, Sea of, 160
Gao, 267
Gaul, 21
Gaza, 16, 46, 199, 202
Genoa, 157
Georgia, 224, 237
Gerard de Ridefort, 175–6
Germany, 149
 Crusaders from, 156, 166–7, 176, 198–201, 210
 Emperors of, 159, 176, 198–9
 and the Ottoman Empire, 255, 256–7, 276
 and North Africa, 266, 269
 and World War I, 272, 278, 279, 299
 and World War II, 281, 283
 post-World War II, 285
Ghana, 96
Ghassan, Beni, tribe, 23, 24
Ghatafan tribe, 37, 38
Ghazan, Il Khan (Mongol, of Persia), 215, 216–17, 219, 228
Ghazna, 126, 132, 187
Ghaznevids, 126, 129, 132, 137
Ghilzai, Mahmood Khan, 235
Ghori, Qansuh al, Sultan (Mamlook, of Egypt), 227
Ghuzz, 129, 131–3, 154, 158, 226; *see also* Seljuqs
Gibraltar, 80, 262
 Straits of, 80, 96, 144
Gilead, 47
Glawi, Thami al, 269
Godfrey de Bouillon, Duke (of Lorraine and Lower Lotharingia), 156–8, 159, 167, 168, 176
Golden Horde, 196, 224
Goliath's Spring, Battle of, 208, 210
Good Hope, Cape of, 241, 255, 289
Goths, 80–1
Gouraud, General, 277
Granada, 151, 191–2, 193, 292; *see also* Spain
Great Khan, 161
Greece, 15, 17, 21, 55, 135, 236, 243, 250, 251, 289–91, 295–6, 297
Greek fire, 81–2
Greeks, 15, 17, 18, 24, 55, 72, 230, 286
Gulhana decrees, 245
Guy de Lusignan, King (of Jerusalem), 159, 175–6, 178, 180, 193
 King (of Cyprus), 183

Habbaniya, 281
Hadhramaut, 18, 43
Hadi, Musa al, Khalif (Abbasid, of Baghdad), 92, 101–2, 111
Hafar, Al, 45
Hafidh, Khalif (Fatimid, of Egypt), 143, 163, 172
Hafsids, 260, 262
Haifa, 213, 257
Hail, 253, 255
Haithum I, King (of Cilicia), 185, 192, 193
Hajjaj ibn Yusuf, 78, 81, 83
Hakam, Merwan I ibn al, Khalif, *see* Merwan I ibn al Hakam, Khalif
Hakam II, Ameer (Umaiyid, of Spain), 148, 150, 152
Hákim, Khalif (Fatimid, of Egypt), 143, 145–6, 153
Hama, 48, 119, 122, 202, 225, 238
 Horns of, 174
Hamadan, 94, 108, 129, 160, 205, 233, 235, 236
Hamdan, Saif al Dowla ibn, 122, 123
Hamdanids, 122, 127
Hammad, Beni, 145
Hamza, Uncle of Muhammad, 37
Handhala ibn Safwan, 87, 97
Haneefa, Beni, tribe, 43
Haritha, Muthanna ibn, *see* Muthanna ibn Haritha
Haroon al Rasheed, Khalif (Abbasid, in Baghdad), 92, 101, 103–8, 109, 111, 138, 294
Harran, 127, 134, 164, 201
Hasa, 255, 272, 275
Hasan I, Al, Sultan (of Morocco), 268
Hasan II, King (of Morocco), 269, 270–1
Hasan, Idris ibn Abdulla ibn, *see* Idris ibn Abdulla ibn Hasan

Hasan ibn Ali, 27, 74, 92, 95, 141
Hasan, Muhammad ibn Abdulla ibn, see Muhammad ibn Abdulla ibn Hasan
Hasan, Pasha, 263
Hasan Pasha Mustafa, 235
Hashim, Beni, tribe, 27, 63–5, 73, 74, 77, 84, 91, 92
Hassan ibn Naaman, 79, 80, 82
Hassan ibn Thabit, 36
Hatim, Yezeed ibn, 95
Hattin, Battle of, 176, 178, 179, 180, 181
Hauran plain, 48
Hejaz, 34, 227, 246, 273, 275, 280, 287
    Railway, 255, 257, 258, 273
Heliopolis, Battle of, 57, 69
Henry of Champagne, King (of Jerusalem), 159, 183, 193
Henry II, King (of England), 164
Henry III, King (of England), 201
Henry VI, Emperor (of Germany), 198–9
Heraclea, 120
Heraclius, Emperor (of Byzantium), 23, 29, 47–9, 54, 59, 69
Herat, 65, 124, 217, 226
Herbiya, Battle of, 202, 210
Hilal, Beni, tribe, 148, 151, 152, 188, 260
Hindu Kush, 129
Hira, 43, 45, 52
Hisham II, Ameer (Umaiyid, of Spain), 148, 150–1, 152
Hisham ibn Abdul Malik, Khalif (Umaiyid, of Damascus), 74, 85, 87, 88, 96, 97, 101
History, the value of, 288–300
Hit, 127
Hitler, 242, 264
Hittites, 15, 55
Hohenstaufens, 159, 176, 198–201, 210
Homs, 47, 48, 51, 119, 122
Honorius, Emperor (Roman), 21, 105
Hudeibiya, oath at, 38–9, 40
Hulagu, II Khan (Mongol, of Persia), 182, 196, 205–8, 210, 211, 213, 215, 217, 220, 226, 228, 231
Hulwan, 54
Humphrey de Toron, 159, 169, 173
Hunain ibn Ishaq, 109
Hungarians, 222, 231
Hungary, 205, 231, 250, 251
    King of, 222
Hurrians, 15
Husain, King (of Hejaz), 272–3, 275, 280, 283, 287
Husain ibn Ali, "The Martyr", 27, 74–7, 82, 83, 90, 91, 92, 94, 95, 101, 111, 141
Husain ibn Ali, Bey (of Tunisia), 266, 270

Ibrahim ibn al Aghlab, ruler (of Ifriqiya), 104, 111, 112, 138
Ibrahim Pasha, 233, 242
Iconium, 166, 174, 185, 197, 201; see also Asia Minor
Idris ibn Abdulla ibn Hasan, ruler (of Maghrib), 92, 95, 103, 107, 111, 112, 138
Idrisid dynasty, 92, 95, 103, 107, 111, 112, 138, 141, 145
Ifriqiya, 72, 79, 82;
    Kharijites in, 87, 90, 95–6, 138
    rebellions in, 87–8, 95–6, 97
    Umaiyids and, 93, 152, 294
    Aghlabids rule, 104, 107, 112, 138, 140, 142, 152
    Ismailis in, 140, 142
    Fatimids in, 142, 144, 145
    Sanhaja in, 144–6, 148
    Beni Hilal and Beni Sulaim in, 148, 151, 152, 188
    Muwahhids occupy, 188–93
    See also Maghrib; North Africa
Imil Valley, 197
India, 21, 24, 26, 61, 85, 104, 109, 110, 126, 197, 217, 224, 241, 255, 273, 275, 288–9, 291, 293
Indian Ocean, 24, 105, 241, 266, 285
Indonesia, 24, 104, 288
Indus, 224
Innocent III, Pope, 183

Iraq, 13, 15, 17, 23, 75, 91, 99, 104, 122, 138, 181
    Christianity in, 26
    Moslems conquer and rule, 45–7, 49–55, 63, 70, 72, 77, 78, 84, 108, 118–19
    Kharijites in, 68, 77, 78, 84, 87
    Abbasids in, 91, 93, 94, 119, 187, 194, 205, 226
    trade of, 124, 145
    Buwaihids and, 127, 129
    Seljuqs in, 158, 161, 226, 233
    Mongols and, 208, 226, 233
    Ottoman Turks and, 233, 235–7, 242, 245, 246, 255
    Safavids and, 233
    "Mamlook" régime in, 237–8
    Wahhabis in, 242
    British in, 275, 279–81, 287
    and Israel, 283, 285
    and Arab League, 285
Ireland, 250
Irene, Empress (of Byzantium), 101, 106, 112
Isabella, Queen (of Castile and Aragon), 191
Isabella, Queen (of Jerusalem), 159, 183
Isfahan, 235
Ishaq, Hunain ibn, 109
Ismail, 140, 141
Ismail, Ahmed ibn, 124
Ismailis, 140, 142, 205
Ismail, Khalif (Fatimid, of Egypt), 143, 144, 153
Ismail Pasha, Khedive (of Egypt), 255, 259
Ismail, Shah (Safavid, of Persia), 227, 233
Israel, 283–5, 286; see also Jews; Palestine
Istanbul, 230–1, 233, 235, 236, 237, 245, 246, 248, 256, 258, 263, 264, 272, 273, 275, 287; see also Constantinople; Ottoman Turks
Italy, 18, 21, 135, 140, 149, 152, 199, 255, 258, 272, 281, 287, 290, 296, 297
Itil, 90

Jaafar ibn Yahya, 105–6
Jaafar the Truthful, 140, 141
Jabiya, 55
Jaffa, 157, 173, 178, 179, 199, 211
Jagatai, 196, 197, 205, 211, 215, 216, 217, 222, 224
Jalair Mongols, 231
Jalula, Battle of, 54
Jamal Pasha the Less, 275
Jamali, Bedr al, see Bedr al Jamali
Janissaries, 227, 230–1, 234, 236, 241, 245, 246, 258, 259, 263–4
Jaráb, Battle of, 275
Jauf, 47
Jaxartes, River, 81, 187, 194, 197
Jazzár, Ahmad Pasha al, 240, 244
Jean de Brienne, King (of Jerusalem), 159, 183, 192, 193, 199, 202
Jebel Druze, 47
Jebel Hauran, 47
Jenghis Khan, (Mongol, of Persia), 194–7, 205, 210, 211, 213, 215, 217, 220, 224, 228
Jerba, Island of, 262
Jerusalem, 23, 49, 57
    Crusaders and, 154, 157–64, 167, 169, 173, 176, 178–9, 183–5, 199–201, 211, 220
    Kings of, 159, 164, 168, 169, 180, 183, 193 198–9, 201
    Saladin captures, 176, 180
    Hohenstaufens and, 198–201
    Ottoman Turks and, 250
    British capture, 273
Jesuits, 240, 253
Jesus, 32, 36; see also Christianity
Jews, 26, 32, 35–6, 38
    Arab attitude to, 56, 84–5, 135, 251, 289
    in Spain, 80–1, 151, 262
    in North Africa, 138
    Mongol Wazeer a Jew, 217
    and Palestine after World War I, 277–8
    and Palestine since World War II, 283
    See also Israel
Jezira, 90, 122–3, 127, 161, 163, 166, 169, 175, 207, 231
Jiza, 59

Johar the Sicilian, 144
John Comnenus, Emperor (of Byzantium), 163, 164, 167, 180
John Tzimisces, Emperor (of Byzantium), 122–3, 127
Jordan, 13, 39, 68, 91, 93, 257, 281, 283, 285, 287; see also Trans-Jordan
Jordan valley, 47
Jourdain, Alfonse, 166
Juheina tribe, 37
Juji, 196, 197, 211, 215, 224
Julian, Count, 80
Justinian, Emperor (of Byzantium), 21, 23, 29
Juwaini, Ala al Deen al, History of the Conqueror of the World, 197

Kaaba, 26, 32, 39
Kabul, 65, 78
Kafr Tab, 160
Kaikhatu, Il Khan (Mongol, of Persia), 215
Kai Qobad I, Sultan (of Iconium), 201
Kamil, Al, Sultan (Ayoubid, of Egypt), 182, 185, 192, 194, 199, 201, 202, 204, 210
Kariun, 59
Kashgar, 81, 82
Kenana, Beni, tribe, 38, 160
Kerak, 39, 91, 175, 219, 257
Kerbela, 75–7, 234
Kerboqa, 157
Kermanshah, 233, 235
Ketama tribe, 140, 142
Khadija, first wife of Muhammad, 29, 30, 33, 36, 40, 41, 68
Khakan of Turks, 87
Khalid ibn al Waleed, 43, 45–9, 54 62
Khalil, Sultan (Mamlook, of Egypt), 216
Kharijites, in Iraq, 68, 77, 78, 84, 87, 90, 91
  in Ifriqiya, 87, 90, 95–6, 138
Khattab, Abdulla ibn Umar ibn al, 43
Khattab, Umar ibn al, Khalif, see Umar ibn al Khattab, Khalif
Khattab, Zeid ibn al, 43
Khayyam, Umar, 133
Khazail tribe, 235
Khazars, 90
Khazraj tribe, 191
Kheibar, 26
Khiva, 94
Khurasan, 87, 91, 93, 95, 103, 107, 108, 111 112, 113, 115, 124 126, 129, 137, 197, 294
Khuwarizm, 185, 192, 193, 194, 224
Khuwarizmi, Al, 109
Khuzistan, 129, 187
King–Crane Commission, 277
Kirkuk, 235, 236
Kitchener, Lord, 256, 273
Konia, 235
  Battle of, 242
Kufa, 55, 62, 64, 65–6, 68, 70, 73, 75, 77 78, 91, 93–4, 104, 119, 127
Kurdistan, 181, 233, 235. 250
Kurds, 17, 127, 158, 172–3, 187, 233, 236
Kusadagh, Battle of, 197
Kuwait, 255, 275

Lakhmi, Dhirgam al, 172
Lakhmids, 23, 24, 45
Las Nevas de Tolosa, Battle of, 191, 192
Latrun, 178
Lawrence, T. E., 273
League of Nations, 278, 279
Lebanese, 16
Lebanon, 13, 122, 146, 231, 238, 240, 244, 250, 253, 258, 275, 276, 277, 279, 281, 283, 285, 286; see also Acre
Leith Amr ibn, 124
Leith, Yaqoob ibn, 124
Leo II, King (of Cilicia), 185, 192
Leo IV, Emperor (of Byzantium), 101
Leo VI, Emperor (of Byzantium), 122–3
Leo the Isaurian, Emperor (of Byzantium), 82, 101

Leon, 148, 150, 151
  King of, 149, 150–1
Lepanto, Battle of, 264, 270
London, 267
Longrigg, S. H., Four Centuries of Modern Iraq, 236
Louis VI, King (of France), 163
Louis VII, King (of France), 166–7
Louis IX, King (of France), 202–4, 210
Louis XIV, King (of France), 98–9, 108, 219
Lubiya, 176
Lusignan family, 159, 175–6, 178, 180, 183, 216
Lyautey, Marshal, 269–71
Lydda, 178

Maan, 273
Macedonia, 222
McMahon, Sir Henry, 275, 283, 287
Maghrib, 72, 95, 103, 104, 107, 112, 138, 144, 151, 152, 187–8, 190–1, 192. 260, 266–70; see also Ifriqiya; Morocco; North Africa
Mahdi, revolt of the, 256
Mahmood Khan Ghilzai, 235
Mahmood II, Sultan (Ottoman), 242, 245, 259
Mahmood ibn Muhammad, Sultan (Seljuq, of Persia), 128, 161
Mahmood ibn Sabuktakeen, Sultan (of Ghazna), 126, 129, 134, 137
Makhazin, Abdul Malik at Wadi, Sultan (of Morocco), 267
Malazkirt, Battle of, 132–3, 137, 156–7, 161, 164, 185
Malik al Dhahir Barqooq, Sultan (Mamlook, of Egypt), 220, 224, 228
Malik al Nasir Muhammad, Sultan (Mamlook, of, Egypt), 217, 219, 220, 228
Malik al Nasir Yusuf, King (of Damascus), 182, 205, 207–8
Malik al Raheem, 131
Malik al Salih Ismail, 174
Malik Shah, Sultan (Seljuq, of Persia), 128, 132, 133–4, 137, 154, 158, 160, 161, 167
Malik Shah I, Sultan (Seljuq, of Asia Minor), 168
Malik Shah, Muhammad ibn, see Muhammad, son of Malik Shah
Malta, 148, 263
Mamlooks, 187, 204, 207–9, 210, 211–13, 216–17, 219–20, 224–8, 230–1, 233, 237–8, 241–3, 244, 255, 263, 272; see also Baghdad; Egypt
Mamoon al Rasheed, Khalif (Abbasid, in Baghdad),, 92, 105, 107–9, 111, 113, 115, 116, 124, 294
Manad, Ziri ibn, 144
Mangonels, 78, 108, 194, 207
Manis, 240, 244
Mangu, Great Khan (Mongol, of Persia), 196, 205, 208, 215
Mansoor, Ahmad al, Sultan (of Morocco), 270–1
Mansoor, Ameer, 144–5
Mansoor, Khalif (Abbasid, of Baghdad), 92–8, 108, 111
Mansoor, Khalif Mehedi ibn, see Mehedi, Khalif
Mansoor, Wazeer (of Spain), 150–2
Mansoor, Yaqoob al, Khalif (Muwahhideen, of North Africa), 189–90, 192, 193
Mansoora, 202, 204
Manuel Comnenus, Emperor (of Byzantium), 169, 171, 174, 180
Marákish, 151, 188, 191, 267
Marash, Battle of, 101
Mardin, 233
Marie, Queen (of Jerusalem), 159, 183, 199
Marj Dabiq, Battle of, 227
Maronites, 240
Martel, Charles, 88
Mascara, 265
Maslama, Muhammad ibn, 59, 62
Masood, Sultan (Ghaznevid), 129
Masood, Sultan (Seljuq, of Iconium), 166, 168
Masudi, 88, 113
Maulay Abdul Rahman, Sultan (of Morocco), 268
Maulay al Rashid, Sultan (of Morocco), 268
Maulay Ismail, Sultan (of Morocco), 268, 271

Mawdood, Ameer, 158, 160
Mazagan, 266
Mecca, 15, 25–6, 28, 62, 66, 75, 77–8, 82, 96, 98, 101, 103, 104, 108, 111, 219, 242, 257, 272–5, 287
   Muhammad and, 30, 32–40, 64, 70
Medain, 46, 53, 55, 63
Medici, 240
Medina, 15, 25, 26, 75, 77, 82, 108, 242, 257, 272–3
   Muhammad and, 33–40
   early khalifs in, 42–7, 50, 56–7, 60, 63, 65, 94, 103
Medinaceli, 150
Mediterranean Sea, 16, 17, 107, 190, 263–4, 276, 288
   countries bordering, 17, 18, 24, 34, 55, 72, 93, 94, 135, 138–53, 264. 288
   commerce of, 72, 135, 241
   Russia and, 251, 276
   Britain and, 251, 276
   pirates in, 262–4
Mehedi, Khalif (Abbasid, of Baghdad), 92, 98–9, 101, 103, 106, 111
Mehediya, 142, 144, 148
Meknes, 268
Melilla, 142
Melisinda, Queen (of Jerusalem), 159, 164, 168
Merida, 80, 149
Merin, Beni, tribe, 191, 192, 260, 267, 270
Merwan, ibn, 127, 182
Merv, 91, 94, 107
Merwan, Abdul Malik ibn, Khalif, see Abdul Malik ibn Merwan, Khalif
Merwan I ibn Al Hakam, Khalif (Umaiyid, of Damascus), 74, 77, 83
Merwan II ibn Muhammad ibn Merwan, Khalif (Umaiyid, of Damascus), 74, 90, 91, 93, 97
Messina, 140
Michael III, Emperor (of Byzantium), 120
Michael VII Ducas, Emperor (of Byzantium), 133
Midhat Pasha, 245–6, 259
Mirdas, Ibn, 127, 132
Mizyeds, 127
Mohaç, Battle of, 231
Mongolia, 208
Mongols, 163, 194–210, 211, 213, 215–17, 220, 224, 226–8, 231, 300
Monophysites, 24
Morocco, 72, 73, 103, 141, 188, 190, 260, 262, 269–71; see also Maghrib; North Africa
Moscow, 224
Mosul, 54, 93, 104, 127, 129, 134, 157, 158, 160, 161, 163, 164, 166, 181, 233, 235, 246, 280
Mota, Battle of, 39, 46
Muadhdham, Al, King (of Damacus), 182, 199
Muawiya, Abdul Rahman I ibn, see Abdul Rahman I
Muawiya I ibn abi Sofian, Khalif (Umaiyid, of Damascus), 27, 64, 66, 68–70, 72–5, 82, 84, 88, 90
Muawiya II, Khalif (Umaiyid, of Damascus), 74, 77
Muawiya, Yezeed I ibn, Khalif, see Yezeed I ibn Muawiya, Khalif
Mudhaffar, Wazeer (of Spain), 151
Mughith, Ala ibn, 96
Muhammad al Darazi, 146
Muhammad Ali, Pasha (of Egypt), 242–4, 245, 246, 253, 255–6, 258, 259
Muhammad al Nasir, Khalif (Muwahhideen, of North Africa), 189, 190–1, 193
Muhammad al Shaikh, 267
Muhammad, Ameer (Umaiyid, of Spain), 148, 152
Muhammad ibn Abdulla ibn Hasan, 95, 103
Muhammad ibn Maslama, 59, 62
Muhammad ibn Nasr, King (of Granada), 191, 193
Muhammad ibn Qasim, 81
Muhammad ibn Rasheed, ruler (of Nejed), 253
Muhammad ibn Saud, 242, 244
Muhammad ibn Toumert, 188, 193
Muhammad, Mahmood ibn, Sultan (Seljuq, of Persia), 128, 161
Muhammad the Prophet, 27–43, 45, 54–6, 63, 64 69, 70, 74, 75, 77, 84–5, 92, 94, 141, 191, 275

Muhammad the Pure Soul, 92, 93, 103, 138
Muhammad Rashád, Sultan (Ottoman), 258
Muhammad, Son of Malik Shah, Sultan (Seljuq, of Persia), 128, 158, 160, 161, 163, 167, 168
Muhammad II, Sultan (Ottoman), 227, 229
Muhammad III, Sultan (of Morocco), 268
Muhammad IV, Sultan (of Morocco), 268
Muhammad V, King (of Morocco), 269, 271
Muhammad VI, Bey (of Tunisia), 266
Muhtadi, Khalif (Abbasid, of Baghdad), 118
Muizz al Dowla ibn Buwaih, 120, 123, 126, 137
Muizz ibn Badees, 145–6, 148
Muizz-li-deen-Allah, Al, Khalif (Fatimid, of Egypt), 143, 144, 145, 152–3
Muktafi, Khalif (Abbasid, of Baghdad), 117, 119
Muljam, Muhammad ibn, 68
Multan, 81, 82
Mundhir, Ameer (Umaiyid, of Spain), 152
Munqidh, Usama ibn, Memoirs, 160,303
Muntasir ibn Mutawakkil, Khalif (Abbasid, o Baghdad), 116, 117, 118
Muntifiq tribe, 235
Muqaddasi, A Description of the Muslim Empire, 127
Muqallad, Ibn, 127, 129
Muqtadi, Khalif (Abbasid, in Baghdad), 193
Muqtafi, Al, Khalif (Abbasid, in Baghdad), 193
Murabits, 151–3, 187–8, 190, 192, 193
Murad I, Sultan (Ottoman), 221–2, 229, 296
Murad IV, Sultan (Ottoman), 234–5, 244
Murad V, Sultan (Ottoman), 246
Murad Bey (of Tunisia), 266
Murad family, 266, 270
Murcia, 191
Musa, Imam, 140, 141
Musa al Hadi, Khalif (Abbasid, of Baghdad), 92, 101–2, 111
Musa ibn Nusair, 80–3, 88
Musa ibn Yahya, 105
Musailima, 43
Muslim ibn Uqba, 77
Muslim, Qutaiba ibn, 81
Mustaali, Khalif (Fatimid, of Egypt), 143, 153
Mustadhi, Al, Khalif (Abbasid, in Baghdad), 193
Mustaeen, Khalif (Abbasid, in Baghdad), 117, 118
Mustafa IV, Sultan (Ottoman), 259
Mustafa Beg, 235
Mustakfi, Khalif (Abbasid, in Baghdad), 117, 120
Mustansir, Khalif (Fatimid, of Egypt), 143, 146, 153
Mustansir, Al, Khalif (Abbasid, in Baghdad), 187, 193, 205
Mustasim, Al, Khalif (Abbasid, in Baghdad), 193, 205, 207
Mutadhid, Khalif (Abbasid, in Baghdad), 117, 119, 124
Mutamid, Khalif (Abbasid, in Baghdad), 117, 118–19
Mutamin ibn Haroon al Rasheed, Khalif (Abbasid, in Baghdad), 92, 105, 113
Mutanabbi, 122, 127
Mutasim ibn Haroon al Rasheed, Khalif (Abbasid, in Baghdad), 92, 113, 115–18, 123
Mutasim, Khalif Mutawakkil ibn, see Mutawakkil ibn Mutasim, Khalif
Mutasim, Khalif Wathiq ibn, see Wathiq ibn Mutasim, Khalif
Mutawakkil ibn Mutasim, Khalif (Abbasid, in Baghdad), 92, 116–20, 123, 134, 144–5, 204
Mutawakkil, Khalif Muntasir ibn, see Muntasir ibn Mutawakkil, Khalif
Mutazz, Khalif (Abbasid, in Baghdad), 116, 117, 118
Muthanna ibn Haritha, 45–7, 49–51, 54
Mutia, Khalif (Abbasid, in Baghdad), 117, 120
Muwahhids, 188–93, 260, 270, 297
Myrio-cephalon, Battle of, 174, 180

Naaman, Hassan ibn, 79, 80, 82
Naaman ibn al Mundhir, Lakhmid prince, 24
Nablus, 283
Nadir Quli Khan, 235–6, 244
Nafi, Uqba ibn, 72–3, 77, 79

Napoleon Bonaparte, 99, 224, 240–2, 244, 264, 268
Napoleon III, Emperor (of France), 253
Narbonne, 88
Nasir i Khusrau, 146
Nasir li Deen Allah, Al, Khalif (Abbasid, in Baghdad), 187, 193, 194
Nasir Muhammad, Malik al, Sultan (Mamlook, of Egypt), 217, 219, 220, 228
Nasir, Muhammad al, Khalif, see Muhammad al Nasir, Khalif
Nasir Yusuf, Malik al, King (of Damascus), 182, 205, 207–8
Nasr, Muhammad ibn, King (of Granada), 191, 193
Nasrids, 191–2
Navarre, 149, 150
  King and Queen of, 149, 150
Nazareth, 122, 199
Nehawand, Battle of, 60–2, 69
Nejed, 253–5, 275, 280; see also Arabia
Nejf, 52
Nejran, 26
Nelson, Lord, 241
Nevers, Jean de, 222
Nicaea, 133, 156, 166
Nicephorus I, Emperor (of Byzantium), 106–7, 111, 112
Nicephorus Botoniates, 133
Nicephorus Phocas, Emperor (of Byzantium), 122–3, 127
Nicodème, Jean, 236
Nicomedia, 156
Nicopolis, Battle of, 222, 228
Nigeria, 96
Nile, River, 17, 59, 173, 185, 202, 241
  Battle of, 241
  Delta, 16, 17
Nimes, 88
Nisapur, 129
Nisibin, 164
Nisibis, 21
Noor al Deen Mahmood, King (of Aleppo), 166, 168, 169, 171, 172–4, 180
Normans:
  in Byzantine army, 133
  in Sicily, 148, 152, 188, 199
  on Crusade, 156–7
  in North Africa, 188
  in England, 290
North Africa, 13, 15, 18, 21, 79, 135, 136, 138–45, 181, 243
  Umaiyids conquer, 72–3, 77, 79–80, 260
  Spain and, 80–1, 262, 266–7
  Berber revolt in, 87–8, 95–6
  Kharijites in, 142, 144–6, 260
  Sanhaja in, 144–6
  Normans in, 188, 192
  Muwahhids in, 188–93, 260
  Beni Merin in, 191–2, 260
  Ottoman Turks in, 246
  Russia and, 251
  religion in, 260, 262
  Portugal and, 262, 266–7
  British in, 265, 275
  Americans in, 265
  France in, 273
  See also Berbers; Egypt; Ifriqiya; Maghrib; Morocco; Tunisia
Numair, Beni, tribe, 127
Nusair, Musa ibn, 80–3, 88

Ogotai, Khaqan (Mongol, of Persia), 196, 197, 205, 215
Oljaitu, Il Khan (Mongol, of Persia), 215
Oman, 43
Oran, 262, 265, 266
Orkhan, 221
Othman, 220–2, 229
Othman ibn Affan, Khalif (Umaiyid, in Damascus), 27, 63, 64–6, 68, 69, 70, 74, 140
Othman, Saeed ibn, 72
Othmanlis, see Ottoman Turks

Ottoman Turks, 13, 220–2, 224, 226–9, 230–44, 245–59, 263–5, 272–3, 275–80, 285, 296
Oxus, River, 62, 65, 70, 126, 205, 211

Pakistan, 72, 81; see also India
Palaeologi, 222
Palermo, 140
Palestine, 15, 16, 24, 46, 54, 55–7, 77, 93, 96, 134–5, 163, 166–7, 227, 230, 238, 240, 244, 246, 257, 273, 276–9, 281, 283, 285, 287; see also Israel
Palmyra, 47
Pamir Mountains, 81, 87
Pamplona, 149
Paris, 257, 265
Pelagius, Cardinal, 185
Peñon, the, 262
Persepolis, 70
Persia, 15, 70, 72, 77, 87, 110, 119, 135, 138 181, 197
  Abbasids in, 91, 93, 94
  Khalif's troops from, 99, 103, 113, 115–16, 123
  Dailamites in, 120
  Ghaznevids rule, 126
  Seljuqs in, 128–37, 146, 157–8, 161, 168, 185–7, 192, 197, 220, 227, 297
  Astronomy in, 133–4
  Khuwarizm Shahs conquer, 187, 192
  Il Khan of, 196
  Mongols in, 197, 208, 209, 210, 211, 213, 215–17, 220, 228
  Ismailis in, 205
  Tamerlane and, 224
  Safavids in, 227, 233–5, 243
  Ottoman Turks and, 227, 233–7, 243
  Britain and, 275
  Russia and, 275
Persian Empire, 16, 21–4, 26, 28, 29, 39, 40, 45–7, 49–56, 60–2, 64, 69, 84, 85, 197, 288, 295–7; see also Persia
Persian Gulf, 24, 45, 118, 235, 246, 257, 272
Persians, 13, 16, 17, 99, 103, 113, 115–16, 124, 126, 134, 158; see also Persia
Peter I, King (of Cyprus), 219–20
Peter the Hermit, 156
Philippe Auguste, King (of France), 176, 178, 180
Philippe le Bel, King (of France), 217
Philistines, 55
Philomelium, 157
Phoenicians, 18, 72, 264
Piacenza, 133
Pirates, 262–4
Plantagenet, Geoffrey, 164
Portugal, 262, 266–7, 268
Provence, 156, 263
Prussian Missionaries, 252
Punjab, 94
Pyrenees, 88, 148

Qadasiya, Battle of, 52–4, 62, 66
Qadhi, 234
Qahtan, 90
Qaim, Khalif (Abbasid, in Baghdad), 117, 129, 131, 134
Qaim, Khalif (Fatimid, of Egypt), 142, 143, 144, 153
Qainuqa, Beni, tribe, 35
Qairawan, 73, 79, 82, 87, 95, 138, 142–4, 145, 148, 152, 153
Qais, 90–1
Qalaun, Sultan (Mamlook, of Egypt), 213, 216, 219, 228
Qansuh al Ghori, Sultan (Mamlook, of Egypt), 227
Qaqaa, 53
Qara Khans, 126, 132, 137
Qara Khitai, 163, 185–7
Qasim, Muhammad ibn, 81
Qasr al Saghir, 267
Qilij Arsan I, Sultan (Seljuq, of Asia Minor), 128, 156, 168
Qilij Arslan II, Sultan (Seljuq, of Asia Minor), 168, 174
Qipchaqs, 213
Qoran, 32, 38, 52, 56, 66, 68, 234

Qubilai, Great Khan (Mongol, of Persia), and Emperor (of China), 196, 211, 215, 228
Quraidha, Beni, tribe, 38
Quraish, 26, 28, 34–9, 42, 46, 51, 63–5, 91, 141
Qusai, 27, 28, 141
Qutaiba ibn Muslim, 81
Qutlumish, 128, 132, 133, 154
Qutlumish, Sulaiman ibn, Sultan (Seljuq, of Asia Minor), 128, 133, 168
Qutuz, Sultan (Mamlook, of Egypt), 207–8, 210
Qutwan, Battle of, 161, 163, 167
Quyuq, Khaqan, (Mongol, of Persia), 196, 205

Rabat, 190, 267
Radhi, Khalif (Abbasid, in Baghdad), 117, 119–20
Radio in the Middle East, 285
Rafah, 57
Raheem, Malik Al, 131
Railways, 255, 256–7
Hejaz, 255, 257, 258, 273
Ramla, 178, 179
Raqqa, 104, 106
Rasheed, Aziz ibn, ruler (of Nejed), 253, 255, 275
Rasheed, Ameen ibn Haroon al, Khalif, see Ameen ibn Haroon al Rasheed, Khalif
Rasheed, Haroon al, Khalif, see Haroon al Rasheed, Khalif
Rasheed, Mamoon al, Khalif, see Mamoon al Rasheed, Khalif
Rasheed, Muhammad ibn, ruler (of Nejed), 253
Rasheed, Mutamin ibn Haroon al, Khalif, see Mutamin ibn Haroon al Rasheed, Khalif
Rasheed, Mutasim ibn Haroon al, Khalif, see Mutasim ibn Haroon al Rasheed, Khalif
Rashid, Maulay al, Sultan (of Morocco), 268
Raymond de Poitiers, Prince (of Antioch), 164, 166, 169
Raymond de Saint Gilles, Count (of Tripoli), 156–8, 160, 167
Raymond III, Count (of Tripoli), 175
Razi, Al, 124, 126
Red Sea, 24, 37, 119, 145, 175, 241, 251, 276
Rei, 108, 129, 132
Renaissance, 289
Renaud de Châtillon, 169, 171, 175, 176
Rhodes, 72, 263
Rhone Valley, 88
Richard I, King (of England), 176–80, 181, 183
Richard, Earl (of Cornwall), 201–2
Ridhwan, King (of Aleppo), 128, 158, 160
Rif Mountains, 269, 271
Riyadh, 16, 255
Robert, Duke (of Normandy), 156, 167
Roderic, King (of the Goths), 80
Roger I, Count (of Sicily), 148, 152
Roger II, King (of Sicily), 188, 192, 193
Roland, 148
Roman Empire, 13, 15, 17, 21, 29, 55, 64, 72, 95, 103, 105, 135, 243 250, 264, 286, 288, 289–90, 295–6, 298, 300; see also Byzantium
Romanis II, Emperor (of Byzantium), 123
Romanus Diogenes, Emperor (of Byzantium), 132–3
Rome, 240
Romelia, 236
Roncesvalles, 148
Roussel de Bailleul, 133, 156
Rueda, Battle of, 150
Rusid, Ibn, 190
Russia, 205. 224, 240, 245–6, 251–2, 273, 275–6, 278, 279, 283, 285, 295, 299
Rustem, 51–4
Rustem, Beni. 95
Ruzzik, Talaia ibn, 172

Saad, Beni, 28, 267–8, 270–1
Saad ibn abi Waqqas, 51–4, 60, 62, 63, 66
Saad ibn al Aasi, 64, 65
Saeed ibn Othman, 72
Saadi, Shawar al, 172–3, 181
Sabuktakeen, Mahmood ibn, Sultan (of Ghazna), 126, 129, 137

Safad, 211
Safavids, 227, 233–5
Saffah, Abdulla al, Khalif (Abbasid, in Kufa), 91, 92, 93, 97, 98
Saffuriya, 175
Safi, 266, 267
Safi, Shah (Safavid, of Persia), 234
Safwan, Handhala ibn, 87, 97
Sagrajas, Battle of, 152
Sahara Desert, 17, 21, 72, 79, 144, 151, 188
Saif al Deen Ghazi I, Prince (of Mosul), 166
Saif al Dowla ibn Hamdan, 122, 123
St. John, Knights of, 263
Saladin, Sultan (Ayoubid, of Egypt), 172–83, 190, 192, 194, 204, 205, 207, 210
Salé, 267–8
Saleem I, Sultan (Ottoman), 227, 229, 231, 233, 244, 262
Saleem III, Sultan (Ottoman), 245, 259
Salih Ayoub, Al, Sultan (Ayoubid, of Egypt), 182, 201–2, 204, 210, 213
Salih Ismail, Al, King (of Damascus), 182, 201, 202, 210
Salih Ismail, Malik al, 174
Salonika, 257
Salt Desert, 161
Samanid dynasty (of East Persia), 124, 126, 135, 137, 297; see also Persia; Persians
Samarqand, 72, 78, 124, 194, 224, 226
Samarra, 113, 116, 118
Samawah, 255
Sanhaja tribe, 144–5, 148, 188; see also Berbers; Hammad, Beni; Ziri, Beni
Sanjar, Sultan (Seljuq, of Persia), 128, 161, 163, 167, 185, 192, 297
Santarem, 190
Santiago di Compostela, 150
Saragossa, 148, 151
Saud, Abdul Aziz ibn, King (of Saudi Arabia), 255, 272, 275, 280, 287
Saud, Feisal ibn, ruler (of Nejed), 253, 255
Saud, Muhammad ibn, 242, 244
Saudi Arabia, 280, 285, 286, 287; see also Hejaz; Nejed
Seleucia, see Medain
Seljuq, 128, 129
Seljuqs:
of Persia, 128–37, 146, 157–8, 168, 185–7, 192, 197, 220, 226, 227, 297
of Asia Minor, 128, 132–3, 134, 154, 156–7, 166, 168, 174, 185, 211, 213, 222, 228
See also Asia Minor; Persia
Serbians, 222
Serbs, 230
Seville, 80, 151, 191
Shaizar, 160, 164
Shammar tribe, 235
Shah Rukh, Sultan (Ottoman), 226
Shaikh, Muhammad al, 267
Shakespear, Captain W. H. I., 275
Shatt al Arab, 54
Shawar al Saadi, 172–3, 181
Shemmer, 77
Shihabi, Basheer II al, Prince (of Lebanon), 240, 244
Shihabis, 240
Shiites, 77, 78, 90–1, 93, 95, 101, 108, 116, 119, 120, 131, 140, 141, 142, 233, 235–6, 240
Shiraz, 120, 217
Shirbin, 204
Shirkuh, 172–3, 180, 182
Shitata, 46
Sibylla, Princess (of Jerusalem), 159, 174–5, 176
Sicily, 262
Arabs raid, 72
Arabs in, 109, 197, 199, 290
Arab culture reaches Europe through, 109, 140, 290
conquered from N. Africa, 140, 144, 152
Normans in, 148, 152, 188, 192, 199, 290
Frederick II in, 198–9
Sidon, 122, 157, 176, 213, 238, 240
Siffeen, Battle of, 68–9

Sijilmassa, 95
Sina, Ibn, 124
Sinai, 57, 148, 208, 243
Sind, 72, 81
  King of, 81
Sinjar, 164
Sivas, 224
Smith, Sir Sidney. 240
Smyrna, 166
Sofian, Muawiya I ibn abi, Khalif, see Muawiya I
  ibn abi Sofian, Khalif
Sophronius, Patriarch (of Jerusalem), 49
Sousse, 72
Spain, 13, 18, 21, 91, 93, 138
  Goths in, 80–1, 148
  Arabs conquer, 80–1, 82, 96, 154
  Christians reconquer, 81, 150, 191–2, 260, 262,
    290
  civil war in, 88
  Abbasids and, 94, 96–7
  Umaiyids in, 96–7, 103, 104, 142, 148–52
  Arab culture reaches Europe through, 109, 110,
    134, 149–50, 179, 191–2, 290–2
  culture of, 109, 110, 124, 135, 149–50, 191–2, 290,
    291–2
  army of, 149
  Murabits in, 151–2, 187–8
  Muwahhids in, 190–1
  American conquests of, 192, 266, 296, 298
  in North Africa, 262, 266–7, 268–9, 270
  Barbary pirates and, 263–4
  at war with England, 267
Spray of Pearls, 202, 204–5, 207, 210
Stack, Sir Lee, 281
Su Bashi, Bekr the, 234
Sudan, 256, 258
Sudanese, 146
Suez Canal, 18, 255, 258, 276
Sugut, 220
Sulaim, Beni, tribe, 37, 38, 148, 188, 260
Sulaiman ibn Abdul Malik, Khalif (Umaiyid), 74,
  81–3, 84, 85
Sulaiman ibn Qutlumish, Sultan (Seljuq, of Asia
  Minor), 128, 133, 168
Sulaiman the Magnificent, Sultan (Ottoman), 231,
  233–4, 243. 244. 245, 251, 262–3, 296
Sulaiman Pasha, 237
Sulaiman, Sultan (of Morocco), 268
Sumaiya, 70
Sumerians, 15
Sunnis, 77, 90, 131, 138, 140, 142, 240; see also
  Umaiyids
Sus, River, 73
Sykes, Sir Mark, 276–7
Sykes–Picot Agreement, 275–7
Syria, 13, 15–17, 21, 23, 24, 26, 28, 29, 77, 91, 119,
  135. 138, 250
  people of, 13, 15, 16–18, 55, 96, 104, 250, 286,
    291–2, 298
  Christians in, 24, 26, 48, 55
  trade of, 28, 34, 37
  Jews in, 35
  Moslems conquer, 46–9, 51–6, 60–1, 64, 66, 77,
    93
  Abbasids and, 94
  Slaves and freedmen in, 99
  Byzantines and, 122–3, 126–7, 137, 163
  Carmathians attack, 122, 137
  Fatimids in, 144–5
  Druzes in, 146, 279, 287
  Seljuqs in, 146, 158–60, 161, 163, 169, 180
  Crusaders and, 156–8, 160, 163, 166, 167, 169
  Ayoubids and, 174, 181–2, 201, 204–5
  Mongols and, 205, 208, 210, 211, 213, 216, 217
  Mamlooks and, 208–9, 211, 216, 227, 230
  Ottoman Turks rule, 227, 228, 230, 234–5, 238,
    240, 242–3, 246, 251, 257, 258, 272–3
  Ahmad al Jazzar governs, 240, 244
  Napoleon and, 240–1
  Wahhabis in, 242
  Muhammad Ali and, 242
  Russia and, 251

Britain and, 276–7, 281, 283, 287
France and, 277, 278–9, 281, 283, 287
General Syrian Congress, 276–7
Arab League Member, 285
See also Damascus

Tabari, 53
Tabriz, 207, 211, 224, 233
Tafilelt, 269
Tagus, River, 190
Tahert, 95
Tahir the Ambidextrous, 108, 111, 112, 124, 137
Tahudha, 73
Tai, tribe, 45
Talaia ibn Ruzzik, 172
Talha ibn Ubaidullah, 66, 68
Talib, Abu, 27, 28–9, 30, 33, 41, 74, 92
Talib, Ali ibn abi, Khalif, see Ali ibn abi Talib,
  Khalif
Tamerlane, 222, 224–6, 228, 229, 231
Tancred, Prince (of Antioch), 161, 163
Tancred of Hauteville, 148
Tangier, 73, 87, 144. 266, 267
Tariq, Tarik, see Zayyad, Tarik ibn
Tarsus, 111, 119, 120, 122, 123
Tashfeen, Yusuf ibn, 151, 153, 187, 188, 192, 193
Taurus Mountains, 49, 101, 106–7, 111, 113, 120,
  122, 156–7, 185, 222; see also Cilicia
Tebessa, 79
Tebook, 40
Tel al Jazar, Battle of, 174
Tel al Kebir, Battle of, 255, 258
Telemsan, 260, 262
Temeem, Abbas ibn, 172
Temeem, Beni, tribe, 52–3
Templars, 175
Tequdar, Il Khan (Mongol, of Persia), 215
Thabit, Hassan ibn, 36
Thami al Glawi, 269
Theodora Comnena, Queen (of Jerusalem), 169, 171
Theodore, Byzantine C. in C., Egypt, 59
Theodorus, brother of Emperor Heraclius, 49
Theodosius, Emperor (of Byzantium), 21, 105
Theophilus, Emperor (of Byzantium), 111, 113
Thrace, 222, 272
Tiberias, 122, 175, 181, 202
Tibet, 288
Tigris, River, 26, 46, 54, 94, 113, 131, 237
Timbuctoo, 267
Toledo, 80, 151
Topal Othman Pasha. 236, 244
Toulouse, 156, 166
Toumert, Muhammad ibn, 188, 193
Tours, Battle of, 88
Trans-Jordan, 238, 257, 276–7, 283; see also Jordan
Trans-Oxiana, 87, 94, 124, 126, 132, 137, 161, 163,
  185, 196, 197. 211. 222. 224
Tripoli (N. Africa), 72, 138, 148, 188, 190, 246,
  258, 260, 272, 287
Tripoli (Syria), 122, 157–8, 169, 179, 183, 202, 211.
  213, 228
Tudela, 149
Tughril Beq, Sultan (Seljuq, of Persia), 128, 129
  131–2, 134, 137
Tughril III, Sultan (Seljuq, of Persia), 185
Tughtekeen, 160
Tukush, Shar (of Khuwarizm), 185–7
Tulaiha, 43
Tului, 196, 197, 205, 211, 215
Tulun, Ahmed ibn, 119, 123
Tunis, 188, 260, 262, 264, 265–6, 270; see also
  Tunisia
Tunisia, 72, 266, 270; see also Tunis
Turan Shah, Sultan (Ayoubid, of Egypt). 182, 204
  210
Turkestan, 91, 113, 161, 197; see also Ottoman
  Turks; Seljuqs; Turks
Turkey, see Ottoman Turks
Turkmans, 129, 133, 156, 158, 185, 220, 226, 233;
  see also Ghuzz; Ottoman Turks; Seljuqs;
  Turkestan
Turks, 17, 87, 129, 194

Turks—*cont.*
  in Khalif's army, 103, 113, 115–16, 149, 208–9
  kill Mutawakkil, 116, 118, 204
  in power in Baghdad, 118–20, 123, 149
  in Samanid army, 126
  Ghazna ruled by, 126, 134
  in Army of Egypt, 146, 204–5, 208–9, 220
  See also Ghuzz; Ottoman Turks; Seljuqs; Turkestan; Turkmans
Tus, 107
Tutush, King (of Damascus), 128, 134, 158
Tyre, 157, 176, 179, 181, 183, 213, 238

Ubaidullah ibn Zayyad, 75–7, 83
Ubaidullah the Mehedi, Khalif (Fatimid, of Egypt), 142, 143, 153
Ubaidullah, Talha ibn, 66, 68
Ucles, Battle of, 188
Udhroh, 68
Uhud, Battle of, 37–9, 40
Ukraine, 224
Umaiya, Beni, tribe, 27, 63–5, 73, 74, 77, 84, 88, 91, 92, 141; *see also* Umaiyids
Umaiyids, 63–6, 68, 95, 97, 124, 299
  the great ones, 70–83, 103, 135, 141
  Abbasids overthrow, 83–98, 101
  a Mediterranean power, 93, 135
  in Spain, 96, 103, 142, 144, 148–52
  power of, 98–9, 104
  and North Africa, 144
  See also Damascus; Spain
Umar, Dhahir al, 240
Umar ibn Abdul Azeez, Khalif (Umaiyid), 74, 82, 84–5, 97
Umar ibn al Khattab, Khalif (Umaiyid, in Medina), 42–3, 47–52, 54–60, 62–5, 69, 84, 103
Umar Khayyam, 133
Underhill, Evelyn, *The School of Charity*, 300
United Nations Organisation, 269, 283, 295
United States of America, 21, 227, 252, 276, 277, 278, 283, 293, 295, 298, 299
Uqail, Beni, tribe, 127, 129
Uqba, 64
Uqba ibn Nafi, 72–3, 77, 79
Uqba, Muslim ibn, 77
Uqba, Waleed ibn, 64
Urban II, Pope, 133, 137, 154, 156, 167
Urfa, *see* Edessa

Val de Junqueras, Battle of, 149
Valencia, 151, 191
Van, 217
Van, Lake, 132
Vandals, 18, 72
Vasco da Gama, 241, 255, 289
Venetians, 251
Vienna, 231
Volga, River, 90, 196
Volubilis, 103

Wadi al Khazindar, Battle of, 216
Wahhabi-ism, 242, 244, 257, 280
Wahran, *see* Oran
Wail, Bekr ibn, tribe, 45, 46, 47, 54
Waleed I ibn Abdul Malik, Khalif (Umaiyid), 74, 80–3, 85, 88
Waleed ibn Uqba, 64
Waleed II ibn Yezeed II, Khalif (Umaiyid, in Damascus), 74, 88, 97

Waleed, Khalid ibn al, 43, 45–9, 54, 62
Waqqas, Saad ibn abi, 51–4, 60, 62, 63
Wathiq ibn Mutasim, Khalif (Abbasid in Baghdad), 92, 116, 117, 123
Wattás, Beni, tribe, 266–7
White Sheep Turkmans, 231, 233
Wilhelm II, Kaiser (of Germany), 242, 264
William I, King (of England), 156
William II, King (of Sicily), 199
William, Marquis (of Montferrat), 159, 174–5, 176
William of Tyre, *A History of Deeds done beyond the Seas*, 157, 303
Wilson, Woodrow, President (of United States of America), 277
Wolseley, Sir Garnet, 255
World War, First, 13, 18, 243, 251, 253, 257, 258, 265, 272–6, 278, 279, 280–1, 287, 299
World War, Second, 13, 265, 266, 270, 281–3, 285, 287

Yahya, Fadhl ibn, 105
Yahya, Jaafar ibn, 105–6
Yahya, Musa ibn, 105
Yahya the Barmecid, 103–6
Yaqoob al Mansoor, Khalif (Muwahhideen, of North Africa), 189–90, 192, 193
Yaqoob ibn Leith, 124
Yarmouk River, 47
  first Battle of, 47, 48, 54
  second Battle of, 51, 54
Yasir, Ammar ibn, 62–3
Yathrib, *see* Medina
Yemama, Battle of, 43
Yemen, 24–6, 34, 45, 90–1, 119, 246, 285
Yemenites, 18, 90–1
Yezdegird, King (of Persia), 46, 49, 51–4, 60, 62, 69
Yezeed I ibn Muawiya, Khalif (Umaiyid, of Damascus), 73, 74, 75–7, 82
Yezeed ibn Hatim, 95
Yezeed II ibn Abdul Malik, Khalif (Umaiyid), 74, 85, 88, 97
Yezeed III, Khalif (Umaiyid, in Damascus), 74, 88, 97
Yolanda, Empress (of Germany), 159, 198–9
Young Turks, 257, 272, 287
Yusuf, Hajjaj ibn, *see* Hajjaj ibn Yusuf
Yusuf ibn Tashfeen, 151, 153, 187, 188, 192, 193

Zab, Battle of the River, 93, 97
Zaghlul Pasha, 281
Zagros Mountains, 54, 60, 197
Zallaka, Battle of, 151–2
Zayyad, Tariq ibn, 80–1
Zayyad, the son-of-his-father, 70, 72, 75, 78, 83
Zayyad, Ubaidullah ibn, 75–7, 83
Zebetra, 113
Zeid, 30
Zeid ibn al Khattab, 43
Zenata, tribe, 79, 145; *see also* Berbers
Zengi, 164, 166, 167, 168, 180
Zengids, 174
Zenj rebels, 118–19
Zionists, 278
Ziri, Beni, 145
Ziri ibn Manad, 144
Zoroastrians, 56
Zubair, Abdulla ibn, Khalif (in Mecca), 77, 78, 79, 82, 83
Zubair ibn Al Awwam, 59, 63, 66–7, 77